# MARGINALITY
# AND
# IDENTITY

# MARGINALITY
# AND
# IDENTITY

*A Colored Creole Family*
*Through Ten Generations*

SISTER FRANCES JEROME WOODS, C.D.P.

LOUISIANA STATE UNIVERSITY PRESS · Baton Rouge

ISBN 0-8071-0241-5

Library of Congress Catalog Card Number 72-79342

Copyright © 1972 by Louisiana State University Press

All rights reserved

Manufactured in the United States of America

Printed by Kingsport Press, Inc., Kingsport, Tennessee

Designed by Albert Crochet

To my sister,
Sister Mary Mercedes Kennedy, C.D.P.,
who first interested me in the
river and its people

# Acknowledgments

I find it difficult to acknowledge all the assistance I have received on a work that has taken more than a decade to complete. But a brief chronology of my preparation will to some extent indicate the debts of gratitude I have incurred along the way.

In 1961 the Religious Education Association sponsored a Research Planning Workshop at Cornell University, where I received help in clarifying the focus of this study and in formulating a research proposal for the National Institutes of Health. In January, 1962, Our Lady of the Lake College gave me a sabbatical, whereupon my colleagues at the college, particularly Mary Vernia, voluntarily assumed my teaching responsibilities. And throughout, the administration, especially President John L. McMahon, encouraged and supported the research endeavor.

In the spring of that year, with a grant from the National Institutes of Health (MH 06093–03), I began to photocopy records and to hire clerical assistance. As the work progressed, the lists of Letoyant Creole population reached unexpected proportions, and the biosocial aspects assumed greater relevance than I had anticipated. In the summer of 1963 I explored the biosocial facets as a participant in an institute on behavioral genetics, sponsored by the Social Science Research Council, at the University of California at Berkeley. The Social Science Research Council's Committee on Simulation of Psychological and Social Processes also awarded me a Computer Simulation grant in 1965. In 1969 the National Research Council of the National Academy of Sciences invited me to participate in discussions on the biology of migrant and urban peoples, with the United States National Committee for the International Biological Program. At these meetings I was encouraged to explore further research possibilities.

Throughout the time the study was in progress I was continuously gratified by willing assistance. James N. Spuhler gave me informal instruction in biogenetics and encouraged one of his students, Jean MacCluer, to incorporate the Letoyant Creole population in her doctoral dissertation and to make available to me the information on inbreeding. Sister Marilyn Molloy helped me compile the statistical data, and Daniel O. Price later reviewed it. Martin Tenney offered to help get the data processed for the computer quickly and economically. Alexander Clark not only helped in the data processing, but he also read the manuscript and was instrumental in involving me in the International Biological Program. I had the use of several Master's theses: Sister Helen Rose Fuchs, "Contact and Prejudice Reaction from the Viewpoint of Colored Creoles"; Florence Alwilda Strom, "The Out-Migration Pattern of a Colored Community in the South"; and Louretha Williams and William H. French, "Attitudes Toward Public Assistance in a Nonwhite Rural Community." Sister Lora Ann Quinonez was an efficient, extremely patient editorial consultant during the final stages of the study.

I was fortunate to have Lynnette Dixon Dukes as research assistant for three years. In the painstaking work of tracing genealogy, she learned early that only substantiated evidence paid off, and disallowed all nicknames or guesses. Jeanette Gerlitz put in extra time typing the manuscript, and Jesus D. Alonso assisted in the final critical reading and editing.

Without the cooperation of the people in the vicinity of Riverville, the study would have been impossible. During the preliminary, exploratory stages the Sisters of Divine Providence not only gave me spiritual support, but also the use of their homes (including the contents of deep freezes), even during the summer months when they were not present. Sister Irene Ceasar spent one entire summer assisting me in the tedious work of perusing records and photocopying them. Without exception, the professional people in Indianola were gracious, encouraging, and hospitable. At the courthouse, it was not unusual to be offered a cup of coffee as well as aid in locating records of various kinds. A well-known lawyer, now deceased, gave me many hours of assistance in tracing and interpreting legal documents, and a social historian spent much time in helping me reconstruct the past.

The most rewarding experience, however, has been afforded by the Letoyant Creoles themselves. They welcomed me, treated me to Creole delicacies, laughed with me, wept with me, prayed with me, and gave me their confidences. I hope I have not betrayed them. To ensure confidentiality, I have used pseudonyms in the text and will here refrain from naming those who have made major contributions to this study. They know who they are.

# Contents

# Tables

# Figures

# PART I
Establishing an Identity

# Chapter 1

# Introduction

The modern era has been called an age of alienation. Today man is particularly conscious of his inability to breach the gulf between his accomplishments and his control over them. Man's feeling of alienation has been given expression in the arts as well as in science. It is reflected in the moods of poets like T. S. Eliot, William Butler Yeats, and Ezra Pound and in writers such as James Joyce, Albert Camus, Ernest Hemingway, and Jean-Paul Sartre. The visual arts, too, portray meaninglessness; surrealistic art, for instance, is deliberately nihilistic. In art—as in ordinary experience—emphasis has shifted from the group to the exploration and definition of selfhood and identity.

Even groups reflect the modern desire to establish an identity. The Black Power movement, for example, arises from the struggle of an ethnic group for self-consciousness and self-identity. It is, in effect, an effort to find an identity with a past that is acknowledged, an effort that can be traced back to its African roots. Negroes are demanding that their accomplishments in the United States be recognized and that their people be aware of their past. An individual who identifies with a people who has a true sense of identity, particularly one that has exemplified courage and an ability to rise above hardships, is not as likely to suffer alienation.

The concept of alienation is not new. In law it has long been used in reference to the transfer of property or of affections, which are regarded as a form of property. Philosophers, psychologists, and sociologists have used *alienation* to refer to a variety of psychosocial disorders: anomie, rootlessness, apathy, meaninglessness, loneliness, isolation, powerlessness, pessimism, self-estrangement, and the loss of beliefs and values. Among those who have been classified as alienated are the mentally disturbed, addicts,

3

the younger generation, juvenile delinquents, the aged, industrial workers, immigrants, and minority groups.[1]

Two general approaches to the phenomenon of alienation are evident in the research of scholars. Psychologists have stressed the estrangement of individuals and have treated alienation as an individual feeling or state of dissociation from self, from other individuals, and from the world at large. The work of Emile Durkheim, at the end of the nineteenth century, however, gave alienation a new focus. In his study of suicide, Durkheim recognized that the norms of society might be such that an individual would dissociate himself from them and subsequently lose his sense of belonging and solidarity with other men. Durkheim also noted that society itself may be in a state of anomie in which guidelines of behavior are not clearly specified. The conditions of society or of the groups to which an individual belongs, therefore, affect man's sense of alienation or belongingness.

Karl Marx, in his analysis of capitalism, also put alienation in a sociological frame of reference when he criticized the system of private property in which a worker is alienated from the product of his labor and from the means of production. In *German Ideology* Marx said explicitly that social conditions influence man's nature and desires and that man cannot be viewed accurately except in relation to the social conditions in which he lives. He wrote: "As individuals express their life, so they are. What they are, therefore, coincides with their production, both with what they produce and with how they produce. The nature of individuals thus depends on the material conditions determining their production." [2] By stressing the effect of modes of production on an individual's thinking and feeling, Marx emphasized that social conditions can determine a person's feeling of alienation or belongingness.

Søren Kierkegaard and Friedrich Nietzsche were concerned

[1] Cf. Orrin E. Klapp, *Collective Search for Identity* (New York: Holt, Rinehart and Winston, 1969); Eric and Mary Josephson, *Man Alone* (New York: Dell Publishing Co., 1962).

[2] Karl Marx and Fredrick Engels, *German Ideology*, ed. with an introduction by R. Pascal (New York: International Publishers, 1939), 14.

with self-alienation as a general human condition resulting from the feeling of nothingness that faces man in a technological, secular, and materialistic society. Major scientific and technological revolutions since their time have compounded the situation. In the impersonal bureaucracies which Max Weber saw as characteristic of modern society, power is concentrated and efficiency made a goal at the expense of the individual. Workers show their frustrations by restricting output, instigating strikes, and resorting to outright sabotage.

Alienation, therefore, obviously has roots in social conditions. In a preindustrial age, the extended kinship group was the primary productive and social unit; since production was centered in the kin group, alienation was unlikely. Work is now almost completely separated from family life; most gainful employment takes place outside the home. In a society where identity is closely associated with occupation, the retired and aged are particularly susceptible to the loss of identity and status that is derived from jobs. They are less likely than ever before to be an integral part of a nuclear family household. In suburbia or in the contemporary urban milieu, the worker's involvement in, and power over, the operation of the community has waned; in many instances, it has become practically nonexistent.

The alienated individual may find a social order nonrelevant or even fraudulent. College and high school students, often from the "respectable" middle or upper social classes, may be sufficiently alienated to lose their former identity and to become "flower children" or "cave dwellers" in the anonymity of the city or in some remote place. Others have recourse to alcohol or drugs. Still others become mentally ill in their quest for a meaningful social order.

In the search for identity and belongingness men have grouped themselves in what Erik Erikson calls pseudospecies.[3] They have set up various kinds of criteria as bases of groupness, such as nationality, language, religion, and race. Differences on which identity can be based have sometimes been visible, like color, and at

[3] Erick Erikson, *Identity* (New York: W. W. Norton Co., 1969), 298.

other times ideological. Ethnicity, although but one of the factors in identity, is especially important since it encompasses not only the visible, material aspects of a people's lives but also attitudes and beliefs.

Ethnicity is ordinarily accompanied by ethnocentrism, the attributing of superiority to one's own people with their distinctive racial and cultural characteristics. Individuals or groups who do not possess these characteristics are deemed inferior and are excluded. Those so excluded, particularly if they have a desire to belong, experience one form of alienation. If enough individuals possessing the same characteristics experience alienation, they may establish a collective identity and form their own distinct ethnic group.

Full-fledged ethnicity is characterized by at least two qualities —a long tradition and a strong tendency toward self-perpetuation.[4] The extent to which an ethnic population is able to maintain itself and promote solidarity depends, in large part, upon the esteem or disesteem accorded it by the dominant society and upon the degree to which the ethnic population fulfills the needs of its members. If an ethnic group is at a disadvantage because of some characteristic which the dominant population devalues, there is a likelihood that the group will be unattractive to its own members. For those of the group who do not possess the devalued characteristic, such as dark skin, the positive forces of attraction within the ethnic group will have to outweigh the negative forces of detraction. Those who are precluded from identifying with the dominant society by color must have positive forces of attraction to offset the tendency toward self-hatred.[5]

The need for a clearcut ethnic identity is compounded if a population is in a minority position and the dominant population refuses to admit the ethnic people to full membership in the larger society and to accord them real recognition. Marginality intensifies

---

[4] L. Singer, "Ethnogenesis and Negro-Americans Today," *Social Research,* XXIX (Winter, 1962), 424.

[5] Cf. Kurt Lewin, *Resolving Social Conflicts* (New York: Harper and Brothers, 1948), 190–92.

the need to develop a sense of identity with, and a feeling of belongingness to, a group that matters. Under these conditions, marginal ethnic people are hypothesized to work out their own identity, based on common characteristics, and form their own social groups to meet their basic psychological and social needs.

## THE CREOLES, A MARGINAL PEOPLE

The marginal group under study is a segment of a population referred to as *Creole*. As the term is generally used in the Western Hemisphere, it is applicable to native-born descendants of French or Spanish colonists, regardless of racial admixture. In the United States the term is most commonly used in reference to the descendants of white persons of French or Spanish extraction who were born in Louisiana. A century or more ago *Creole*, as used in Louisiana, designated a native of the state, regardless of his racial origin. In 1840, for example, the New Orleans *Picayune* used the term in reference to nonwhite slaves.[6] But, in the last quarter of the nineteenth century, George Washington Cable, the New Orleans novelist, excluded the descendants of French and Spanish colonial stock who had a Negro strain, and his restricted application of the term became popularly accepted.

The Creoles in the present study are Creoles of color. They comprise a population of 8,901 persons who are direct descendants of one couple, a Frenchman named Letoyant (pseudonym) and Marie, a woman of uncertain racial origin but who was known to have African ancestry. Also included in the study population are the 1,246 "outsiders," which term refers to the nondirect descent population who married Letoyants during the last two centuries. Although the nondirect descent population includes whites, Indians, Negroes, and racially mixed people, Creoles predominate among

---

[6] "Creole," *Dictionary of American English on Historical Principles*, II (Chicago: University of Chicago Press, 1942), 677. Although *nonwhite* is popularly used in reference to persons with *any* African ancestry, many of them also have white ancestry, therefore they resent this usage. See Albert Murray, *Omni-Americans* (New York: E. P. Dalton, 1970), 78–80. For consistency, however, the popular usage is followed here.

the outsiders, and the offspring of all these unions are considered in this study as direct descent Letoyants through one parent. The study population, then, consists of a total of 10,147 persons. The direct descendants, called Letoyant, settled initially in a Louisiana community called here Riverville.

The Letoyants take pride in being called Creole, a label that denotes their French ancestry. In this study "other Creoles," meaning Louisiana Creoles not related to the Letoyants, will be so designated. In Figures and Tables based on the study population both direct descent Letoyants and the nondirect descent population are included under the general caption of *Creole*.[7] Despite the Letoyant emphasis on their French origin, they possess Negroid characteristics introduced by Marie in the first filial generation (referred to hereafter simply as the first generation). The oldest first-generation male, Nicholas, who subsequently became known as Grand Pere because of his many descendants, married a Canadian "half-breed" who was French and Indian. Others with Mongoloid (Indian) characteristics subsequently intermarried with these people.

The Letoyant Creoles are a marginal people set apart not only by racial characteristics but also by a distinctive culture. When they became identity-conscious, prior to the Civil War, they emulated the early French settlers in language, religion, family patterns, and style of life. They lived in semi-isolation, however, and their culture took on its own flavor. This cultural distinctiveness, where it has been preserved, has contributed to the Letoyants' sense of identity. Familiarity with their own history and culture has been a strong force uniting the Letoyant Creole population.

Individual identity is influenced not only by the prevailing conditions at a given time but also by historical circumstances and by the vision of the future. The history of the Letoyant Creoles is very significant, for it explains, in large part, their motivation in creating an ethnic group. But the future is equally important, if not more so, for no ethnic group can persist without some vision of their future as a people.

[7] For the manner in which other populations are defined and referred to in this study, see the Appendix, p. 390.

Even though, as a racially mixed people, the Letoyants are marginal in the total American society, they nonetheless have a clear concept of themselves as a distinct people. This self-concept is immediately apparent to anyone who becomes acquainted with them. *Our people, the people,* or simply *we, the people* are common expressions. A journalist from Chicago, who visited their rural homeland, asked one of them, "Just what kind of people are you? You are not white nor are you colored." The response was, "We are the forgotten people." Perhaps the respondent had in mind that prior to the Civil War the Letoyants enjoyed a special status which was lost when the distinction between free people of color and their slaves was obliterated.

Letoyant Creole awareness of a distinct identity is evident in the ability of many living Letoyants to trace their ancestry back through nine or ten generations and to do the same for relatives and acquaintances. Moreover, the vast majority claim a common ancestor—the eldest son of the Frenchman Letoyant—to whom they refer as Grand Pere. Sometimes he is the common ancestor on the paternal as well as the maternal side. Stories about ancestors have been handed down by word of mouth for ten generations, and pre–Civil War episodes are recounted vividly as though they took place within the lifetime of the narrator. Heirlooms and portraits are treasured by families that claim them. Old trunks contain ledgers with entries about purchases of slaves and shipments of goods from New Orleans or France, letters or first drafts of letters that date back more than a century, and old French textbooks.

Non-Creole residents in the vicinity of Riverville are also aware of the distinctive identity and group solidarity of the Letoyants. The white people who have resided in the area for years make remarks such as the following: "These people are fine, they are not like the regular Negro today. They have pride. They try to educate their children and to live like us. They are nearly all of them Catholics. They just live to themselves. They don't have anything to do with others. It's just like a colony of people that live for themselves. They think, a lot of them believe, they are white, or they act like they are white."

A white resident of old-family descent said, "Records show that before the Civil War, some of these people owned as many as 150 slaves. They had race horses, stables, sets of silver, and valuables imported from France. These things were recorded on the inventory of a man's possessions when he died. The people were also accepted by the officials. The circuit judges were entertained in their homes when they went around making their circuit."

A perceptive, educated white man, a resident in the area for little more than a decade, remarked, "These people are a self-contained unit. They are different from the ordinary Negro. They look different with their thin lips, long narrow noses, and long faces. Whatever Negro background they have must be superior to that of other Negroes in the vicinity. These people remind me of the Gullahs of the Carolinas who are also distinctive. They must have been smart to keep their land—the best farmland in the parish —all these years. It is a kind of bond holding them to this vicinity."

On the other hand, Negroes in Louisiana are very sensitive to the exclusiveness of the Letoyant Creoles, and their opinions of them are quite different from those of the white people. An old Negro man who has lived in Riverville all his life made the following statement: "The mulatto is not your pure race, but yet he will try to style himself above me, and I am pure. Now there are a few of those mulattoes here that put themselves on the same quality with me, but most of them try to class up with the whites. If I was mulatto, I would be looking for the darker race to try to get with them."

The people who marry into the population usually become absorbed by it and are quick to note its distinctiveness. One of these persons, a trainman, commented that among the passengers he could always pick out Letoyant Creoles, even though he did not know them personally. He said that they had a distinctive appearance, a noticeable dialect, and recognizable names. He indicated that he thought their physical appearance is attributable to their mixed racial origins and close inbreeding over ten generations.

The spelling or pronounciation of surnames is often a clue to Letoyant Creole identity. Many of the surnames are peculiar to this population; others have a spelling characteristic of the people. Since Letoyant Creoles have many of the same surnames as the old-family whites, a different syllabic accent or a peculiar spelling was used by the whites in referring to the Letoyants. Thus, Letoyant is pronounced La toy awnt' for the whites bearing that surname and La twa' yant for the nonwhites with the same surname. In the case of a surname commonly used by both the French and the Irish, but spelled slightly differently by each, the Letoyant Creoles use the Irish version while most of the other natives of Louisiana use the French.

Letoyant Creole speech patterns have traces of both southern and Negro dialects as well as some peculiar expressions. The upper social classes reveal little of the prevailing dialect, and educated Letoyants who have moved out of the South have a less readily discernible dialect than those who remain in the South. Final r's and t's are generally not pronounced. *Hoot* owl becomes a *who* owl and *door* is generally pronounced *dō*. Similarly, *here* is pronounced *heah*. *Some* is very often used instead of *very*. A costly item is said to be *some high;* or a garment is described as *some pretty*. An old person may be called an *ageable* person and a single item may be referred to as the *onliest* one. Word order is frequently peculiar. A person will say "I yet am [tired]" for "I am still tired."

RESEARCH IMPLICATIONS

SPECIFIC APPLICABILITY

The Creole population under study is a marginal one that has not been totally accepted by the dominant population. As such, many of its experiences over the past two hundred years are unique and, therefore, have limited applicability to other populations.

Among the questions explored in this study that are germane

specifically, though not always exclusively, to the Letoyant Creoles are the following: Why have these people set themselves apart and developed their own identity? What kind of self-image have they developed? How have they gone about establishing themselves as a group? Have any of the norms set up prior to the Civil War been preserved, and if so, to what extent? How have they managed to maintain their identity over a span of two centuries? What threats to solidarity have they had to overcome? With whom do they come into contact, and how do they relate to others whom they consider outsiders?

Has the Black Power movement had any effect on the Letoyants? If so, to what extent? Have the Letoyants been leaders to the Negroes? Are Negroes resentful of the Letoyants, especially of their pride in their past?

What happens to the sense of identity of American nonwhites when they move out of their rural isolation to larger communities? Do light-complexioned nonwhites attempt to pass into the dominant white population? Do those who leave isolation marry outsiders with increasing frequency?

As Creoles of color, the Letoyants differed from most other Creoles in that they had rural roots and were physically, as well as socially, isolated. When world wars brought the United States increasingly into international affairs, the Letoyants were jolted out of their isolation and had to travel and to fight abroad, to mix with many kinds of people; eventually some settled in predominantly urban areas. Other Creoles, in general, however, were typically more urban than rural, interacting with other populations in the urban milieu.

The case study approach to the Creoles is a comprehensive and intensive analysis of a total situation, with evidence derived from a multiplicity of sources. It affords a microscopic view of a total, though limited, society of some ten thousand individuals. This approach is essentially narrative and descriptive. The quantitative data are based upon the total population, or specific components of it; therefore, there is no sampling or application of tests of reliability. This type of approach affords an assessment of intangible, immeasurable qualities and an in-depth perspective.

The time span covered by the story of this group also affords an unusual perspective. The population consists of descendants of one couple traced through ten generations over a period of two centuries—from colonial times, through the early years of statehood, Civil War, and Reconstruction, into the mid-twentieth century. Over fifty fourth-generation Creoles are still alive, and some of them can recount with clarity events which took place during the Reconstruction era, as well as relate stories of the past told by their parents and grandparents.

The population investigated has clear parameters limited to the descendants of one couple and those whom they married; it is relatively small, yet nonetheless large in comparison with those of other studies of this kind.[8] It sets discernible limits to observation and affords insights into human social behavior that are not ordinarily possible for group analyses.

The Letoyant Creoles are viewed in a natural environment, not in an artificial laboratory setting. Although much of the focus is necessarily on the community of origin, Riverville, the population is also studied in the "colonies" to which they migrated. These Creoles, then, are a natural group interacting in their ordinary habitats, that is, in Riverville and in all the other places to which they have migrated in appreciable numbers.

The Letoyant Creole has achieved what Negro Americans are now striving to attain, namely, a recognizable identity and a homeland—something that most Americans can boast about if they so choose. In the vicinity of their homeland, at least, they do not share the Negro's burden of being nameless. On the contrary, they have a historical heritage and a unique identity that are sources of psychological security.

GENERAL APPLICABILITY

Despite the uniqueness of the population under study, the findings do, in several instances, have general applicability. Thus,

[8] See E. Franklin Frazier, *The Negro Family in the United States* (Rev. and abr.; New York: The Dryden Press, 1948), 164–89; and Brewton Berry, *Almost White* (New York: The Macmillan Co., 1963), for accounts of similar racially hybrid populations.

the two hypotheses that dominated this research are relevant, in particular, to marginal ethnic populations: (1) A people who possesses a marginal ethnic status in society and is geographically isolated for a long period of time will develop a unique sense of identity and strong bonds of group solidarity. This identity will be maintained through the institutionalization of what is most important to identity. (2) As individuals move from isolation into the larger society, their sense of identity will be weakened and they will gradually become assimilated into other groups. The study, therefore, takes a sociological approach to identity and alienation by focusing on the historical and social characteristics of an ethnic group and on the impact that belonging to the group has on its constituents.

The process of ethnogenesis by which a people develops a sense of ethnic identity may vary from one group to another, but there will be many similarities. In the process of attaining a recognizable ethnic identity these people look for a territory or a homeland where they can take root. Then they either assume some culture, or aspects of a culture, that is deemed useful, as the Black Muslims have done, or espouse aspects of the culture of the dominant population. They may take on aspects such as attitudes toward racial characteristics that are a source of shame to dark-complexioned group members. They may even emulate the dominant population by discriminating against people darker than themselves.

In the course of time, some norms and values, such as those that contribute to ethnic identity and pride, become more meaningful than others. Group members who deviate from these norms and values incur group displeasure and may be excluded from important group activities.

A population that has been physically and socially isolated for a long period of time and has reinforced group norms and values through this isolation will experience some cultural shock when large numbers move into an alien environment. Identity as a distinctive group is reexamined. Unless there are frequent and sustained opportunities for interaction among group members, there is a risk of losing identity and of becoming assimilated by other groups.

Insights into the effects of rapid social change are needed. This study exemplifies the social change occurring in the Deep South over a long period of time and culminating in modifications of farming practices and particularly the decline of family farms. Moreover, it exemplifies the acceleration of mobility from rural to urban places and such effects of that exodus as the loss of insularity and reliance on kinfold, particularly the extended family.

Information on "passing" of nonwhites into the white population is fragmented and meager. The Letoyant Creole population, with its definite parameters, affords additional data on a topic about which there is much speculation but little hard data.

A population, such as the Letoyants, that constitutes a social group at once marginal and yet dynamically involved with both the dominant white population and the minority Negro population further affords an insight into the complexity of intergroup relations, especially interracial relations in the United States. Within the population classified as Negro, there is a variety of populations with Negroid background. Creoles are one of the "mixed blood" or "half-breed" populations found in any society.[9] They are very conscious of color differences and rarely classify themselves as white, nor do they call themselves blacks as the Negroes now commonly refer to themselves. They have no objection to being called colored, or Creole. Research on intergroup relations concerning minorities has thus far been primarily limited to the study of the relationships between given minority groups and the dominant white Anglo-Saxon Protestant American. There is little research on intergroup relations among minority groups themselves, especially within the nonwhite population. Therefore, an aim of this study is to contribute to the understanding of racial attitudes and discriminatory practices among American minority peoples.

[9] For a list of similar populations, their size, and location by state and county, see Calvin L. Beale, "American Triracial Isolates," *Eugenics Quarterly*, IV (December, 1957), 187–96.

Thus, even though the study is limited to one population that is in many respects unique and atypical, it does, nevertheless, provide insights and partial answers to questions that are of concern to society at large.

## ORGANIZATION OF DATA

Findings are organized into four parts: (1) Establishing an Identity, (2) Maintaining an Identity in the Southland, (3) The Diaspora and Subsequent Identity, and (4) an Epilogue. Part I affords a glance into the past of the Letoyants: their origin, their history, and the process of building up their identity during the first century of their existence, prior to the Civil War.

Part II traces the development of social institutions designed to maintain their identity in the South, their goals, norms, and social roles, and their interaction patterns with other populations. The guiding hypothesis of Parts I and II is that a marginal people, geographically isolated for a long period of time, will tend to develop a sense of identity and strong feelings of group solidarity.

Part III, concerned with the dispersal of the Letoyant Creoles and the survival of their institutions, treats the hypothesis that individuals who move from isolation into the larger society will gradually become assimilated.

Part IV presents an overview of the study and conclusions. It is followed by an Appendix which gives the method used in the investigation of the hypotheses, particularly personal interviews and historical records including family albums, legal documents, and church records. Terminology used for various populations referred to in the study is explained, as well as the manner in which Letoyant genealogy was traced. The reader will find it helpful to consult the Appendix before proceeding with the text.

*Chapter 2*

---

# Letoyant Creole Identity as Free People of Color

Since the identity of the present-day Letoyant Creoles has its origin in the past, a knowledge of their history is essential to an understanding of their feelings of identity. The very appellation *Creole* commonly implies descent from French or Spanish settlers. The perpetuation of this line of descent and a claim to use the surname of Letoyant was particularly important to the first generations of the people.

Related to their descent from a respectable, well-known colonizer was their identity as free people of color prior to the Civil War. The French and Spanish settlers in Louisiana who had nonwhite children were inclined to show concern for them. One of the most obvious expressions of this concern was to liberate any of these offspring born into slavery and to see that legislation favorable to them was written into law when their happiness was threatened.

In the present chapter some perspective is given on the Letoyants by focusing on the first century of their history when, labeled as nonwhites, they enjoyed the status of free people of color. Their identity was shaped by the laws pertaining to people of Negro origin in the United States, and especially in Louisiana. The extent to which they prospered economically, increased biologically, and earned the good will and recognition of their contemporaries helped to forge their initial identity. Their beginnings remain as much a part of their cultural heritage as do the beginnings of the descendants of the Mayflower passengers or of the Main Line in Philadelphia.

### Free People of Color in America

Soon after the first slaves were brought to the American colonies in 1619, some became free. Many escaped from captivity; others were freed legally through diverse means such as self-liberation through paying the master's estimated monetary value of the slave; liberation by the master for various reasons, such as religious scruples or sentiment; and liberation in recognition of military valor. One slave, for instance, was emancipated and given a reward of $500 by the Louisiana legislature in recognition of "meritorious service."[1]

A slave who was baptized was probably accorded more dignity and had a greater possibility for freedom than one who was not, for baptism by its nature recognized that the slave was not merely a chattel, but a human being, and initiated him into the society of Christians. Early records show that among the slaves brought to Virginia in 1619 were some with Christian names who were probably baptized by the Spanish missionaries prior to their sale to the colonists. E. Franklin Frazier believes it probable that the distinction between Christian and heathen, or baptized and unbaptized, had as much significance at that time as the distinction between white and black at a later date. However, by 1667 Negro labor became so profitable that the Virginia legislature enacted a law stating that "the conferring of baptisme doth not alter the condition of the person as to his bondage or freedome."[2]

During the seventeenth and eighteenth centuries the free Negro population within the boundaries of the present United States grew three times as rapidly as the slave population.[3] In addition to natural population increase through the birth of children to the freedman, the numbers of the free people of color were augmented by the manumission of slave women by whom white masters had children, as well as by the progeny of such unions.

[1] Kenneth M. Stampp, *The Peculiar Institution* (New York: Alfred A. Knopf, 1956), 233.

[2] E. Franklin Frazier, *The Negro Family in the United States* (Rev. and abr.; New York: The Dryden Press, 1948), 142–43.

[3] *Ibid.*, 143.

The most striking feature among free people of color was the incidence of "mixed blood." In 1850, about three-eighths of the free people of color in the United States were classified by the Bureau of the Census as mulattoes—persons of mixed Caucasian and Negro ancestry—whereas only about one-twelfth of the slave population was so classified.[4]

Until the early nineteenth century, the freed Negro had a relatively secure place in society. He had the right to own and to alienate property, though not the right to own whites as servants. In most states, free Negroes could bring suit against persons doing them an injury. When charged with crime, they had a right to trial by jury and could, after indictment, give bond for liberty. In the South, where the free Negroes were concentrated, they had a more secure economic position in the cities than they did in rural areas, for urban freedmen were employed in factories and in skilled occupations, and they acquired sufficient property to be taxpayers.[5]

After the first quarter of the nineteenth century, the status of free people of color became uncertain. They were under suspicion as possible sources of discontent and as instigators of revolt among the slaves. Race riots in New York City and Philadelphia between 1830 and 1840 aroused an even greater fear that the free Negro would support the cause of the slave.[6] This explains, in part, the increasing legislation in the slaveholding states to restrict the number of free Negroes. By the mid-1800's there was some restriction of the movement of free Negroes from one state to another. In 1849 the Virginia legislature was petitioned to make an appropriation for the gradual removal of free Negroes to Liberia. One Virginia master offered freedom to his fourteen slaves if they would agree to move to Liberia at the expense of the

[4] *Ibid.*, 145. Creole attitudes toward being called *mulatto* are discussed in Chap. 3.
[5] E. Franklin Frazier, *The Negro in the United States* (New York: The Macmillan Co., 1949), 70.
[6] John Hope Franklin, "History of Racial Segregation in the United States," *Annals of the American Academy of Political and Social Science*, CCCIV (March, 1956), 2.

American Colonization Society. In 1859 the Arkansas legislature required sheriffs to order the state's free Negroes to leave the state.[7]

Immediately prior to the Civil War, then, the condition of free people of color was relatively precarious in most of the southern states. Many liberated slaves were, understandably, not sympathetic with the system of slavery. As the tension between the North and South became increasingly serious and inflammatory, the southern states often tightened the restrictions on manumission and curtailed the rights of free people of color.

## LOUISIANA'S "GENS DE COULEUR LIBRE"

The early French colonists were not favorably disposed toward tilling the soil, nor were they particularly successful in their attempts to get the Indians to do so. Therefore, in 1708 the French Canadian explorer, Jean Baptiste le Moyne (called Bienville), who was in charge of a colony at the mouth of the Mississippi established by him and his brother Pierre (called Iberville), asked the French government to authorize the exchange of Louisiana Indians for Negroes in the French West Indian Islands. However, it was Anthony Crozat who, in 1712, obtained from the king of France an exclusive fifteen-year privilege of trading in the immense territory that France claimed as Louisiana. The following year the first Negro slaves were recorded in the census of a little colony on the site of the present settlement of Biloxi, Mississippi.[8]

The exact origin of the Negroes of colonial Louisiana cannot be traced accurately; records show, however, that the slaves were a diverse group. Many of those directly from Africa came from Senegal, the Congo, and Guinea. Other slaves originated along the west coast of Africa but were taken to the West Indies and brought from there to the American colonies. Soon after landing in the West Indies, these Africans began to mingle with the whites

[7] Stampp, *The Peculiar Institution*, 216, 94.
[8] Alice Dunbar-Nelson, "People of Color in Louisiana," *Journal of Negro History*, I (October, 1916), 362.

as well as with the Indians in the area. In the West Indies a person of Negro-white ancestry was recognized as colored and formed a special class, intermediate between whites and blacks. In French Louisiana all Negroes who were pure-blooded Africans were called Negro; those not pure-blooded African were known as *gens de couleur*.

Among the *gens de couleur* in Louisiana, distinctions were made on the basis of the degree of white and Negro ancestry. The mulatto was half white and half Negro; the griffe was the offspring of a mulatto and a Negro; the quadroon was one-fourth Negro; and the octoroon, one-eighth Negro. Of all the Negroes emancipated after 1803 about three-fourths had a large measure of white blood, and by 1860 no less than 81 percent were largely white.[9]

Louisiana had the reputation for being the most liberal of the southern states in the treatment of nonwhites.[10] In the territory there were 1,303 free people of color in 1785; in 1810, when the first United States census was taken in Louisiana, their number had increased to 7,585.[11] This rapid increase can be attributed in part to the natural population increase through the freeborn progeny of freemen and in part to the manumission of slaves. But the numbers were increased considerably by thousands of mixed-blooded refugees from Haiti who formed a distinct class in New Orleans and objected to associating with Negroes on terms of equality. They amassed fortunes, educated their children in France or in non-segregated schools, and attained distinction in scientific and literary circles.[12] Particularly through their influence, early laws restricting free people of color were mitigated.

Many of the daughters of these wealthy free men of color were educated in France, and much time and expense were involved in

[9] Joe Gray Taylor, *Negro Slavery in Louisiana* (Baton Rouge: Louisiana Historical Assn., 1963), 10, 12, 162.

[10] Stampp, *The Peculiar Institution*, 232.

[11] Annie Lee West Stahl, "The Free Negro in Ante-Bellum Louisiana," *Louisiana Historical Quarterly*, XXV (April, 1942), 381.

[12] Grace E. King, *New Orleans: The Place and the People* (New York: The Macmillan Co., 1895), 342.

training them to develop their natural charm. In 1788, however, restrictions were decreed by Governor Miro in an ordinance making these women liable for punishment if they walked "abroad in silks, jewels, or plumes." The only head covering they were permitted to use was the *tignon*, a kerchief tied around the head.[13]

At the time of the Louisiana Purchase, in 1803, the free Negroes protested against not being included among the colonists who signed a memorial to Congress on the status of the colonists under the United States government.[14] They participated in every war and were accorded a separate identity, from the Revolutionary War through the Civil War. During the American Revolution, when Louisiana was a Spanish province, the Spaniards waged a successful war against the British on the Gulf Coast. During the campaign colored freedmen constituted part of the regular force of Galvez.[15] During the Spanish regime, a battalion of free men of color, under the command of Colonel Fortier, a rich merchant of New Orleans, were organized as a part of the militia of New Orleans, and on several occasions they showed great courage in battle. During the war of 1812 General Andrew Jackson was so pleased with the battalion of freedmen from New Orleans that he levied a new battalion of the same people.[16] During the Civil War the free people of color were, as a rule, separated in fact and in sympathy from the slaves, and at the outbreak of the war many of them volunteered their services to the Confederacy.[17]

MANUMISSION

Manumission was not too difficult to arrange in colonial Louisiana provided the slaves were freed by their owners. If, however (as in the case of the family in this study), children were born to

[13] *Ibid.*, 307–310.
[14] E. Franklin Frazier, *The Negro in the United States* (Rev. ed.; New York: The Macmillan Co., 1957), 77.
[15] Charles B. Rousseve, *The Negro in Louisiana* (New Orleans: Xavier University Press, 1937), 27.
[16] Stahl, "The Free Negro in Ante-Bellum Louisiana," 327.
[17] Edward B. Reuter, *The Mulatto in the United States* (Boston: Richard G. Badger, 1918), 340.

a slave woman belonging to someone else, then economic resources had to be available to purchase the children's freedom.
Just as indentured servants could secure their freedom by repay-
ing the debts which they had incurred, so, too, it was possible in
some instances for slaves to purchase their own freedom.

Shortly after the Louisiana Purchase, however, the Louisiana
legislature began passing laws restricting the emancipation of
slaves. In 1807 an act was passed stating that no slave could be
freed unless he was at least thirty years of age and had not been
guilty of bad conduct for the preceding four years. The only exception was in the case of a slave who saved the life of a member
of his master's family. Emancipation of slaves under the age of
thirty required a special act of the legislature. Requests to the
legislature were so numerous that, in 1827, the legislature ruled
that a master who wished to free a slave who had not attained the
age of thirty had to present a petition setting forth his motives to
his parish police jury. If three-fourths of the members of the police
jury approved, the slave might be freed.[18] In 1830 another act
provided that any person who freed a slave must post a bond of
$1,000 to guarantee that the freedman would leave the state
within thirty days. An amendment to the act of 1830 was passed
the following year providing that a master would not be required to post bonds nor would the freedman be required to leave
the state if the manumission were for meritorious service.

Numerous other legislative acts were passed in the 1840's. By
1852 the Louisiana legislature ruled that no slave could be emancipated under any condition unless he was to be sent out of the
United States within the year. A master who set a slave free was
required to post $150 to be used to pay for transportation to
Africa. Manumitted slaves who did not leave within the year
were to revert to slave status; however, this act resulted in another
flood of petitions for special authorizations to emancipate
slaves. Of the Negroes who were emancipated between 1852 and
1855, only six were actually required to leave the state and, in

[18] Taylor, *Negro Slavery in Louisiana*, 154.

1855 the obligation to send manumitted slaves to Africa was removed. A person who desired to emancipate a slave under the 1855 act had to bring suit against the state in a district court and pay all costs of his suit regardless of the outcome.[19]

Immediately before the outbreak of the Civil War, the position of the free men of color became increasingly tenuous. Freedmen were suspected of having a "most pernicious effect" on the slave population and of inciting the slaves to insurrection. In fact, in 1859 provision was made for a freed slave to choose a master and voluntarily resume status of a slave.[20]

LEGAL STATUS

Suits for freedom by Negro slaves were nowhere else so common and successful as in Louisiana.[21] Louisiana made legal provisions not only for manumission, but also for a variety of matters of consequence to freemen. Like the other southern states, Louisiana had general policies regarding the nonwhite population embodied in a mass of legislation known as the Black Code, which were changed from time to time. The first of these statutes, enacted in 1724, was adapted from the existing law of Santo Domingo and reflected the strong influence of the Catholic Church upon legislation concerning slaves in the New World where the Spanish and French colonized.[22] Laws favorable to the slaves entitled them to be baptized and to be instructed in Catholicism; to worship; to enjoy all the Church rights pertaining to marriage—with the exception of parental consent; to be free from servile work on Sundays and holy days; and to be buried in consecrated ground.[23] Once a slave was manumitted he enjoyed the same rights, privileges, and immunities as persons born free.

In some respects Louisiana was unique in the manner in which its citizens regarded people of color. The French and Spanish

---

[19] *Ibid.,* 155.

[20] Stahl, "The Free Negro in Ante-Bellum Louisiana," 326.

[21] Taylor, *Negro Slavery in Louisiana,* 313, 376.

[22] Herbert Asbury, *The French Quarter* (New York: Pocket Books, 1936), 15.

[23] Taylor, *Negro Slavery in Louisiana,* 17, 195.

colonists who took wives from among native Indian or Negro women often acknowledged the paternity of their children and evidenced concern about restrictive legislation affecting their offspring. Many of the nonwhites in Louisiana were descended from influential white persons who intervened between them and the law and who provided private education, religious instruction, and a home life for their colored children. With the exception of political rights, certain social privileges, and the obligations of jury and militia service, the free man of color in Louisiana was distinguished from the slave to the same extent as the white man was legally distinguished from the slave.

*Marital Proscriptions.* Legislation concerning marriage had one onerous restriction that applied to free men of color as well as to slaves. A marital union between a white person and the descendant of a Negro, regardless of how remote the Negro ancestry, was illegal. Before such a marriage could be legally performed, the white party was required to take an oath that he had Negro blood. By such an oath, of course, the white person voluntarily severed himself permanently from the society of his people.[24] This law put the daughters of white men and "half-blooded" mothers in an anomalous position, for regardless of their personal charm and mental qualities, they were forbidden by law to marry white men.

The quadroon balls, attended only by quadroon girls and white men, for example, were considered the amusement par excellence in New Orleans. At these balls, the young quadroon girls displayed their accomplishments in dancing and conversation. They were watched over by their mothers until they found a white man who was attractive to them and who was to become their protector. A businesslike arrangement would be made between the mother and the suitor to "place" the girl if the suitor could provide adequately for her and for the children who might be born to the union. After the bargain was made, the daughter was regarded as a prospective bride and was feted by her acquaintances. The

[24] Stahl, "The Free Negro in Ante-Bellum Louisiana," 309–10.

young woman was then set up in a household very much the same as if a marriage had taken place.

In 1788 the New Orleans directory listed fifteen hundred unmarried free women of color who lived in little houses near the ramparts. They were esteemed as honorable and virtuous as long as they remained faithful to the men who "placed" them and instances of infidelity were rare. Children born to these unions were illegitimate, but the fathers were expected to provide for them. French and Spanish settlers tended to entertain warm feelings toward their children of mixed racial backgrounds. To many of the French and Spanish, there was little if any disgrace attached to having such children and to showing regard for them.[25]

*Property Rights.* Manumission had little value unless the freedman had opportunities to earn a livelihood and to safeguard himself against economic reverses by enjoying property rights. Louisiana had comparatively favorable attitudes toward the economic rights of the free Negro and there were some wealthy persons of color. Since the opportunities for securing work were greater in the cities, most freedmen lived there. In New Orleans, at least one-fifth of the taxable property was in the hands of free Negroes.[26] One of the few restrictions on property ownership was a prohibition against retailing intoxicating liquors, either for oneself or as an employee.[27]

Although the countryside afforded comparatively few economic opportunities, some freedmen, including the Letoyants, did acquire large land holdings and invest in slaves. In some instances, they developed and operated large plantations with slave labor and had sufficient economic resources to become money-vendors. All of a freedman's private property could be passed on to succeeding generations under Louisiana's inheritance laws.

Freedmen in Louisiana were represented in practically all economic endeavors and made such an economic contribution to the

[25] *Ibid.*, 307, 312.
[26] Otto Klineberg, *Characteristics of the American Negro* (New York: Harper & Brothers, 1944), 343.
[27] Stahl, "The Free Negro in Ante-Bellum Louisiana," 396.

state that the laws relating to deportation for various causes were never enforced. Even when laws restricted mobility, the freedmen were permitted to enter and leave the state both for business and for social reasons. Most important, however, the freedman had the privilege of being party to suits involving the rights of white persons—a privilege he enjoyed only in Louisiana. Moreover, in cases of seeming injustice, appeals could be made to a higher court.[28]

*Mobility*. The Black Code placed certain restrictions upon mobility. Among the first nonwhites to be restricted were those convicted of crime and who had a prison sentence. In 1817 Louisiana passed a law severely penalizing anyone who imported such a slave. Another category of Negroes prohibited from entering the state was a group referred to as *statu liberi*, a term designating slaves entitled to future freedom. Presumably, these persons would unduly increase the number of freedmen in the state. All free persons of color, however, except those going to and from the West Indies, who were permanent residents and owners of property within the state were permitted to leave and return as their business required.[29]

Nearly all of the southern states had laws from time to time that restricted the mobility of the freedman. These laws were more stringent in time of economic upheaval or depression and also during the years immediately preceding the Civil War. They were not designed to work a hardship upon the free people of color who were well known and established in a particular locality, especially the slaveholders who had an economic investment in the southern way of life. But they were intended to deter "outside agitators" from moving about freely, instigating riots, and urging the slaves to revolt.

By the 1840's the controversy over slavery was intensified, and freedmen who were strangers were increasingly suspect. In 1842, legislation was passed prohibiting free persons of color from

[28] *Ibid.*, 335, 375.
[29] *Ibid.*, 331.

coming into Louisiana on board vessels either as employees or passengers. In the following year this act was amended to allow free people of color who came into the state prior to the year 1838 and had constantly resided there to remain in the state without their residency being challenged. Free people of color who had lived within the state since the first of January, 1825, were allowed to leave and return, a right they had formerly enjoyed, provided they did not change their domicile from Louisiana to another state. The old maxim "Once free for an hour, free forever" remained in effect until 1846. Finally, in 1852, a law was passed which forced a manumitted slave to leave the state within three months after the act of liberation unless he was granted a permit to remain.[30]

Such legislation provides a backdrop against which to view the Letoyants. During the first few generations, when they were establishing themselves as an ethnic group, they were undoubtedly influenced by prevailing social conditions, their experiences, and those of their contemporaries. Knowledge of these conditions is essential to interpreting the documents that afford evidence about the aspirations and accomplishments of the Letoyants and to appreciating the distinctiveness that became characteristic of the ethnic group.

## GENESIS OF THE PEOPLE

Anthropologists have found that peoples throughout the world who have a strong sense of identity tend to regard themselves as *the* people and to express ethnocentrism. In fact, when the name by which a people is identified is translated it is often "*the* people," indicating that this tribe or population holds itself above others as *the* people who matter. Similarly, as the Letoyants, who were free people of color set apart by law from slaves, developed a distinctive identity, they came to refer to themselves as "we, *the* people," and to this day the expression is used. The evolution of one family into a people with a peculiar identity, like the chronol-

[30] *Ibid.*, 317, 333–34, 374.

ogy of legislation affecting their lives because of their special status, affords insight into the contemporary Letoyant ethnic group.

The setting in which the ethnogenesis of the Letoyants occurred was in the vicinity of a fort, Indianola.[31] Early in the eighteenth century the French, accompanied by a few Indian scouts, established the fort on a tributary of the Mississippi, New River. The fort was strategically located at the northernmost navigable point on the river at a place beyond which boats could not go because of a great log jam that flooded the upper valley. The settlement was established to protect the French title to a disputed strip of land adjoining the Spanish territory to the West and to develop a lucrative trade with the Indians of the area and with the Spaniards of Mexico. Since the French were soldiers, explorers, and trappers rather than tillers of the soil, the early land grants around Indianola were issued to persons who agreed to furnish supplies for the military post.

At this time wealth consisted largely of personal property, chiefly slaves who were regarded as the highest species of property. Land, though plentiful, was valuable only when it had been cleared and improved. In a census taken at the fort in the third quarter of the eighteenth century, there were about 50 Caucasian adult men, the same number of women, and some 250 children. In addition there were free people of mixed racial origin: 9 French and Indian half-breeds, 2 Indian women, and 4 mulattoes. Negro slaves numbered 94 males, 67 females, and 63 children.

The country was full of game judging from the exports listed the year the census was taken—thirty-six thousand deer skins and five thousand pots of bear oil taken from approximately twenty-five thousand bears. Other exports giving a clue to the economy were over eighteen hundred head of cattle and over one thousand head of hogs, sheep, and goats. In addition, there were large shipments of tobacco and indigo. Sugarcane became a major crop at

---

[31] All names of specific places and people are fictitious.

the end of the century, after the slave uprising in Santo Domingo, when the planters from the island fled to Louisiana.[32] It was in this environment that the first generation of Letoyants was born and reared.

THE "FIRST FAMILY"

Pierre Letoyant, a soldier at Indianola, was born in France in 1744. Marie, his common-law spouse, who was baptized in 1742, was a slave belonging to an official at the fort of Indianola. Although Baptism registers often designated the racial or ethnic origin of slaves, no such identification was recorded for Marie.

In 1758, when the official's estate was divided among his heirs, Marie was given to his daughter. Pierre paid the official's daughter for the services of Marie, and, in 1767, when Pierre was twenty-three years of age and Marie approximately twenty-five, they began to live together as man and wife. The first children of this union were twins, Nicholas and Suzanne, born in 1768. Between 1768 and 1778 children were born at two-year intervals.

In 1776, after the birth of the sixth child, Eulalie, Pierre purchased four of his children. The legal documents recording the transaction read that on the 31st day of May in the year 1776, before the lieutenant governor of the post, the daughter of the official acknowledged and declared that she "sold, transferred, and delivered, now and forever," to Mr. Pierre "to have and to hold for himself and his heirs and assigns with full warranty against all troubles and evictions whatsoever, four head of mulatto slaves," namely, Nicholas, Suzanne, Louis, and Pierre.

Two years later, Pierre purchased and freed his common-law wife, Marie, and his baby son, Joseph, born that year. Apparently he did not have sufficient funds for an outright purchase since he issued a certificate of mortgage to secure the freedom of the infant and his mother. Two years later, in 1780, two of the other children, Dominique and Eulalie, were purchased. After Marie's liberation, Touissant and François were born. The youngest

---

[32] Since the source of this information identifies the fort by name, it cannot be cited here.

child was born in 1787, nineteen years after the birth of the twins. (For the names of the first generation in order of birth, see Fig. 14, Appendix.)

About a year after the birth of the last child, a priest, new to the area, was instrumental in breaking up Pierre's alliance with Marie, and shortly thereafter Pierre entered into a marriage contract with a white widow by whom he subsequently had three children. But he assisted Marie in her application to the government for a tract of land of about 800 arpents[33] (677 acres) near Indianola. This land, with 20 arpents on a bayou front and 40 arpents extending into the hill country in the rear, was not the only land that Marie acquired. In 1794 she claimed two more tracts of land on East River, one having 800 arpents, and another smaller in size.

Pierre Letoyant lived approximately fifteen years after signing his last will and testament in 1801. During this time he continued to maintain ties with his colored children. In fact, he followed the planter's custom of lending to one of his colored sons, Dominique, a slightly older slave boy, stipulating that if the slave had not been liberated by the time of his master's death, he was to be freed at that time.

In his will Letoyant mentioned a brother, also stationed at the fort, to whom the loan of a Negro woman had been made in the year 1792. Pierre stipulated that if, at the time of his death, his brother had not paid 400 piasters for the slave, she should be sold as property belonging to himself and his wife, since he did not wish to wrong his wife and her children by her first marriage.

Among the descendants of Letoyant, there is some confusion about the number of Letoyant brothers who came from France, all of whom reputedly received land from the French government. According to one reconstructed version of the family, the only brother of Pierre who came to Louisiana married into a very prominent family and had children. The first cousins, colored and white, collaborated on business deals. A colored cousin often furnished financial resources, and a white cousin made the invest-

[33] The French measured land by the arpent instead of the acre. An arpent is slightly smaller in size than an acre.

ments. However, this investigator found no records to substantiate the assertion that Pierre's brother had children. It is more likely that collaboration took place between Pierre's white and colored descendants.

All of Pierre's white descendants along the male line, bearing his surname, have since moved away from the area of Riverville. In fact, in no instance in the search for Letoyant Creoles was a living white Letoyant, bearing that surname, found by this researcher; therefore, the name Letoyant always refers to Creoles.

The account of the colored Letoyants reconstructed from legal and ecclesiastical records differs from the version popularly believed in the vicinity of Riverville. One informant, a descendant of the white Letoyant line, said, "It was against the laws of the United States for a white man to marry a Negro. So this white Joe Letoyant who never married had these two women. And I have always been told that they were like these women [quadroons] in New Orleans. They have a great deal of white blood in them, and they don't look colored; they look white. These women had straight hair. That's where that Letoyant business started. They took the name of their owner." [34] Other white informants believe that the Letoyants are the descendants of slaves who cannot trace their descent to the Frenchman Pierre Letoyant, but who merely took his surname.

One of the accounts given by the Letoyants is as follows: "Grandpa's mother was an African woman from New Guinea. I don't know whether she was a slave or what, but I do know that all this land was given to her by the government of Louisiana. And then, in turn, she and some co-workers cleared this plantation, and started her money by making indigo. They claim her children was slaves, and she free, but that ain't so. The people who really helped her work, my grandmother say, were her co-workers. She bought their freedom. And then after that this man

---

[34] The given names of Joseph and Marie are used repeatedly since they occur with great frequency in the Creole population; they are not used in reference to any particular persons who may bear them. Hereafter, in all direct quotations, the pseudonym Letoyant is used for the family name.

came from Lyon, France. Pierre, and he married her. That was Grand Pere's father. He was French. Beginning we were mixed with French and Indian. But, that's the beginning. The blood got mixed further, later." The buildup given the "African woman" by some informants may be a reiteration of a more recent reconstruction of the past by a local white scholar rather than tradition passed by word of mouth through the generations.

Although there is disparity in the accounts reconstructing the early history of the Letoyants, there is, nevertheless, a consensus that the early generations of Letoyants were people of importance. Not only were they born into a family tracing descent from one of the first French settlers, but they achieved status through their financial dealings and their social behavior.

THE ACQUISITION OF STATUS

The early Letoyants probably aspired to an identity as a distinctive, and even remarkable, people of color. At any rate, they were motivated to acquire the same status symbols as their prestigious white contemporaries: large plantations with spacious homes, exceptionally large slaveholdings, speculation in investments of capital, and a reputation as devout and loyal adherents to the church of the original French settlers. Their success is noteworthy not only because they were nonwhite, but also because (judging from signatures on legal records) only one of the first-generation Letoyants, *petit* Pierre, was literate.

Through ingenuity and hard work the stretch along New River that was to become Riverville was transformed into thriving plantation country, some of the richest land under cultivation in the South. The two eldest sons, Nicholas and Louis, were the best financiers in the family. Property appraisals and records of succession give some indication of the extent to which the first generation must have taken risks and speculated to acquire the material status symbols that assured them recognition and contributed to their identity.

Gifts of money and property to children at the time of their marriage give some clue to prosperity. When Nicholas' oldest children married, he gave each of them 600 piasters and property ranging from 200–400 arpents as a wedding present. The two youngest sons brought their wives to live with their father and helped him operate the plantation. Nicholas later equalized land-holdings, taking into account the assessed valuation of the land and the extent of his children's indebtedness to him. Apparently Nicholas made investments for his twin, Suzanne, who similarly made gifts of land and money to her children at the time of their marriage. Since all but one of her children married Nicholas' children, they began marriage under exceptionally favorable financial circumstances (Fig. 14, Appendix).

All of Nicholas' property was assessed in 1840, prior to his distribution of it to his children who were in financial distress. Their distress was probably due to speculation in the preceding decade and to the decline in the worth of the dollar from 270 cents in 1833 to 198 cents in 1837.[35] Even after distributing 1,746 arpents of land to his children at the time of their marriages, Nicholas still had 1,754 arpents on New River and 756 arpents on East River, making a total of 2,500 arpents worth more than $50,000. His most valuable investment, after property, was in slaves. He had twenty-seven male and eighteen female slaves valued at $33,160.[36] Other property included his home valued at $2,000, two cotton mills valued at $2,000 and $1,200, respectively, and farm animals worth approximately $2,000. The total value of all his property in 1840 was $100,360 (or $240,864 in terms of the 1939 dollar),[37] and in addition he undoubtedly had cash assets.

Louis' acumen in acquiring status symbols was also extraordinary. Since his one legitimate son continued to live in the paternal plantation home, Louis had no occasion to distribute lands prior to his death in 1832. He left an estate valued at

[35] The purchasing value of the dollar is measured in terms of the consumer's price index in January, 1939, when the dollar was worth 100 cents.

[36] Since the average slaveholder in the census of 1860 owned fewer than ten slaves, the Letoyants were comparatively large slaveholders.

[37] In 1840 the value of a dollar was 240 cents.

nearly $113,000. Included in his property were sixty-six slaves, a flatboat, a barouche, a stud horse, silverware, mahogany furniture, and a plantation home that was near completion.

Just how affluent the other first-generation Letoyants were prior to the panic of 1837 cannot be determined because there are no records of the value of the holdings prior to the assessment at the time of their deaths. They, like Nicholas' children, undoubtedly suffered financial reverses. Nicholas' siblings Suzanne and Joseph died in 1838, and Dominique in 1839, immediately following the year of deep depression. Suzanne left an estate worth approximately $62,000; Joseph had property worth $31,000; and Dominique had accumulated approximately $43,000, including three hundred slaves.

The Letoyants also engaged in activities characteristic of people of importance. Nicholas made a voyage to France, the land of his forebears on his father's side, and purchased, among other things, an altar for the church. In 1836, he had his portrait painted by Feuville, an artist who traveled along the river during the summer and made portraits of people of means. Louis had erected a church to serve primarily the free people of color, and he had developed one of the outstanding plantations with a beautiful mansion. Other first-generation homes were equally impressive with billiard parlors, wine cellars, and miniature schoolhouses where children were taught by private tutors.

Of all the symbols of status, slaveholding undoubtedly had great significance, for it set the Letoyants apart in a special way from those who, like themselves, bore the mark of color. Although slaves were essential for the clearing of land and the operation of plantations, the comparatively large holdings of the Letoyants suggest that they took particular care to satisfy the need for this kind of property. Some clue to the aggregate number of slaves owned by the Letoyants is given in the christening records of the Riverville church during the twelve-year period between the time the church was accorded its parish status and the end of the Civil War. Between 1852 and 1864, 158 slaves belonging to the Letoyants were christened—an average of 20 to 25 each year.[38]

One of the Letoyants recalled what she had been told about her slaveholding ancestors: "But all these people were slave owners at one time. That's a little before the Civil War. In fact, was just our people. Was nobody else here. No American people here at all. In those days, it was strictly a mixture of French and Indian. The other mixture came in after the Civil War. And these people are very proud of themselves. Most of the people were slave owners, you know. We shouldn't be proud of that, but then, that was a way of life in that time, you know."

Like their white counterparts in Louisiana, the Letoyants apparently took relatively good care of their slaves.[39] The old adobe house which they used as a hospital is called the "slave hospital" to this day. One informant gave the following account of conditions as described by her grandmother: "The slave huts were of logs and dirt. Joe'd have them white washed every three months. They say he was a peculiar man. And he had a line of toilets 'way back from the house. All of them white washed. He would see that his hundred slaves kept up being clean because he was fastidious about things like that! He was very strict man, rigid man! And he wanted slaves in the house to be starched, dressed, you know."

Apparently this slaveholder had a premonition of hard times to come prior to the Civil War, and he attempted to prepare his children. In the words of the informant, "And he made his children, mind you, every week one of those daughters had to

[38] The slave birthrate was highest in 1861, when forty-three infants were christened. Slave christening records read as follows: "On June 5, 1852, I baptized Eugenie, born on December 2, 1851 of Julia, of the family of Nicholas Letoyant of Riverville." The slave owner's name took the place of a surname; no names were entered in the spaces provided for the father's name or for the names of the godparents.
[39] Sick records of Louisiana plantation owners during the 1840's and 1850's noted an average loss of time from work per slave as eleven or twelve days a year —a comparatively good health record and an indication that physical abuse of slaves was not common. Clement Eaton, *The Growth of Southern Civilization: 1790–1860* (New York: Harper & Row, 1963), 64.

cook and another would take the house. Learning housekeeping. Because he saw that things were going to change. He told them its going to be different. You going to have to do—to work."

For the most part, the second-generation Letoyants were, like their fathers, industrious, enterprising, and respected. When Nicholas' oldest son died in 1854, after having suffered losses in the depression of 1837, he left property valued at $84,000, including thirty-nine slaves.[40] But some of the second generation must have regarded conspicuous consumption as a meaningful way to give evidence of their importance. Two of Nicholas' sons borrowed from their father without paying their debts. When Nicholas divided his property in 1840, the youngest son owed him nearly $7,000 and the son who was his namesake owed him $24,000. When the latter died in 1857, his property was worth only $1,500, and he had debts of over $2,000, which his widow had to pay.

The third generation had similar experiences, sometimes compounded by the need to maintain status when white persons accorded them recognition by asking for financial backing. Thus, Theophile, the only son of Louis' son, was constrained to offer his plantation as collateral when he was asked to do so by a white man who needed financial backing for a business venture that failed. By 1844 Theophile was indebted to two attorneys for the sum of $3,800 for which he gave promissory notes. As security for the payment of the notes, he mortgaged forty arpents of land; forty slaves and his title and interest in twenty-five slaves held in common between him and his mother; a strip of land containing ninety-eight acres; and his plantation home together with the buildings and improvements. His mother, who shared with him the ownership of over $67,000 worth of property, lost no time having her property separated from that of her son.

During the first half of the nineteenth century, then, the Letoyants had become well established in the area of Riverville and were recognized as a family with tremendous drive, an esteem for culture and the finer things in life, and a southern

---

[40] Seventeen slave children were not included in the property evaluation.

outlook similar to that of other Louisiana planters. Not all of the second- and third-generation Letoyants realized the ideals set before them by Nicholas and his siblings, but the goals of family consciousness and pride in their heritage were clearly delineated during the long lives of the first-generation Letoyants.

## THE CIVIL WAR AND ITS AFTERMATH

Although five of the first-generation Letoyants who lived to adulthood died during the 1830's, Nicholas lived to be eighty-eight and died in 1856 when the Civil War was threatening. The two youngest brothers lived through the war years and died in 1864, aged sixty-seven and sixty-nine. In the decade preceding the war, the surviving Letoyants could look back with pride on the accomplishments of the family. Nicholas, known as Grand Pere to 161 of his descendants in 1856, had lived to see the family increase in the civil parish where Riverville is located from 15½ percent of the total nonwhite population in 1820 to 34 percent in 1840, and at the time of his death to about 50 percent. By 1860 the Letoyants constituted 56 percent of the nonwhite population in the parish—a parish that ranked fourth in the state in the number of free men of color.

When secession and war were pending, the Letoyants were as concerned as other Southerners were about its impact on the southern way of life. The attitudes of the free people of color were expressed in a statement sent to a New Orleans newspaper shortly before the outbreak of the war: "The free people of color of Louisiana . . . own slaves, and they are ready to shed their blood for her defense. They have no sympathy for abolitionism; no love for the North, but they have plenty for Louisiana. . . . They will fight for her in 1861 as they fought in 1814–'15." [41] Although there were numerous acts of manumission involving individual slaves, there was no recorded instance of nonwhite slave owners voluntarily liberating all of their slaves. During the

[41] Stahl, "The Free Negro in Ante-Bellum Louisiana," 323.

war, at least one of the Letoyants was a captain in the cavalry, and another free man of color from the area, whose children married into the Letoyant family at a later date, was a colonel.

Although the Letoyants had many reverses as a consequence of the Civil War, they did make efforts to recoup their losses. Land was one type of property that was frequently used in bartering during the postwar era. But loss of land could mean eventual loss of hegemony in Riverville; therefore, serious attempts were made to regain land lost as a consequence of a failure to repay debts. One old-family descendant kept a record of transactions on forty-six acres of land: it was lost in 1886 because of failure to pay taxes, then sold for $250; in 1894 it was again lost and purchased for $351; in 1896 the land was again repurchased; it was lost again in 1897. Whether or not such an exchange of land was typical is uncertain. What is certain is that the Letoyants regretted having to part with their land.

When the carpetbaggers took over, some of the former free men of color who were literate and educated were called for jury service and became deputies or justices of the peace. They began slowly to regain some of their material losses. Their psychological losses were more difficult to bear. The third- and fourth-generation Letoyants were generally not as enterprising as some with whom they made matrimonial alliances. Moreover, the generations reared in the 1870's and 1880's were, for the most part, illiterate because the people were not able to pay teachers.

Apart from the personal and property damage inflicted by the war, there was disturbance in the relationships between the Letoyants and other populations in the area. The Letoyants not only suffered a loss of slaves, homes, cattle, and crops, but they also suffered the loss of their special status as free persons of color and came to be identified as "simple colored folks"—with the same legal status as their former slaves. Moreover, the "po' white folks" from the hill country began to come down into the fertile lowlands and to make demands on this erstwhile prosperous colored population that had fought valiantly for the Confederacy.

Sometimes the Letoyants were defrauded by white persons with whom they attempted to do business. A peddler in the vicinity persuaded one of the Letoyants, who owned a plantation store, to set up a partnership in business. The Letoyant reputedly kept advancing money for merchandise while the peddler pocketed cash from sales. Eventually, of course, the business went bankrupt. When the Letoyant attempted to get legal help, the peddler outwitted him and bribed the lawyer, and, in time, the peddler bought up all the colored man's land.

Letoyant family scrapbooks and ledgers still extant contain copies of promissory note forms in use during this era. On one form, the borrower agreed to pay the attorney's fee, in the event that suit was instituted at the time the note matured, and waived the benefit of all laws exempting from seizure and sale any property owned by the borrower or any that was thereafter acquired. Many Letoyants were victims of fraud because they signed contracts which they could not comprehend. To this day, some of their descendants contend that this manner of obtaining property was illegal but that there is no longer any legal recourse.

Some living family descendants resent the implication that their ancestors were defrauded or that they were not good business men in the postwar era. A white planter in Riverville remarked to one of the Letoyants that the reason they suffered great financial losses was that their own people were too good to their children. Commenting on this remark, the informant said, "Imagine, they was too good to us! Why, our own people worked for what they had; they gave it to us. Why is it too good for us? When you worked for it yourself, it certainly is good enough for you. As far as the American people is concerned, if your skin isn't white, you're not suppose to have nothing. You know, don't be a Mexican, don't be anything. They should have their foot on our neck. That's their belief. They have that from England. That's all there is to it. It's down deep, I guess. They can't help themselves, but they can't see that." Although the Letoyants may criticize themselves, commenting on the lack of discipline and initiative among some of their ancestors, they are unaccepting of this kind of criticism from a white person.

The postwar changes in Letoyant relationships with whites in the area were reflected in the altered attitudes of the whites toward the community of Riverville. Apparently, as the Letoyant population increased, the people in the vicinity began to identify Riverville as a nonwhite settlement.

An informant gave this account of what transpired: "I'd say just before the Civil War when they began to draw strong lines between the white and colored, a lot of the people being here identified with this place, which was given by a Letoyant, and he had specified in his will that it was going to be given for the free people of color. Well now, there was many people who lived here that was actually white, and some that weren't. When they saw that they were going to be identified as colored if they stayed, a lot of them left. Because, say for instance, one particular family that I know of. There are many of them that live near here today. They are actually white, and when they seen that they were going to be branded as colored, well, they moved on away. They started setting up one church out at East River, and another one on Little Bayou and they withdrew from this place. I think that if Nicholas had never specified in his will that he was building this place for his free people of color, it would have probably just passed on, through the ages, as just another place. A lot of white people used to come to this church—belong to this church. But as time went by, the people began to be identified as Nicholas' children. Well, they know that he wasn't more than about half white, and they are still branded as colored."

Attempts to trace some families whose name appeared in the original genealogy revealed that they are still in the vicinity, but, as one woman said: "They went as Caucasian. Those people all grew up together. They grew together and went to school together. A number of years back they moved out of this parish. Then, they went as Caucasian, completely Caucasian. And they moved. Now I see them. Right now. Every now and then. But I don't know them. I don't remember them at all."

The identity of the present-day Letoyants has strong historical roots. The special status they once had as free people of color set them apart from those who were slaves; moreover, they were Creoles who could trace descent to a respectable French colonizer who acknowledged his paternity and gave them evidence of his affection for them. In the first generation, particularly, identity as Letoyant's offspring with a free status and recognition as people of importance were undoubtedly goals which they attained as a group. The first generation could not foretell exactly how recognition of their identity would be perpetuated. They did not foresee that a priest in Riverville would record their genealogy shortly after they went into the second century of their existence, nor that one of their plantation homes would become a tourist attraction, nor that a novel would be written about them. They did, however, provide a firm groundwork for the perpetuation of their identity.

# Chapter 3

# Why Letoyant Creoles
# Set Themselves Apart

A feeling of belongingness to a meaningful social group is very important to psychological security. Since the Letoyants were not accepted as equals by the dominant white population, they chose to set themselves apart, develop their own distinctive identity, and give their progeny a sense of dignity and worth as well as a feeling of security.

Like other underprivileged groups, the Letoyants emulated the white people of high status in the types of goals which they set for themselves. The early Letoyants were planters who acquired and developed large landholdings. They were slave owners and connoisseurs of the good things of life—stud horses, imported furniture, portraits, and other possessions. They also adhered to Catholicism, the dominant religion of colonial Louisiana. Even more important, however, was their emulation of the familial roles of the Caucasian population where males were semipatriarchs and women relatively subordinate to them.

If the Letoyants had remained near the fort in Indianola, where power definitely rested with the predominantly white population, they would probably have had to seek external protection with greater frequency than was necessary in a rather isolated rural community where the population was almost wholly nonwhite. Seeking external protection may become a form of depersonalization if the protected person feels constrained to adhere to norms not of his own choosing or believes it necessary to play socially approved roles such as those prescribed for nonwhites. While these forms of externalization would offer protection, they would in some cases simultaneously lead to a diminution of the sense of personal worth and even to diminished personal identity.[1] For

---

[1] Helen Merrell Lynd, *On Shame and the Search for Identity* (New York: Harcourt, Brace & Co., 1958), 184–85.

in playing expected, approved roles, one acts in a drama that one has had no part in writing or casting.

## PHYSICAL DISTINCTIVENESS

### RACIAL TRAITS

Perhaps one of the most obvious reasons the Letoyants set themselves apart is that they had already been set apart from both the dominant population and the darker nonwhites because of distinctive racial characteristics. The first generation was presumably half Caucasian and half Negroid, assuming that Marie was a "full-blooded" Negro. Nicholas, the eldest son, married a Canadian whose father was French and whose mother was Indian. Their children, then, would have been about one-fourth Indian, one-fourth Negroid, and one-half white, if such crude measures can be used. Nicholas' brothers married women who were, like themselves, at least half French with some Negroid ancestry. The majority of the direct descent Letoyants, then, were predominantly Caucasian with Negroid and slight Indian (or Mongoloid) admixtures.

The physical appearance of living Letoyant Creoles is difficult to describe because there have been ten generations of mixture from three main physical stocks, Caucasoid, Mongoloid, and Negroid, and there are exceptions to any description. The Letoyants tend to have *café au lait* complexions, although some of them are noticeably brown and others are very light-skinned. As a rule, they have dark wavy hair, but again there are exceptions—there are some with straight hair and some with "kinky" hair, with color ranging from blond to black. Some Letoyants are tall and thin with high cheekbones and aquiline noses; others are short and inclined to be stocky. For the most part, however, the height of the people ranges from medium to tall, with long heads prevailing over round heads. Noses are generally neither very broad nor very thin, and lips are of medium thickness. In many Letoyants, Indian-Negroid phenotypes are sufficiently discernible for these people to be identified readily as having a distinctive racial origin.

Within the boundaries of the present United States, even in colonial times, non-Caucasians generally suffered discrimination by virtue of their phenotype. This type of prejudice, sometimes referred to as prejudice of mark, differs from prejudice of origin; where the latter prevails, a nonwhite individual may compensate for physical disadvantages by a superiority of intelligence, education, and economic condition.[2]

Living Letoyants are well aware of this pattern of discrimination and generally profess ignorance of the source of dark skin color genes. They seem to be sure of their ancestry along *both* lines of descent only as far back as Nicholas and his siblings. They also take pride in the tradition that Nicholas' father was a French-born Caucasian, but they appear to have forgotten about their nonwhite mother. Perhaps the provision of the Black Code that the status of children born to mixed racial unions was dependent upon the status of their mother was a contributing factor.

The affectional ties between Marie and her children must not have been sufficiently strong to counteract her children's desire to obliterate her memory. Pierre Letoyant in his will used threats to be sure that his colored children assumed the responsibility for the financial payments which he had contracted to make to their mother at the time of his separation from her. Another indication that Marie's children did not intend to perpetuate her memory is their failure to have her buried in the cemetery beside the church which they built for their own ethnic group. Even if Marie died prior to the erection of the church, her burial place must have been known to her children. With the great emphasis Creoles placed upon ancestry and reverence for the dead, the failure to have her remains rest with those of her children can only be interpreted as deliberate.

There is slight evidence that some knowledge of Marie was passed down through the generations. Marie's nickname, *Coin-Coin*, which is French for quack-quack, may have been derived

[2] See Oracy Nogueira, "Skin Color and Social Class," *Plantation Systems of the New World* (Washington, D.C.: Pan American Union, 1959), 169.

from her conversational ability. An incident that lends credibility to this supposition and illustrates attitudes toward her was observed by a stranger in Riverville who was visiting an elderly Creole woman whose grandchild was misbehaving in the presence of guests. The grandmother attempted to admonish the child without attracting attention. When the child did not respond, the grandmother leaned over and whispered in French, "Do you want these people to think you are related to that old nigger quackquack?"

The hesitancy of the Letoyants to acknowledge any Negroid genes was expressed by an informant in these words: "Even though we are considered colored, we look about ourselves, and see such a striking physical difference between ourselves and Negroes, that we cannot quite accept the story that we, too, are Negroes." One mother commented that it was very important that she teach her children who they are, especially that they are not Negroes. She maintained that her people are a mixture of American, French, and Spanish but emphatically denied any Negroid mixture attributable to intermarriage with Negroes since the first generation. Another parent remarked, "I don't think we're training the children to know *who* they are. They really don't know who they are, until they be old enough to know that they are *not* considered white. They don't call themselves Negroes, but they know that they are recognized as colored as far as race is concerned, so more or less they stick to one another."

Color consciousness in Riverville is evident when conversations turn to describing a person's appearance. In describing her sons and daughters-in-law, one elderly woman consistently used color in speaking about them. Of one son-in-law she said, "Sister, he's the color of your [black] dress." Other in-laws were described as "looking just like a white person with blue eyes and blond hair." If a child has kinky hair, the mother will brush it vigorously and comb it as flat as possible. One mother, whose small daughter has kinky hair, brushed the child's hair with her hand and remarked to the child, "You are *so* lively; that's why your hair looks that way."

This investigator received another clue to color consciousness when making inquiries about one family whose children were not enrolled in the Catholic school at a time when 99 percent of Riverville Creole children were in that school. The consensus of the people was that these children were dark-complexioned and that their mother felt they would not be very welcome. Elaborating on the description of the family, informants usually noted that the mother was herself dark-complexioned but that she had "nice" hair.

HARDY BIOLOGICAL STOCK

Even if the Creoles wanted to set themselves apart, they could not have succeeded in establishing and maintaining the group unless they had enough progeny [3] and the leaders had a sufficiently long life to carry out their objectives. From the first to the tenth generation they have tended to place a high value on marriage and children. Their religious tenets were undoubtedly a factor in the development of these values. The early generations of Letoyants had sufficient economic stability to allow them to have children without considering them as either an asset or a liability. In the post-Reconstruction era, when the population had become large and impoverished, the economic factor probably took on a new importance, and children were considered economic assets on the farm. But as the population migrated from the South to urban areas, children could no longer be so considered.

Of the nine children born to Pierre Letoyant and his nonwhite spouse, all but Eulalie, who died in her seventh year, reached maturity. One of the younger males, Touissant, is reported to

[3] The term *mulatto*, derived from the Spanish and Portuguese *mulato* and translated *mule*, is particularly offensive to the Letoyants. To these Creoles, who have rural backgrounds, the term *mule* implies sterility and is inappropriate because as a people they have been very fertile. As commonly used, *mulatto* refers to people of mixed racial origin, particularly Caucasoid and Negroid, and does not necessarily imply inferiority. To the Letoyants, however, the term is one of opprobrium wholly inappropriate to them. They not only have a low proportion of childless unions, but also question the source of their colored ancestry inasmuch as they have never consciously acknowledged that their white progenitor may have had a Negro spouse.

have remained single even though there is a record of one child. The seven remaining first-generation Letoyants had at least nine thousand descendants over the past two centuries. If childless families are excluded, the mean size of a Letoyant family is nearly seven persons. Population increase by generation shows that the

*Figure 1*

GROWTH OF CREOLE POPULATION

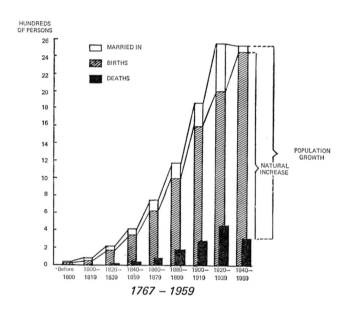

1767 – 1959

second generation was five times larger than the first, the third nearly four times the size of the second, and the fourth slightly more than one and one-half times that of the third [4] (Fig. 1).

Length of life is another indication of biological fitness. The first generation, consisting of nine persons, had the longest life span, 63.4 years, despite the death of Eulalie at age 7. The second

[4] The rate of Creole natural increase, that is, the excess of births over deaths per 1000 individuals, has recently declined from 20.3 in 1940 to 15.8 in 1960. The 1960 rate, however, is higher than the rate of 13.2 for the total U.S. white population but lower than the nonwhite rate of 22.0.

generation had a life span 7.5 years shorter than that of the first; however, for the late eighteenth and early nineteenth centuries, the span was comparatively long. Subsequent generations showed a decrease of approximately 7 or 8 years in life span. In the fourth and fifth generations, this decrease is attributable in part to the hardships following the Civil War. Since a vast proportion of the seventh, eighth, and ninth generations are still alive, it is not meaningful to calculate mean life span for them.

The Letoyants, then, have not been a sickly people. On the contrary, they have shown an immense vitality, a high fecundity, a comparatively balanced sex ratio (102.9 males for every 100 females), and a determination to maintain themselves as a people.

## GEOGRAPHIC ISOLATION

An eighteenth-century traveler in Louisiana depicted the environment of this ethnic population during the time when the first generation was being "established" and identified. He stated that the river which flows through the Riverville area would have been as great as the Mississippi if the waters had not been diverted into small streams or bayous and into a multitude of lakes. It resembled the Nile in that the soil along its banks was the most fertile in the country. At that time, the traveler further commented, nearly all travel was by water, and all principal settlements were established along waterways.[5]

Although the white progenitor of the Letoyants established his offspring with their mother on a tract of land when the union was forcibly broken up, this land did not become their eventual homeland. It was at least fifteen miles distant from the strip of land along New River (called by the Letoyants "the river"), where all first-generation Letoyants staked a claim. The site where the first-generation siblings settled was not far from the land-holdings of a prominent white planter whose colored daughters became the wives of Louis and one of the younger Letoyants,

[5] Henry Marie Brackenridge, *Views of Louisiana* (Chicago: Quadrangle Books), 1962.

Joseph. At that time the land was unimproved and there was no bridge across New River.

Both the French and Spanish crowns were generous with undeveloped land, provided applicants for the land followed established procedures. Apparently the Letoyants knew how to obtain land and had the "right connections" through their French father and his white descendants. They undoubtedly obtained the unimproved land along New River by petitions to the French government. Early land maps, however, show that hundreds of arpents of land had already been claimed by other persons. The Letoyants must have purchased this land or acquired it through matrimonial alliances.

In at least one instance the Letoyants had to defend their claims in court against white contenders. A white man who had once had a claim to the unimproved property of Louis Letoyant but had renounced it, tried to reclaim the property when the government of the United States was attempting to clarify land records of the newly acquired Louisiana Purchase. Louis, however, successfully verified his claim in the ensuing legal battle. By the mid-1830's, the Letoyants owned practically all the land along both sides of New River near the present center of Riverville. There were white inhabitants in Riverville prior to the reactionary period following Reconstruction; because of the large number of nonwhite families, however, the white inhabitants subsequently withdrew from the immediate area. Perhaps the Creoles isolated themselves on this stretch of river in an effort to consolidate the social group. Riverville was sufficiently near the French fort to permit commuting by riverboat without undue hardship and sufficiently removed to permit the Creoles to develop their own community without much interaction with, or interference from, outsiders. Their physical withdrawal reinforced their self-isolation and at a later time led to the withdrawal of most of the whites who had initially settled there.

In their semi-isolated homeland the Creoles organized effectively to protect and promote their interests. During the pre-Civil War era, organization was informal and simple because the population had solidarity based upon close blood ties and joint economic endeavors.[6] In their own community the Creoles also realized the goal of self-government, at least in matters that did not pertain to the outlying areas. Their environment permitted the development of leaders and the exercise of social controls from within the Letoyant population, both of which were quite important to group development. Group conflicts and minor feuds were settled within the community, and the Creoles developed an autonomy that contributed to their cohesiveness. Only through the exercise of social control in Riverville could the Creoles restrain deviancy and present to the outside world a favorable image.

## DEVELOPMENT OF A LETOYANT CREOLE SELF-IMAGE

In addition to environmental and physical factors, certain social needs contributed to the Letoyant Creoles' urge to set themselves apart as a distinct social group. One of these was their attempt to establish status for themselves. A relatively low status is accorded individuals and groups who bear a stigma, a designation that is deeply discrediting in the eyes of people from whom they wish to attract respect. These Creoles with a visible Negroid or Mongoloid phenotype may be said to have a stigma, since American society is color-conscious and anyone with Negroid characteristics tends to be stigmatized. One Creole objective in seeking status, then, was to be differentiated from the Negro.

### THE NEGRO'S IMAGE

For more than three centuries after the Negroes were first brought to America, there was little public esteem for them. Initially, the majority were slaves, and color was a factor in keeping them in a state of oppression since they could not secure independence under the same conditions as Caucasian indentured servants.

[6] Creole leadership and organizational efforts are discussed at length in the next chapter.

In the years following the Civil War, the efforts of the Negroes to attain status made little headway. They were predominantly a southern rural people bound to the soil, for the plantation system had some resemblance to medieval feudalism. A tenant was, in a sense, bound to a plantation by virtue of the debt which he owed to the planter. Although there was some migration out of the South in the post–World War I era, it did not reach its greatest proportions until after World War II.

In the area which the Letoyant Creole population regards as its homeland, the image of the Negro has always been especially unfavorable. Negroes have not had the means to purchase land along the waterfront despite availability, nor has their condition been much better in the civil parish in which Riverville is situated. The image of the Negro, held by the Caucasians in the area, was depicted by a monument (removed in the 1960's) intended to be a tribute to the arduous and faithful service of the good "darkies." This type of recognition, of course, has always been strongly resented by all nonwhites in the area because of the inferiority implicit in it.

Since the public image of the Negro has traditionally been derogatory, Letoyant Creoles are understandably loath to be considered Negroes. Creoles are, in a sense, caught in the crossfire between the Negro and the dominant Caucasian population. Their peculiar situation has contributed in no small measure to their developing their own self-image.

SELF-IDENTITY IN THE RURAL ENVIRONMENT

Their first generation of Letoyants did not ordinarily use the family name of their father in official transactions, nor were they so identified in the Church. Early records affixed the nickname of their mother, "Coin-Coin," as a surname. After the Louisiana Purchase, however, when members of the first generation began to acquire property and to establish themselves as astute businessmen, the name of their father was used in official documents. It is doubtful that they ever used their mother's nickname as a surname since it would be a reminder of her low status. The probability is that this identification was given to them by the officials or clergy, for in the eighteenth and early nineteenth centuries it was not customary for nonwhite offspring of French or Spanish parentage who could not be legitimized to be identified by the surname of their father.

The Letoyant Creoles cultivated the image of a proud, free people of color, who (after the first quarter of the nineteenth century) bore the name of an early French settler. They had little, if any, recollection of any status other than that of free people, and since they constituted the majority of the *gens de couleur libre* in the area, they personified that status in a special way. After the Civil War, when the Creoles lost their special status as free people of color, they ran the risk of being identified as Negroes and assigned the low status accorded to freed slaves.[7] This predicament was compounded by the loss of many status symbols, such as servants, mansions, and wealth. Therefore, the search for a new identity intensified.

The following incident was related by a present-day Letoyant to show the strong feelings these people have about maintaining an identity distinct from the Negroes: "Marie was the youngest of thirteen children. The baby. She was a pet. And anything she wanted, her father would give her. All right, she *had* to have Joe C. and her parents couldn't see it. Because he was the son of a slave. But anyway, she got to crying and she didn't want to eat any more. And she'd lock herself in her room. And, well, her father finally gave in.

"For the wedding they had a big reception. And they had stairs in those days. The long table was spread upstairs. And they were drinking toasts. When Marie's father was given a drink, he threw his glass away saying in French, 'To think, that I am

---

[7] Reconstruction did, however, afford the Creoles some new types of recognition. They served in the capacity of nonwhite citizens on civic bodies such as the police jury, probably because they were literate and better prepared than any of the other nonwhites in the area. Newspaper notices in family ledgers, naming the Creoles who served in such a capacity, indicate that they took pride in this service—despite the knowledge that they were probably selected for the service primarily because they were "colored."

drinking with the son of a slave to marry my daughter!' Her father cursed and pitched his glass in the punchbowl and walked out of the room. Anyway, she married him, and *that was that.*

"In those days people were legally married. They were chaperoned, too. They were really nice people. You had to be nice to be considered."

The seemingly irrelevant reference to the Letoyants' being chaperoned during courtship and to their contracting legal marriages was in fact highly significant. It signified that the Letoyants knew they were different from the freed slaves and that they wanted others to have an awareness of their uniqueness as a strong (nonwhite) family.

Obviously the Letoyant Creoles were not amenable to internalizing the newly assigned status of colored people without the qualification of "free"; therefore, history and tradition assumed even greater importance than before. In their attempt to retain some of the status which they enjoyed prior to the Civil War, Creoles placed emphasis upon their French descent, for this implied not only old-family status but also Caucasian descent and Catholicity. Appellations which are most acceptable to these people are *Creoles, Catholics, French people,* or simply *Frenchmen.* Early in the present century, one of the musically inclined Letoyants proclaimed his French origin in these verses which he put to music:

> "France, so they say, is the home of the French,
>    And Paris, the city that holds them.
> This we all know is true, but just take it from me,
>    You don't have to go across the ocean to find them.
> Oh what a swell bunch of Frenchmen
>    Oh, what beautiful Creole girls;
> They are thousands of miles from Paris the city of styles,
>    But they are French just the same."

Dark-complexioned Letoyants try to forestall any identification as Negro or as colored. One man acknowledged that he had never registered to vote because he feared that he would be listed as Negro. In a small community near Riverville, the Creole boys presumably volunteered for military service in World War II because they feared being classified as nonwhite if they were drafted, and they definitely did not want to be placed in segregated, Negro regiments. An informant in the South remarked that a "good many of them died because they were the first to go overseas, but they preferred this to the dishonor of being labeled Negro."

During World War II, one of the young men from Riverville who was drafted was placed in a segregated regiment. When he protested that he was not Negro, some officers came to Riverville to make inquiries about his ethnic origin. The boy's parents consistently maintained that they were not colored and suggested that the officers talk to the parish priest. When the priest was questioned about the boy, he answered, "I have not made a chemical analysis of the 'blood.' I don't know how you would classify them, but they are different from other so-called Negro people." As a consequence, the boy was assigned to another regiment.

The father of this young man related an incident about a train trip when the conductor attempted to put him in a segregated coach. Of course, he refused. When he recounted the incident, one of his white friends attempted to placate him with the comment, "Well, one time shouldn't make so much difference." The old man said, "Well, one time was just *one time too many.*" Developing a favorable self-image is, then, rather complicated for the Creole, since, as a young urban Creole noted: "We are in the cotton-pickin' middle; we *can't* belong to the one group that is above us in status, and we *won't* belong to the other."

SOCIALIZATION OF CHILDREN

Awareness of identity is essential for both security and maturity. A child needs to have trust in his world and in the persons who are its interpreters. If he cannot identify clearly with the social situation—family, neighborhood, community, ethnic group, or even nation—of which he is a part, he will find it very difficult to develop a sure sense of himself. He develops a stable self-identity only when he knows what his relationships are in the groups to which he is committed and what he is expected to do.

In Riverville, particularly, it was and still is, to some extent, possible for a child to develop a clear sense of identity, because in semi-isolated, stable surroundings his family and other members of his ethnic group exert great influence on his conception of who he is and is not. Here he learns what is right and wrong and defines goals which he deems worth striving for. As he acquires a sense of belongingness, he assumes a place or a status in the groups to which he belongs and this status affects his performance in a group task at any given time. If he loses acceptance by the groups that are important to him, or if the ties that bind him to group members are weakened, he will have intense feelings of aloneness and personal rejection.

In the company of other children, in particular, a child develops stable relationships. He learns to give and to take as he participates in play activity with other children. In the semi-isolation of Riverville, where his companions are Creoles like himself, self-identification is simpler than in other environments. Riverville is not, however, completely isolated, for Negro children live in the community and the Creole children also come into contact with the white population in the surrounding area where goods and services have always been obtained.

Negro and Creole homes in Riverville are sometimes adjacent to one another; however, Creole children are seldom allowed to play with Negro children. Even organized school activities such as ball games, which formerly put the children of the Riverville Catholic school in competition with the Negro children from the public school in the community, were disapproved by many parents. If anything, the scheduling of such activities gave Creole parents an opportunity to point out their distinctiveness to their children. The settlement pattern in Riverville facilitates segregation because the plantation with the largest number of Negro tenants belongs to a white family.

A young Letoyant woman, reminiscing on how she learned

her ethnic identity and how, in general, her people had maintained this identity over the centuries, commented: "I don't know how they do it. I guess by just staying together and caring about everybody down there in Riverville and being interested about them, keeping up with all your family and being told about dead relatives and all the good times they had in the old days and all that. I guess that's how they know who they are." This remark reflects the importance of history and of tradition in the lives of these people.

To this day the people of Riverville and vicinity are a family-centered people who value progeny and whose preferential mating pattern is to seek a spouse from within the ethnic group. Moreover, they see themselves as upright, moral, God-fearing Catholics who have supported their own church since its inception in Riverville. They further see themselves as a people with fortitude and ability, who has throughout its history been more or less affluent. They have had the ingenuity to establish themselves on the most fertile stretch of river land in Louisiana, to establish and maintain social control over their own community of origin, and to have amicable relationships with both whites and Negroes.

# Chapter 4

# Evolution of an Identity

A sense of identity is not gained or maintained by a group once and for all; it undergoes a continuous process of development. As group members interact among themselves in achieving the goals of the group, and as they come into contact with out-group members, their sense of group identity may either intensify or decline. If the group experiences an increasing sense of identity, it has a concomitant sense of psychosocial well-being. There is a sense of knowing where the group is going and an assurance of anticipated recognition from those within the group who are important and, to some extent, from others outside the group.[1]

A group's sense of identity develops from its consciousness as a group entity. This consciousness enables leaders to emerge, goals and norms to be defined, and social roles and patterns of interaction to evolve. If a group becomes conscious of itself in a marginal position, it may undergo a process of establishing a unique group identity. The Letoyant Creoles, as a marginal group, experienced this process of group formation and group identity.

Through the first century of Letoyant family history, its members experienced the ups and downs that accompany the establishment of a sense of identity. Although the vision of the leaders was generally optimistic and hopeful, there were times when the legal restrictions on free people of color must have contributed to a serious questioning of the attainment of this identity. In the period prior to the Civil War, the Letoyants no doubt resented the prohibition on in-migration of other free people of color, and, as large slaveholders, they must have chafed at being categorized

[1] Cf. Erik H. Erikson, "The Problem of Ego Identity," *Journal of the American Psychoanalytic Association*, IV (No. 1, 1956), 74.

with those suspected of encouraging revolt among the slaves.[2]

After the Civil War, however, the Letoyants' identity faced even greater threats than before. They were then merely non-whites in the same legal category as the large number of former slaves. Moreover, the carpetbaggers must have looked upon them as collaborators with the Confederacy in the war effort.

## LEADERSHIP

In the struggle to achieve an identity, not only distinct but also distinctive, the Creoles had a strong leader in Nicholas who had, as the firstborn male, a natural advantage over his younger siblings. Nicholas had a longer association with his father than any of the other children. At the time the union between his father and mother was dissolved, he was about twenty. When he was thirty-one, Nicholas went to France to visit his father's birthplace. His correspondence from France and objets d'art of the Napoleonic Era that he brought back with him are still treasured by his descendants as testimony to his "Frenchness." His amiable relationships with his white relatives undoubtedly contributed to his success.

Nicholas was endowed with unusual vitality and intelligence. He lived long enough to witness the establishment of his Creole group. At the time of his death, in 1856, some fifth-generation Letoyant infants had been born, among them his great-great-grandchildren. Grand Pere Nicholas, who had eight children, had more descendants than any of the first-generation Letoyants, despite the fact that his brother Dominique had eighteen children.

The vast majority of Letoyant Creoles trace their ancestry to Nicholas with whom they almost totally identify. Although, because of the close intermarriage within this population, many could also trace descent from Nicholas' siblings, they usually give priority to Nicholas as their ancestor probably because of his

[2] Free Negroes employed in river boats, for example, occasionally concealed fugitive slaves. Kenneth M. Stampp, *The Peculiar Institution* (New York: Alfred A. Knopf, 1956), 120–21.

leadership qualities. Before his death Nicholas had 161 descendants; 5,044 were born after he died, giving him a total of 5,205 descendants.

Louis was only two years younger than Nicholas, and he, too, benefited from the constant association with his father during his formative years. Although Louis was a shrewd businessman, who developed a large plantation and erected one of the most attractive mansions on New River, he had only one legitimate child; consequently, his influence in the years after his death was not as great as that of Nicholas.

His mansion, however, has been preserved in much of its pristine beauty, and legends are still told about his affluence. According to one legend, Louis predicted that the freedom of the slaves would mean ruination to the South and that a long period of impoverishment would result from the war. Therefore, he converted securities into gold coins that he carefully hid. But someone learned where he had hidden his wealth and stole the strongbox with all the money. In the hope that he would be able to get back at least a part of his fortune, he did not report the theft to the authorities. His descendants are still trying to trace the reputed fortune.

Over the past thirty years a lawyer in the civil parish has had periodic requests from the descendants of Louis who moved away from the area to recover the fortune of diamonds, pearls, rubies, and land deeds. Some of the inquirers believe that there is an immense estate of valuable land where oil is being produced. One such claimant wrote to the lawyer: "Since you proved us to be the heirs of the money that's in the bank, now just what do we have to do to get it? If you would help us get this money, we would rather reward you than anyone else. We have already made our identification, so there shouldn't be any trouble getting this money. That's why we ask for your help."

Although Grand Pere Nicholas was titular leader of the Letoyants until his death, in his declining years new leaders were coming to the fore. Not all of them bore the surname of Letoyant; some were descended from the females.

At the close of the Civil War, a nonwhite man, originally from one of the border states, who was familiar with Riverville prior to the Civil War, began to acquire huge landholdings and eventually settled his family in Riverville. Nearly all of his children married Letoyants and became leaders in the community in the post-Civil War period. Even though these so-called newcomers married into the Letoyant family and acquired large landholdings and other symbols of wealth, they never had the same status as the pre-Civil War Letoyants who earned their fortunes at a much earlier time.

## IMPORTANCE OF A NAME

A name indicates group boundaries and delineates the group to its members and to outsiders. The name by which a people refers to itself is an important clue to identity since it reflects a self-image. The use of a name can also solidify the group by reinforcing a sense of distinctiveness.

Letoyant Creoles, especially older ones, seldom refer to themselves as Negroes. The term *Negro* is decidedly not a status-conferring one, for only pure-blooded Africans were so called in colonial Louisiana; the "mixed bloods" were called *colored*. Since all peoples who are not albinos have some coloring, the term *colored* is not particularly offensive. But the concept to which it refers is not looked upon with favor by all Letoyants. Many prefer the title "Creole" because it implies French ancestry.

The Letoyants are well aware of the resistance they meet from white Louisiana Creoles when they apply the term to themselves. Although white people of French descent may acknowledge that the Letoyants are descended from a Frenchman, they question the Letoyants' use of the French surname since, under the Black Code, the first generation of Letoyant Creoles could not be legitimized. An incident that occurred at the parish fair in Indianola in the early 1950's typifies local attitudes. According to custom, nonwhite persons who submitted entries to the fair were obliged to enter them in a section where they would not be in competition with the whites. At the nonwhite section, the Letoyants designated their booths with a sign: CREOLE. When the Caucasian authorities saw the sign, they forced the Letoyants to remove it, and the Letoyants were thenceforth more cautious in using the term in the presence of native white Louisianians who also claimed the title.

One informant said: "Sister, don't call us mulattoes; don't call us colored. Just say 'the people on the river.' And don't call names or nationalities. You'd be surprised, but the young people don't pay no attention. But, the old timers, they know!"

The Letoyants' claim to being Creole is supported by the longstanding prevalence of French given names among them. One informant said: "Creoles make their names sound so pretty. They rhyme their names. Now John is Jean, then there's Angeline, Victorine, Meline, Severine, Adolphine, and Celine. You see, one family. Now look at their neighbors, Eulalie, Elodie, Leonie, and Octavie. See how it rhymes? That's how we do." The Creoles also follow the custom prevalent in colonial times of using Saint before a given name and also of naming a child for the saint on whose feast day he was born. A boy, for instance, born on the feast of St. Ann could hardly be called Ann but could be christened St. Ann.

A boy named for his father is commonly called *petit* or simply T followed by his given name. Instead of being called Jean, Jr., he is called T Jean, to stand for little Jean. Nicknames serve a very useful function since it is not uncommon to have two or three cousins with identical given names and surnames. The nicknames also reflect emphasis upon the French background. A woman known as T Be has an abbreviation of the French *petit bebe* or little baby—a nickname which she was given as a child. A man known as T Mit derived his nickname from *petit mitron*—or little jack-of-all-trades. These nicknames have been used throughout Letoyant history. Their prevalence made it especially difficult to identify members of the first generation whose christening names were used on records but who are known to their descendants only by nicknames.

The use of certain names also shows the unity and family ties of the group. Many titles of consanguinity, for example, are extended far beyond their ordinary bounds of meaning. Nicholas is spoken of as Grand Pere, grandfather, even by seventh- and eighth-generation descendants, and many elderly women are called *tante* or *cousine* by distant relatives. Spiritual relationships, such as *parrain* (godfather) or *nanaine* (godmother), reinforce the feeling of relatedness among group members.

## DELINEATION OF GOALS AND NORMS

Groups originate and develop a sense of "we-ness" in attaining certain goals; norms, guidelines of behavior, are established to assure that all members of the group will strive for the achievement of those goals. Frequently, group goals are not entirely conscious in the beginning of the group's formation but evolve with its development. If all of the first-generation Letoyants had had small families, they would hardly have envisioned a strong Letoyant family group with an identity of its own as a solution to marginality. Instead, they might have merged with several other families of mixed racial origin like themselves to achieve the same goal. A distinct group identity is founded on important goals, namely, the general and enduring preferences that govern behavior.[3] Goals and norms most essential to the formation and maintenance of the Letoyants, as well as to their sense of identity, were of an institutional order, namely, perpetuity and maintenance of blood ties through the family, a concept of sacredness and morality through religion, and financial security through the economy.

### MARRIAGE, FAMILY, AND PROGENY

The privilege of using the Letoyant name was, in the beginning, questioned even though Pierre Letoyant, the French male progenitor, identified his nonwhite offspring as his children. The first-

[3] Cf. Allen Wheelis, *The Quest for Identity* (New York: W. W. Norton & Co., 1958), 200.

generation Letoyant Creoles, however, probably wished to be recognized by the surname Letoyant and, furthermore, to realize their goal of having a sufficient number of progeny to constitute eventually a people bound together by consanguinity and by identity with this family name. Therefore, norms regarding marriage and progeny soon evolved in the development of the group. Although there were free people of color unrelated to the Letoyants in the vicinity of Riverville, in no instance did these other free men build up a recognizable people descended from common ancestors with strong blood ties.

What was initially a concern of the early Letoyants became an extended family venture. Even when the Letoyant daughters married outsiders who also had French origin, they continued to regard themselves as Letoyants, and almost invariably their spouses, too, came to be regarded as group members. Identity as a Letoyant in the area of Riverville was in itself status-conferring. This status, of course, had upper limits principally because of the stigma of color, but the Letoyants did enjoy an esteem based upon the values with which they came to be identified.

Approximately 93 percent of the unrelated persons with whom the Letoyants had marital unions before 1865 were, like themselves, free people of color with French or Spanish ancestry. Less than one-half of one percent were Negro. The remainder were predominantly Indian and French. Even though Creoles had sexual relations with slaves, in no known instance before the Civil War was a fiancée's freedom purchased; Letoyant Creoles became affianced only to persons who were already free.

First-generation Letoyant siblings did not marry one another, but some of their children did intermarry, and as soon as the population became large enough, in-group marriage was the preferred pattern. Cousin marriage was quite common at least until the Civil War, especially within the fourth generation, which had a greater incidence of close intermarriage than any other generation.[4] This was due in part to the fact that the family was not

[4] The median year of the fourth generation was 1863. Offspring of this generation contained 1,385 inbred sibships with a mean inbreeding coefficient of

yet dispersed. Population pressures were not so great that the area of Riverville could not afford them economic prosperity. Before 1865 approximately three-fourths of the marital unions were in-group unions, that is, they were unions between descendants of the early Letoyants. In the words of one elderly informant, "We's all related. There is a tangle—you know how a spool of thread gets tangled. That's the way we are."

In order to perpetuate the Letoyant family, marriage was important. Of the population born before 1865, about 87 percent of those over fourteen years of age married. Moreover, the Letoyants of the early generations usually remarried on the death of a spouse. Grand Pere Nicholas married only once; his first wife, who was about his own age, lived to be seventy. But not all of the Letoyants were as long-lived as Grand Pere and his wife. Approximately 18 percent of the males and 13 percent of the females who married prior to 1865 had second unions. The difference in the percentages between sexes is probably attributable to the relatively high rate of maternal mortality in an isolated area where medical care was not readily available. Prior to 1865, 9.1 percent of the males and 2.5 percent of the females had third marital unions, and a few of them were married four or five times.

Large families were also important to the Letoyants. The average number of children born to the first-generation Letoyants was 6.7. Another index of the importance of children, to be discussed at greater length in the next chapter, is the reproductive span of the mothers.

CATHOLICISM

Although marginal people may use given characteristics, such as religion or language, as means of identification, such charac-

---

.0200, nearly as high as the most inbred generation of the Ramah Navaho which had .0205 in the seventh generation. For a more complete treatment of inbreeding, see Jean Ann Walters MacCluer, "Studies in Genetic Demography by Monte Carlo Simulation" (Ph.D. dissertation, University of Michigan, 1968).

teristics need not be exclusively those of the marginal group. In fact, a marginal group may simultaneously use a characteristic in a given locale as a means of solidifying the group and attempting to exclude others, and yet take pride in identifying with a church that is regarded as universal or in speaking a language that is widely spoken.

Being Catholic reinforced the Letoyants' claim to being old-family French because, under French colonial rule, the state religion was Catholicism. Moreover, Pierre Letoyant, their white progenitor, was himself closely identified with Catholicism; in his will he mentions the church in France where he was christened, and he notes that he has a priest uncle. His piety undoubtedly contributed to his nonwhite offspring's resolve to make Catholicism an essential element in their identity and to make the behavioral norms of Catholicism their own.

According to tradition, Nicholas erected the first chapel in Riverville in 1803, probably as a part of his plantation home because devout planters often set aside a chapel within their mansions. After the Louisiana Purchase, there were few priests to serve the spiritual needs of the people and no resident bishop. But the priests who traveled through the countryside were always welcomed by the Letoyant Creoles, who regarded Catholicism as a part of their heritage and an integral element in their identity.

When the Letoyants became sufficiently numerous to warrant a large church, Louis erected one on land given by Nicholas, adjacent to the latter's home. The church structure followed the prevailing architectural patterns in Louisiana and had a single nave covered by a gabled roof that extended over the sides providing galleries along the sides of the structure where the worshipers tied their horses. The slaves attended services on the gallery by looking through the church windows. After the Civil War when the population needed a larger church, the galleries were enclosed and, significantly, excluded former slaves.

The importance of the Letoyants' identification as Catholics is evident from their insistence that the church in Riverville—which was designated a parish church shortly before Nicholas' death—be known as *their* church. Identification as Catholic was to take on a very special meaning following the Civil War when it would differentiate the former free people of color from the darker people who had been slaves. Identification with Catholicism was so important that less than one-half of one percent of the Creoles born during the first century converted to another religion or failed to have their offspring christened. Of the population that married the Letoyant Creoles before 1865, about 95 percent were christened Catholics at birth. Only one-half of one percent were known to have religious convictions other than Catholic.

According to tradition, the first generation was not well acquainted with the laws of the Catholic Church restricting marriage between close relatives. Grand Pere was reputedly told by a priest that he should make an effort to see that the young Letoyants had more choice of potential mates. In-group marriage, however, continued to be highly preferred. Deviance from the accepted Church standards was seemingly regarded as a justifiable price for perpetuation of the group value of Creole intermarriage.

One device for obtaining the necessary church dispensation for a cousin marriage was to confront a priest with an already existing common-law union. Dispensations were, under such circumstances, nearly always granted, particularly if the girl was pregnant. If the spouse of a common-law union was a nongroup member, out-of-wedlock pregnancy was a potentially effective pressure for acceptance of the spouse by the group.

Despite the emphasis the Letoyants placed upon legal marital unions sanctioned by church and state, there was some deviancy during the early generations. Louis, as already noted, had only one child by his legitimate wife; subsequently he had three daughters, each by a different woman. One of Nicholas' sons had a child, probably by a slave woman, before he contracted a legal marriage with someone else. The fact that these deviancies were noted for posterity can be interpreted as an indication of the strength of group disapproval. In every instance, however, the children born to these unions were regarded as part of the family, and most of them married Letoyant relatives.

Very early in their history, the Letoyants recognized the necessity and desirability of possessing material goods, for freedom could place a person of color in a precarious position if he had neither property nor means of livelihood. Freemen were hardly able to compete on an equal footing either with whites or with slave labor, nor did they have the kind of security which slavery afforded.

The precarious situation of free people of color in the decades immediately preceding the Civil War made it imperative that they be economically self-sufficient or even affluent. Material goods can assist a people in courting the goodwill and favor of those who are powerful. Although there is no evidence that the Letoyants ever used their wealth in bribery, the very fact that they were recognized as people of financial means precluded any efforts to depreciate them as n'er-do-wells or as business subordinates.

By the mid-1800's the Letoyants had become well-to-do plantation owners. As they began to accumulate wealth, they built mansions on the property and used their initial homes for other purposes. Louis' second home, which was completed in 1833, a year after his death, is still intact. It has walls two feet thick and floors of slave-made bricks. The veranda in front has brick pillars, which were popular in plantation homes. On the grounds of the plantation are several other structures: the kitchen, the dwelling used by the family until 1833, and a storehouse. Nicholas' home, a two-story mansion located in the very center of the settlement with a gallery facing the river, was destroyed by fire in the 1920's. Two other homes of the first generation are still preserved. One has a 120-foot gallery with three large drawing rooms opening onto it. The first-floor rooms have walls two feet thick and large handhewn timbers of choice cypress and built-in bookcases. It also has a wine cellar.

Furnishings were in harmony with the elegance of the houses. Not only did the Letoyants have their portraits painted, but they also invested in other works of art, including religious art.

They imported fine glassware and china from France and had a variety of sewing and serving silverware. They were also connoisseurs of fine music, and they imported pianos so that their children could take music lessons.

As the first-generation Letoyants became wealthier, they also invested in leisure-time pursuits. One of the homes had a billiard parlor. Some early French books are preserved by their descendants as testimony to the emphasis placed upon literacy. The second generation had tutors who lived with the families and taught the younger generations not only classroom knowledge but lessons in the manners of polite society.

Financial security, then, was a goal from the time that Pierre Letoyant broke up his union with Marie. He not only provided an annuity for her, but he also saw that she had a plot of land on which she could dwell with their children. Financial security became increasingly bound up with emotional security and with status, as legislation concerning free people of color became more and more restrictive, as economic depressions took their toll of financial reserves, and as the loss of investment in slave labor became a possibility.

## Definition of Social Roles

Suzette was the only female first-generation Letoyant who survived childhood. The launching of the group, then, was predominantly a male venture, especially since all but one of Suzette's children married the children of her twin brother, Nicholas. Following the example and precedent set by the first generation, the males of the next two generations were also planters and overseers of large landholdings and personnel. Most of the males who married into the Letoyant family were men with business ability and social status. Therefore, a strong male role became part of the Creole tradition.

Since Suzette and the spouses of the first generation were free women and, in two instances, daughters of a Frenchman who had even higher prestige than Pierre Letoyant, the female role was not one of subservience but rather complemented that of the male. Even though Suzette was midwife for the slaves of her father's second household, under terms of his will Pierre specifically indicated that she was to be paid for these services. Suzette undoubtedly did as her father wished, a circumstance that probably explains her postponement of marriage until she was twenty-six.

The fact that Louis' wife sued for a separation of property from her son indicates that women took legal measures when necessary. Legal documents, however, seldom contained the names of the women unless they were the instigators of a suit. When Nicholas left property to his children, his daughters' shares were given in the names of their husbands.

The Letoyants, then, emulated the role behavior of the French. In contrast to the Negro family, where the mother was chiefly responsible for providing for the children, the Letoyant male made the decisions about financial matters, while the woman's place was primarily in the home. The elderly male as well as the female was highly respected and cared for, as were dependent children.

## INTERACTION PATTERNS

Interaction patterns among whites, free people of color, and slaves had been established early in the history of the region. Socially, the free man of color was never the white man's equal. A white man out on a hunt might sit down and take refreshments at a free colored man's table and yet never shake hands with him because there was supposed social contagion in the touch. Places of recreation, including theater boxes in New Orleans, were segregated. Moreover, segregation in the churches began quite early. Even in cemeteries the ground was subdivided into sections for whites, free Negroes and slaves.[5] Church records during this period often had sections for free persons of color. In their contacts with white men, the free men of color did not assume "the creeping posture of debasement—nor did the whites expect it."

[5] Joe Gray Taylor, *Negro Slavery in Louisiana* (Baton Rouge: Louisiana Historical Association, 1963), 230.

While the whites were considered superior to the free men of color, the free men saw themselves, in turn, as infinitely superior to the blacks and had as much objection to associating with the blacks on terms of equality as any white man did.[6]

In 1801 Pierre Letoyant made his will in which he acknowledged his nonwhite children as well as the three white children born to his marriage with the widow. This will reveals several facts about relationships between the two families. Apparently, the widow knew about Pierre's other family and the arrangements which he had made to support them. At the time Pierre established Marie in a household of her own, he made a promise to give her a life annuity of 150 piasters, anticipating, as he said in his will, "that she must have means to live and for upkeep for herself and for the children." In his will Pierre requested his nonwhite children "out of gratitude" to release him as well as his white family from paying to their mother the above-mentioned annuity by taking it upon themselves as a group to pay the annuity for him and to annul forever the contract made concerning the annuity before the notary of the post. He stated that if the nonwhite children refused to show this "slight and last mark of obedience to his wishes," he "ordains and directs" that the two of them whose act of manumission had not been signed before the notary (*petit* Pierre and Suzanne, his only living daughter) remain slaves of his succession until they did annul the said contract.

Suzanne was charged to serve the widow throughout her lifetime and, after the widow's death, to rear the youngest son. Suzanne was also asked to "remain with my wife as long as they please each other." The wife, in return, was asked "to repay her [Suzanne] both for me and for herself—according to the services she has rendered me and those she will render her [my wife]."

Although Pierre had affection for all of his children and lent his support to them in their economic endeavors, his nonwhite children were at a disadvantage when compared with his white children. Even though he recognized that the nonwhite Letoyants

[6] Grace E. King, *New Orleans: The Place and the People* (New York: The Macmillan Co., 1895), 347.

were his offspring and named each of them in his will, he did not leave any of his earthly goods to them. On the contrary, he expected them to take responsibility for and to render assistance to his white wife and to their white half-siblings, for in his will, Pierre states: "If through some unforeseen event my [white] children would happen to find themselves in indigence, I hope that the said mulattos, mentioned here above, will assist them according to their means."

The Letoyants and the whites in their vicinity lived on neighborly terms. They were all engaged in similar work and were all slaveholders in comfortable financial circumstances with adequate means for developing intellectual and aesthetic tastes. Both nonwhite and white neighbors engaged in land speculation, and both occasionally incurred losses. Sometimes they collaborated on business deals. The Creole Letoyants occasionally asked their white relatives to underwrite their signatures on legal papers. The white father of the two Creole sisters who married into the first generation, for example, underwrote the signatures of his sons-in-law.

Intergroup relations extended occasionally to social activities. The Letoyants were noted for their hospitality, and white businessmen and travelers often arranged their trips to allow for an overnight stay in the community, when they might as easily have chosen to stay with the white planters to the north or south of Riverville. When hospitality was offered a white person, however, the nonwhite host did not presume strict social equality. White guests seldom ate at the family table but were served alone or at a table apart. At one plantation, the white guests were informed that a certain room was reserved for white company and that no person of color had ever occupied the room.

By the time of the Civil War, however, Creole-white relations had become strained over several issues. In 1840 the plantation that Louis Letoyant had with much effort developed was lost through the chicanery of whites. Another issue that began to divide the whites and Creoles immediately prior to the Civil War was the identification of Creoles with the slaves. The free people of color who were big planters and slaveholders were not an integrated part of southern white society. They had fought in every war and, according to the testimony of their descendants, their sympathies were predominantly those of the white southern slaveholders. Yet their color served as a badge to remind the public that they were not part of white society. Their marginal position, especially at the time of the Civil War, led the Creoles to a greater sense of having an identity all their own.

By 1865 the Letoyant Creoles, who then numbered 933, had become well established as a distinct social group. Because of the able leadership of Nicholas and his brothers, they had maintained their distinctiveness as Letoyants. Norms regarding the importance of family, religion, and financial stability were well defined. Interaction patterns with whites in the vicinity were, on the whole, harmonious, and the Creoles were respected as an enterprising and upright people. Although the Civil War and Reconstruction era jolted the whole social structure of the South, the Letoyants had become sufficiently established to survive the crisis and retain their identity in the troublesome years ahead. Their semi-isolation in Riverville and the establishment of their own social institutions played an important part in the retention of identity.

# PART II
# Maintaining an Identity
# in the Southland

During the second century, those group characteristics that were considered sufficiently important to remain marks of identification became rooted in social institutions. Through these institutions a way of thinking and a manner of life were perpetuated. Just what these enduring characteristics are can be gleaned from a brief exposure to ethnic-conscious Letoyant Creoles. In the course of a long conversation they are sure to refer to the Letoyant family and possibly to Grand Pere. To be descended from *the* family on both paternal and maternal lines gives a real sense of belonging, especially if the persons have maintained family values. In addition, Letoyants identify themselves with the Catholic Church, particularly in Riverville, where the darker people are very seldom so identified.

Although the Letoyants lived predominantly in Riverville and its vicinity until the late nineteenth century, out-migration gained momentum early in the twentieth century. Regardless of where they live, however, Letoyants seem to have some knowledge about Riverville as their place of origin and to desire firsthand information about the place. These three characteristics—belonging to *the* family, being a Catholic, and having roots in the community of Riverville—are peculiar to the Letoyants. The manner in which they enact their social roles according to approved norms of behavior and interact with outsiders is socially prescribed and reflects what is important to the group.

Along the stretch of New River known as Riverville, the Letoyant family developed what amounted to their own little kingdom. As the family increased in size, it became an ethnic group, and the account of this group is, in effect, an account of the Letoyant family. One of the distinctive features of the population studied here is its origin in one family. To this day, despite the large numerical increase and the geographic dispersion, this family is still relatively synonymous with the population. Not only do the members of this population conceive of themselves as part of the mixed-blood, nonwhite population; they also regard themselves as a very special kind of people, namely, Creoles who have a rich tradition to be transmitted to future generations.

The focus in Chapter 5 is on the family as a force in ethnic identity. There are varying degrees of completeness of data due to the nature of specific data as well as their availability. Thus, data on marital status were not as readily accessible as those on number of children. The other two strong forces in ethnic identity, religion and the homeland, are the topics of Chapters 6 and 7. Subsequent chapters in this section deal with Letoyant Creole norms, roles, and goals and with their interaction with other populations in the Southland. The cutoff date for the statistical data in this section of the study is 1964; interview material, however, was collected through 1971. Although, as the title of Part II indicates, the emphasis is on the Southland and interview material is generally so restricted, statistics such as those on the family have a broader scope.

# Chapter 5

# A Strong Nonwhite Family

Recent studies of nonwhite families, particularly Negro families, point to basic weaknesses: broken families, families with female heads, families lacking economic stability, and children growing up in an unfavorable environment. The Letoyant Creoles, however, like many other former free people of color, had established a stable family system in many parts of the South prior to the Civil War. The manner in which they have perpetuated family values associated with the proud name Letoyant is, perhaps, more characteristic of their identity than any other single element. Their family strengths are particularly evident when they are contrasted with other nonwhite families.

The real test of a people's value system is in the extent to which they realize their ideals in everyday life. In conversation the Letoyants verbalize the importance of a strong, honorable family. They maintain that their family behavior is as "Creole" as that of the whites who resent their use of the appellation. Moreover, they allege that there has been a continuity in their family values, from the time they were free people of color to the present, which distinguishes them from the Negro family. The realization of Creole family ideals is demonstrated by a study of these areas: importance of marriage and type of union contracted; size of family and extent of illegitimacy; household composition and kind of household head; and family dissolution, particularly through divorce. Interspersed with demographic data obtained from interviews and records are comments from informants. Comparative figures on all nonwhites or Negroes and on the dominant white population attest to the Creole assertions that they constitute a strong family.

The relevance of descent has already been evident in the background and early history of the ethnic group. After ten generations, however, the relative ease with which group members in the South identify one another—even though they are distantly related or not related consanguineously at all—indicates the importance of descent to the population. When this investigator made inquiries concerning the identity of persons whose genealogy could not be traced beyond their parents, the answers usually cited the length of time a particular conjugal family had lived in Riverville, the relative prosperity of this family prior to the Civil War, or the way in which the family was related to other Letoyants. When one elderly woman who referred to someone as a relative was asked to explain the relationship, she replied, "Well, her husband was my husband's uncle." Tracing the genealogy of group members who have moved away from Riverville was not exceptionally difficult because these people correspond or visit regularly with relatives or friends in the community of Riverville.

## MARITAL STATUS

### IMPORTANCE OF "I DO"

The Letoyants have, since the first generation, been a marrying people; they regard marriage as the only acceptable status in which to propagate the ethnic group. Of the population born before 1865 all but 9 percent married; most of the unmarried were young people who died before maturity. Of the living direct descent Creole population in 1964, 70.9 percent of the males and 73.6 percent of the females over fourteen years of age were married, percentages that are higher than in either the total Negro population (62.0 percent of the males and 60.6 percent of the females) or the white population (68.9 percent of the males and 64.8 percent of the females) (Table 1).

There were always a few bachelors and unmarried women. In the first generation, one of the male Letoyants, Touissant, never married. He did have one child through an illicit union, but the line through this child cannot be traced by the rest of the population, and it is probable that the child did not live to maturity or

*Table 1*

MARITAL STATUS OF NEGROES, CREOLES, AND WHITES
AGED 14 AND OVER, BY SEX, 1964 *

| Marital Status | Negro | | Creole | | White | |
|---|---|---|---|---|---|---|
| | Male | Female | Male | Female | Male | Female |
| Persons 14 years old and over | 6138 | 6970 | 1686 | 1837 | 57,480 | 62,040 |
| Percent single | 31.8 | 21.9 | 28.1 | 20.6 | 25.7 | 20.1 |
| Percent married | 62.0 | 60.6 | 70.9 | 73.6 | 68.9 | 64.8 |
| Percent separated | 5.9 | 9.6 | 4.3 | 4.5 | 1.1 | 1.4 |
| Percent widowed | 3.8 | 13.5 | .7 | 5.0 | 3.3 | 12.2 |
| Percent divorced | 2.3 | 4.1 | .3 | .5 | 2.1 | 2.9 |

* Negro and white numbers in thousands. Taken from *Population Characteristics* (Bureau of Census, Ser. P–20, No. 145, December 27, 1965), 2. Creole percentage based on population where data were available.

had no issue. This bachelor lived through the Civil War period, and several of the old people recall conversations of their parents and grandparents about him. Apparently he was mentally normal and remained a bachelor by preference.

There are unmarried adults among the Letoyants, today, who prefer to lead single lives and whose decision is respected. However, some reason is generally proffered to explain the fact that these persons have not conformed to the social expectation that adults marry. In some instances those who remain unmarried are mentally deficient, and a few of them are somewhat eccentric in behavior. Generally, however, they are accepted by their people and are welcomed into the homes of relatives for gatherings and meals. Riverville has several single adults residing in the parental home or with relatives.

As a rule, the choice of the celibate life in religion does not occasion the same degree of inquisitiveness as the decision to remain unmarried and live at home. As Catholics, the Creoles have always emphasized religion, and the celibate clergy and religious have been held in high esteem; however, no Letoyants entered religious life in the early generations, probably because of the failure of Catholic congregations in the South to recruit candidates among them, and because of segregation within religious congregations.

Another indication of the importance of marriage is seen in the strong tendency to remarry, especially on the part of the men (Table 2). Many of the men who are widowed do not feel competent to care for a house and rear children unaided. In Riverville small scale farming is primarily a cooperative family enterprise, and the farmer who has no wife to care for his home and no children to assist him is at an economic disadvantage. One man whose wife died leaving him with four children said that he gave the babies to relatives and tried to get along, but it was hard. The father, who was himself orphaned, had not been reared with his brothers and sisters, and he did not want to deprive his children of sibling companionship. After a second marriage he was able to keep the family together. Men who do not remarry are usually elderly persons, who look to adult children for familial relationships.

SHADES OF MATRIMONY

The status of "married" among Letoyant Creoles has many shades of meaning, for they differentiate between a civil marriage that is later "blessed" or revalidated by the Church; a civil union that has never been "blessed" by the Church; a common-law union that is recognized as relatively stable and that could readily be legalized but has not been; a common-law union that has been legalized and "blessed" by the Church; concubinage, which involves at least one party who is married to someone else and endures for a time; and a temporary illicit union. Remarriage after divorce is legally valid but is deviant from Church norms since it incurs excommunication. An illicit union following separation from a legal spouse is also deviant behavior but does not necessarily incur excommunication.

Among the living direct descent population with marital unions, deviancy from marital norms is not great. In the South, over 85 percent of the unions were initially Church marriages; another

## Table 2

MARITAL UNIONS PER PERSON BY SEX AND TYPE OF DESCENT, BEFORE AND AFTER 1865 *

| Number of Unions | Before 1865 | | | | After 1865 | | | | Total | | Grand Total | |
|---|---|---|---|---|---|---|---|---|---|---|---|---|
| | Direct Descent | | Not Direct Descent † | | Direct Descent | | Not Direct Descent | | Direct Descent | | | |
| | M | F | M | F | M | F | M | F | Number | Percent | Number | Percent |
| One | 87 | 98 | 37 | 37 | 1566 | 1705 | 671 | 479 | 3456 | 86.18 | 4680 | 89.04 |
| Two | 22 | 16 | 1 | 2 | 195 | 264 | 6 | 11 | 497 | 12.39 | 517 | 9.84 |
| Three | 11 | 3 | 0 | 0 | 16 | 18 | 1 | 1 | 48 | 1.20 | 50 | .95 |
| Four | 0 | 2 | 0 | 0 | 3 | 3 | 0 | 0 | 8 | .20 | 8 | .15 |
| Five | 1 | 0 | 0 | 0 | 0 | 0 | 0 | 0 | 1 | .02 | 1 | .02 |
| Totals | 121 | 119 | 38 | 39 | 1780 | 1990 | 678 | 491 | 4010 | 100.00 | 5256 | 100.00 |
| No Data | 28 | 16 | 0 | 0 | 909 | 776 | 0 | 0 | 1685 | | | |

* Where dates of marriage not available, unions estimated at age twenty.
† Population associated with direct descent prior to 1865 not included here.

8 percent were civil revalidated unions, making a total of 94 percent of the unions in good standing with the Church. The common-law revalidated unions constituted only .2 percent of the total unions. Another 2.1 percent of the unions are civil unions and in many of these cases there is an impediment to a Church union.

What may appear to be a serious involvement between Letoyant Creoles ineligible for a Church marriage may not be as deviant as it appears. For example, a Riverville woman who was deserted by her husband thought he might return to her if she could make him jealous. Therefore, she went out several times with a man who had shown an interest in her, a Creole widower who did not have very strong religious values. In speaking of this incident, the Creole woman said that one thing she could not condone was intimacy with a man who was not her legal husband. The widower asked the priest about the possibility of marriage and was told that the woman was still lawfully married to her first husband, even though he had deserted her. The man was ready to contract a civil marriage following a divorce on the part of the woman, but the woman would not countenance a civil marriage because of her religion.

Family honor and conformity to religious norms often cause conflict. In families where children have deviated from marital norms there is a tendency to be protective of the deviants, to excuse them on the grounds that they had difficult decisions to make, or to categorize a particular case as an exception. There is less tolerance, however, towards other Creoles who are similarly deviant.

## PROGENY

### IMPORTANCE

Children, the lifeblood of any population, have always been valued by the Letoyants. An index of the importance of progeny is the size of completed families where mothers have lived through the childbearing years. The mean number of children per completed Letoyant family (mothers who were born in 1920 or before) from the first through the ninth generation is 4.64, or nearly 5 children per family. Another meaningful index of the importance of children is the contraharmonic mean, a little-known statistic that is particularly useful for telling the mean size of the family

*Table 3*

ARITHMETIC MEAN AND CONTRAHARMONIC MEAN NUMBER OF CHILDREN
PER KNOWN COMPLETED CREOLE FAMILY, 1964

| Number of Children Per Family, X | Arithmetic Mean | | Contraharmonic Mean * | |
|---|---|---|---|---|
| | Number of Families With Given Number of Children, f | fX | Number of Children in Families of a Given Size, f' | f'X |
| 0 | 66 | 0 | 0 | 0 |
| 1 | 137 | 137 | 137 | 137 |
| 2 | 134 | 268 | 268 | 536 |
| 3 | 113 | 339 | 339 | 1017 |
| 4 | 102 | 408 | 408 | 1632 |
| 5 | 121 | 605 | 605 | 3025 |
| 6 | 98 | 588 | 588 | 3528 |
| 7 | 81 | 567 | 567 | 3969 |
| 8 | 60 | 480 | 480 | 3840 |
| 9 | 61 | 549 | 549 | 4941 |
| 10 | 37 | 370 | 370 | 3700 |
| 11 | 16 | 176 | 176 | 1936 |
| 12 | 14 | 168 | 168 | 2016 |
| 13 | 6 | 78 | 78 | 1014 |
| 14 | 5 | 70 | 70 | 980 |
| 15 | 5 | 75 | 75 | 1125 |
| 16 | 1 | 16 | 16 | 256 |
| 17 | 1 | 17 | 17 | 289 |
| Totals | 1058 | 4911 | 4911 | 33941 |
| Mean | 4.64 | | 6.91 | |

* $CM = \dfrac{\Sigma f'X}{\Sigma f}$

into which children are born,[1] namely 6.91. Most Letoyant children, then, tend to be born into a 7-child family rather than a 5-child family (Table 3).

The number of childless unions among direct descent married females was minimal. In the first and second generations there were no childless married females. Of over ninety direct descent married females in the third generation, approximately 2 percent were childless. In the fourth and fifth generations, the percentage was slightly higher.

Childless families often adopt children, at least informally. Wherever possible, they rear the children of relatives as their own. Legal adoptions are relatively rare probably because the Letoyants are disinclined to become involved in "the white man's law." When one or both parents die and leave small children, relatives usually take care of the orphans. One woman related the experience in her own family in the following words: "The little boy we raised . . . his mother died and his father wasn't able to work and take care of the family, so he had to give away all the children. We grew him up as our own, and we did all we could for him. It was very hard then because the depression was on, and we had our own children to take care of. We had to work in the field to try to make a living for them. Until today he loves us very much, and he helps us whenever he can."

Another index of the importance of children is the relative length of the childbearing period. The reproductive span, the interval between the date of birth of the first child and the date of birth of the last child, of direct descent mothers having more than one child was 16.5 years for the second generation.[2] In the third generation the span was 15.5 years, in the fourth generation 14.3, and in the fifth generation 12.7 years. Since the sixth, seventh, and eighth generations still have appreciable numbers of mothers in the childbearing years, information on these families is inconclusive.

[1] See Virginia L. Senders, *Measurement and Statistics* (New York: Oxford University Press, 1958), 317–18.
[2] Suzanne, the only female who married in the first generation, did not marry until she was twenty-six.

In 1964 the average Letoyant population per household for all ages was identical with the nonwhite population per household, 3.8 persons. The population for white households was smaller by .57. Letoyant households had a slightly larger number of children under eighteen years of age in 1964 than did white or nonwhite households: the Creoles had 1.8 compared to 1.7 for nonwhites and 1.2 for whites. When a breakdown is made by regions, the

*Table 4*

AVERAGE POPULATION PER HOUSEHOLD BY COLOR,
U.S. AND SOUTH, 1964 *

| Region and Color | Average Population per Household | | |
|---|---|---|---|
| | All Ages | Under 18 | 18+ |
| U.S. | | | |
| Total | 3.33 | 1.24 | 2.10 |
| White | 3.28 | 1.18 | 2.09 |
| Nonwhite | 3.85 | 1.73 | 2.12 |
| Creole | 3.85 | 1.82 | 2.03 |
| South | | | |
| Total | 3.43 | 1.31 | 2.12 |
| White | 3.31 | 1.20 | 2.11 |
| Nonwhite | 4.02 | 1.85 | 2.16 |
| Creole | 4.20 | 2.14 | 2.06 |

* Data on U.S. and South from *Population Characteristics* (Bureau of Census, Ser. P–20, No. 139, June, 1965), 5. Creole data from household census.

largest number of children under eighteen years of age per household is to be found in the South where Letoyants have 2.1 children per household as compared to 1.9 for nonwhites and 1.2 for whites (Table 4).

ILLEGITIMACY

Large families are characteristic of both Letoyant Creoles and Negroes in the United States. However, the two populations have different rates of illegitimacy, probably due to the stress tra-ditionally placed by Creoles upon a Church marriage prior to marital relations and to pride in family heritage. Illegitimacy is frowned upon by the Letoyants, and a comparison of theirs and the Negro rates reveals that Creoles have lower rates than other nonwhites.

Statistics on illegitimacy are difficult to obtain and have a low degree of reliability. The United States Office of Vital Statistics points out that the legitimacy of a child is more likely to be mis-represented by white families than by nonwhite families. The former are better able to conceal an illegitimate birth by having the unwed mother leave the community before the birth of the child. They are also more likely to resort to abortion than are nonwhite families.

Letoyant illegitimacy ratios (illegitimate births per one thousand live births) are higher than white ratios and lower than nonwhite ratios. The most noticeable trend is a decline in Creole ratios and an increase in nonwhite and white ratios in the last ten years (Fig. 2). Due to the relatively small number of Letoyant illegitimate births, the Creole trend shows rather sharp differences from year to year rather than a curve.

Letoyant Creoles exhibit a wide range of attitudes toward il-legitimacy. A priest who has lived and worked among them for many years believes that their attitudes have been influenced, in large part, by their knowledge that "legitimacy is a Church rule." In his experience, however, the illegitimate child is not particularly disadvantaged within the ethnic population for he belongs to the family and, as a child of the family, he is entitled to stay there. In the early generations there was more illegitimacy than there is in the present population, and probably there was more acceptance of it. The records show that Letoyant children born out of wed-lock in the early generations married into the population and were no more likely to become "lost" to the population than were children born in wedlock. Children born out of wedlock to a Negro mother, however, had a double disadvantage, especially if

Figure 2

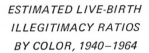

ESTIMATED LIVE-BIRTH
ILLEGITIMACY RATIOS
BY COLOR, 1940–1964

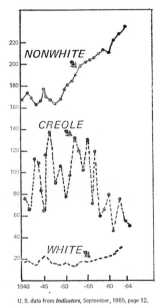

U. S. data from *Indicators*, September, 1965, page 12.

they were darker than the average Creole, for they were not likely to intermarry with other Letoyants.

Although there were probably some deviants in every Letoyant generation and age group, the incidence does not appear high compared to other populations. Among the middle and upper classes young couples who have had extramarital relations may be urged to marry before the birth of a child, particularly if both young people are from similar class backgrounds. If the mother is a Negro, there may be little possibility of having a child legitimated; sometimes an existing marriage precludes it. Some Creole women bearing illegitimate children have had a legal marriage and are separated from their husbands; others have never been married. At least one woman who has had a relatively large number of children out of wedlock is regarded as being mentally subnormal.[3]

It is not customary for Letoyant men to maintain two households, one with the legitimate children and another with children by another woman. However, in at least one instance in Riverville, a Creole man has almost consistently maintained a second household. His behavior is interpreted by some of the people as an effort to prove his manliness and by others as an attempt to gain publicity. He does, however, provide for his legal children and is regarded as a good father to them.

Illegitimate children who are "adopted" by their grandparents are usually reared with much affection and attention. They are more likely to be left with grandparents if the mother remarries or if the mother had the child out of wedlock and later contracted a marriage. Grandparents and older couples often assert that if a child had a baby "that way," they would take care of the daughter and the baby and would not force a marriage until they had "a good look" at the boy. Unless they approved of the match, there would be no marriage. Although many of these people could afford an abortion, religious norms prohibit it. In all probability, the grandparents assume responsibility for the child born out of wedlock.

Since Creoles are predominantly Catholic and their marital norms predominantly those of the Catholic Church, children born of civil marriage would be regarded as illegitimate even though they would not be legally so categorized. Of the direct descent [4] living Creoles in 1964, 2.5 percent were born of civil unions.[5]

Children born out of wedlock where no marriage took place between their parents constitute 7.2 percent of the total direct descent living Creoles. The highest incidence of this type of ir-

---

[3] The genealogical charts reveal a high incidence of illegitimacy in families that have a high prevalence of mental and physical disorders.

[4] The direct descent population can trace their origin to Pierre Letoyant and Marie; nondirect descent are those who married into this population.

[5] Based on known parental marital irregularities.

regularity is found in urban areas: 4.5 percent as against 2.7 percent in the rural community.

The force of social control within the Creole population is evidenced in the number of rectifications of illicit unions by individuals with premarital irregularities, 93.5 percent of whom had a Church marriage. Some of those who did not marry could not do so according to Church norms. Among those who married after some premarital irregularity, 78.3 percent of the unions were stable.

The incidence of premarital irregularity as measured by Church norms is about 13.8 percent. As used here, the incidence of premarital irregularity was determined by the notation of a christening record that the father of the child is unknown, or by a notation that a marriage is rectified according to Church laws after a child has been born. In either instance, the child is born out of wedlock according to Church norms. The incidence of irregularity was also revealed by the date of birth of the child and the date of the marital union. If a child was born prior to nine months after the date of marriage, premarital irregularity was presumed. No allowance was made for premature birth, but neither was there any way of determining the extent of premarital irregularity where there was no issue.

## HOUSEHOLD COMPOSITION

### HOUSEHOLD HEADS

One index of family strength is the presence of both husband and wife in a household. A Negro family characteristic dating back to the days of slavery is a proportionately high number of female family heads. When contrasted with both white and nonwhite (Negroes, American Indians, Japanese, Chinese, Filipinos, and other) families in the United States, the Letoyant family is considerably stronger as measured by this index. In 1964, 83.4 percent of Creole households were headed by both a husband and wife compared to 75.1 of white households and 61.3 percent of non-

*Table 5*

HOUSEHOLDS BY TYPE AND COLOR OF HEAD, 1964 *
(Whites and Nonwhites in thousands)

| | Color of Head | | | | | |
| | Nonwhite | | Creole | | White | |
| Household Type | Number | Percent | Number | Percent | Number | Percent |
|---|---|---|---|---|---|---|
| All households | 5,709 | 100.0 | 813 | 100.0 | 50,287 | 100.0 |
| Primary families | 4,711 | 82.5 | 736 | 90.5 | 42,568 | 84.7 |
| Husband-wife | 3,497 | 61.3 | 678 | 83.4 | 37,760 | 75.1 |
| Other male head | 158 | 2.8 | 15 | 1.8 | 1,045 | 2.1 |
| Female head | 1,056 | 18.5 | 43 | 5.3 | 3,763 | 7.5 |
| Primary individuals | 998 | 17.5 | 77 | 9.5 | 7,719 | 15.3 |
| Male | 383 | 6.7 | 31 | 3.8 | 2,577 | 5.1 |
| Female | 615 | 10.8 | 46 | 5.7 | 5,142 | 10.2 |

* Data on whites and nonwhites from *Current Population Reports* (Bureau of Census, Ser. P–20, No. 130, July 27, 1964), 1.

white households (Table 5). Households headed by females are also fewer among Letoyants: 5.3 percent of Letoyant primary families, 7.5 percent of white families, and 18.5 percent of nonwhite families. Where the primary family is headed by a male other than a husband (for example, a brother or a father) the Letoyant couple is almost always separated; in a few instances they are divorced.

Some households are headed by primary individuals, that is, heads of households who are not living with relatives. Most of these households among the Letoyants are headed by widows or by single males. The percentages of households headed by primary individuals in 1964 were 9.5 percent of the Creole, 15.3 percent of the white, and 17.5 percent of the nonwhite.

COMPOSITION BY RESIDENCE

Although the Letoyant Creoles were initially a rural people, they have, in the present century, migrated from the rural South in large numbers. Today 20.5 percent of the total Letoyant population is rural-farm. This compares with 6.9 percent of the Negro population and 6.6 percent of the white population. In comparison to the Negro, the Letoyants remain relatively rural even though only one in five of them still lives in a rural environment.

A comparison of the composition of Letoyant and total United States households by residence shows that a greater proportion of nonfarm than farm Creole households have husbands and wives present (89 percent nonfarm and 70.9 percent farm) while in the total U.S. population more farm (83.8 percent) than nonfarm (73.0 percent) households have husbands and wives present. This is probably due to the large number of young Letoyant couples who have settled in nonfarm areas in recent years. Another difference in the two populations is the number of farm and nonfarm households with a female head: among Letoyants, 10.9 percent farm and 2.7 percent nonfarm; among the U.S. population, 5.3 percent farm and 8.8 percent nonfarm (Table 6).

Households headed by primary individuals are comparable in percentages, except that Letoyant females who are living on the farm correspond roughly to United States females who are living in nonfarm areas. This difference is due largely to the prevalence of widows in the rural areas who maintain a household separate from their children. The small number of Creole females living alone in nonfarm areas is due to the large number of Letoyants who recently migrated from the South and to the tendency of relatively young household heads to bring an aged parent into their household in the city or to send a grandchild to live with the aged parent in the rural environment.

CONJUGAL AND EXTENDED UNITS

*Conjugal Units.* The comparatively strong role of the Letoyant Creole male is probably responsible in large part for the predominance of households having both husbands and wives. A priest who had worked among Louisiana Creoles for many years said that he attributed the dominance of men to tradition. He said, "It isn't that women are not industrious or that they do not earn money; it is just that the male has always been dominant among the Creoles, and women learn this from their parents and pass it on to

## Table 6

HOUSEHOLDS BY TYPE AND RESIDENCE, U.S. AND CREOLE POPULATIONS, 1964 *

(U.S. population total in thousands)

| Household Type | Residence of Total U.S. Population | | | | Residence of Creole Population | | | |
|---|---|---|---|---|---|---|---|---|
| | Farm | | Nonfarm | | Farm | | Nonfarm | |
| | Number | Percent | Number | Percent | Number | Percent | Number | Percent |
| All households | 3,345 | 100.0 | 52,651 | 100.0 | 258 | 100.0 | 555 | 100.0 |
| Primary families | 3,082 | 92.1 | 44,197 | 83.9 | 219 | 84.9 | 517 | 93.2 |
| Husband-wife | 2,804 | 83.8 | 38,453 | 73.0 | 183 | 70.9 | 495 | 89.2 |
| Other male head | 100 | 3.0 | 1,103 | 2.1 | 8 | 3.1 | 7 | 1.3 |
| Female head | 178 | 5.3 | 4,641 | 8.8 | 28 | 10.9 | 15 | 2.7 |
| Primary individuals | 263 | 7.9 | 8,454 | 16.1 | 39 | 15.1 | 38 | 6.8 |
| Male | 137 | 4.1 | 2,823 | 5.4 | 11 | 4.2 | 20 | 3.6 |
| Female | 126 | 3.8 | 5,631 | 10.7 | 28 | 10.9 | 18 | 3.2 |

* U.S. population data from *Current Population Reports* (Bureau of Census, Ser. P–20, No. 130, July 27, 1964), 1.

their children." Teachers who worked among the Letoyants for years also observed that the father was the primary disciplinarian in the family and that he played a very important part in all family decisions. In Riverville, the teachers seldom had disciplinary problems.

In the rural economy where family tradition developed and where Grand Pere's influence was very strong, the cooperative efforts of husband and wife were important. Since the Civil War, the husband has done most of the heavy work, and emphasis has been placed upon his economic productiveness. These circumstances, coupled with the importance of his role as a disciplinarian, are primary factors accounting for the high incidence of unbroken Creole families. Religious values, however, are also important.

In most conjugal family units, children leave home after they finish high school, at about age eighteen. Among the Letoyants, however, there is a relatively high proportion of children over eighteen still living with their parents. Among the major Letoyant settlements, Indianola has the highest proportion of households with children over eighteen, namely 26 percent. Riverville is second with more than 19 percent. Southern communities with large Letoyant settlements have from 10 to 15 percent of the households with children over eighteen.[6] Of the 813 households for whom census data were available, approximately 13 percent have children over eighteen years of age living in the household with their parents. There is a higher predominance among Letoyants in the South than in other parts of the country and particularly in southern communities where work opportunities are available or in Riverville, where the family has deep roots and owns property. The other large rural community, Riverton, where property ownership is less extensive and where farms are not as large, has a lower incidence.

*Extended Units.* In a closely knit ethnic population, a relatively high incidence of extended family households may be expected.

[6] Percentages were calculated from the church parishes that had censuses on households available.

Among nonwhite families the composition of a household is usually not restricted to the conjugal unit, since grandchildren are commonly found in them.

Approximately 10 percent of the Letoyant families have relatives of the parents living in the household. The incidence is highest, at 15 percent, in Riverville and in Southern City. A comparative study of extended family members in Riverville over a ten-year interval between 1954 and 1964 showed a numerical decrease in the incidence of relatives living in the households, with the exception of grandchildren. In 1954, grandchildren constituted 2.6

*Table 7*

RELATION OF RIVERVILLE CREOLE HOUSEHOLD HEADS TO
HOUSEHOLD MEMBERS OTHER THAN SPOUSE, 1954 AND 1964

| Relationship | Percent in 1954 | Percent in 1964 |
|---|---|---|
| Children | 79.1 | 86.7 |
| Grandchildren | 2.6 | 7.2 |
| Siblings | 5.3 | 1.9 |
| Nieces and nephews | 3.9 | 1.5 |
| Sons and daughters-in-law | 3.9 | .8 |
| Parents | 1.3 | 1.5 |
| Cousins | 1.3 | 0 |
| Aunts and uncles | 1.3 | 0 |
| Stepchildren | 0 | .4 |
| Other | 1.3 | 0 |
| Total | 100.0 | 100.0 |

percent of the household members; in 1964, 7.2 percent. This increase is due, in part, to the concern which people who have moved from Riverville have for their elderly parents. When the elderly balk at leaving their homes, grandchildren are sometimes sent to live with them. One grandmother voiced her expectation of having a grandchild in her home when she said, "I have sixty grandchildren and not a child to stay with me." The only other increase in the ten-year period was a very slight proportion of elderly parents. The incidence of siblings living in a household declined from 5.3 percent to 1.9 percent because of the paucity of cash-paying jobs in the rural community (Table 7).

Although financial assistance is not a primary consideration in children's willingness to care for elderly persons, it probably is a factor in the rural economy where cash is not plentiful. Old folks who stay with their children in Riverville are generally welcomed not only because of the responsibility the child feels toward his parents but also because today the parent usually has old-age benefits and a regular cash income. Sometimes children vie with one another to take care of their parents. Elderly parents who are senile or mentally disturbed are as well cared for as those who are mentally alert. Very few old persons are put in homes for the aged.

Godparents, especially if they are distant relatives, are an important part of the extended family, even though they usually do not reside in the household. A person who would like to take on the role of godparent may indicate to parents expecting a child that he would feel honored to be chosen. If the parents have not already made a decision, they usually act on the suggestion. Godparents are expected to give gifts at Christmas, Easter, and special occasions, i.e., birthdays, First Communion, Confirmation, and graduation. In families where one child has an attentive and generous godparent and another child has a godparent who does not live up to expectations, this difference is a topic of comment. A family with several teenage girls decided to ask cousins who lived in a large city where a university was located to let the eldest girl stay with them and attend college. The cousin was reluctant because as she said, "The second girl is my godchild, and I had hoped that she would come and live with me while she attended college." Apparently the godmother felt that she could not offer the same opportunities to both sisters, and she felt an obligation toward her godchild. The exchange of attention and of gifts is reversed when the godchild reaches adulthood, especially when godparents become elderly or ill. A visitor to the hospital, for example, will identify himself as the godchild of an ailing person.

## Broken Families

Dissolution of a family through the death of one of the spouses is to be expected in the course of the family life cycle. In the United States, there are more widows than widowers. Negroes have the highest proportion of widows, 13.5 percent, which is slightly higher than the percentage for the total United States, 12.2 percent. The Letoyant percentage is much less, 5.0 percent. For males, the incidence of being widowed is 3.8 percent for Negroes, 3.3 percent for whites, and .7 percent for Letoyants. (Table 1, p. 79).

Statistics on incidence of widowhood according to age reveal the following comparisons between Letoyant Creoles and total United States population: The percentage under age thirty-five is very small, less than 2 percent among the total population and practically nonexistent in the Letoyant population. Between the ages of forty-five and fifty-four the proportion of those widowed is approximately the same in both populations. From age fifty-five through seventy-four the proportion of widowed Letoyants is slightly higher. In the age bracket seventy-five and over there are relatively fewer widowed Letoyants than there are in the total population.

Desertion, often referred to as the poor man's divorce, has been relatively frequent among Negroes. Separation, too, which may be temporary or sporadic, has a comparatively higher incidence among Negroes than among either whites or Letoyants. Letoyants have a low incidence of family dissolution due to separation as compared to the Negro (5.9 percent of Negro males and 4.3 percent of Letoyant males; 9.6 percent of Negro females and 4.5 percent of Letoyant females), but a comparatively high incidence as compared to the whites, whose rates are 1.1 percent of the males and 1.4 percent of the females. This difference between the

Letoyants and each of the other populations is more than offset by the relatively low proportion of Letoyant divorces: .5 percent of males and .3 percent for females as compared to 2.3 percent of Negro males and 4.1 percent of Negro females and 2.1 percent of white males and 2.9 percent of white females (Table 1, p. 79).

Riverville women who either separated or divorced and are having children out of wedlock are occasionally defended by Creoles who explain that these women had cruel husbands. One woman's husband allegedly shot himself and threatened to kill his wife in order to intimidate her. Another woman in Riverville, who has had several illegitimate children, is believed to have had these by her legal husband even though she asks for welfare support and claims that the children are illegitimate.

When Letoyant couples who have moved away from Riverville experience difficulty in personal relations, and the wife decides to take the children home to her parents, both husband and wife can normally expect pressure from their parents to effect a reconciliation. They may leave the daughter out of their social planning and treat her as though she has disgraced the family. The wife may hear constant reminders of the importance of going back to her husband.

In some instances, separation is attributed to lower social-class behavior. One family that had children who were not living with their spouses was described as "a rowdy people." Sometimes marriages were forced upon the young couple. In one instance, a young man who took a girl to a dance stayed out with her all night. They allegedly became intoxicated; the man was unable to drive; and they went to sleep in the parked car. When he returned the girl to her home the next morning, her parents insisted that they marry. Observers commented that the young people were really not sufficiently interested in one another, and such a marriage could not be expected to endure. In at least two instances in Riverville this same explanation was given for couples who are separated. The marriage was forced upon the couple after their families decided that they had been imprudent in some way. One informant gave the following account: "Most of the women-chasers on the river support their families. They don't really intend to give up their wife and children. Some of them get married to please their families, and that don't usually work out. I have a brother that married like that, and he and his wife stayed together for about fourteen years. But they never did get along. So he finally quit. That hurts us. I don't think they should do that."

DIVORCE

Letoyant Creoles are more averse to divorce than to separation. A person divorced and remarried is prohibited from receiving the sacraments and is excommunicated from the Church. Within the family these relatives are usually defended, at least by their parents and siblings. The strength of family ties is partially responsible for this defense. Sometimes, however, parents or siblings are openly critical of those who have divorced and remarried.

If physical abuse or a threat to health or life is involved in the legal separation and divorce, it is more likely to be condoned, at least by relatives. Some marriages to servicemen who were strangers have ended in divorce. Of the total living married Letoyant population, only 1.1 percent is known to be divorced. The divorce rate is higher in urban places outside Louisiana than it is in the rural communities. It is more common where there is a mixed religious marriage than it is if both parties are Catholic. The proportion of divorces between the partners where one is not a direct descendant is, surprisingly, proportionately less than where both are direct descendants, due in large part to the preference for outsiders who are culturally and racially similar to themselves.

Compared to other nonwhite families, Letoyant families are strong according to the indices presented in this chapter. While marital unions and progeny in large numbers have been important to both Creoles and other nonwhites, Creoles seem to place more emphasis upon the legitimate status of children than do Negroes. Among Letoyant Creoles, remarriage after the death of a spouse is common; divorce rates in the population are negligible when compared with other populations. There are many factors which contribute to family solidarity such as the strength of tradition and the importance of reunions where children from all parts of the United States and from other countries come to celebrate weddings, anniversaries, and birthdays. The Letoyant family system places a high value on family unity, a tradition that continues to be imparted to children today as it has been through past generations.

# Chapter 6

# Religion as a Force in Ethnic Identity

Historically, the culture of the Letoyants has deep roots in Catholicism. Pierre Letoyant was unmistakably Catholic. As stated earlier, in his will he refers to the church in France where he was christened and to an uncle who was a priest. The beginning of Letoyant's last testimony reads like a prayer:

> "In the name of the Most Holy and Undivisible Trinity, Father, Son and the Holy Ghost. A true Christian, Catholic, apostolic and Roman, I recommend humbly my soul to God when it pleases Him to separate it from my body, begging His Divine Majesty and goodness, by the infinite merits of the passion and death of His only son, our Lord and saviour Jesus Christ, by the intercession of the glorious Virgin Mary and of all the saints and of the heavenly court to take it and place it in the Kingdom of God among the number of the Blessed."

Catholicism was the state religion in colonial Louisiana, and slave owners were required by law to see that their slaves received religious instruction. When some priests complained to the king of Spain that slaves in outlying plantations were not observing the Sabbath and were not receiving the sacrament of matrimony, Charles IV ordered, in 1789, that chaplains be installed on such plantations, that quarters for unmarried men and women be segregated, and that particular attention be given to slave marriages.[1] Negro slaves generally had marital unions without benefit of clergy, and marital partners were likely to be separated since masters did not ordinarily respect the family groups among their slaves. After emancipation, many of the freedmen continued to live in the family styles they had known in the past; those who had

[1] Joe Gray Taylor, *Negro Slavery in Louisiana* (Baton Rouge: Louisiana Historical Association, 1963), 134–35.

stable, legal unions generally enjoyed a relatively high economic and social status. Unions among whites and nonwhites were forbidden and could not be legitimized according to the laws; therefore, a legal union between Letoyant and Marie was impossible. French royal decrees concerning the welfare of Negroes and Indians were not always observed, and the decree on slave marriages did not affect the union of Letoyant and his spouse. However, the very year the Spanish royal decree was promulgated was the year a new priest in the locality was instrumental in breaking up the union since it could not be regularized under the law.

Despite the shortage of priests after the Louisiana Purchase in 1800, religion continued to be a primary factor in the identification of the Letoyant Creoles. This kind of identity can have special significance for members of a minority group. If there is little or no recognition from the dominant population, those who believe in spiritual powers may find some compensation in the sense of acceptance from transcendent powers. A religious perspective permits an individual belonging to a minority group to define himself in relation not only to the natural world in which he lives but also to a supernatural world. He can view himself as an individual loved, desired, and approved by supernatural beings if not by other human beings. God becomes a "significant other" in his life, and he has a destiny unbounded by earthly restrictions.[2]

The first Creole church, erected on Grand Pere's plantation, became a place for worship, whether or not there was a priest. Grand Pere undoubtedly communicated directly with the Pope about the church and about the identification of the Letoyants with Catholicism. In 1823 Pope Leo XII wrote Grand Pere a letter of commendation for providing a house of worship on his estate. Grand Pere established a precedent in writing directly to Rome, and some of his descendants have since followed his example. Thus, a Letoyant woman living in Northern City, indignant over being charged $10 for a burial place in Riverville, appealed to the Louisiana bishop. When she received no reply from him, she wrote to

[2] Cf. Glenn Vernon, *Sociology of Religion* (New York: McGraw-Hill, 1962), 97.

Rome, and the bishop heard directly from Rome. In a subsequent letter to the Riverville pastor, the woman wrote: "Leo XII wrote a letter to our Grand Pere in 1823 and the letter was read to the congregation at a Sunday High Mass." It is highly improbable that this woman would have known the name of the 1823 pontiff unless this information came down through tradition as a very significant episode in family history.

The church on Grand Pere's plantation was not formally blessed until 1829, due in large part to the scarcity of clergy. In Grand Pere's official portrait the church is in the background, and he points proudly to it as if to signify that one of his greatest accomplishments was the transmission of religion as a part of Letoyant Creole cultural heritage. Shortly before his death, in 1856, when the Creoles numbered more than two hundred, this edifice was designated as a parish church, and the priests stationed there served the outlying missions; it was the first instance of a non-white church parish having missions whose congregations were predominantly or wholly white.

The concern of the people for their spiritual welfare during the intervals when they were temporarily without a minister can be detected in drafts of letters found in family ledgers. One letter, dated December 4, 1877, states: "I received your letter dated October 8 on the 29 of last month, day of the First Communion and Confirmation on the West River, where I had the happiness of seeing and talking with His Excellency, the Bishop. . . . He promised to give us a priest soon. I believe that he will leave Father M. until he receives another priest from France." Another letter written to a priest-godfather on July 10, 1889, states: "Father D. is leaving today for France, with no hope of returning. How long, then, will we be without a priest? When will you come to see us?" Religion as a continuing mark of identity to the Creoles was evidenced by the comment made concerning a conjugal family whose descendants could not be traced. An informant wrote: "I went all over the hills, but those people forgot all about each other together with their religion." Apparently the lost kinsmen not only contracted out-group marriages but also neglected to practice their religion; hence, they were outside the ethnic fold on two scores.

In the two centuries since the origin of the Letoyant family, only .27 percent of the population are known not to have identified with Catholicism, either by not having their offspring christened or by converting to another denomination.[3] Of those who are not Catholic, eleven children came from three families where the father was not a Catholic, and four from two families where the mother was not a Catholic; eight children came from a family that lived on a remote bayou with no means of transportation; and one adult, who moved to a metropolitan area, became an Episcopalian during the Reconstruction period when he gained prominence as the first colored notary public in Louisiana.

Common or parallel religious experience can be an integrative force, particularly if a religion has adherents throughout the world who share both ideology and norms of prescribed behavior. Catholic missionaries, who were adept at syncretizing religion and other aspects of culture, converted large numbers of aborigines who shared a common culture. But with the Negroes who were imported from heterogeneous cultures and who were enslaved, the success of the missionary was dependent, in large part, upon the good will of their owners and the enforcement of royal decrees.

To the freedmen of mixed racial origin, particularly if their culture approximated that of the French or Spanish, religion was generally a source of cohesion. The Letoyants, for instance, chose French or Spanish patron saints, and the saints for whom Grand Pere and Louis were named became in a sense the special patrons of their descendants.

For Letoyant Creoles, religion was also an instrument in strengthening and weakening relationships with other groups. Religion strengthened the ideological and behavioral resemblance of the Creoles to the white status-conscious descendants of the first settlers. Their blood ties with their white progenitor, who

[3] There are strong possibilities that two other families, located after data processing had begun, have not had their children christened as Catholics because there is no church in the area where they live.

was a professed religious man, constituted an additional bond of unity, even though their white counterparts were reluctant to acknowledge this tie.

On the other hand, the Letoyant Creoles used religion to further differentiate themselves from the lower-status Negro population, with whom they generally disavowed any ties of blood. Former slaves who had been practicing Catholics, and their descendants, were gradually and effectively excluded from the Church in Riverville.[4]

When the Letoyants began migrating to Indianola about the time of the Civil War, they attended services in the only church in that community. One of the priests became concerned about the lack of educational opportunities for them and arranged to have some classes taught in a former seminary building adjacent to the church. Through his efforts, a church was eventually erected to serve the Creole and Negro Catholics, and a parish school was subsequently added. When the second Riverville church was ready for services, the Creoles attempted to use it as a focal point for ethnic activities and to exclude others; however, they were not completely successful because they could not obtain the collaboration of the clergy.

An elderly white informant in Indianola related the incident concerning the Creoles there in the following words: "The bishop had a lot of trouble with those people. You know, they didn't want the niggers to come to their church. The bishop, for a while, thought he was going to have to build another church for the niggers. They usually don't push, but they really didn't want those niggers in church with them."

There is evidence that the Letoyants in other Louisiana communities give preference to fellow Creoles in church activities; however, they were not successful in establishing predominantly Creole churches in other places where they settled in large num-

---

[4] To this day, Catholicism continues to be a clue to Creole identity. Joseph H. Fichter estimates that only 5 percent of American Negroes are Catholic, despite a high rate of urban conversions. In Louisiana, especially in the area of the Letoyant's origin, nonwhite Catholics are almost exclusively Creole. "American Religion and the Negro," *Daedalus*, XCIV (Fall, 1965), 1091.

bers. In at least one instance, they were forceful in the establishment of a second parish in a section of a city where they congregated, although others living within the parish boundaries were not excluded from parish functions.

The sacraments confer status upon the Creoles, as well as a sense of identity. The four of the sacraments of the Catholic Church that are of more particular concern to the Letoyants are baptism, confirmation, marriage, and extreme unction. Letoyant Creole children like most Catholic children are ordinarily baptized within four weeks after birth; relatives, friends, and neighbors can be expected to ask for an explanation if baptism is delayed. The most frequently used names among the Creoles have been Marie for the girls and Joseph for boys, especially during the first generations, followed by a second name by which the child would ordinarily be called. And as with most Catholics, it was not uncommon to name a child for the saint on whose birthday the birth occurred, a circumstance that explains some of the unusual names found among these people: Prospar, Ligouri, Philogue, Chrysostom, Faustina, and Hippolite. Among Letoyants, godparents assumed the traditional responsibilities, including that of seeing to it that the godchild remained a good Catholic. One informant explained the character of the godparent-godchild relationship as follows: "It used to be years ago if I was your godmother and your parents died, I'm supposed to take you and raise you. I'd be forced to raise you as my own. They used to follow that rule. Very much so. I don't know about now, but it used to be a very, very rigid thing. Being a godchild, and a godparent was something wonderful, an honor. They wanted to be sure you were all right."

Among Letoyants, confirmation is conferred less frequently than baptism, since it is ordinarily administered by a bishop, and, in the past, bishops could not visit all parishes regularly, especially in rural areas. Moreover, there, as everywhere, parents have less control over young adults than they do over children. They have been known to induce their offspring to receive this sacrament by offering them gifts of money. Failure to be confirmed provokes unfavorable comment. Speaking of a man who was courting her daughter, a Letoyant mother said in a disdainful tone, "Why, that old rascal never even made his confirmation."

Great solemnity and ceremony were often associated with confirmation. A pastor of Centerville who accompanied the bishop on a confirmation tour relates the manner in which the clergy were received by the Riverville people. They arrived in the late evening at Milltown, the nearest railroad station, and were met by some three hundred men mounted on horses, each man carrying a torch. When the procession started toward the church over the two-mile country lane, without a house on either side, the horsemen stretched out in double file for over a quarter of a mile ahead of the carriages conveying the bishop and the clergy—their torches casting a weird light on the woods that lined the road.

Marriage, the sacrament so vital to the perpetuation of the Letoyant group, is of great importance to them. A marriage rite is preceded, as a rule, by publication of the banns, that is, announcements at Masses on three consecutive Sundays of a couple's intention to marry. Anyone who knows of an impediment to the union is expected to make it known to church authorities. The ceremony takes place in public and gives an opportunity for as much celebration as can be afforded by the parties involved.

The rite of marriage, like that of baptism, reinforces ethnicity by affirming the recipients' membership in the society of Catholic Creoles. In the case of matrimony, however, the Church's proscription against unions within the third degree of kinship sometimes comes into conflict with the Letoyant Creole group norm of in-group marriage. This conflict may be resolved by a couple's decision to resort to a civil ceremony and later having the union "blessed" by the Church. In this way they can eventually comply with two divergent norms.

Rites of passage at death are regarded as very important to the Letoyants, and a funeral is more likely to draw a host of friends and acquaintances than any other rite, especially in communities to which the Creoles have migrated. In rural areas, particularly, word of a critical illness spreads swiftly.

When a person dies in the rural community, a Negro funeral director is called. (There is no Creole in the mortuary business locally.) The body is brought to the home the evening before the funeral and the community turns out for the wake. Shortly after the body arrives, in the late afternoon, the Sisters who live in the community are expected to come and lead the mourners in saying the rosary. In the evening, the priest comes and leads another rosary. The home and yard overflow with relatives and friends, many of whom spend the night. Early on the morning of the funeral the gravediggers work in the cemetery. Those who are asked to dig seldom refuse, for as one gravedigger commented, "Someone will be asked to dig for me someday."

The site of the graves in Riverville has been a cause of controversy for several years. Only the land immediately behind the church is suitable for use because a bayou behind the church property often floods the low lands adjacent to it. With a high premium being placed upon burial in the homeland and on the front lots, it is difficult to get suitable lots for all the deceased. If lots are reused, relatives in distant places protest loudly; very often relatives intend to use the plot themselves. The priest is, moreover, expected to find a burial place for many of the Letoyants who have migrated and died elsewhere. This note, found in an old ledger, points out the importance of the Riverville cemetery: "Charly died October 31—1914 and was burry at the big Cross in the grave yard. He was bury 5 days after his death on the 4 of november at 12 o'clock. It surely was a sad burry that every one shuld always remember. He died in Centerville and he asked to the Bishop to carry him to his church." One old lady who moved to Northern City wrote to the priest in Riverville protesting about the re-use of cemetery space: "Father, I am disappointed in you for tearing our old tombs down. And selling our graves space. That was already ours. With the money you take from us in the grave yard, you could of kept it up real nice like the others in Louisiana. I know you have no right to do this, as the land is there for our use."

## Church Norms

Although the Letoyants identify with Catholicism verbally, the best index of the importance of this self-identification is the extent to which they conform to the behavioral norms of Catholicism. The Church serves as an agent of social control because it sets norms or guidelines for the behavior of its adherents and implements these norms both directly and indirectly through various means: confession, threat of excommunication, and admonition. Especially in the rural community, where people are related by ties of blood—as well as by the rural party line—almost any deviancy becomes common knowledge. Under these circumstances, the Sunday sermon may have a particular thrust that would not be felt in an urban congregation.

### RELIGIOUS OBSERVANCE

Attendance at Sunday Mass and annual reception of the Sacrament of the Eucharist during Eastertime is the commonplace index for distinguishing practicing Catholics from nonpracticing ones. Of the 1,947 Letoyants for whom a religious census was available,[5] 86.3 percent complied with these two prescriptions. Of the 6.5 percent of the Letoyants who are classified as irregular in their observance, some couples go to Mass regularly but cannot receive the sacraments because of marriage irregularities. Others are infirm or dependent, either small children or aged persons; a few are without means of transportation. About 7.2 percent do not attend any services throughout the year nor do they receive the sacraments (Table 8).

The highest percentage of regular observance is in urban communities outside the South, while the highest percentages of irregularity and nonattendance—at least 10 percent—occur in rural Louisiana communities. However, the highest percentages of dependents are also found in rural communities where the distance from a church is greater than in most urban communities.

Religious observance is most regular among young people, aged

[5] All Creoles on whom data were available are included in the analysis of religious observance, regardless of place of residence.

## Table 8

### Religious Observance of Living Creoles by Age and Community Type, 1964

| Observance by Community Types | Years of Age | | | | | | | Totals |
|---|---|---|---|---|---|---|---|---|
| | 0–5 | 6–9 | 10–19 | 20–29 | 30–34 | 35–39 | 40+ | |
| **Regular** | | | | | | | | |
| Rural Louisiana | 125 | 87 | 236 | 67 | 29 | 46 | 284 | 874 |
| Urban Louisiana | 66 | 50 | 133 | 57 | 20 | 27 | 168 | 521 |
| Urban Elsewhere | 51 | 42 | 53 | 30 | 29 | 25 | 55 | 285 |
| Total | 242 | 179 | 422 | 154 | 78 | 98 | 507 | 1680 |
| Percent | 85.8 | 85.7 | 93.2 | 87.0 | 77.2 | 83.8 | 83.4 | 86.3 |
| **Irregular** | | | | | | | | |
| Rural Louisiana | 17 | 6 | 11 | 5 | 4 | 5 | 30 | 78 |
| Urban Louisiana | 3 | 4 | 8 | 3 | 1 | 4 | 12 | 35 |
| Urban Elsewhere | 3 | 2 | 0 | 3 | 2 | 1 | 2 | 13 |
| Total | 23 | 12 | 19 | 11 | 7 | 10 | 44 | 126 |
| Percent | 8.2 | 5.7 | 4.2 | 6.2 | 7.0 | 8.5 | 7.2 | 6.5 |
| **Non-Attendance** | | | | | | | | |
| Rural Louisiana | 16 | 17 | 12 | 11 | 11 | 8 | 46 | 121 |
| Urban Louisiana | 0 | 0 | 0 | 1 | 5 | 1 | 9 | 16 |
| Urban Elsewhere | 1 | 1 | 0 | 0 | 0 | 0 | 2 | 4 |
| Total | 17 | 18 | 12 | 12 | 16 | 9 | 57 | 141 |
| Percent | 6.0 | 8.6 | 2.6 | 6.8 | 15.8 | 7.7 | 9.4 | 7.2 |
| Grand Total | 282 | 209 | 453 | 177 | 101 | 117 | 608 | 1947 |

ten to nineteen, where attendance is 93.2 percent. Approximately 86 percent of the children under ten years of age also attend Mass regularly; however, they are more dependent upon their parents than are adolescents. Church attendance is more irregular during the years twenty to twenty-nine; 87 percent of these Letoyants attend regularly. Irregularity is sharpest, however, between the ages of thirty to thirty-five when religious observance drops to 77.2 percent. At age thirty-five it rises again to over 83 percent—a level that is maintained in later years (Table 8).

These findings place the Letoyant Creoles within Fichter's profile [6] of the modal Catholic who is very religious during adolescence and postadolescence, negligent during his twenties, and a religious delinquent between the ages of thirty and thirty-nine— except that the religious observance of the Letoyant Creoles becomes stabilized at age thirty-five.

Women are slightly more observant than men, with the exception of urban communities outside Louisiana (Table 9). In the complete sample of Letoyants where data on religious observance were available, the greatest difference between the sexes was only 2.5 percent. In general, both men and women are observant Catholics, and migration from the home community does not have an adverse effect upon religious practice.

One of the clearest types of identification with the Church is dedication to its service in the priesthood or religious life. That there were no priestly or religious candidates among the Letoyants until the twentieth century can be attributed, in part, to the segregation that prevailed in religious orders in the South. The Letoyants, who had drawn a fine line of distinction between themselves and Negroes, were not eager to join a Negro religious order. Since the Letoyants exodus from the South, there has been a threefold increase in religious vocations, primarily to congregations outside the South.

If Letoyants have not evidenced religiosity by entering religious life in large numbers, they have been respectful of and devoted to

[6] Joseph H. Fichter, *Social Relations in the Urban Parish* (Chicago: University of Chicago Press, 1954), 91.

*Table 9*

RELIGIOUS OBSERVANCE OF LIVING CREOLES BY SEX AND COMMUNITY TYPE, 1964

| | Religious Observance | | | | | | | |
| | Regular | | Irregular | | Non Attendance | | Totals | |
| | | Per- | | Per- | | Per- | | Per- |
| Community Type | No. | cent | No. | cent | No. | cent | No. | cent |
|---|---|---|---|---|---|---|---|---|
| Rural Louisiana | | | | | | | | |
| Males | 412 | 79.7 | 42 | 8.1 | 63 | 12.2 | 517 | 100 |
| Females | 462 | 83.1 | 36 | 6.5 | 58 | 10.4 | 556 | 100 |
| Urban Louisiana | | | | | | | | |
| Males | 253 | 89.4 | 20 | 7.1 | 10 | 3.5 | 283 | 100 |
| Females | 268 | 92.7 | 15 | 5.2 | 6 | 2.1 | 289 | 100 |
| Urban Elsewhere | | | | | | | | |
| Males | 153 | 94.4 | 8 | 5.0 | 1 | .6 | 162 | 100 |
| Females | 132 | 94.3 | 5 | 3.6 | 3 | 2.1 | 140 | 100 |
| Totals | | | | | | | | |
| Males | 818 | 85.0 | 70 | 7.3 | 74 | 7.7 | 962 | 100 |
| Females | 862 | 87.5 | 56 | 5.7 | 67 | 6.8 | 985 | 100 |
| Grand Total | 1680 | 86.3 | 126 | 6.5 | 141 | 7.2 | 1947 | 100 |

religious persons. Being a Sister undoubtedly gave this investigator advantages she would not otherwise have had. In making home visits, she was often greeted by, "Come in, Sister, and bring God's blessings to our home." When the Letoyants leave the South, they continue to exhibit devotion to religious persons. An emigrant from Riverville to Northern City is proud of his acknowledged role as guardian and benefactor of his fellow factory workers, the Sisters of Jesus and Mary—religious who live and labor among workingmen.

MARITAL NORMS

Another measure of adherence to Church norms is the observance of the Church marriage ceremony. As previously noted, 94 percent of the marriages of the living, direct descent population in the South are recognized by the Church as valid.[7] More than

[7] See Chap. 5, p. 82.

7 percent of the revalidated civil marital unions are with persons who are not direct descendants; and less than half of one percent occurs within the ethnic population. Among the latter are instances where a couple decided not to wait for a dispensation from a Church impediment; where there was parental objection; or where couples did not wish to follow the advice of the priest or their parents about delaying marriage.

Since their Church stresses the permanence of the marriage bond, separation and especially divorce are not normally viewed by Letoyants as solutions to marital problems. If separation or divorce occurs, the Catholic is not free to remarry in the Church unless the previous union has been invalidated by the Church. Divorce is rare among Letoyant Creoles. Fewer than one in every one hundred is divorced, regardless of place of residence. Where divorce does occur, it is likely to be in an urban place outside of Louisiana, for only one-third of the divorces take place in that state. With a high incidence of in-group unions to fellow Catholic Letoyants, about five-sixths of the divorces occur among couples who are both Catholic and direct descent Letoyant Creoles.

The degrees of deviancy from Church norms regarding marriage can be gauged by the number of living direct descent individuals who are excommunicated because they have contracted a second marriage following divorce. Of all living, direct descent Letoyants, regardless of place of residence, only 0.5 percent have contracted a second marriage after divorce and only 1.4 percent have had another union after separation, making a total of 1.9 percent.

Creoles who are divorced and remarried "outside the Church" tend to rear their children as Catholics and to send them to Catholic schools. Of a divorcée's son, an acquaintance remarked, "She brings that kid of hers up strict in Mass." Of another couple the comment was made that "they keep hoping something will happen so they can straighten out their marriage." An elderly woman who returned to the sacraments when her marriage was rectified said: "I was the most happiest person in the world. I was awake almost all the night before, just like I was making my first communion."

HOODOO AND OTHER SUPERSTITIONS

Adherence to any type of superstitious cult or magical practice has been forbidden by the Church and is, therefore, some index of deviancy from Church norms. The Creoles refer to most magical beliefs as *hoodoo*, a colloquial version of *voodoo*. In Southern City, known as "the hoodoo capital of the world," there was often an amalgam of Catholicism and magic. No doubt the Letoyants became acquainted with many of these magical beliefs through their contacts in Southern City or in areas to which the beliefs spread from there.

While there is now no local hoodoo doctor in Riverville, the people have contact with hoodoo men and women in Southern City and elsewhere. One elderly Letoyant woman sees herself as having supernatural powers; however, she would never countenance being called a hoodoo lady. She attributed the acquisition of these powers to her grandmother who was a semiofficial "intercessor" for group members—especially during the days when there was no resident priest. When her grandmother was in her last illness, she expressed the desire of having her daughter perform this role, but the daughter, who had a large family and many responsibilities, was reluctant to do so. Then the dying woman called her grandchild to her bedside, took the child's hand, and gave her "the power of intercession." According to the recipient, the role is an exacting one. The hoodoo person needs freedom from distractions, especially when making novenas, as well as association only with people who lead a "good life."

A common use of hoodoo is to cast a spell of bewitchment on some enemy. One hoodoo woman supposedly alienated the affections of a husband from his wife. Their daughter related the episode in the following words: "I really know that this woman had my father so he didn't care nothing about us. It was just plumb ridiculous! And then, he got so he was helpless. And some old man—I don't know what they call him—well, he was a hoodoo man, too. And he told my father that if he'd come to him, and do as he said, he'd get that off of him. And sure enough, my father started going to this man."

There are ways of casting and of breaking spells. Among the former is the procurement of some property of the person to be bewitched; entering a dwelling and uttering magical words is among the latter. An attempt to break a spell was described as follows: "This hoodoo lady came over here with a man from Texas. I was out in the yard a raking, and he say, 'This is where Joe stay?'

"And I say, 'Yes.'

"And he say, 'I was sent here to ask you a question—to ask you —could I go into your house? They's something put on you, and that's why you working so hard. Just work and work—don't never stop. As long as you can go, go. Never do any stopping. They's something put on you. And if you let me in your house, I can get it off of you. But if you don't want me in your house, I can't go in.'

"So I say, 'Joe ain't here'—and he wouldn't want him to come in like this.

"So he told me he could come back again.

"And so when Joe came, I told Joe about what the man said. And he told me I'd better not let this man come in this house. Didn't want him in!"

The persistence of a malady may be attributed to failure to have recourse to magic. A pyromaniac who had to be institutionalized allegedly became "sick" because someone put a dead cat under her front door steps. The ill woman went to the hoodoo man once, but her husband lacked confidence in hoodoo, and she never completed the treatment. Some relatives thought that the woman could have been cured if she had been allowed to continue treatments. One of them declared that she saw a man with a shovel dig up a dead cat from the front porch after the sick woman was institutionalized.

The Letoyants are reluctant to discuss their superstitions with anyone identified with the Church because they are painfully aware that they are liable to censure. In speaking of the pyromaniac, the informant commented that "Catholics are not supposed to do this or to believe in hoodoo, but you take these things as you see them." Some Letoyants are quite outspoken in their condemnation of those who have recourse to hoodooism, and they, too, recite illustrations of the high price superstitious people pay, as in the case of the man who procrastinated about visiting a medical doctor when he had trouble with his legs and eventually had to have both of them amputated. One woman voiced her indignation against believers in magic: "That's where people gets all them ideas about their neighbors doing them wrong. If you lose money or want to bet on the races, or feel sick, you can see the hoodoo man. They don't tell the truth; they just accuses your neighbor."

In general, patronage of hoodoo does not contribute to status among Creoles; it is predominantly a lower social class phenomenon. If, however, one believes that trouble ensues from superhuman causes, recourse to the superhuman is thought to be the most logical remedy—be it recourse to the hoodoo man or to the intercession of the saints.

## OTHER ROLES OF THE CHURCH IN THE LETOYANT CREOLE COMMUNITY

Although the Church's role is primarily a religious one, that role is interrelated with many other roles. Religion, an integral part of Letoyant Creole ethnic identity, permeates many aspects of their lives. This is especially the case in the rural environment of Riverville.

### EDUCATIONAL

A parish school was opened in Riverville immediately after the establishment of the parish, and French Sisters were brought to the community to teach. The more affluent Letoyant Creoles sent their daughters to board at the convent "to draw better advantage of the lessons." After seventeen years, however, hardships following the Civil War forced the school to close. It was not reopened for fifteen years, and in the interim many fourth-generation Creoles who were not tutored privately grew up illiterate. In three communities not far from Riverville the Creoles were largely instrumental in the establishment of Catholic schools, even though all of these schools have since been closed, as has the school in Riverville.[8] Moreover, they were staunch supporters of these schools.

One of the functions of the school, before and after the Civil War, was to impart religious instruction. When asked about their educational attainment, many of the older persons in Riverville comment: "None too long . . . just long enough to make the First Communion." Speaking of the role of the school, one educated man, who was reared in Riverville, made the following comment: "And no matter how poor they were, this is one thing that I think all of them share in common that they do want to try to live decently. Not extravagantly but decently. I think this probably can be attributed to a religious background. One of the big things—the school, the training—that if they went to the third grade, they got this one thing out of school."

SOCIAL AND CIVIC

Church property in the rural community is the hub of many social and civic activities because it is centrally located and is sufficiently large for community-wide events: religious, charitable, educational, civic, economic, and recreational. Some of these activities are church-sponsored and extend to the entire congregation, for example, a periodic call to clean the church or the cemetery. Others are little more than announcements or perfunctory collections for various causes: collections for a cancer drive and notices pertaining to agriculture.

[8] Until 1967 the Riverville school was the focal point of parish activities. The PTA was one of the most active organizations in the community. In 1966, with the opening of a new integrated Catholic school in the parish (county) seat, less than twenty miles away, the upper elementary grades were discontinued in Riverville, and one year later the school was closed. Since 1967, resident Sisters have provided for the religious education of Letoyants attending the public school.

Most rural community-wide activities are sponsored by church organizations. May Day festivities, for example, were formerly planned and sponsored by the school but the entire church parish usually participated in the procession, the crowning of the Blessed Virgin, and the religious service that concluded the celebration. All organizations also participate in the annual church fair that is the chief fund-raising activity of the year; all parishioners are expected to take part in this fair, whether or not they are members of organizations.

*Table 10*

CREOLE ADULT MEMBERSHIP IN CHURCH
ORGANIZATIONS IN RIVERVILLE BY HOUSEHOLDS, 1964

| Households | Number | Percent |
|---|---|---|
| Total | 138 | 100.0 |
| With no membership | 66 | 47.8 |
| With membership | | |
| Husband-wife | 37 | 26.8 |
| Husband only | 2 | 1.5 |
| Wife only | 22 | 15.9 |
| Widows | 11 | 8.0 |

Moreover, the Church affords the Letoyant Creoles an opportunity to become "joiners," like other Americans. In a familiar, comfortable atmosphere they participate in meetings and learn how to conduct them. Slightly more than half of the adults in Riverville are members of church organizations. The three organizations for adults are the Holy Name Society for men, the Christian Mothers for women, and the Knights (and Ladies) of St. Peter Claver for men and their wives. In more than a quarter of the households, both husbands and wives have membership. In about 16 percent of the households only women (nearly 8 percent are widows) are members; in only two instances do men belong to organizations where their wives do not (Table 10).

In 1954 the Riverville Holy Name Society had a hundred men enrolled; in 1964 less than a third of that number claimed membership. Older men gradually withdrew, and leadership was assumed by a few. One man voiced disapproval of these leaders because they allegedly came to meetings with plans already formulated and decisions already reached. Another man maintained that the Society was practically defunct; activities consisted chiefly in carrying banners in church processions and having Masses said for deceased members.

The most active church organization in Riverville is the women's society known as the Christian Mothers, which has twice the membership of the men's society. The official purpose of this organization is "the Christian home education of the children by truly Christian Mothers"; however, Riverville women describe their purpose as "fixing up the church" or "raising money for things we need at church." Membership is a mark of prestige in that it gives the members recognition as practicing and socially involved Catholics.

The Knights and Ladies of St. Peter Claver (the nonwhite counterpart of the Knights of Columbus) aims "to assist the Hierarchy and Clergy in the Apostolic work to which they have dedicated their lives." Of Riverville's thirty members in 1964, nine were women (Table 11). In Riverville, membership is confined largely to those of the upper classes who can afford to pay dues or who are regarded as social climbers. Meetings are held three or four times a year. The feast of St. Peter Claver, September 9, is the occasion for a special celebration, usually a field Mass in the school yard with a Negro priest officiating.

## Threats to Religious Identity Today

### OUT-GROUP MARRIAGE

A potential threat to Letoyant Creole ethnic identity is out-group marriage. Insistence upon in-group marriage suggests that they are well aware of this threat. Because religion is an essential element in Creole identity, marriage to a non-Catholic constitutes an out-group marriage just as much as does marriage to a Negro or a white.

## Table 11

TYPES OF ADULT MEMBERSHIP * IN CHURCH ORGANIZATIONS IN RIVERVILLE BY SEX AND RESIDENTIAL AREA, 1964

| Organization | Membership by Area of Residence † | | | | | | | | Totals |
|---|---|---|---|---|---|---|---|---|---|
| | N. Right Bank | | N. Left Bank | | S. Right Bank | | S. Left Bank | | |
| | M | F | M | F | M | F | M | F | |
| Holy Name | 18 | — | 5 | — | 3 | — | 4 | — | 30 |
| Christian Mothers | — | 32 | — | 13 | — | 7 | — | 10 | 62 |
| Knights | 8 | 5 | 7 | 2 | 2 | 0 | 4 | 2 | 30 |
| Total | 26 | 37 | 12 | 15 | 5 | 7 | 8 | 12 | 122 |
| Percent | 21.3 | 30.3 | 9.8 | 12.3 | 4.1 | 5.8 | 6.6 | 9.8 | 100.0 |
| No. with no membership | 17 | 8 | 8 | 9 | 6 | 5 | 32 | 19 | 104 |
| Percent | 16.3 | 7.7 | 7.7 | 8.7 | 5.8 | 4.8 | 30.7 | 18.3 | 100.0 |

* Some persons have membership in more than one organization.
† Parishioners beyond the boundaries of New River are not included.

Of the 275 persons who married into the population before 1865, about 95 percent were Catholic. Due to wide geographic dispersion, information was not available on 44.2 percent who married in after 1865. Of the remainder, 43.2 percent were Catholics, and another 3 percent became converts, making a total of 46.2 percent known to be Catholics. Baptists ranked second in religious affiliation, both before and after the Civil War, but they constituted only 4.4 percent after the war and less than 1 percent before it (Table 12). In the South, of the 2,393 living Letoyant Creoles who are married, only 17.9 percent have married outsiders.

The nondirect descent who are not Catholics are more likely to be accepted in an urban environment than in a rural one. A young woman from a Louisiana city observed: "We accept these people as long as the man or woman who isn't Catholic goes to church, as long as the children are Catholic, as long as the children are going to the church, going to a Catholic school, and the man goes to a church—who just doesn't seem a very Baptist Baptist and a very Methodist Methodist. If he goes to the Church with his wife, and comes to family things, it's all right."

Conversely, if the nondirect descent who contract civil marriages do not have a marriage rectified or conform to group mores, they are not likely to be accepted by group members. Traditionally, Letoyant Creoles who married outsiders were not "received," and a relative who was a "fallen away" could not be taken around by his family to visit friends and neighbors. Today censure is not so obvious, but there is strong likelihood that these persons will be reminded of their deviancy through slight, if not ostracism.

NEGRO CONVERTS

In Riverville, intergroup relations are quite sensitive between the Creoles and the so-called "dark" residents who live on several of the big plantations there. The Creoles are deeply religious and belong to a missionary church that places strong emphasis upon spreading the faith, and yet the nonbelievers who live in their midst and are the most likely subjects of conversion are not en-

## Table 12

## RELIGION OF NONDIRECT DESCENT BY SEX, BEFORE AND AFTER 1865

| Religious Affiliation | Before 1865 * | | | | After 1865 | | | |
|---|---|---|---|---|---|---|---|---|
| | Male | Female | Total | Percent | Male | Female | Total | Percent |
| Catholic | | | | | | | | |
| Christened at birth | 130 | 131 | 261 | 94.9 | 222 | 197 | 419 | 43.2 |
| Convert | 0 | 1 | 1 | .4 | 20 | 9 | 29 | 3.0 |
| Baptist | 1 | 1 | 2 | .7 | 26 | 17 | 43 | 4.4 |
| Other | 1 | 2 | 3 | 1.1 | 36 | 15 | 51 | 5.2 |
| No Data | 3 | 5 | 8 | 2.9 | 277 | 152 | 429 | 44.2 |
| Totals | 135 | 140 | 275 | 100.0 | 581 | 390 | 971 | 100.0 |

* Includes the population that associated with the Letoyants as free people of color prior to 1865 and intermarried with them after 1865.

couraged to become members of the church in that locality. One Negro woman who decided to visit the church on Christmas Eve recounted her experience: "When we walked in the door everyone turned around and looked at us. The cold, hard look we got told us plainly that we weren't wanted and this was my last time going into *that* church."

Another Negro informant noted, "I can't understand those Catholics. They'll ask you for money and when you ask them to help you, they'll say it is against their religion. My husband bought a raffle ticket on a calf and the person that sold him the ticket said that if he didn't win the calf the money that he denoted would be put to good use by the priests—but it would be a sin to contribute to something *our* church is putting on!"

Several years ago a letter from the bishop asking Catholics to participate in a "campaign for souls" met with mixed reactions. The only "souls" in Riverville who were not Catholics were those of the Negro people. According to one opponent of the campaign, bringing those folks into the church might result in its being labeled a "Negro" church. Some Catholic Creoles in Riverville did invite dark-skinned neighbors to come to church with them and encouraged them to take instruction, but these Creoles were not, for the most part, of direct descent.

A similar episode occurred when a mission was scheduled and the priest asked that posters be placed throughout the Riverville area inviting everyone to attend. This caused consternation among the direct descent Creole population. One of them stated: "We have a mission and Father ask him to put some posters to let the people know, and he put in the posters the date—the whole week it was going to be, and who was preaching and everyone was supposed to come to the mission to be welcomed. Everybody was welcome to come, and he also went around . . . to tell the people that had black people in the plantations to tell to be sure and encourage all those people to come to the mission . . . even in the houses I guess he must have gone." Then he recited a litany of Creole names, noting who had brought whom and what a mixture there was in church. "There were white people sitting in the front.

Father must have told them they could go to the front. Everywhere, they mix with the others." None of this admixture, of course, was approved. The white folk had no business in the front pews, when they relegate the nonwhites to the last pews in "their" churches, and the Negro people interspersed with everyone only added to the confusion.

In short, Negro conversions to Catholicism, especially in the rural environment, complicate the already involved process of identification. In this instance, religious norms come into conflict with racial norms, and the latter usually take precedence.

The Riverville church, then, is the place where the religion of the Letoyant Creoles was implanted, where their forebears were christened, married, and buried. That church is regarded as "our church," and Letoyants who have established residence elsewhere come back to it periodically and visit the cemetery where their ancestors rest. Grand Pere's attention to the church in his portrait is symbolic of the emphasis placed by his descendants on the religious element in their identity. The regularity of their religious observance and the tendency to marry fellow Creole Catholics attest to the strength of this aspect of their cultural heritage.

*Chapter 7*

---

# Riverville's Role in Letoyant Creole Ethnic Identity

Riverville, as the name implies, is a rural settlement along the banks of a river in an area characterized by a network of waterways. The community is located along a twelve-mile stretch of New River, so called because the stream flows through the bed of a once-navigable tributary of the Mississippi. Other rivers on either side of New River flow almost parallel to it. West River to the west of Riverville flows into the Mississippi River; and the whole area is honeycombed with bayous.

The river basin is almost surrounded by low hills. The hills to the northeast are beyond the Mississippi tributary, more than ten miles distant from Riverville; on the west the hills are less than five miles away. The hilly land, unsuitable for farming, is settled by "po' whites," a familiar and casual term among Rivervillers. Part of the hill country is a forest preserve thickly covered by pine trees, native shrubs, and undergrowth. In the hills, water is at a premium (Fig. 3).

Identification with the community of Riverville ranks with descent from the Letoyant family and with Catholicity as a strong index of Creole ethnic identity. Riverville is the place where the Letoyant family took roots, laid their ancestors to rest, and preserved evidence of the glory of the past. Here they enjoyed a geographical and social isolation that allowed them freedom to associate among themselves or among other people like themselves. In such circumstances, they established their own social institutions and their children were reared with a feeling of belonging and of security.

*Figure 3*

*Riverville & Vicinity*

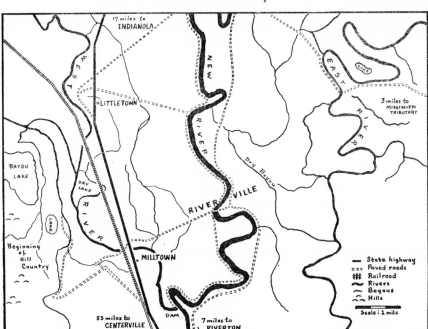

## THE HOMELAND

The Letoyants succeeded in acquiring most of the land that now constitutes the community, either through business transactions or through intermarriage. Homes were built along the riverbank, a circumstance which fostered neighborliness and social activity. This settlement pattern, the so-called "French line village," required less road-building than the traditional American gridiron arrangement that prevailed in the plains area. Every family was assured of having water, rich sandy soil, and woodland, as well as access to the main route of transportation.

In the course of time, as progeny increased, the large land-holdings were divided into narrow strips, all having frontage on

New River. With each succeeding generation the practice of giving heirs a strip of land extending from the riverbank into woodland was continued. Girls and boys received comparatively equal shares in the inheritance.

To contemporary Letoyants, however modified the bloodline or whatever the current address, Riverville is the homeland, the land of their forefathers. Here it was that the people known as "our people" originated. Here it was that Grand Pere established a church and eventually a school, both of which have been considered "ours" by the Letoyant Creoles. Behind the church is a cemetery where ancestors are buried—mute testimony that the church has placed her seal upon their marriage and that the Letoyant Creoles date back to the time of French colonization and have a claim to be called Creoles. In a special way the people belong to Riverville, and the land belongs to them.

Here they have their own community institutions. Here they operate large plantations, cotton gins, and small stores. Here they have tenant farmers working for them just as their forebears, who were planters, had slaves or hired hands. Here they exercise the franchise and have a voice in civil affairs. Here their children can grow up with little confusion as to their identity because they can associate primarily with their own people.

The relevance of the community of Riverville to the Letoyant Creoles is indicated by the frequency with which those who have moved away return to visit. When they come back, they visit relatives if there are any close enough to host them, and they invariably visit the cemetery where they pray for their deceased ancestors and study the history of their people recorded on the tombstones.

A Letoyant woman who was forced to move to a Louisiana community approximately ninety miles from Riverville made the following comment when she visited one of her children: "We had to leave. Times was so tight. What was the use of staying here when my husband could work? So we left. But you see, my husband isn't able to haul wood. And that's two things you have to have here—wood and water." She did not dislike her present home, she said, but when she returned to Riverville, she felt "like a bird out of a cage." Asked to elucidate, she responded, "Oh, I am out. I can sit on my back steps and see what's going on. Sit on my front steps. But up there I don't meddle. I latch my front door and sit—just like a bird in a cage."

When young adults leave the community, they still tend to think of it as the homeland. Even if they marry outsiders, they bring their spouses and children back to visit relatives and friends; they attend services again in their own church; they visit the cemetery; and in various other ways they strengthen their ties with Riverville. So important is the community to the Letoyant Creoles that children who have moved away sometimes offer to send support money to their parents to keep them there on the homestead. Since Riverville is the place to which migrants wish to return on vacations, it is desirable to have relatives or friends to offer hospitality.

The Letoyants consider it in "the bad taste" to declare openly a preference for living elsewhere. One informant stated that of all the people he knows who have left Riverville "not one has said that he prefers to live elsewhere—if he could make a living for his family here."

## IMPORTANCE OF LAND

Riverville has remained a nonwhite community with fewer than ten white household heads, including those at the church and the convent. White residents are usually large landholders, some of whom allegedly obtained their holdings through questionable means following the Civil War, or they are smaller landholders who purchased property for a home along the riverbanks—usually a summer home. Riverville also had, in 1964, ninety-four Negro households. Most of these Negroes are descendants of the slaves who lived there prior to the Civil War, and almost all of them reside on one of the two large white plantations near the heart of the community.

Although Negro and white households constitute 43 percent of the total households in the area defined as Riverville, the community is predominantly Letoyant in many respects. Only two white planters live near the center of the community, and both have strong ties with Indianola; in fact, in only one instance does the planter live in his Riverville home. Other white planters are on the periphery of the community. The northern boundaries of the community extend farther on one side of the river than on the other since the inhabitants on one side of the river are predominantly Letoyant while on the other side they are not, and they do not identify with the community. The Negroes belong to Riverville, but their belongingness is different; their ancestors had no choice in the matter, were relegated to an inferior status, and denied access to Letoyant social life. Moreover, the Negro people were not able to acquire property in Riverville.

Strong feelings are attached to the sale of property to outsiders. When land is sold, norms prescribe that relatives or other Letoyant Creoles have preference as buyers. White landowners occasionally acquire holdings adjacent to their plantations if they offer a high price or if they have a mortgage or similar type of option. But Negroes have never been in a position to secure a foothold along the riverbanks by foreclosing on mortgages.

The importance of the land is emphasized repeatedly by the Creoles. One tenant farmer made the following comment: "We love it here, but the only way to own the roof over your head is move somewhere else. The person who does not own land is never going to get very far in Riverville, no matter how hard he works."

MEANS OF LIVELIHOOD

Riverville is strictly a farm community. With few exceptions everyone is engaged in cultivating the land for himself or for someone else. Many of the farms are small in acreage—eighteen of the sixty-one landholders have less than twenty acres of land each—an amount insufficient to make a "fair living." Much of Riverville's land today is held as it was originally in small estates operated by day hands, i.e., laborers who work by the hour on someone else's property, instead of slaves. Only seven Creole families own large enough tracts of land to be considered plantation owners; each of these plantations is at least three hundred acres. A planter is often spoken of as a landlord since he has on his property the homes of many of his field workers.

Renters generally share the crops with the landowners. Since many renters who have their own equipment agree to give the landowner one-fourth of their crops, they are called "tenants on the fourth." Other renters may agree to pay a fixed amount of cash instead of part of a crop. In the latter instance, a tenant is said to pay "standing rent." Under such conditions he takes risks and needs to have sufficient cash reserves to tide him over the poor crop years. As a rule, landlords rent "on the fourth" those strips of land that are not contiguous to the plantation proper. Most of these strips were purchased from heirs who no longer live in Riverville.

Cotton is now the major cash crop, but it became important after the nineteenth century. The government limits cotton acreage, and, once the cotton is planted, farm representatives check the measurements. A penalty is attached to violations. Indigo, once in great demand for making dyes, was formerly one of the principal cash crops. After experiencing several crop failures because of caterpillars, the people of Riverville ceased to plant it. Other early crops were perique tobacco—a strong variety which was discontinued because of a limited market—and sugar cane, which was planted until early in the present century.

Apart from the major cash crops there are several other sources of income. The pecan tree is native to Riverville, and nearly every farm has several in the woods which extend beyond the stiff land—the untilled land several acres from the river that was not enriched by alluvial deposits from the river. Cattle raising has become important as a source of revenue in the last three decades. The stiff land which every Riverville farm has is used for pasture. At one time the plantation owners butchered their cows and hogs and sold the meat to the plantation stores, but the law now requires that the cattle be inspected and the meat stamped. Housewives often keep the money they make from selling eggs or poultry, both of which are intended primarily for home consumption. Occasionally a housewife realizes small cash sums from the sale of vegetables. Since red pepper is a popular seasoning in that area, some housewives plant more pepper than they need for their own use. When ripe, the peppers are dried and ground into fine powder for sale. Fillet, made from the dried leaves of the sassafras tree, is another source of income. Like the pepper, the leaves are dried and ground and usually packaged in pint size whiskey bottles which sell for fifty cents.

STATUS SYMBOLS

Land ownership is considered important as a status symbol by the Letoyants. Location of land in Riverville is also a factor in status. Land on the periphery of the community is generally not as important as land in the heart of the community near the cross-roads, close to the church property where most of the social activities in the community take place.

Riverville is divided roughly into four sections. A branch road from the main highway leads to the center of the community where the church, the school building, a cotton gin, and a plantation store are located. At this point there is a bridge over the river. It was here that Grand Pere and Louis established their plantations. North of the bridge is called "up the river"; to the left of the bridge, facing north, is the "upper west bank"; to the right the "upper east bank"; south of the bridge are a "lower west bank" and a "lower east bank." The system of waterways furnishes a convenient means of identifying place of residence, and the inhabitants of the vicinity popularly use it when referring to their neighbors. Thus, in addition to identification by name, a family is said to live on East River, on West River, "up the river," or "down the river" (along New River), or on a particular bayou.

The upper west bank contains the highest proportion of Creole households. Near the center of the community the landholdings are relatively small and houses are quite close to one another. Near the northern part of the bank are stretches of farmland, about six in number, that were acquired as homesteads under federal land grants in the 1930's. Slightly south of these homesteads are plantations. In the central area of the upper west bank, then, are to be found plantations, but to the north and to the south of these plantations are relatively small landholdings (Fig. 4).

The majority of the inhabitants on the northern west bank are Creole landowners who pride themselves on their old Letoyant family status and who consider themselves high ranking because of it. The upper east bank is second in rank by status. It, too, has a relatively large number of Creoles. North of Whitefield plantation are relatively small landholdings with a sizable number of homesteads. The center and northern sections of the upper east bank, however, are owned almost wholly by planters, and settlement is not only sparser than on the west bank, but the upper east bank has, on Whitefield plantation, a higher proportion of Negro residents who are day hands.

Third in importance by rank is the lower west bank. One large plantation extends through the dividing line of the north and south banks as well into the lower west bank. There are fewer Creole landholders in this area, and these Creoles do not enjoy the same status as those on the upper banks.

The lower east bank ranks lowest in status. With a few exceptions this bank is largely plantation property owned by two white planters, one of whom has predominantly Negro residents. Many of the residents on the lower east bank are in-migrants from Riverton. The relatively small number of landholders contributes to the low status of this area.

## A DECADE OF CHANGE
### 1954–1964

In the decade between 1954 and 1964 Riverville became less and less isolated. Nearly every home had acquired a television set by 1964. In 1954 only 23 percent of the households had telephones; by 1964 nearly two-thirds of them had telephones. Car rides to town could be arranged so readily that it was no longer necessary for plantation stores to stock many of the items that they had traditionally sold to the people.

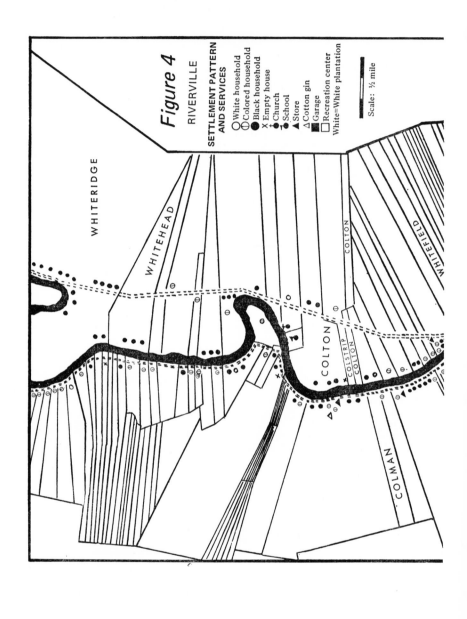

*Figure 4*

RIVERVILLE

**SETTLEMENT PATTERN AND SERVICES**

○ White household
⊖ Colored household
● Black household
✕ Empty house
† Church
🕈 School
▲ Store
△ Cotton gin
■ Garage
□ Recreation center
White=White plantation

Scale: ½ mile

WHITERIDGE

WHITEHEAD

COLTON

COLSTRIP COLTON

COLTON

WHITEFIELD

COLMAN

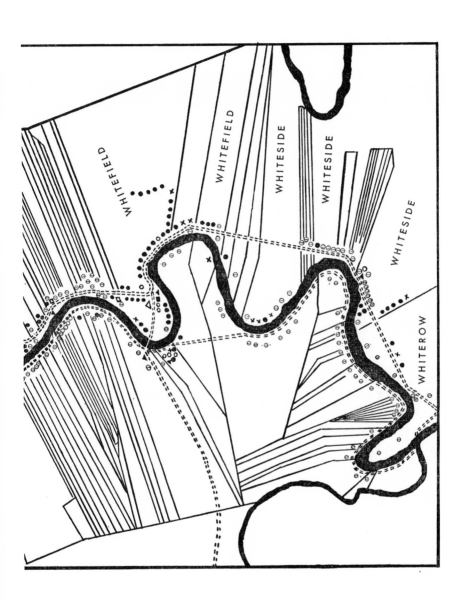

WHITEFIELD

WHITEFIELD

WHITESIDE

WHITESIDE

WHITESIDE

WHITESIDE

WHITEROW

Between 1954 and 1964 Riverville lost a total of 28 households, 14 Negro and 14 Creole. In 1954 Riverville had 152 Creole households, constituting 56.3 percent of the total; 108 Negro households, constituting 40 percent of the total; and 10 white households, constituting 3.7 percent of the total. Although the number of white households remained the same, their percentage increased within the decade from 3.7 to 4.1 percent because of the overall decrease in the number of households, and the percentage of Negro households decreased to 38.9 percent of the total, while the percentage of Creole households increased slightly to 57 percent (Table 13).

A significant change occurred during this ten-year interval. The number of women in the childbearing years decreased, a circumstance that could threaten the survival of the community. In 1954, 22.4 percent of Riverville's Creole families had wives under thirty years of age. By 1964 this percentage had dropped to 9.9 percent. Families in which the wife was over thirty and still in the childbearing years constituted 38.5 percent of the families in 1954, but only 26.7 percent in 1964. Completed families where the wife was over forty-five years of age were 39.1 percent of the total 1954 and 63.4 percent in 1964.

Another trend was the increasing number of widowed older people. In 1954, 8.83 percent of the adult population was widowed; in 1964, 13.31 percent. Older Creoles or widows often rent their farmland to relatives or friends since they are no longer able to do the farm work themselves. As a consequence, there has been an increase in the acreage farmed by those engaged in agriculture, particularly small farmers who have elderly relatives. Of the population married and living with spouse, the percentage was 84.81 in 1954; by 1964 it had fallen by almost 5 percent to 79.83 percent. The number of individuals who were either single or separated was approximately the same at both times (Table 14).

Within the decade sharecroppers completely disappeared. In 1954 about 12.5 percent of the farmers were sharecroppers, but between 1954 and 1957 farmers had so many bad crop years that they either moved from the farm or become day hands. In 1954

## Table 13

### RIVERVILLE'S POPULATION CHANGE BY ETHNICITY AND RESIDENTIAL AREA, 1954 AND 1964 *

#### Ethnicity of Households

| Area | Negro | | | Creole | | | White | | | Totals | | |
|---|---|---|---|---|---|---|---|---|---|---|---|---|
| | 1954 | 1964 | Change | 1954 | 1964 | Change | 1954 | 1964 | Change | 1954 | 1964 | Change |
| Upper West Bank | 21 | 20 | −1 | 43 | 43 | 0 | 1 | 2 | +1 | 65 | 65 | 0 |
| Upper East Bank | 50 | 43 | −7 | 33 | 35 | +2 | 4 | 4 | 0 | 87 | 82 | −5 |
| Lower West Bank | 0 | 1 | +1 | 36 | 30 | −6 | 2 | 2 | 0 | 38 | 33 | −5 |
| Lower East Bank | 37 | 30 | −7 | 40 | 30 | −10 | 3 | 2 | −1 | 80 | 62 | −18 |
| Totals | 108 | 94 | −14 | 152 | 138 | −14 | 10 | 10 | 0 | 270 | 242 | −28 |
| Percent of Total | 40.0 | 38.9 | | 56.3 | 57.0 | | 3.7 | 4.1 | | 100. | 100. | |
| Percent change over decade | | | −13.0 | | | −9.2 | | | 0 | | | −10.4 |

* A crossroads to the west, approximately two miles south of the northern bridge, constitutes the boundary on the upper west bank. The upper east bank has very few Creoles.

*Table 14*

CREOLE ADULTS IN RIVERVILLE BY MARITAL STATUS, 1954 AND 1964

| | 1954 | | 1964 | |
|---|---|---|---|---|
| Marital Status | Number | Percent | Number | Percent |
| Single | 7 | 2.47 | 7 | 3.00 |
| Separated | 11 | 3.89 | 9 | 3.86 |
| Widowed | 25 | 8.83 | 31 | 13.31 |
| Married, living with spouse | 240 | 84.81 | 186 | 79.83 |

about 12 percent of the Creoles were day hands; in 1964 the percentage was slightly less. Wages of day hands varied from three to five dollars a day. Renters declined from approximately 14 percent of the total households in 1954 to about 8 percent in 1964. Less than 2 percent of the households having nonproperty owners had family heads who were not renting, sharecropping, or working as day hands in 1954. By 1964 nearly 30 percent of the households had other arrangements: paying rent or subsisting on welfare or on old age assistance.

Even though the living family members are scattered and the home community now has less than 20 percent of the population, Riverville remains a sort of Mecca to which the Creoles return. Here in comparative isolation they interact freely with one another, and their children learn their identity through association with other members of the group. Although their school has been closed, the church retains its identification as their own social institution and the community is still known as their homeland.

# Chapter 8

# Self-Image of a Southern People: Norms, Roles, and Controls

In the semi-isolation of Riverville there was an exclusiveness and a positive attitude toward Letoyant Creole group identity that was not altered appreciably even by the reverses of the post-Civil War years. As the Creoles moved to other places in the South, however, there was a strong possibility that they might develop attitudes of self-deprecation, especially when stereotyped as Negroes, and negativism as a way out of anxiety-arousing situations.[1] The incidence of suicide among Riverville Creoles affords some clue to their self-image. Suicide is an index of alienation and a lack of solidarity, both within a group as well as among individuals in it.[2] Of the 653 known causes of death recorded in the necrology in Riverville, 1908–1964,[3] only 7 were suicides; a percentage of 1.1 percent. This percentage is very low, the same as that for the United States in 1963 alone, even if the people attempted dissimulation—something difficult to do in a small, close-knit community. As a people, the Creoles have a feeling of being honorable, proud, cohesive, and self-sufficient.

## CREOLE COHESIVENESS

### SOLIDARITY

Group cohesiveness stems primarily from the chief marks of their identification. Since they are all descendants from the same ancestors, blood ties are one of the strongest sources of solidarity.

---

[1] Cf. Ernest G. Schachtel, "On Alienated Concepts of Identity," *The American Journal of Psychoanalysis,* XXI (1961), 125.

[2] Emile Durkheim, *Suicide* (Reprint; Glencoe, Ill.: The Free Press, 1951).

[3] This is 26 percent of the 2,524 deceased Letoyants. Only entries in official registers were used for causes of death other than suicides and infant deaths. Testimony was also used in the latter instances.

Moreover, their identification with a common place of origin, Riverville, and with the same religion serves to bind them together. But as the Creoles dispersed over a wide area even in the South, solidarity has become difficult to maintain.

Solidarity is usually most evident among family members. Parent-child relationships are particularly strong. The child who leaves home in adolescence or young adulthood usually maintains close ties with his family, particularly his parents. On nearly all special occasions it is customary to give gifts. One woman who had fifteen brothers and sisters commented that she made a practice to give everyone "a little something" and that it took planning, particularly when she was short of money. Adolescent children who leave the South may express their love and concern for their parents and siblings by sending gifts shortly after receiving their first paychecks. A Riverville mother whose husband is a tenant farmer expressed great happiness over the gift of a refrigerator from her two sons who had moved to Northern City and found work there. She added that they had asked their parents to be on the lookout for any land up for sale because they intend to purchase it for their parents. Then when their father is unable to work for a living, he will be secure on his own property in the Creole home community.

When parents are aged or ill, children are expected to show a special interest in them. If the parents wish to continue living alone, every effort is made to see that they have adequate care. Sometimes the adolescent children of neighbors are paid to do chores for an old couple, or a grandchild is sent to live with them. At other times a son or daughter may return to the South and live with aged parents. On weekends children often travel long distances to be with their parents and take turns in commuting home. Occasionally a couple will retire to Riverville and take care of aged or ailing parents.

Solidarity is also evident among those who are not closely related, particularly in time of trouble. At a public recreation center at Riverville, proceeds from a particular event may be earmarked for assistance to a needy family. Thus, when a home was destroyed by fire, an announcement was made in church on Sunday that the proceeds of a dance the following weekend would be given to the family. Another benefit dance was given for a widow with a very sick son who was in the hospital about seventy miles from home. The boy's grandfather said, "If it takes everything I can rake and scrape, he's going to come back here." With the help of friends, enough money was cleared at the dance to enable the widow to bring her son closer to home. Regarding this family a neighbor said, "The mother is a good woman. She is quiet and well liked. If she'd be running around, no one would have any sympathy for her." This comment indicates that group solidarity is more in evidence for Letoyants who conform to group norms.

Letoyant Creoles are more likely than Negroes to show cohesiveness by concealing deviancy from outsiders. When both Riverville populations were asked if a person on welfare should be reported for misconduct by his neighbors, the Negroes were more inclined to agree than were the Creoles. About 27.6 percent of the Creoles stated that the Welfare Department should be informed, while about 47.6 percent of the Negroes were inclined to agree that misconduct should be reported, a differential of 20 percent.[4]

Solidarity is also evidenced by the extent of borrowing and relying upon fellow Creoles in one's absence. Borrowing, which implies reciprocity, is usually most prevalent among close neighbors. One woman bragged, "I'm the only somebody Marie borrows from." Neighbors, relatives, or close friends are usually relied upon to take care of fowl, livestock, and utilities when a family is away on vacation or on a short trip.

One form of social interaction that promotes solidarity is visiting. In the rural South, visitors may be welcomed at any time of day whether or not they are expected. In urban communities there is more likelihood that no one may be at home or that a call is

---

[4] For data on attitudes toward welfare services in Riverville, the author is indebted to William H. French and Louretha Williams, "Attitudes toward Public Assistance in a Nonwhite Rural Community" (M.A. thesis, Worden School of Social Service, Our Lady of the Lake College, San Antonio, Tex., 1963), 83, 86.

expected prior to a visit. If a rural Creole does not have many visitors, this may be an indication of social disapproval. One woman who complained that she had had very few visitors during her first year on the river was a divorcée who was necessarily married by the justice of the peace. She was, moreover, from another community even though she was a direct descent Letoyant. A Creole who moved to Northern City and married an outsider was shocked when one of her husband's relatives offered to pay her for baby-sitting with their children. Among relatives an exchange of services such as making minor repairs in the home is taken for granted.

The telephone, perhaps more than any other medium, has promoted interaction among the Creoles. In the rural community, where there are from six to eight people on the party line, "listening in" is an accepted practice, though no one relishes having others listen in on a conversation. One grandmother called her grandchild to listen in to a neighboring girl's conversation. Afterwards she cautioned the grandchild not to "take on" with boys like her neighbor. In the course of an interview, an informant answered her telephone and complained loudly that someone was listening in, preventing her hearing clearly. Yet a few minutes later when another party on her line had a call, she listened in to the conversation and proceeded to inform everyone what was said. The telephone has been an important link between Letoyants who are geographically scattered. For the elderly to whom writing is a chore, the telephone has become a popular means of communication with their children. Several families said that the chief reason they installed a telephone was to facilitate communication with friends and relatives in distant places.

Visits to Riverville from people who have moved away also promote solidarity. One woman said, "People come here more often because they can come on weekends. They come down here to take their children to parties because there is people they been knowing all their lives. I have sisters and brothers that live about ninety-five miles away. They comes regularly." The father of a large family cited another motive for hospitality to relatives, friends, and acquaintances from distant places. "The way we look at it, we all have large families, and we are raising our families primarily for the day when they will have to go off somewhere to get a job, having few industries here. And the reasons we seem to go out of our way to be nice to our relatives and the people who visit here is because you can't tell the day where those kids might wind up. I know how it is always with the people from home. If they're in a position where they can give a newcomer some kind of helping hand, they will."

One informant estimated that 90 to 95 percent of the people who ever lived in Riverville come back at one time or another to visit. Even if they have no relatives or friends, they wish to show the community to their children and to see the cemetery where their ancestors are buried. Riverville is a regular summer vacation place for many Letoyants. Another informant said, "In the city the children have to go to the park to have a picnic. Here, as soon as they get here, they can all take to the yard and go under the tree. If they go to town they're all stuck up there in the house where they don't have a lawn or yard."

Holidays are occasions for intense interaction, particularly religious festivals, which involve church-going. In many southern communities, the parish church gives a fair annually to raise funds for the support of the church. These fairs last all day attracting the sponsoring group and many who come to patronize it. The planning involved is long-range and sustained. The success of the fair is a matter of pride and satisfaction; it gives the Creoles an opportunity to be hosts to outsiders and to share with them their handiwork and, in particular, their characteristic good cooking.

Communication with the non-Creole world has increased, especially with the widespread ownership of television sets. Even in relatively isolated rural areas, the Creoles are now informed of national and local issues. Since the advent of television, the circulation of newspapers has declined in the rural area with the exception of the local weekly.

Despite the relatively high degree of solidarity that Letoyants exhibit, many of them express dissatisfaction with the degree of cohesiveness they now have. Geographic dispersal and increased communication and interaction with outsiders, in the opinion of some Letoyants, are to blame. Even in Riverville, there is some dissatisfaction. One affluent farmer commented that "everyone around here roots for himself too much. We all make our own investments in farm machinery, and we still have too many of our own stores." Then he added, referring to a cooperative venture, "If we could get together, we would be able to sell more to the people here."

SELF-RELIANCE AND MUTUAL AID

The Letoyants, like most Americans, have a tradition of self-sufficiency, but it has been coupled with mutual aid. In the early years of group formation, when Riverville was isolated, these characteristics were essential. Even at the present time, they continue to be guarded as the *sine qua non* of group survival. As in other ethnic groups, mutual aid within the group and freedom from debts and responsibility to outsiders promote group strength and interaction. One woman described the attitudes of her parents in the following words: "My mother sewed for people. All those people at that time (it was horse and buggy style, you know), they would go, and do their doing, and stay all day. People had plenty of everything, you know, and they just always live like that, together."

When the present adults in Riverville were children, there was less exchange of money for services than at present; reliance was placed upon cooperation among group members. Older people relate that in their childhood there was much sharing of work at peak seasons. One woman said: "We helped one another at cotton time. Sometimes we even picked cotton by moonlight. Paying for a day's work was not common. We helped one another at planting and picking." Even today, there is this type of mutual aid with no expectation of financial remuneration. But since farming has become highly mechanized, and machinery is costly, there is more financial exchange for the use of equipment than was feasible at an earlier time when more reliance was placed on human labor.

During peak seasons, when it is important to harvest quickly lest a crop be damaged, relatives and close friends have priority over other group members in renting equipment.

As American society became increasingly welfare-conscious in the twentieth century, enacting legislation to provide a wide range of assistance programs involving the farm, the school, surplus commodities, and aid to the dependent, the Creoles had the option to use the support for which they were eligible as citizens or to continue to rely on the group.

Federally sponsored programs are generally not viewed as inimical to group solidarity; on the contrary, contemporary Letoyants take advantage of the benefits accruing to them as citizens. Nevertheless, they entertain reservations about public assistance programs, per se. Riverville attitudes toward these programs were probed through several salient questions.

In response to a question on whether public assistance encourages dependency, approximately 43 percent of the Riverville Creoles expressed the opinion that people will become accustomed to receiving financial assistance and will not make an effort to become self-supporting. Concern was expressed about children who grow up in this atmosphere. One informant commented, "A lot of people raise their children on the welfare. And their children are growing up with a check coming in every month—some of them'll do a little outside work, and some of them won't. It makes those children grow up with the idea of receiving a check. I think that some of those things bring on socialism. So, I think children should be made to go to school, and be encouraged by the parents to try and get a job and better their conditions. When you ain't got nothing and the welfare's taking care of you, it's natural to expect that check every month."

Riverville Creoles were also asked whether public assistance should be limited to those people who have a desire to help themselves. Over 91 percent of the respondents agreed that persons who are not concerned with bettering their circumstances should not qualify for welfare services; about 6 percent expressed the opposite point of view; and 3 percent made no judgment.

When asked whether people prefer work to being on welfare, nearly 97 percent agreed.[5]

## SOCIAL NORMS

As any group evolves, patterns for aggregate behavior develop. The larger the group or society, the greater the possible heterogeneity in norms. The most important norms usually become embodied in precepts or laws, but these norms are not equally acceptable to members of the society, and there will be varying degrees of compliance with them. Since the Letoyant Creoles have become numerically large, there are exceptions to generalizations about their norms. Not all Letoyants subscribe to norms which have been handed down by tradition. Thus, older Letoyants may be more tradition-bound than younger ones. Those in the rural South may entertain values and norms that vary from those in urban areas outside the South.

An individual learns what is expected of him during the socialization process. He may accept the validity and desirability of aggregate norms and yet act contrary to them. The decision to conform to or deviate from norms is, in part, conditioned by the evaluation one anticipates from oneself or others. The individual who repeatedly conforms to group norms eventually adopts as his own these aggregate evaluations. Such a compliant individual tends to enjoy favorable self-attitudes at least within the confines of the ethnic group. When he conforms to the norms of the larger society, he similarly may entertain favorable self-attitudes stemming from his compliance; however, compliance with norms per se does not assure acceptance in the larger society since there is a physiologically based Creole visibility which may interfere with acceptance in the larger society and, consequently, with self-attitudes.

As long as group values and norms are shared and cherished by group members, compliance with and deviation from them

[5] *Ibid.,* 91.

are ever-present concerns. Neither conformity nor deviance can be considered in the abstract. There has to be conformity to and deviance from some referent or norm. Conformity and nonconformity are more readily apparent also in behavior towards significant other persons, often related to the individual in terms of membership in groups: family, church, work group, and so on.

Norms provide motivational and emotional warmth. Norms that bring members of a group together initially may assume great importance; deviation from them generally evokes severe penalties. At any rate, conformity to norms governing matters of great consequence to a group—that is, its very existence, its perpetuation, its solidarity, and its effective functioning toward its central goals—has high priority. Deviation from these norms incurs greater penalties than deviation from lesser norms.

Once young Creoles have internalized group norms, the process of identification is well underway. Internalization implies that one will defend and maintain a norm even in the face of strong external pressures. Those who have not truly internalized norms but conform because they are under surveillance have relatively high rates of deviance. Once norms are internalized, an individual attempts to make his behavior consistent with his self-image. As a consequence of socialization, members punish themselves internally if their behavior violates the social norm; self-control and self-punishment are primary goals in the socialization process.[6]

The Letoyant norms that were largely responsible for initiating the group, that is, the family (and the related question of biological heritage), religion, and place of origin are in a sense crucial to group preservation. Marriage outside of the group, particularly to those who have a high Negro admixture, is generally considered deviant behavior. Violation of church norms also ranks high as a type of deviation. Riverville continues to have an importance in the group analogous to that of Mecca—at least in the eyes of the southern Letoyant Creole.

There are, in addition, more peripheral norms; the more periph-

[6] Ernest Q. Campbell, "The Internalization of Moral Norms," *Sociometry,* XXVII (December, 1964), 391–412.

eral an issue the greater the latitude of acceptable behavior. "The concept of latitude of acceptable behavior indicates that no two individuals in the same group uphold the same norms to the same degree, nor that the penalties attached to the violation of norms are always the same. Leaders in a group have a broader latitude of acceptable behavior in matters of lesser consequence than do other group members." [7] Thus, cleanliness, which is a Letoyant norm peripheral to identity, nonetheless contributes to the status of someone who ranks relatively low on the social ladder. A clue to its importance in such an instance was given by a remark concerning a young couple: "That poor girl had to marry the boy, and he wasn't ready to support her. They have the poorest excuse for a house you ever seen, but *it is spotless*. You can eat off the floor!" A high-ranking Creole can violate this peripheral norm, however, and still enjoy status.

ACQUISITION OF NORMS

Socialization, the *process* through which group members learn prescribed norms and social roles and internalize them in such a way that conformity to them in daily life becomes habitual, is important in any group. Much of the socialization of a child takes place through direct training; however, a child is believed to learn vicariously by active imitation of attitudes and patterns of behavior not directly taught. [8] During the socialization process, for instance, Letoyant Creole children develop attitudes about both whites and Negroes. A three-year-old Creole child who was playing by herself with dolls was heard to say, "Nigger, get off that sidewalk!" Although she probably did not know what the expression meant, the tone of voice in which she said it indicated that she had learned the accompanying attitudes.

Children also learn the difference between themselves and whites. One Riverville Creole father described the training of his

[7] Muzafer and Carolyn W. Sherif, *Reference Groups* (New York: Harper & Row, 1964), 180.

[8] Albert Bandura and Aletha C. Huston, "Identification as a Process of Incidental Learning," *Journal of Abnormal and Social Psychology,* LXIII (September, 1961), 311.

children thus: "I believe as long as the colored people stay in their place, I believe they'll make it. But if they get to where they think that they rank with the white folk, well, that's what mess up things. Some of them want to be too smart, you know."

When asked how Letoyant children are taught who they are, a father responded, "Well, I think that at a kind of an early age, the parents usually show them their place. Most of them intermarry among themselves. They seem to have gotten along much better than by marrying in the dark people or the white people. I think the girls here are willing to put up with a whole lot more, you know, to make a marriage a success than the other people."

Some of the older Creoles believe that members of the younger generation are failing to socialize their children adequately and thus threatening to undermine group identity. One grandmother said, "When we got married and had children, we raised our children. But nowadays, oh, those children. It is a shame. Oh, I don't like all of that, the way they dances. I guess if I was young, I'd like it. Going to church doesn't keep them from being bad. I'm telling you, yes, indeed, it's a shame. And then they go to church and receive communion. I say, what's the use for that? Now when I was young, my mother would not let us go to parties by ourselves. She would make one of my old aunts go with us and we better be straight. That's the way I was raised. That's how come I don't like this wild life they're carrying on now. Oh, it's a shame and a sin the way some of them let their children go."

Another elderly woman who was ashamed of the behavior of one of her adult daughters reflected on her experiences as a mother and her efforts to rear her children properly. She said, "She hasn't been that far away from me that she doesn't know how we raised her and tried to bring her up right. My oldest son, I tell you he'd have the recommendation of all the colored in the world. My youngest son is in his thirties and we never had no trouble with him. I tell him all the time he treats me like nothing in the world is too good for me. But this daughter, she's letting that man court her. He came to my door and I told him to get out. I didn't want him in here." The daughter was being courted by a man who was not free to marry her. Since she was aware of her mother's dissatisfaction, she avoided visiting her mother, and the elderly woman was distraught at her daughter's behavior, particularly since she had "raised her right."

Premature independence on the part of adolescents is frowned upon by adult Letoyants. "Some youngsters think they know better than their elders or they can manage things for themselves," said one mother. "When Joe was finishing the eighth grade, they had a prom and youngsters decided they didn't want no parents there. Marie and I set outside in the car to see how it would turn out. As soon as the priests walked out of the hall, a boy jumped up and grabbed a piece of the paper decorations. That one jerk brought down most of the decorations. Marie said, 'Let them dance on the paper now that they're so smart.' When it was time to serve, the girls decided that they didn't want to get their evening dresses messed up, and they came out to the car and asked us to help them. I said, 'You didn't want any parents here, so you just go on and do it yourselves. Do you think you'd be dancing on paper decorations if some parents were there?' They pleaded and begged, so we finally decided to go in. When we were working at the legs of a table to put it up, a boy whose parents were very strict kept letting out deep roars like an animal. It got on my nerves, and I finally asked him where he thought he was—in the field with the cattles? There was a silence so you could hear a pin drop. The boy apologized later."

In every neighborhood, there are a few delinquent adolescents who are the talk of the neighbors. Of some of these young people, one woman said, "That boy look like he try to be an outlaw or something. They had an old automobile, the oldest boy wanted to take it. The mother didn't want him to take the automobile, so he got some kind of iron or something and he put out every glass. If my child had been something like that, I don't know if I wouldn't have knocked him in the head with a stick. And the youngest one, I tell you, he take that automobile and he hit the road—she behind him on foot—he going about 75 or 80 miles an hour and he ain't got no license and he not of age. That day the mother took the car—hid it back there and took the two front wheels and let the air out of them plumb flat—that boy went back there and she followed behind him, and he got in that automobile and run on them two flat tires as far as the store. The father borrowed a pump and he pumped one tire up. The boy looked and he seen his mother coming behind him and he got in that automobile and went on three wheels, and the other one flat. How he didn't wreck that car, I don't know."

Sometimes parents move from the urban area back to Riverville to be sure that their children are socialized in an environment that will maximize their sense of security. One mother said: "There are advantages to rearing children out here. You don't have to go looking for them, you know where they are. If I don't know where they are, I can call and find them in a little while 'cause they don't have all those honky-tonks as we call them. They are either at some friend's house or they may be at a little dance. We do raise good children. They may get a little mischievous some time, but it's nothing bad. They get into a fight over a girl or something like that, but other than that we don't have any trouble with our children. They go to work as soon as they have to go to work, they make a good living for themselves. They don't steal, they don't run the streets, or anything of this sort. We never had any trouble with our children and we have ten. We have six that have gone away from home and they all take care of themselves. We never had any trouble with them whatsoever."

A mother who moved back to Riverville with her family said she did so because she didn't want her boys to join gangs where they would be with non-Creoles. When they are finished with school she is willing to move back to town. She said, "It seems that we work and work and never have anything to show for it. The boys don't have much spending money, but we think it is better training for them to appreciate what they have and to work for it."

Concerning town children, a Riverville mother said, "Children is bad all about. Take them children in town. When they come in the country, you can't hardly do anything with them. They go loose. I believe people handle children in the country better than in town. You see, we give them something to do on the farm and their mind is occupied. But in town, they don't do nothing but study. There ain't nothing for them to do. And work don't hurt them. You take children and put them out there on the field. If you feed them, that work ain't going to hurt them." This comment highlights the value placed upon industry in child training, particularly in the rural community. In urban places, especially where both parents are gainfully employed and opportunities for adolescents to obtain remunerative jobs are limited, the same patterns cannot prevail.

Socialization in the urban southern community takes on a different character from that in the vicinity of Riverville, which is predominantly nonwhite and has greater homogeneity than is found elsewhere. In a homogeneous rural society, much of the socialization of children is inadvertent, for the child observes the reactions of those about him and responds to them. In a more heterogeneous urban society, socialization becomes more complex; at the inadvertent level, attitudes and behavior toward outsiders are much more of a factor in the socialization process simply because of the heterogeneous circumstances. Even at the advertent level, where parents socialize verbally and purposely, the behavior of children toward outsiders enters into socialization to a much greater extent than it does in the homogeneous community of Riverville.

DEVIANCE

Deviance is not a property inherent in any particular kind of behavior, it is a property conferred upon that behavior by the people who come into contact with it. When a people consider conduct dangerous or embarrassing or irritating to the extent that they bring special sanctions to bear upon the persons who exhibit it, deviant behavior has taken place. The response of an audience, then, to a type of behavior indicates whether or not that behavior is deviant.[9]

Even the same action performed in the same society may be considered deviant in one instance and not in another. Whether or not a given person is considered deviant is contingent upon many factors, such as his past record, his social class, the amount of remorse he conveys, and so on. The community filters out and codes the many details of behavior that earn one man the title of deviant while another escapes that label.[10]

A community or a group establishes its own boundaries of behavior. The ethos of the community sets it apart as a special place and provides an important point of reference for its members. Within its confines members know what is appropriate and what is inappropriate. The official agents of the community set limits to the variability and diversity that can be tolerated before the community or group begins to lose its unique identity. When there is a confrontation with persons who venture out to the periphery and are met by policing agents who guard the integrity of the community, members very often participate in these confrontations. Boundaries remain a meaningful point of reference only as long as they are repeatedly tested by persons on the fringes of the group and repeatedly defended by persons chosen to represent the group's inner morality.[11]

The type of boundaries set by a community ipso facto influences the style of deviant behavior. Thus, where a high premium is placed on ownership of property, theft is likely to be relatively common and also highly censured. In every society there are people who choose a deviant style simply *because* it offends against an important value of the group, and the deviant individual often has an inner need to challenge this value in a direct test. The thief and his victim, then, both share a common respect for the value of

[9] Kai T. Erikson, *Wayward Puritans* (New York: John Wiley & Sons, 1966), 6.
[10] *Ibid.*, 7.
[11] *Ibid.*, 11, 13.

property. The community will impose more severe sanctions against theft and devote more time and energy to rooting it out than they will in other types of deviance.[12]

Contemporary theorists maintain that deviant as well as non-deviant action is, then, typically not contrived by a solitary individual but is part of a collaborative social activity in which the things that other people say and do give meaning, value, and effect to one's own behavior. Even if there is not an established deviant social organization, individuals with similar problems who are in effective communication with one another may join together to do what they cannot do singly. They may collectively contrive a subculture to replace or neutralize conventional culture and lend support to one another in their deviance. They need not be people with similar problems; they may have variant problems which lend themselves to a common solution in which each participates in different ways. Each by his deviance serves the interest of the others.[13]

A negative self-identity is often expressed in a hostility toward group norms and the roles offered as proper and desirable. Much of the deviance from Letoyant Creole norms may be, in part, a reflection of this sense of negative identity. Estrangement from ethnic norms and even ethnic origin, however, rarely lead to a complete denial of personal identity. The deviant may take on a new name, denying the identity of Creole, for instance, and insisting upon being called Negro. A negative identity is based on all those identifications and roles which at critical stages of development have been presented to the individual as most undesirable or dangerous. Negative identity may also be dictated by the necessity of finding and defending a niche of one's own against the ideals demanded by ambitious parents or a proud ethnic population. When a person is unable to perform acceptably the roles which are prescribed, he may find it easier to derive a sense of identity out of

[12] *Ibid.,* 20.
[13] Albert K. Cohen, "The Sociology of the Deviant Act: Anomie Theory and Beyond," *American Sociological Review,* XXX (February, 1965), 8.

a total identification with that which he is least supposed to be.[14]

Some kinds of offenses are more damaging to the self-image of the Letoyants than are others. Among the less image-marring types of deviance are those known primarily or exclusively within the ethnic population, such as deviance from religious norms of church attendance. Other deviations project a stereotype of dependency that is not palatable to a people with pride in their group autonomy and self-reliance. Mothers with many illegitimate children, fathered by several men, who appear to be using their deviance to secure welfare benefits, violate not only the norms of self-reliance and family solidarity but also the norms of religious behavior. Another serious deviation consists in cohabiting with or marrying a Negro (discussed in Chapter 10, under Use of Sanctions).

Most legal offenses, even those that are not related to the essential norms of the group, project an unfavorable image that is not consonant with Creole identity as a proud, respectable people. The types of offense and frequency by type give some insight into the Creole image projected to outsiders.[15]

According to incidence, Letoyant legal offenses reported in the local paper can be classified as (1) traffic violations, 33 percent; (2) aggravated assault, 23 percent; (3) offenses against property, 22 percent (4) disturbance of the peace, generally accompanied by drunkenness, 20 percent; and (5) family neglect, 2 percent.

Traffic violations included failure to have a license, a misdemeanor not considered serious in a rural area where adolescents often drive before they apply for a license; failure to yield the right of way, which may have been unintentional; and leaving the scene of an accident, an understandable tendency on the part

[14] Erik Homburger Erikson, "The Problem of Ego Identity," *Journal of the American Psychoanalytic Association*, IV (No. 1, 1965), 85–88.

[15] The weekly paper circulated in the Riverville area prints all cases before the court, listing the names of offenders and identifying the nonwhites by CM or CW for a colored man or a colored woman. Over a period of three years (1962–65) this paper was scrutinized and note taken of every violation.

of a people who may have been in trouble with the law before or who fear the "white man's law."

All cases of aggravated assault involved males, and the incidence was affected by the indictment of three men for multiple offenses. The most serious was an arraignment for attempted murder involving a man estranged from the ethnic group because of family irregularities and geographic distance. Many of the cases involved family feuds, and some of them were settled out of court.

Theft is one of the most common offenses against property, and it occurs most frequently among adolescent males. In one instance, a five-dollar bill was taken from the desk of a policeman, probably as a test of skill to see if something could be put over on the police. Many instances of theft are not reported to the police, such as stealing pecans, fruit, or liquor. Another type of offense is the destruction of property, or attempted arson, an offense that may be intended to "get even" with an antagonist.

Although intoxication may incur civil penalties, unless it is accompanied by aberrant behavior, it is not regarded as "intrinsically evil" by the Letoyants. Like other Catholics, Creoles reacted against the prohibition laws as the last major example of a synthesis of Protestantism and Americanism, and against the Protestant ethic that proscribes smoking, dancing, and cardplaying. One woman commented that "all the men do a little drinking; that is the one way they relax." Some wives, however, will not tolerate intoxication on the part of their husbands, even if it does not lead to violence. One woman commented: "If my husband was like Joe, I wouldn't stay with him. His wife went in to buy clothes for the children and when she came out she saw him hugging the parking meter. I just wouldn't stay with a man who drinks like that." Women also object to teenage drinking, as one mother noted when she said: "The boys around here have a hard time keeping straight. No one enforces the law about their not drinking. If they don't buy it, someone gives them a drink. If a boy wants to mind his mother and stay away, he is not part of the gang." Wife-beating, disturbing the peace, and nonsupport of a family are the most frequent legal charges associated with drunkenness. Drunkenness has been the cause for separation between spouses and for calling in the police when behavior becomes unmanageable.

Although deviations from legal norms are readily perceptible, there are other forms of deviation. Slight norm deviations occur throughout the course of the socialization process when a group member is learning how to behave. Moreover, some deviation is to be expected from time to time. In fact, the reputation of those who are held in disesteem by a group may be attributable primarily to norm violation or deviance. Conversely, those who enjoy a relatively high prestige tend to be conformists, at least in matters of consequence to the group.

## SOCIAL ROLES

### SEX ROLES

All societies provide the young with role models, that is, models of expected behavior in particular places and at particular times, upon which to pattern their behavior. During the process of maturation, a child defines a self-concept [16] and establishes an identity such as male or female, colored or white, important or unimportant, and as a member of a particular family. Sex roles, which are not subject to much change, afford insight into characteristic expectations in a society.

Since the first generation, in which only one of the Letoyants to reach adulthood was a woman, males have played forceful roles. First-generation Letoyants probably had no experience of servitude, since they lived in the household with their white father who purchased their freedom. The tradition of male supremacy has been handed down through the generations to the Letoyant Creoles now living, particularly in the rural South where they are predominantly property owners.

The husband and father generally has the final word on any sizable expenditure of money. In forty-nine Riverville house-

[16] Samuel I. Hayakawa, *Symbol, Status, and Personality* (New York: Harcourt, Brace & Co., 1963), 44.

holds, where husband and wife are living together—excluding the widowed, the single, and the households where a young couple lives with a parent in the parental house—63 percent of the males were found to be responsible for handling the household finances. In 35 percent of the households both husband and wife shared in the financial decisions, and in one percent the woman made the decisions alone. Where husband and wife share responsibility, both may have independent incomes, sometimes from social security, sometimes from inheritance. In urban communities where women are often gainfully employed or where they are co-owners of a business, they are more likely to participate actively in financial matters than they are in the rural community.

In one family the mother, who had been hospitalized for mental illness, complained that her husband had had the welfare check, previously made out in her name, "fixed in his name—like—just signed to him." She particularly resented the manner in which her husband handled the money, saying: "He ain't never come and say, 'Here's a few dollars to buy stuff for the baby or something.' He even buy the groceries and let that woman take what she want to her house." (The woman referred to was engaged by the welfare office to assist in the care of the informant's children.) The sick woman resented being unable to exercise judgment in the purchase of clothing for the children or groceries, both of which would ordinarily be within her province.

Since the husband is expected to be the household head and provider, he generally decides where the family will live. One rural tenant family whose older children had established themselves in Northern City were invited to come live in the city. The mother looked forward to helping with her grandchildren. She enjoyed city life and was eager for her husband to accept the invitation and to find work in the city. The father, who was skilled in more than one type of work, was hesitant; however, he agreed to go for a short time and to see what kind of life he could expect to have there. After a few weeks he decided to bring his family back to the river. His wife later commented, "In the city, many men give their paychecks to their wives. But here, a wife don't know just how much her husband earns. My husband wears the pants at home. Since he wants to stay, we'll stay."

Regardless of how vocal and influential a wife may be, farming entails heavy work, and since this is a male prerogative, the husband has prestige stemming from his work. Moreover, children participate in the work on the farm, and the father is with his children often enough to share with the mother in disciplining them. For no matter how busy he happens to be, he usually comes home for meals, and during the slack winter season, he frequently works near the house.

Sex roles are evident in the driving of a car. Of the forty-nine Riverville families where husband and wife are living together, only the husbands do the driving in 57 percent of the cases; both spouses drive in 33 percent of the cases; in 9 percent neither drives; and in one percent only the woman drives. Some women have no desire to learn how to drive, which means that they cannot "take off" for town or anywhere else on their own. An old woman expressed her disapproval of a woman's driving when she said: "No one finds me ripping down the road." In urban communities, where more women tend to be occupied outside the home, different attitudes toward driving probably prevail.

A husband is expected to be a good provider for his family and to enjoy sufficiently good health to be able to do a "good day's work." Elderly women occasionally express dissatisfaction with a daughter's marriage when the son-in-law is neither particularly healthy nor sufficiently energetic to make a good living for his family. In the rural environment, an able-bodied man who does not earn a living for his family is likely to be considered lazy.

Although the father tends to be dominant, the mother is indispensable to the household. The mother not only cares for the children but also works incessantly. Women, especially in the middle classes, seem to be expected to work despite disabilities. A woman who was said to be suffering from pains around her heart, for instance, could not "think of resting in the middle of the day." Another woman with small children managed to do domestic work every morning in order to supplement the cash income of her family. In the afternoon she had her own work to do at home. In rural areas, women seldom participate in plowing, but on the small farms they do help hoe and pick cotton. The importance of the family, and especially of the woman, was expressed in these words: "If a woman ain't working with a man, he don't get nowhere!"

Riverville women seldom participate actively in meetings called to settle community matters, nor are they included in the "bull sessions" held after church services. When community meetings are called, some women will attend, but they are seldom as vocal as the men.

In certain areas, however, women may assume the initiative. Women who have independent incomes or who inherit money or property, for instance, may not give their husbands control over either. Thus, a woman who inherited considerable property from a deceased husband decided to dispose of it without consulting her second husband. The second husband became so angry when he found out that she had sold some of the property that he went on a binge and stayed out until early the next morning. When he did go back to the house, his wife refused to let him in, and he was forced to spend the night in the cold. According to his wife, he had no right to expect sharing in the decision since the property was hers by a previous marriage. Another woman who had inherited property from her first husband discovered that her second husband was not astute with finances. Concerning the manner in which this woman handled financial matters in her second marriage, a relative said, "She'd do anything for him. But she didn't let him get mussed up either. That was the good part of it. They tell me if he was on that side of the road where his honky-tonk is, and she is on this side with her store, and what have you—if they borrowed a case of coke from each other, they paid for it. But they say, she gave him his share. Now, she say, 'If he's going to throw it away, let him throw it away!' When he gave her money she didn't say, 'No, I don't want this money.' She took it. If he just run up and down the road and give it to other women and gamble, and drink it up, no one would have it. But then when he needed it, she would let him have it."

Some men take advantage of male dominance, even when they are not good providers and are not faithful to their wives. One widow remarked that she had had a hard time living with her husband. "I should've done like my sister-in-law," she stated. "She say what she thought and meant what she say. Her husband didn't go no fooling around with other women or get lax about going to church!"

PARENT-CHILD ROLES

The Letoyant child is ordinarily reared in a family with several other siblings.[17] Regardless of the size of the family, he is generally warmly welcomed and, as a baby, is the center of attention and affection. Although the mother takes care of most of his needs, the father also shares the parental function by being a good provider and by taking an interest in the rearing of the child. Concerning a workman who was picking cotton for her, a grandmother remarked that the man was a good worker but "much too slack to be a father." Of another man, who was away from home working by the day, remarks were made "that he ain't worth a killing, but he's still somebody. That old good-for-nothing gadabout! He's a winsome devil all right, but he ain't no father! That poor woman, trying to raise all them children by herself."

Creoles feel very strongly about the parents' right to have the care of their children even in detrimental circumstances. A Letoyant mother who had tuberculosis and was unable to provide hygienic conditions for her children was threatened with having them placed in foster homes. The reaction to the social worker who had a court order to remove the small children from this home was described by another Creole: "This woman, she and her children, they went to court, and the judge take her children away. And she and her daddy make such a fuss at the courthouse

---

[17] Cf. Chap. 5, p. 48.

and on the street 'til they had to call the sheriff's department to quiet them down. It ain't fair to take children away from their mother, because the worst women can be good mothers to their children."

Parents experience great shame when their adult children fail to conform to family roles. A father who was "running around with another woman" was discussed by his mother and his mother-in-law. His mother's response was to "just cry. She can't do a thing with him, I don't think. All she say is, 'Lord, what's going to happen next? I didn't think my son, with the family like he got, would turn out to be such a no good thing like what he is.'" A father who was going with a woman other than his wife was also severely castigated, especially because his children were aware of his behavior.

An elderly woman was similarly shamed by her adult daughter's behavior. She recalled her efforts to rear her own children properly and pondered what she could have done differently to forestall such a catastrophe in the family. She related her experiences as a young mother in the following words; "I come out of the field about four o'clock in the afternoon, and I make a big fire on the pot. Wash a big wash for people outside, and the next evening I iron. I works all day to keep my little children presentable to go to school, with shoes and good decent clothes and books, and I fix their little lunch buckets. The Lord took my little boy when he was just six years old. I had ten of my own and I helped raise three half sisters and brothers until they got grown up. That makes us thirteen—we were fifteen in the house. I kept those children up, I worked, I washed, I ironed—sometimes I had three washes without my own. After my little children got bigger, my oldest girl worked for sister. And she helped me iron, my boys helped me iron. We used a washboard. We didn't have such things as washing machines. We washed on the washboard."

Grown children usually respect their parents and adhere to norms which parents have instilled into them. One woman said she picked up a habit of smoking after she married, but she never smoked in front of her father. Another elderly woman upbraided her adult son in front of relatives and visitors for drinking with an old schoolmate. The son defended himself by saying the schoolmate stayed until he "finished the bottle." His mother chided him for drinking in front of his daughter. She said that her son should have told the visitor when to stop drinking and both men should have watched their language.

Letoyant Creole children usually expect to be disciplined and recognize that it is intended for their welfare. The older people, of course, experienced more discipline than their grandchildren do today. One old woman said, "My father was a strict man. The old man just had to look at us, that was all. We'd better go straight. The baby, you know, we had him spoiled, but the other children—we just look at them and that was all."

Children who leave home to find work elsewhere can expect support from their family. They are nearly always welcomed back home when they are out of a job, sick, or temporarily separated from marital partners because of military service. Parents may not be in agreement on the advisability of giving financial assistance to children who have left home. In one instance, a boy who was away from home working wrote to his mother for money. The father thought it would be a good lesson for the boy to learn to manage for himself, but the mother said she had to respond to the boy's plea. Without the father's knowledge, she wired the boy some money that she had saved.

The elderly, like the children, are the recipients of much affection and care. In the memory of the present inhabitants, only two persons ever left Riverville to live in an institution for the aged. One was an unmarried woman who had been a housekeeper at the rectory for years. Since she had savings, she made her own decision to retire to an institution. The other was not a Letoyant descendant but the father of a woman who had married into the family. Since the elderly man was unable to care for his physical needs, his daughter had him institutionalized. Among the comments made were: "She put him in an old Negro rest home in Indianola to die," and "He was covered with bed sores and very poorly cared for." The Letoyants felt that this old man had not reared his children properly, and that the one remaining child had shown very little feeling for her father by confining him to an institution.

## SOCIAL CONTROL

If the Letoyants are to maintain solidarity and project a favorable image to outsiders, thus enhancing their chances of enjoying a desirable self-image, then they must exercise control over the behavior of their members. Society itself exercises some control in the form of law. Deviation from many of these civil laws is not regarded by the Creoles as serious. Traffic violations and drinking, for instance, are not generally regarded as serious deviancy. Even more serious deviancy, such as stealing, particularly from outsiders, may not be taken too seriously. When a Letoyant was made a deputy in the Riverville area, some concern was expressed by Creoles who feared that he might be placed in a position where he would be expected to arrest one of his own people for violating "the white man's law." A white person who is well acquainted with the Creoles in Riverville said that they never tell on one another. When questioned by outsiders, they give the impression that they do not know what has happened, even though they have been victimized by one of their own people. They do not trust the law; it is not reliable since it is a white man's law.

Many of the controls within the group are informal, though more pervasive than formal controls. The group usually brings pressure upon its members who violate norms in a number of ways. They are the subject of conversation, for news is largely a report of deviant behavior and its consequences. Reputation within the ethnic group is highly significant. A Riverville mother related an experience that exemplifies internal controls and reaction to them. When a man, who was a heavy drinker and was not legally free to contract another marital union, was courting her daughter, she became very upset. "He's a drunk," she said. "I hate to tell you all this, but he's drunk with every woman that ever was there. He takes his so-called wife and drags her by the hair. He came in the church the night of the missions. Never had put his foot inside the church, but during the mission, he'd sit right behind our backs, but I'm glad I didn't see him until it was all over. Drunk until he couldn't stand, sitting in the pew. It makes me so shamed, makes me so shamed that I wouldn't want people even to see me. Now I'm so shamed to go any place. I go to Mass and come back home and then I lie down and sleep. I can't go to sleep because if somebody told me something about that, it would hurt me clear through to my heart."

This Creole woman was, in effect, experiencing what theorists call degradation ceremonies. As she envisioned the situation, her daughter was degrading herself and running the risk of changing her identity from a respectable Creole to a lower class "no-count" person. Her daughter *should* have been experiencing shame. Since she apparently was not, the mother was removing herself from public view out of shame for her disgrace as a mother, as well as the disgrace to the family.[18] The mother's shame was based upon disapproval coming from outside the family and stemming from her failure to reach group ideals. She was ashamed because the intimate vulnerable aspects of the self were exposed. She had hoped to deter her daughter, and when she failed, her impulse was to conceal her daughter's behavior. When this failed, however, because the man appeared in a public place with her daughter, her vulnerability was exposed.

The primary group, then, often uses positive sentiments and informal controls. When family and group order have been violated, affectional ties are strained. Within the ethnic group where respect is very important, one experiences shame. This type of control, which affects one's acceptance by one's own people, is generally much more forceful than external controls enforcing a law written by outsiders and generally enforced by them.

[18] Harold Garfinkel, "Conditions of Successful Degradation Ceremonies," *American Journal of Sociology*, LXI (March, 1956), 421.

# Chapter 9

# Self-Image of a Southern People: Prestige Variables

In addition to conformity to social roles and the observance of social norms enforced through internal control, status within the group also affects the Letoyant Creole's self-image. A realistic image is contingent upon one's status among group members who know an individual personally. Within the Letoyant Creole group there is a subjective element in prestige, applicable specifically to Creoles as opposed to other nonwhites and based on the group's evaluation of the elements that confer status.

Place of burial in the Riverville cemetery is some indication of one's standing in the prestige hierarchy during life. The front places in the cemetery, in particular, belong to the old families. Grand Pere's tomb, for instance, is in the most prominent place with a large headstone on which is inscribed, in French, his name and the dates of his birth and death. One Letoyant voiced his opinion of the importance of place of burial in these words: "The old families ought to have the front of the cemetery where we can get to the graves and fix them up and pray for the dead. We were here first!" A fracas occurred when an old man died and his daughter (who had come to Riverville only after her marriage to a planter) made arrangements for a plot near the front of the cemetery. "She isn't from here, and her mother is buried in Centerville," proclaimed an old-family spokesman. "Why couldn't the old man have been sent there—or put in the back of the cemetery?"

Burial in Riverville is usually preferred to burial in the places to which the Letoyants have migrated. After two centuries, the little cemetery is crowded. If a plot has been left untended for a few years, it is customary to bury the dead on top of one another. News about a body being shipped in for interment is always likely to raise some queries. When one man heard the news, he asked, "Are they digging near the fence by the schoolyard, and about two rows from the back?" Receiving an affirmative response he said, "Oh, then, that's the right place." He explained, "When people die somewhere else and they bring them back here, they don't always know where to dig the grave—and they takes our places." As previously noted, a Northern City resident who was informed by friends that some of her relatives' graves had been reused was indignant and set up a chain of correspondence to remedy the matter.

One elderly informant in Riverville spoke at length about the importance of the cemetery. She said: "We don't know where Gus was buried, and we're trying to save those tombs if we can. They used to be twenty-five of those tombs. Gus's parents, my grandparents, great-grandparents, all buried there. Every time a priest comes, they'd sell the bricks from the old tombs. Sister Joan didn't know very much about fixing things, but whatever they did, they did it the best way they could. They fixed all those old tombs. I remember as a child, I could see Gus's mother and father in that cemetery in their graves. But that was nineteen seven."

To forestall such calamities as having the dead disturbed, some of the more affluent Letoyants have had vaults constructed in the cemetery. An old family representative who could not afford such a luxury opposed it by saying, "Vaults ain't right either. You can't bury nobody on top of a vault once it's put up. The cemetery will be filled in no time that a way." By 1970 the popularity of vaults prompted the erection of a mausoleum where the less affluent could also be interred.

Some Letoyant prestige variables are the same as those found in similar populations: education, occupation, income, and respectability.[1] Among the Letoyants, prestige seems to be directly re-

[1] An analysis of the bases of prestige among Negroes based on sixteen empirical studies reveals that the criteria which recur most frequently are, in order of frequency: education, occupation, wealth or income, and respectability or morality. All of these criteria were mentioned in at least half of the empirical studies analyzed. Other criteria appearing less frequently were: refinement of

lated to those aspects of identity rated highly by the group, namely, family, religion, and physical attributes. Since these variables have already been discussed at length, they are not unduly reemphasized as discrete variables. Emphasis is placed upon the important variables of education and life style.

## MARRIAGE, FAMILY, AND PHYSICAL ATTRIBUTES

Marriage usually implies equality of status between the parties. As a consequence of marriage, husband and wife share a common name, common living quarters, and common offspring. Especially among the Letoyants, marriage takes on the nature of a reciprocal agreement, and—if one's spouse is an outsider—of an agreement between ethnic groups. Even within the ethnic population, families want their children to marry into other families who have at least as high a status as their own. Despite the psychological preparedness of a couple for a mixed union, the offspring will run the risk of bearing the mark of the lower status parent.

In Riverville, for instance, a union with a black native invariably leads to a loss of status and, in some instances, to identification of the children with the Negroes. In other parts of the South it might be viewed differently, but a Letoyant who elects to live or cohabit with a black person almost always puts social distance between himself and his ethnic group. Therefore, the safest course is to marry within the ethnic population.

On the other hand, union with higher status whites does not necessarily confer status. The incidence of Letoyant Creole-white intermarriage in the South has been negligible since interracial

---

"culture," skin color or white ancestry, family background, and property ownership. The last criterion was important only in studies based on the southern region. In all of the studies, education took precedence over either occupation or income. The preeminence given to education may indicate the comparative scarcity of a good education among Negroes as compared to whites and its unequal distribution among Negroes. Moreover, education may be of greater utility in the acquisition of other prestige bases than the other valued attributes—although the reverse is usually assumed to be true. Norval D. Glenn, "Negro Prestige Criteria: A Case Study in the Bases of Prestige," *American Journal of Sociology,* LXVIII (May, 1963), 647–49.

marriage has until recently been proscribed by law; therefore, a union with a white person in the South usually implies extramarital relations. Some Letoyants maintain that a child born out of wedlock of a Creole-white union is more acceptable than a child born of Creole-Negroid parents who are not properly married. Illegitimate children who have a white parent carry a stigma that is a deterrent to contracting a "good" marriage. A southern Letoyant who has a legal union with a white person has been forced in the past to "pass" into the white population in order to contract the union. Such persons are, in a sense, lost to the ethnic population.

Not all southern Letoyants regard marital relations with white persons as objectionable, regardless of the type of union. Since Caucasian racial characteristics are preferred, they favor the infiltration of Caucasian genes. Unions with whites, therefore, may be not only condoned but, at times, deemed status-conferring, despite their illegality, especially if the union endures.

A Letoyant woman who was born into a "good" family lost status by associating too much with Negroes and by marrying a man who had a Negro mother and a white father. Although other Letoyants think of her as "lost," she draws a line between herself and the Negroes among whom she lives. She says, "When you are poor, you must live wherever you can, but I don't meddle with those people here. I do for them and am nice to them. I let them borrow ice and use my refrigerator, but I don't meddle with them." Her daughter, an attractive young woman, was going with a "white looking" Creole boy whose grandmother was white. She thought a marriage could be forthcoming, but the boy's mother broke up the affair saying, "We're not her class and not her people."

The girl's mother recalled the advice she gave her children, "I was always telling them not to mix too much with the old French people because they might hurt our feelings." When the informant's son dated a Creole girl he, too, had trouble. "He was told after the first car ride that he'd be shot if he didn't marry the girl. We learned later the old man got all his daughters married that a way. The marriage broke up because the girl said she wasn't used to living with *white* people."

The unacceptability of Negroes as spouses is prevalent in the South. A young man in the army brought his Negro girl friend to meet his grandmother. She was very cool and inhospitable to the girl; after the girl left, she asked her grandson, "Why did you bring that black girl into my house?" The boy said that he and his brother were considered outcasts because they were dating Negro girls. Even when the children of such unions appear more Creole than Negroid, a stigma is attached to their lineage. Of one family, it was said, "They were lovely, fair children, but the father was a black man." Letoyants who have been forced to move out of the South, primarily for economic reasons, and who married either Negro or Caucasian outsiders threaten the kinship structure, for the in-law who has a diverse racial origin cannot visit comfortably with his spouse's parents, at least in the rural South. In urban southern communities there is a greater likelihood of social tolerance, but an obstacle is generally introduced into group interaction by bringing into the kinship circle someone who has a different racial background.

A Northern City Letoyant woman who was married to a dark man came to Riverville to visit relatives. She warned him in advance that he might not be acceptable. He just laughed about the situation and said to his wife, "If they don't want me, I don't want them. I can't help it because God made a mistake. He just should have made me white!" When the man returned to Northern City, his wife reported that he was teasing people about Riverville saying, "Man, you should see that place! All the pretty girls! I *like* to go there. That's the kissing place. You go to church on Sunday, and you get to kiss everybody!" His wife said, "Huh, nigger, that's all you squawking on?" She then added, "I say, he really had his nerve. He might have gotten shot any minute going around and kissing all the pretty girls."

Letoyants, who place a high value on physical characteristics, see themselves as highly coveted mates for Negroes. One woman said she thought Negroes were proud to have their children marry

Creoles because their grandchildren would be light complexioned, and this would be a step up the social ladder. But to the Letoyant Creole such a union would lower status. She indicated that if her children left home and married white persons, they would be going up the social ladder, but she would discourage it because she preferred for her children to marry their own people.

By contracting out-group unions, then, the Letoyants incur risks. One of the greatest risks is loss of identity as a Creole if the union results either in passing into the white population or in being identified as Negro. Status is most likely to be enhanced through marriage to a Creole, particularly to one who enjoys prestige within the group.

Contracting marital unions with blacks that will lead to increasing the Negroid phenotypes in the Creole population is also regarded as a form of deviance that incurs loss of status. When young people run away from home to marry outsiders, parents consider them deviant. Speaking of a son whom she called wayward, a mother deplored the fact that his wife was black. Since the girl had economic resources and was unmarried, the union was contracted in the church; but the son was still regarded as wayward for contracting a marriage with an outsider. Occasionally, a priest will hesitate to rectify a union that has been contracted before the justice of the peace, particularly if one party is an outsider. In one instance, where the union did not endure, the young woman's mother supported the priest's decision by saying, "He knowed our species of people, and he didn't want to mess you up." After the civil divorce, the girl later married in the church.

Letoyants give many indications that Negroid characteristics are undesirable. No doubt, the obscurity that has befallen Marie, the mother of the first-generation Letoyants, is attributable to her Negroid characteristics. A "bright" Creole, that is, one who has a light complexion, is favorably regarded. One wife commented approvingly that her husband was "a big man with blue eyes, looks just like white." An elderly Letoyant woman gave evidence of the disapproval which Letoyants usually have for dark-complexioned people when she displayed a family album to a stranger and identified relatives. One relative had married a Negro, and the child was comparatively dark-complexioned. When a visitor pointed out the picture of the child in a family album and was going to ask for some identification, the hostess began to interrupt before the visitor could voice the question. She started rubbing the picture, saying that it was not a good picture since it made the little boy darker than he really was. Then she added that he was her niece's child and that the father was not "one of the people." She went on to say that the child's parents did not stay together very long, noting, "When my people marries other people [Negroes], they never stays together long."

Although Caucasoid characteristics are preferred to dark complexion and very kinky hair, blond, light-complexioned Creole may also be uncomfortable because of his Caucasoid traits, particularly if he belongs to the poor folk who attend segregated schools where his physical appearance will undoubtedly set him apart from others.

## RELIGION

Catholicity is a clue to social status as well as Letoyant identity. There are external rituals that accompany church membership and attendance. The place a family occupies in church, for instance, may be a form of deference ritual indicative of social status. In the Riverville church, certain pews are passed down from one generation to the other. Pew rent initially gave families a claim to a certain place, and tradition has perpetuated this practice. In the rural South, places in church have been the cause of emotional tension, primarily because nonwhites have been expected to occupy the last pews in churches where whites predominate. A similar situation prevails in Riverville because of the non-Creoles who go to church there. A few white families who live in the vicinity generally occupy the first places on one side of the church, the nuns the other side. The few Negro converts and any other visitors are expected to take the back pews.

Church-going, moreover, gives an opportunity to display the trappings of social class. Church services provide an occasion for putting on new clothes or clothes that are reserved for special events to display these marks of status. One elderly woman to whom clothing was of no great importance observed: "Sister, they'd do better staying home. Specially those coming after Mass is half over. Why are they going? To look at the others—what we got on or something? I figure God will look at me just as good with my dress clean. Some people, they can't even tell you a word what the priest said."

Lower-class Creoles can use religion to help establish relationships with those in the upper classes by asking the latter to be godparents for their children. Although relatives generally serve in this capacity, others, too, are asked.

The church also gives the Creoles an opportunity to show leadership both in the activities it sponsors and in its formal organizations. Some of the latter are identified as society or status associations. The one called "knights" implies by its very name that it is for the elite. The dues required for membership and the type of people who are invited to join testify to their status.

In Louisiana, to call the Letoyants "Catholic" is not necessarily a mark of distinction. The degree to which they live up to Catholic behavioral norms, however, is generally a clue to their social position in the group, whether they are urban or rural dwellers. Of particular relevance are the norms that relate to identification by distinguishing Creoles from the Negroes who are not Catholic. Thus, to be married "properly" is a norm that confers status, and a marriage contracted before civil authority is more clearly a deviation from a religious norm than from any kind of norm.

### EDUCATION

To a nonwhite population in the South, education is understandably of value and a help to social status. Prior to the Civil War, nonwhites were traditionally slaves with little or no provision for formal education. But the Black Code in early Louisiana guaranteed religious instruction to the slaves, thus providing them with the rudiments of reading and writing. Louisiana slaves had "religion with letters" as opposed to the scheme devised by the English colonists for their slaves, "religion without letters." [2] When the Ursuline Sisters arrived in New Orleans in 1727 to open a school, they did not restrict their mission to the whites. They had seven slave boarders and many black and Indian women who came every day for several hours for some type of instruction.[3] Nor did the New Orleans whites feel they were condescending in teaching the nonwhites, and Caucasian children attended special schools accessible to both races.[4] Approximately two thousand wealthy free people of color provided for their children's education by sending them to boarding schools in the North or in France.[5] The first-generation Letoyants had tutors for their children, and one of them from France has descendants among living Creoles. As already noted, the Letoyants brought French nuns to Riverville, where they purchased property and built a private school. When the economic hardships following the Civil War forced the nuns to leave Riverville, some Creoles tutored their children, but only the comparatively well-to-do could then afford tutors. Even though the generation that grew up in the late nineteenth century was nearly illiterate, the very scarcity of education contributed to its status value.

Louisiana's rate of illiteracy in 1962 was the highest in the country—24.9 percent,[6] much of it among nonwhites. A study of two rural southern civil parishes, based upon interviews in households, showed that Negro household heads had very little formal

[2] Charles B. Rousseve, *The Negro in Louisiana* (New Orleans: Xavier University Press, 1937), 42.

[3] Betty Porter, "The History of Negro Education in Louisiana," *Louisiana Historical Quarterly*, XXV (July, 1942), 729–30.

[4] E. Franklin Frazier, "The Negro Family," in Ruth N. Anshen (ed.), *The Family: Its Function and Destiny* (New York: Harper, 1949), 147.

[5] Annie Lee West Stahl, "The Free Negro in Ante-Bellum Louisiana," *Louisiana Historical Quarterly*, XXV (April, 1942), 359.

[6] Based upon the percentage of persons aged eighteen or over who completed less than six years of schooling.

schooling. Their median education was only 2.3 years compared to 7.3 years for whites. One-third of the Negroes had not completed even one year of schooling.[7] Statistics from the Bureau of the Census report the comparative educational attainment of Negroes and whites by type of residence. In 1969, over the entire nation, Negroes twenty-five years of age or over had completed 10.5 median school years compared to 12.3 among whites. In nonmetropolitan areas, Negroes had completed only 7.5 years of school, compared to 11.8 among whites.[8]

Among many southern Creoles today, education continues to be regarded as very important. Although many of the very elderly people are illiterate or have only the rudimentary skills of reading and writing, there are some who were tutored. One woman, who lived too far from a Catholic school to attend regular classes, was sent to Centerville to be tutored by the nuns who taught in the exclusively white schools. She commented on her educational experiences as follows: "I went to school when I was seven years old. We had a colored school there near home. But you know, they wouldn't let us go to that colored school. Well, you know, people weren't civilized as they are now—then. All those old—low down—people. It was a Catholic school, but I didn't go. I went to the white school." As this informant indicated, the socioeconomic status of the other nonwhite children attending the school closest to home was not acceptable to her parents, and, therefore, children in her family were sent off to the nearest large community where they were given special instruction by the nuns.

The whole issue of education as a social elevator is clouded by the circumstances under which an education was available to the Creoles in the deep South. In Riverville, for instance, where Creoles had their own elementary school, and where attendance was restricted to Catholic children, all of whom were Creole, the

[7] Alvin L. Bertrand and Calvin L. Beale, *The French and Non-French in Rural Louisiana* (Baton Rouge: Louisiana State University Press, 1965), 28.

[8] "Educational Attainment: March, 1969," *Population Characteristics* (Bureau of Census, Ser. P–20, February 19, 1970), 15–16.

question of interaction did not enter into decisions about education. However, in nearby Riverton, where there were two schools on the church property, both conducted by the same religious congregation but one restricted to white children and the other to nonwhite children, the nonwhites were likely to associate that schooling with an effort to segregate them from white children. Moreover, the nonwhite population in Riverton, even though it was predominantly Creole, consisted of a high proportion of children from low-income families. Consequently, people from Riverton who had the means were likely to prefer boarding schools where segregation was not as noticeable and where interaction would be with Creoles of the same socioeconomic status or with white children.

In Indianola, toward the end of the nineteenth century, one of the priests became greatly concerned about the lack of educational opportunities for the nonwhite Catholic children, most of whom were Creole. He arranged for the nuns who taught in the Catholic school in that community to set up classes for nonwhite children. Eventually, a school was established in Indianola for nonwhites, and it soon began to attract non-Catholics and Negroes as well as the Creoles. This school became attached eventually to a second parish, which also served the nonwhite population who had previously attended the only Catholic church in Indianola.

Limited educational opportunities in Riverville and the inaccessibility of a school were given as a chief reason for out-mobility. One informant said that education was "what I was getting away from there for! My children couldn't go to school. I was living way back out there in the hills. I had built me a nice house out there, and well furnished. I had everything out there—a nice well, running water, and everything. But my children couldn't go to school out there. That's why I wanted to get where my children could go to school. I didn't have no schooling, so I didn't want them to come up like I did. They couldn't make a living now with no experience. You got to have a high school education to get any kind of job."

Letoyant Creoles who moved into central and northern Louisiana at greater distances from Riverville also succeeded in setting up schools attached to their parish churches serving only the nonwhite population. However, in these urban centers, interaction in the school could not be restricted to Creoles. The Creoles did not object strenuously to going to school with other nonwhites in Indianola and Centerville because in both instances the non-Creoles apparently had more socioeconomic resources. One mother, whose children attended the nonwhite Catholic school in Centerville, said, "Of course, that was a mixed school, but it was Catholic and it didn't bother too much. They were all Catholic; looks like they were better raised, or something." She went on to talk about the Catholic school in the northern Louisiana community where she had lived for awhile, and of it she said, "But now, Father there was taking the non-Catholics, too. You could always tell the children to be friendly, but leave them [non-Catholic] alone." This remark indicates that the proportion of non-Catholics attending the Catholic school and their behavior as well as their socioeconomic status were important factors in the rating Creoles gave the school. Education, then, cannot be isolated from the type of schoolchildren with whom the Creoles associated during the educational process.

An elementary education is deemed essential by the rural Letoyant Creoles. Those who are not landholders, however, and who have a limited income take a different view of education from those who are more secure economically. Many parents have a low level of educational attainment themselves, and they rely upon the assistance of their childen to provide the necessities of life. If a crop is harvested by hand picking, then children are expected to remain at home and help. Although there are now truancy laws to penalize parents for utilizing the labor of their children on school days, some parents still disregard the law. One Creole plantation owner made the following comment about conditions on his plantation: "Those tenants don't care whether or not the children attend school. A truant officer from town told us he'd fine us the next time it happened that the children were in the cotton field during school time. We sent word to one child's father, and he said, 'The child works for me, not for you.' Another time a tenant said, 'If he doesn't work here, I'll send him out to work!' Some children don't go to school until Christmas if the cotton isn't in!" This attitude is not restricted to tenants. One small landholder said in defense of his son who was having trouble in school, "They ain't going to school to learn from books to go up and down the cotton fields."

Many of the elderly Creoles who live in rural areas had only three or four years of schooling. There was no bus service for children in the Catholic school until 1952. Many children walked from five to seven miles to school and some of them forded the river until after World War II; others rode horseback. When they were old enough to walk to school, they were usually overage for their grade level, also, and uninterested in repeating primary-level work. Children very often missed the first month of school because it was time to pick cotton.[9]

Among Letoyant Creoles, as among other nonwhites, intellectuals are a special symbol of racial achievement. Intellectuals are in themselves a refutation of the inferiority of nonwhites, since they have seldom had the same educational advantages as whites. Moreover, activities of intellectuals often involve "advancing the race." These intellectuals have been among the principal instruments, at least until very recently, through which the nonwhite community expressed its feelings about the American biracial system and exerted pressures upon the dominant society.[10]

The status accorded teachers among the Letoyant Creoles lends support to the idea that education is closely related to status. In Riverville, this is also true of Negro teachers. One young Negro teacher in the local public school is addressed as "Mister" by Creole children and by Negroes who are older than he. When

---

[9] Permanent school records yielded figures of withdrawal from school over a twenty-year period, 1934–54. When a child was absent for the first six weeks of school, from September through mid-October it was assumed that he was kept home to help with cotton picking. Such children withdrew from school at an earlier grade level than those who did not pick cotton.

[10] Wilson Record, "Social Stratification and Intellectual Roles in the Negro Community," *British Journal of Sociology*, VIII (September, 1957), 235–55.

one older Negro man was questioned about using this honorific title when addressing a young man, he explained that he uses the title "Mister" because "he's higher than I am," meaning that the teacher had attained a higher level of education. There is some envy of Creole teachers in Riverville. One family, in particular, is said to be "great for marrying teachers" and for holding positions in the local public school. An old-family Letoyant who was not in favorable economic circumstances noted, "The one that gets the education, they get fixed; then they teach school. An ordinary person, if he is not fixed with the right people, he will never stay at home to teach. They have to go off to teach. It's just a family doing. They are the leading people—the top people." This informant indicated that teaching in the local public school system necessitates not only having a higher education but, even more important, being "fixed" with the top people.

One test of the strength of a value is its relative importance when it competes with another value. When a public high school opened in Riverville, the Creoles who could not afford to send their children from Riverville to other communities to school had an opportunity to educate their children on the high school level in their own community. Many Creoles, however, hesitated to take advantage of the opportunity to give their children a high school education at home because the school population was predominantly Negro. One woman told her social worker that she would like to move where her children would have access to a good education. She said that while it was true that the school bus passed by going to the high school, she just could not send her children to a "black school."

These attitudes are not peculiar to the Letoyants. In places where other Catholic Creoles had an option to send their children to school with darker children or terminate the child's education in the elementary school, many decided in favor of the latter. Of one such situation, an investigator wrote, "No Creole [not specifically Letoyants] would lower himself by allowing his child to go to school with 'niggers.' As a result, they are completely cut off from outside associations, and their persistence for some time to come seems to be guaranteed by their inability, on the one hand, to enter into another world, and the refusal, on the other, to assimilate with the Negro group."[11]

Another woman said concerning the public school in Riverville, "Those people are not like the Catholic people. You understand what I'm talking about? Some doesn't belong to any religion at all that goes there. But if you can keep them in that Catholic school until that age, they're pretty well grown up by that time." This mother expressed concern that children associate only with their own kind until they finish high school, which would be about the time they are ready to get married. A parent who decided to send her children to a nonwhite public school said: "I always teach my children to be friendly. Everybody, anybody, be friendly. Just to a point, however, you know. I always try to make them understand that you can get along with people without mixing with them. So, I hated to let them go. Some of those black people just don't care what they do. If they accept some, they will accept others." This mother indicated that a loss of status and a lack of discrimination in the choice of friends might result from mixing freely with the Negro children at the public school.

Another mother explained: "We really needs a Catholic high school because so many of the children have to go away to school. They can't stay home. And parents would do just anything they can to send the children to school—even miles away—than to send them to a public school. They would prefer a high school for the Catholics. The children from Indianola would come here to this high school if they could. It is just getting so bad at the public schools that we are just getting afraid to send the children there. It is just a risk we are taking. If we had our Catholic schools then our children could be more to themselves —I call it—and if it was run by Catholics it would be a much better school, I think. I don't know. There are so many things

[11] Horace Mann Bond, "Two Racial Islands in Alabama," *American Journal of Sociology,* XXXVI (January, 1931), 560.

a Catholic people can do or will do that non-Catholics are not allowed to do."

The mother of a Letoyant Creole who finished high school in Riverville at the age of seventeen expressed the wish to send the girl away to a "good Catholic boarding school for a year at least," associating such an experience with a "finishing school." With some hesitation, the mother continued, "Marie probably thinks she knows better than me since she has a better education. My parents wouldn't let me go to school with those black people, and I have only the schooling I got at the Catholic school here."

Higher education, in particular, contributes to social status. Grandparents brag about the educational attainment of their grandchildren. One elderly woman whose daughter married a widower spoke with great approval of this match. She said that the children by the first marriage are in graduate school, one studying for a doctorate at a Catholic university and the other for a degree in nursing at another Catholic institution. Although the stepmother of these young people had been educated in Riverville schools and had no higher education herself, she remarked, "One cannot get anywhere today without a college education. If you go for a job, the first thing they do is ask you how much education you've had. If you've had only one or two years and there are applicants with a degree, you are automatically ruled out."

Among the older Letoyants, very few people had an opportunity for a higher education. Those who went to college were either sent somewhere in the North or attended a segregated Catholic college in Southern City. Indianola has long had a publicly supported college, but Creoles were not admitted there until 1965. There was considerable speculation among the Creoles that the first nonwhite student there might risk physical harm; however, the small number who attended initially did so without incident. For the most part, they were intellectually capable and well-mannered. Since the state college has been integrated without incident, Creoles in the vicinity of Indianola now anticipate that their children will have an opportunity for a college education. Their chief concern is that they have a high school education that will equip them to compete at the college level.

## LIFE STYLES

A realistic self-image has to encompass the fine gradations of status that are present only within a population where there are many shades of valuation placed upon group-defined norms and where deviations from these norms have many more meanings than would be apparent to outsiders. There are differences in life styles and in behavior patterns among the various prestige strata in the Creole population. These differences are most evident in such material possessions as property holdings, homes, and wearing apparel, all of which are indices of economic resources. They are also discernible in language, which usually reflects culture as well as educational level. Even more important, differences are noticeable in behavior patterns, especially in social relationships among Creoles themselves.

Creole awareness of social status differences are evidenced frequently. After this researcher had visited several of the "better" homes in Riverville, she decided to go to some of the lower-class homes. This decision was questioned by an upper-status person who declared, "You've been *everywhere* already," implying the unimportance attached to those of less prestige. The taking of refreshments in these homes was also questioned. "I wouldn't eat after *just anyone* handled the food," said one planter's wife in a tone of disapproval.

One day when this investigator was visiting in an unpretentious home, she was interrupted by a message to go to the telephone in the home of a more prosperous neighbor. The hostess from the first home accompanied the investigator. In the latter home, the investigator was immediately offered a drink of fruit juice and a slice of cake. However, the lower-status woman companion was not offered any refreshment. When the investigator shared her cake with this woman, the neighbor offered a very thin slice of cake but no drink. The companion, who had been very expressive in her own home, assumed a subordinate role and spoke very little.

When the investigator was in another home, toast and coffee were served. Everyone except the Creole handyman was offered two pieces of toast and a saucer with the cup. He was offered only one piece of toast and a cup without a saucer. At dinnertime, everyone except him had gumbo. In the afternoon when a freshly baked cake was served, the handyman got a piece of leftover pie. Obviously he did not measure up socially.

The ability to be a good hostess is expected of every Letoyant woman. A wife who does not know how to entertain or to serve good meals lowers her husband's status. A prominent Creole complained that his wife was a failure as a hostess and that, as a consequence, his friends and people of importance would not visit him there. In his last illness, he left his wife and went back to his paternal home so that his friends would visit him.

Language helps to make possible the discovery of one's identity. Older Creoles take great pride in their knowledge of French and they cherish the ledgers and textbooks written in French which have been handed down by their ancestors. The very name by which one is called is an important clue to identity. In a society where epithets are commonly used in reference to racial groups, the Letoyants are highly sensitive to language and to their identity as expressed by other people in addressing them. For this reason, being identified as *Creole* is important because it denotes native-born descendants of French ancestry. They are particularly resistant to being called *nigger* or even *Negro* and use of courtesy titles such as *Mr.* or *Mrs.* is quite significant to them.

Lower-status Creoles are occasionally ridiculed by the better educated because of speech habits. One prominent woman asked a friend if she had heard how another woman had pronounced *pneumonia*. The speaker went on to comment that the woman had said "lumonia" and that she might greet a person with "How you all is?" and talk about going to the "prieses." Better educated Creoles have certain speech patterns similar to those of southern whites. They have a southern drawl but do not use many of the expressions that are more characteristic of the Negro than of the white southern population.

The status classifications used here are those used by many of the people of Riverville. Variations in the classifications are no doubt used in the larger urban settlements; however, the three-fold Riverville classification has some applicability beyond the confines of the rural homeland because of the regular and frequent contacts of other southern Creoles with it.

Among Letoyant Creoles there are at least three prestige groups—the "big fellows," "we Frenchmen," and the "po' folk." None of these categories, however, is airtight, for there are Frenchmen who are big fellows and some who are po' folk. However, the big fellows tend to be big primarily in proportion to their economic strength, the po' folk in proportion to their economic weakness, and the Frenchmen are somewhere between these two extremes.

THE BIG FELLOWS

As with all people of rural heritage, land is an important index of strength and importance. In urban places, property ownership has high priority, particularly ownership of a place of business or of an apartment. Extent of land acreage is a clue to the status of rural dwellers. As the map of Riverville shows,[12] some landholdings are more than a thousand acres and others are at least five hundred acres, with valuations up to $30,000. The bigness of the large landholder not only affords him a disproportionate share of the homeland, but it also enables him to bargain for good prices, buy wholesale, and invest in labor-saving devices such as mechanical cotton pickers. The big fellows "employ" the tenants to operate their farm machinery as they direct.

In urban communities in the South, the Creoles of importance are undoubtedly more affluent than others. They may be proprietors of businesses or employed by someone else, but in an occupa-

[12] See Fig. 4, pp. 132–33.

tion that ultimately accords them high status. One Riverville woman who came from an adjoining community responded to the question about her feeling of belonging to Riverville as follows: "I feel that I belong to the people here, and I feel that I belong to the people down the river. But I'll tell you, down the river, most of the people was right people. They are mostly families in school here."

The big fellows who are set apart by their prosperity may indulge in some ostentation. They may have a lodge or clubhouse overlooking the river. Annual vacations may also be a part of their behavior pattern. The wife and daughter of one retired Letoyant Creole took a trip around the world. Creoles who freely use their money for enjoyment, though, are usually subject to criticism, even among those in the same social status. Public opinion approves expenditures on homes, cars, equipment, and education but not on "foolish" things such as expensive clothes and luxurious travel.

Even the upper-class women do not, as a rule, have servants. For the most part these women do their own housework and cooking. They take pride in their culinary skills and in their clean houses. They rarely do any field work such as hoeing and picking cotton. They may gather pecans, care for the poultry, and take some responsibility for the garden, but the wives of tenants can be called in to help. In the urban communities, these women never become domestics. They may, however, be teachers or do white-collar work requiring skill and education. In fact, their employment in an office where they are ostensibly the peers of white women may be status-conferring.

The educational opportunities of upper-class Creoles also set them apart. Their children usually have music lessons and sometimes dancing lessons. Until the Catholic high school in Indianola became accessible to them in 1965, Creoles from Indianola and Riverville sent their children to Catholic schools away from home. Less affluent Creoles resent the lack of opportunities which their children have, even though they recognize that in every known society the possibilities for full realization of individual capacities have always been restricted to a small part of the population. Of the upper classes, other Rivervillers say, "The big fellows say they like the public school here fine. But *they* do not send their children there. They have to say it's fine because they work there or their relatives work there."

Type and condition of dwelling is another index of status. Preservation of stately rural homes attests to old-family standing. Well-preserved structures have the inside walls sheetrocked and either painted or papered. Tenant houses are almost always old structures that have had very little improvement or frame dwellings made from old lumber. Creoles who are small landholders also make extensive use of lumber that has been salvaged; but they spend freely on the upkeep of their houses and they have more conveniences than do tenants. In urban areas, Creole dwellings are generally indistinguishable from those of any others in their socioeconomic status. These homes, however, are usually concentrated in a section of town populated almost exclusively by nonwhites.

Even more important to life style than material possessions and educational opportunities is the power exercised by the big fellows, who tend to be in positions of leadership. They seem to contribute more than others to the process of setting social norms and defining social roles. Major norms, as delineated by these leaders, become internalized as members interact toward common goals.[13] Their power can be viewed as potential capacity for action or as a latent force that will put them in positions to carry out their own wills despite resistance.[14]

The potential of the leaders to have their own way was exemplified in Riverville in August, 1962, when the church school was still in operation. The small farmers and plantation tenants who wished to have the assistance of their children during the

[13] Muzafer Sherif, "Some Effects of Power Relations in Molding Opinion and Behavior," *Southwestern Social Science Quarterly*, XXXIII (March, 1963), 289.

[14] M. Herbert Danzger, "Community Power Structure: Problems in Continuity," *American Sociological Review*, XXIX (October, 1964), 713.

cotton-picking season asked that the school year begin early in August and that the children be released in late September and October when it was time to pick cotton. What happened subsequently was related by a small landholder as follows: "Father called a meeting in the church hall and we voted to close the school. But not enough important people were there to get their way. Then the next Sunday there was *another* meeting called, and this time all the important people were there and they voted to have school. I don't know how they could do that when we had *already* made a decision. They had so much to say about how important it was for children to go to school. That was fine for their children, but ours had to miss school."

There is, of course, divergence among the upper classes. A lower-status informant noted with some satisfaction that a Creole landholder who had some ideas about a recreation place had been "told off" by the wife of another prominent person at one of the church meetings so that the pastor could not "get a word in." Nor do all of the upper social classes behave strictly according to established norms. In at least one instance, a Riverville couple is ineligible to receive the sacraments because the wife was married previously and divorced. In other matters, however, their behavior conforms to that of their social class, for those who deviate from group norms frequently, particularly in matters of great importance, risk losing status.

Rivervillers who are large property holders and have purity of lineage probably have a higher status than have other southern Creoles. But not all wealthy Creoles can claim to be Frenchmen with purity of lineage. The big fellows who have land and economic resources and, perhaps, old-family lineage also are clearly distinguishable from others who live nearby. When the basis for this distinction was explored, an informant responded, "They even *look* different." By way of elaboration, the informant added that the nearby people "make trouble at dances here," "dirty the bathrooms," and "even do some shooting at weddings."

When job opportunities are open to Creoles, preference may

be given to the important people. One woman related that when the Head Start Program was inaugurated on the river, the upper crust applicants for jobs were given preference over her niece who had applied and who was as well qualified. According to this interpretation, status factors superseded other qualifications. An Indianola Creole girl, whose father was a proprietor, supposedly went to the Riverville high school because she had been assured that she was going to be valedictorian.

One clue to the identity of the big fellows is the choice of individuals to head drives and to represent the ethnic group. When one woman was asked how the leaders were chosen to take up collections for charitable purposes, she answered, "Well, there are people who are the leaders. People from town do it. They come to Father and he makes announcements in church. My son was appointed. I heard some remarks a few years ago that all this collecting from door to door, they didn't approve of." She went on to say that when a door-to-door collection was made, the response depended in large part on the person appointed to the job. She said, "Jim told me, 'If Son comes along and collects, I'm going to have my dollar. But if Tom, Dick, and Harry comes along, I won't have any.' "

Another clue to status is the choice of officers for organizations. Since religion is very meaningful to the Creoles, the trustees in their churches generally enjoy relatively high status; they are men who get things accomplished. Even a cursory examination of nominees for such honors indicates that they are persons who, by virtue of their economic position and moral behavior, enjoy social status in the population.

There is some resistance to accepting as equals outsiders who marry into the population and come with their spouses to live among the Creoles, particularly if these outsiders are dark-complexioned. One such woman, a college-educated Catholic, was coolly received. She did not hesitate to speak when the occasion called for it, but she never became part of the "in-group." Another woman from a prominent Creole family married into an equally prominent family but lived out of Louisiana for twenty years. When she returned to Riverville, she was not warmly welcomed into the social life of the upper strata. Her reception did not reflect on her ethnic origin, her family, her religious or socioeconomic status. She had simply been "out of things" for at least two decades, and the women who had achieved status in the community were not inclined to be enthusiastic, particularly when she made an effort to exert leadership.

The upper social strata appear to be more organization-minded than others. They are active in long-established organizations such as the Holy Name Society and the Christian Mothers. The Knights of St. Peter Claver is predominantly upper class. Concerning membership in the Knights, one middle-class woman said, "That's society most of it. But the Holy Name is everyone. I'll tell about those groups. Lots of the society people invited them in to join, and they have groups that get together and have different things, and some of the groups are left out. That is very discouraging and disgusting, you know that yourself. The Christian Mothers' Society have groups that get together and and have different things by groups and that ain't so good. I have been free with everybody, so whether they group it off or not, I stick with my Christian Mothers' Society because I like it, and I want to be a good mother." One of the men from the middle social strata said he had joined some of the men's church organizations but stopped attending because he resented the tendency of a few important men to come to the meeting with plans for action already drawn up.

The big fellows, who form a subgroup of their own, are accused of "barely saying howdy" to some of the po' folk. One small landholder's wife noted that the big fellows "belong to that social club, but they don't never invite none of us to their parties." Riverville's social club, restricted to the "upper crust," has at least one dance at Christmastime. Invitations may be extended to couples outside this small circle. One such invitation, clearly meant to restrict the attendance to those who were acceptable to the host organization, read, "Admission $1 per person. Present card. Non-transferable."

WE FRENCHMEN

If the "gentry," the persons with the "landed estates," and the proprietors fail to take cognizance of the importance of the family, the distinction is nonetheless evident to everyone who claims to belong to "we Frenchmen." The old families are the *noblesse* who have lineage—something that money cannot buy! Most of the small landholders and their counterparts in the towns claim descent from Grand Pere. Equally important, they have preserved "integrity," although they suffered the loss of much property. Residentially, the upper west bank in Riverville is their stronghold. Some farms are only an acre or two in size; and proximity, as well as ideology, serves to fortify this bulwark. Opinions are formed in conversations over the fenceposts or by the side of the road. The "big fellows get up and talk at meetings," said one Frenchman, "and we don't get up and make speeches or say what we think at a meeting, but we have tempers and we knows what we want!"

The small landholders—especially of old family stock—have their own little coterie. They, too, have bull sessions—not necessarily in a plantation store or lodge but by the side of the road or around a fireplace. One of the most opportune times for such gatherings is after the early Sunday Mass.

Although the Letoyants are of mixed racial origin and new strains have constantly been introduced, the newcomers who entered the population after the Louisiana Purchase in the early nineteenth century found it especially difficult to become accepted by the "first families." Even today families who cannot trace their origin beyond the nineteenth century are not considered a part of "our people" by the old families, despite the fact that much intermarriage has taken place. Some families who came in the mid-nineteenth century are said to have come to Riverville "not too long ago." Even though the newly arrived families in question could "buy and sell the lot of them [old families]," the latter have lineage and can trace their ancestry back to the first generation. This attitude was evident when the Creoles were asked to pledge money for some improvements on the church. When an old timer, who had naught but name and dignity left, was approached, she wanted to know how much a planter with a mere century's residence was giving. When told that the planter had pledged $100, she protested, "Don't take it! That church belongs to us!"

Most of the Frenchmen are small property holders or renters who can afford to be independent. Loss of property means dependency and a threat to status and to ethnic survival. Grand Pere's descendants appear to be particularly ethnic conscious, and preservation of ethnicity assumes the nature of a life-mission with many of them. Hence, they oppose any attempts to confuse their identity with that of the blacks, and in the past they have proved to be a formidable obstacle to the functioning of the NAACP in Indianola and in Riverville.

Old-family Letoyants have carefully preserved those possessions they regard as heirlooms. Some of these things are not of great monetary value, but to Creoles, who emphasize ancestry, they are very important. The most common item which they have kept is the old ledgers in which were kept notations of financial transactions and occasionally drafts of letters and notes of births, christenings, marriages, and deaths. They have also retained silver, glassware, and china, much of which was imported from France during the heyday of Letoyant prominence. In one home, an old trunk contains many such treasures. Among them is a thick glass mug with an etching of Napoleon's bust. The owner said that Grand Pere brought back a set of these mugs when he visited France and left one to each of his children when he died. In her family, the mug was carefully kept and handed down from generation to generation.

Among the remnants of French culture that characterize these Frenchmen are food preferences, often known by French names. Rice and gravy make a choice, cheap dish. Gumbo, another favorite, is seasoned with filé, a powder made from the ground, dried leaves of the sassafras tree. Filé thickens and flavors the soup. Jambalaya is a highly seasoned stew made of seafoods or chicken. "Dirty rice," is prepared with chicken giblets and is well-seasoned. Coffee, served thick and black and blended with chicory, is a favorite drink. Meat pies made of breadlike dough filled with well-seasoned ground meat that may contain a little rabbit or wild meat for flavor and fried in deep fat are other specialties. Cakes, "stirred up" without consulting recipes and with a minimum of measuring, are called by whatever filling or icing is spread on them.

Most Frenchmen cannot afford to send their children away to school, but they do make use of the public high school, as much as they dislike close association with the Negroes. The parental group among the small landholders seldom has had more than an elementary education. At times, certain colloquialisms and a slight patois are evident.

Social-class values were evident in the interaction among children who attended the Catholic school in Riverville. One mother regretted that a daughter's classmates were not highly desirable friends. She said there were "illegitimate children" in the class, and some of these children were leaders. "If the others didn't follow through on what they wanted to do, they weren't included in games. In choosing sides for a ball game, the girls who would not go along with the leaders were just not chosen." The mother continued by saying that while these girls occasionally came to her house to play, she would not allow her daughter to return the visit. She feared that her daughter's attitudes had been influenced by these classmates, who have "no ambition to make anything out of themselves, and who may follow in the footsteps of their mothers." Attendance at the Catholic school did not, in itself, guarantee association with one's social equals because all Creole children, regardless of social status, attended that school.

Individuals in the middle-class range are careful to make distinctions between themselves and others who violate group norms. When one woman was asked about a particular family, she preferred not to talk about them. When pressured, she said, "Don't ask anything about those people. I don't know anything about them." And yet, when the conversation eventually got down to specifics about a member of the family who had moved away, she knew not only the whereabouts but the names of each of the children and the communities in which they were born. Although she was quite well informed, she initially resisted communicating this knowledge lest she be associated with their social status.

People in this social range usually have strong feelings about participation in group activities. They are not financially able to make monetary contributions, but they give unstintingly of their time and energy and show their concern in other ways. When a benefit style show was being planned, one Creole woman regretted her inability to purchase clothes for the event. She was, however, willing to lend a blouse which her mother had worn for her wedding. Another woman in this category expressed her desire to participate in projects such as rebuilding a house that was destroyed by a fire for another group member. She could make only a small monetary contribution, but she worked diligently at a Christian Mothers' fund raising project.

The ability to make fine distinctions between the big fellows and the middle social stratum, "we Frenchmen," is not possessed by Creoles unfamiliar with Riverville and environs. The more remote the individuals in a stratum are from the position of an informant, the less clearly can that informant make distinctions. He can place only those of whom he is aware, and he is particularly aware of those with whom he has social contacts. In Northern City, for instance, the Creoles are labeled simply "from the river," and any class difference between the upper and middle strata is, to all intents and purposes, obscured if not lost. This is particularly true of the population coming from Riverville and Centerville. Similarly, the white population even in the environs of Riverville is not always able to make distinctions based upon social behavior. They can make distinctions based upon economic resources if they are knowledgeable about such resources. One of the mothers from this middle stratum, noting the lack of discernment among the white people, said she would prefer that her children go to school with the whites in town rather than with the nonwhites on the river because the former would be more likely to accept her children for their individual worth rather than for their social position. Another woman, who enjoyed a relatively high social status, de-emphasized the economic basis of her status by noting, "Money don't do everything; there's something deep down in you has to make you what you are."

PO' FOLKS

To be categorized as po' folks implies lack of material possessions. Ownership of land and property is so important to the Creoles that one of them commented, "If you don't own your own house, some people won't look at you when you're in a group of more than three people. If you are alone or there is only two or three people, they will speak. Otherwise, they put their nose in the air." The homes in which the po' folks usually live have hinged board windows without screens and have few conveniences. Since money is either scarce or used "foolishly," their homes are usually poorly furnished.

Poverty does not in itself relegate everyone to the same status. Some po' folks are recognized as honorable if they have good morals, attend church regularly, and contribute their labor, if not their cash, to worthy causes. Those with French ancestry value hospitality highly, and they will borrow or use credit in order to entertain visitors "properly." The wives of the big fellows often employ the high caliber po' folk. At times social-class barriers are ignored when the women work side by side. One employer related that she and a tenant helper "got so chummy" that "they never did ice that cake" and the family eventually ate it without icing. A tenant farmer and a widow on relief who are nearly destitute may enjoy dignity based upon group membership and adherence to group values despite their financial distress. If they are from "good" families and observe the norms of morality, they enjoy a dignity not shared with the economically secure but nonconforming Creole.

Since most Riverville po' folks are sharecroppers or day hands, they usually have "boss mans" in the persons of plantation owners, who with one exception are Letoyants. The tendency to stay under boss-rule was explained by a landholder as follows: "These fellows aren't educated, and an uneducated man with a family to support isn't going to do as well in town." These po' folks were "raised on the soil and know nothing but farming —poverty!" The po' folks in urban areas are usually the non-propertied, the unemployed, or the part-time employed.

As the industrious Creoles in the lower classes view the economic situation, it is very difficult for them to make a living. Their situation in Riverville was described in the following words: "It's very hard to make a living unless you work as much as you can. The family always tries to help out, but it's hard if you don't own the land that you work. You get a very small wage for the long hours you put in. Now we go to work in the morning early, at seven o'clock. We have to be in the fields at seven o'clock and we work until eleven and again at one we go out and until six in the evening, and we get $3.15 a day." She continued that they would have left long ago except for her husband. "He is uneducated. He has talents, but no education to go with it. He doubts himself. That's why we remain here."

Creoles on the periphery of lower class status, if they are not clearly in that category, resent being "used" by their cohorts who are higher on the status ladder. One woman said, "Some people don't seem to recognize others." She went on to say that when the nonwhites were making an effort to enter the state university in Indianola, they were fearful of having their own children apply. They were not hesitant, however, about getting a lower-class friend's son to apply in order to see what would happen.

But another perspective was given by a Creole landholder who hires help: "The people who were industrious left here long ago. The help you get now is not dependable. Very few people have day hands they can count on. If you hire someone from town, they come out asking how much you will give them. They start asking $2.00, then the next day they say they are getting $2.50 somewhere else, and eventually they want $4.00. If you pay them that much, you have nothing left. They really are not getting that much other places; they just want to see how much you will give." He went on to describe the type of work that could be expected from these people. "Those who hire to pick cotton leave a patch and go up where they can talk to their friend in another row who is a faster picker. They don't care. Or you hire them to hoe, and they leave big patches of huckle-burrs."

Concerning a lower-class woman who was being paid for staying with an elderly white woman through the night, and who was dismissed from her job, an upper-class woman said, "She complained about all she had to do and get so little for it. I knows better. They just won't work. I'll tell you what she did. I told her. I say, 'You put in a night's sleep and then come here and boast.' She wouldn't work at night, and worked somewhere else at day. They was used to her; she had been taking care of the old lady all along. Then she quit because they didn't pay her what they paid the nurse during the day. I know that's the truth."

Po' folks are often regarded as ne'er-do-wells who lack ambition and fail to support their families. They seldom enjoy either the respect or the friendship of those above them on the social ladder. If they have to go to town and have no means of conveyance, they may find few offers of a ride from their thrifty neighbors. "I needs to go to a doctor," a woman complained, "but I'd have to pay someone to take me!"

There may be less stress on cleanliness than among the respected folk. In one home, chickens were allowed to come into the house. When an upper-class woman visited a bereaved family in one of the tenant homes, the man in the house was eating some bread soaked in coffee. The woman recalled, "He'd dip up a spoonful, eat it, and the next spoonful would go to the chickens." The woman became so disgusted that she said to her companion, "Come on. Let's get out of here."

Some of the po' folks are considered rowdy in expressing emotions. One wife "broke a broom over her husband and had the poor man all bruised up." Another mother has boys who "can hardly read or write and when she hits them they strike back." A woman described an encounter with her husband in the following words, "When I was playing with this baby, he shoved me in the kitchen against the wall. Next door is Miss Marie. I call her. I told her that he was fighting me. He told me if I said another word, he'd knock my guts out. So, his uncle and this man down the road come to get a hambone. I was crying. I walk in the front room where they was, and I told them what this all about, that Joe was fighting me, and hurt me up in the chest, and shoved me back and was pulling my hair. They told him not to do that."

Another upper-class woman said of the lower classes: "These people are always carrying grudges, and they want to settle things themselves. They may stick you with a knife, shoot you, or hit you on the head with something. I tell them to say what is the matter and get it over with." Concerning the person who had been the subject of conversation, she added as an afterthought, "He is nothing and you can't do nothing with nothing."

Concerning one "no count" family, an upper-class informant said, "The children stop school before finishing and spend their time in the honky-tonks. They got money, but never save any of it for a rainy day or spend it on good, sensible clothes or medicine. When the children gets sick, she comes over here for aspirins or cough syrup. That woman can do anything. She's tough like a man, and gets out there with a team and plows her land. She's rough and tough, and insanely jealous. She fusses at her man and cusses him awful. Even the baby cusses. You can hear them fighting way over here!"

A store owner's wife related her experience with the lower social classes as follows: "These families will charge without ever intending to pay their bills. Some have bills standing for three years. Those women with 'outside' children try to get my husband to wait on them because he is soft-hearted and cannot turn down a plea for food for hungry children, especially around Christmas or holiday time. During the pecan picking season one family gets $70 a week, but they never spend it on shoes, or clothes, or furniture. When it's time to get clothes, they are always looking for someone to give them things. One of those women drinks everything she gets."

Women who have several children out of wedlock and who are simultaneously on welfare generally fall into the "no count" category. One of these mothers, who was reminded by a welfare worker that she was jeopardizing her chances of a marriage by having several children by different fathers, responded "with arrogance and rudeness" that it was "impossible to live without a man on occasion, and that she doubted if she would be able to dispense with one in the future."

In the lower social classes men are not likely to be members of church organizations. One of these men said that a missionary had given him a penance to go to communion once a month and strongly suggested that if he would join the Holy Name Society he would be reminded to go. He talked the "joining" part over with his friends, and they advised him not to do so. He said, "I didn't have to join; I could remember to go without being a member." Then, as though he were rationalizing, he said that he often had to work on Sundays, and "it just might be" that he would be working on "Holy Name Sunday."

There are many ways in which people seek psychological compensation. One man who is indifferent to religion and who has a mistress attempts to pick the first bale of cotton of the year. This is a legitimate form of compensation as contrasted to the deviant forms of having a mistress and showing indifference to religion. Since he does not, in the latter instances, receive status or recognition by following group norms, he receives recognition for outstanding deviance. A Creole mother similarly has recognition throughout the state as a hard-core welfare recipient who has had so many children out of wedlock that hers, according to a caseworker, is almost a classic case in public assistance annals. Presently, one of her older daughters is beginning to follow her footsteps.

In many respects, the po' folks at the bottom of the social scale live and act very much like some of the lower-class blacks. They may, in fact, lose their identity as ethnic group members if they fail to observe ethnic norms and if they cohabit or inter-marry with blacks.

# Chapter 10

# Maintaining a Letoyant Creole Image Distinct from the Negro's

Just as an individual's personality is built on his relations with other persons, and the individual can be understood only in terms of the whole system that produced him,[1] so, too, a group's identity can be understood only in terms of its social relationships. Letoyant Creole identity has been shaped by the kind of personal relations they have had with certain other groups.

In the deep South there are basically two populations to which the Creoles project their image—the Negro or black population and the Caucasian or white population. The Negroes probably have a much more distinct image of the Letoyants than the whites have because there is more frequent interaction between Creoles and Negroes than between Creoles and whites. Moreover, whites often confuse Letoyants with Negroes, giving evidence of their inability to make clear distinctions between these populations. Any generalization about the image which the southern Letoyant projects to these outsiders needs qualification. In rural areas, for instance, they probably have an image distinct from that in the urban areas. Older Creoles, moreover, probably project a different image from the younger ones. In effect, there is a generation gap between school-age Letoyants and their parents. Their image is further contingent upon the social-class level with which the other populations are familiar. As previously noted in the discussion of social class, there is within the southern Letoyant population a broad spectrum of interaction and behavior. Therefore, the image projected will be related to the kind of Creoles with which the other populations come into contact.

[1] See Henry Stack Sullivan's theory as quoted in Helen Merrell Lynd, *On Shame and the Search for Identity* (New York: Harcourt, Brace, & Co., 1958), 156.

Whatever image the Letoyants project is obviously related to those members with whom outsiders have been associated and the kind of interaction that has taken place. Traditional interaction patterns, best exemplified in Riverville, are "exported" by those who move away. Letoyants who are several generations removed from the homeland and who have infrequent contacts with it probably have interaction patterns somewhat different from those of Riverville Creoles. But for southern Letoyants who are not at such a distance from their homeland to preclude periodic travel, the attitudes and environment of Riverville are quite pervasive. Southern Letoyants frequently return to Riverville on weekends or holidays, and particularly during summer vacation months, to visit and to recreate. Therefore, interaction in the Riverville area has far-reaching effects.

Many factors are involved in any group's attitudes toward an out-group. Among them are the attitudes toward the out-group held and conveyed by earlier generations; the concrete out-group experiences encountered during socialization, particularly childhood and adolescence; the in-group attitudes prevailing in an immediate area and fostered in its institutions; and the sense of personal security which the in-group fosters in its members.[2] On the basis of their tradition, socialization, self-reliance, self-sufficiency, and exclusiveness, it is hypothesized that a chief concern of Letoyants in relation to the predominantly lower-class Negro will be to maintain the traditional social distance. In their relations with the whites, who represent power and status, however, emphasis will be on lessening the social distance.

Another factor that has been explored in regard to intergroup relations is the effect on attitudes of out-group contacts and interaction. Among the hypotheses that have been supported in studies on the effects of contact in various situations are: Groups in contact, consisting of individuals who are not susceptible to change, may become more prejudiced than they initially were

[2] Cf. Victor D. Samua, "Social Science Research Relevance to American Jewish Education," *Jewish Education*, XXXIII (Spring, 1963), 164.

at the outset; [3] when contacts between two groups are intimate, however, prejudice tends to be reduced on the part of both groups; [4] where the two groups have similar socioeconomic status, contact tends to reduce prejudice, but where statuses are different, interaction intensifies rivalry; [5] and if a relationship is to exist, it must provide minimally satisfactory reward-cost outcomes to its members, that is, in terms of the rewards (pleasures, satisfactions, and gratifications) received as a result of the contact as well as the costs incurred (embarrassment or anxiety). [6] All of these hypotheses are reexamined in the Creole-Negro relationships in Riverville.

In this chapter, Letoyant perspectives of the blacks are viewed prior to a discussion of the image the blacks have of the Creole. Such perspectives provide background information, afford a glimpse of intergroup relations, and undoubtedly affect the image that an out-group entertains.

## CREOLE PERSPECTIVES OF THE BLACKS

In Riverville, the black folk are decidedly "beyond the pale." Unless they are tenants of the Creoles, the latter may ignore their presence in the community. In answer to direct questions about the names of black persons, Creoles may profess not to know names even of next-door neighbors. An old-family spokesman commented as follows: "We don't have anything against these people. They are friendly, and when someone is sick we

[3] Paul H. Mussenfi, "Some Personality and Social Factors Related to Change in Children's Attitudes toward Negroes," *Journal of Abnormal and Social Psychology*, XLV (July, 1950), 423–41.

[4] Daniel M. Wilner, Rosabelle Price Walkley, and Stuart W. Cook, *Human Relations in Interracial Housing* (Minneapolis: University of Minnesota Press, 1955), 95; Ernest Works, "The Prejudice-Interaction Hypothesis from the Point of View of the Negro Minority Group," *American Journal of Sociology*, LVII (July, 1961), 47–52.

[5] Gordon W. Allport and Bernard Y. Kramer, "Some Roots of Prejudice," *Journal of Psychology*, XXII (No. 4, 1946), 9–39.

[6] J. Allen Williams, Jr., "Reduction of Tension Through Intergroup Contact: A Social Psychological Interpretation," *Pacific Sociological Review*, I (Fall, 1964), 81–88.

help them out, but we don't go to their houses just to visit and we don't want them in our church. They aren't our people!"

Even the Letoyant babies are said to protest at association with Negroes. A Creole mother maintains that her son "never cared for darkies," and once when he was a baby he "started crying when he saw a darky in a doctor's waiting room." The mother was "so embarrassed" because the Negro woman said, "He's crying because he's not used to us!"

A Riverville Creole does not like to be called a Negro. A resident of Riverville bragged that when he went to Indianola to register as a voter, the official "knowed the difference" between him and the blacks and registered him not as *Negro,* but as *colored.*

A Letoyant teenager who was born and reared in an urban center beyond the immediate vicinity of Riverville commented on the racial classification among her people. She said, "They wouldn't just say that they were Negroes. It's all the same thing, but I think they would more or less say they were colored before they would say they were Negroes. If they can't be Frenchmen, then they're colored. But when anybody calls them Negro, then it's all right because they know that's what they are to everybody, but they just don't go around calling themselves that. After a while a lot of the older people that have been there for a long time think about it, and will call themselves Negroes, but not at first—not the people that are coming up from the river. At first they won't do that, not even the teenagers."

The term most commonly used for the Negro people near Riverville is *blacks,* but *Baptists* is also used with great frequency since religion is a basis for differentiation there. *Negro* is used occasionally. Although whites use *nigger* indiscriminately to refer to either the blacks or the Creoles, neither of these groups makes use of that term except in derision or in teasing. The blacks are seldom called *colored* by Riverville Creoles even though outsiders often confuse the terms.

Many Creoles are quite explicit about their feelings toward the blacks and do not hesitate to call them names. "They's God's people, but they ain't my kind," said one woman. "Why they's black as crows," she continued, reflecting the racial bias prevalent among whites especially in the South and simultaneously differentiating Creoles from Negroes.

"Respectable" po' folks, like the Frenchmen, seldom get "messed up" with the blacks, and if they do they never publicize any friendly relationships with black neighbors. A Creole, who was recalling an incident, stated inadvertently that he was "talking to" a black man. Immediately he added, "I mean I *overheard* him." This afterthought was intended to minimize the possibility of this investigator's concluding that there was any friendship and informality in the relations between Creoles and Negroes.

When visiting a family who referred to the Negroes residing nearby as though the latter were really neighbors, this investigator witnessed the effect of a third party—especially a white person—on their relationship. The Negro came to borrow a tool. When he noticed the investigator he appeared reserved and looked at the host with a half-hopeful smile. There was nothing to hope for under the circumstances, however. The tool was lent without question, but there were no other overtures such as an introduction, small talk, or a friendly inquiry about the family.

Attitudes toward Negroes were further revealed by a Creole woman who owned property adjacent to a large plantation with Negro tenants. She commented to a friend that she had a house for rent and that it had been empty for several months. A friend responded that the plantation owner was moving his tenants from the outlying areas into the center of the community and that she could probably rent it to a day hand. The owner replied, "But I just couldn't let one of those people [Negroes] move in there."

In Riverville, as the map (Fig. 4) depicts, plantations tend to have predominantly Negro or predominantly Creole tenants. Since Negroes are not landowners, they are, by this very fact, at a disadvantage socially and can be very effectively isolated by Creole landowners. This situation exists even though Negro tenants may live adjacent to Creoles, and the Creoles on whose plantations they work may be empathetic toward them.

In Louisiana towns and cities, the exclusion by Letoyant Creoles of Negroes from neighborhood activities is not as marked as in rural places. An Indianola Creole said, "We have those people as neighbors, and they are the best neighbors you ever seen, but they never visit us and we never visit them unless someone is sick or they are invited for something. If someone gets married in the family, or something, these people will come, but they come in not at the time of the wedding or the reception or something. They come afterwards or before. They never come in. It seems like they know they are different, and they never come in." She continued, comparing the younger generation with her own generation, "The children are more together, but they don't visit too much or do things different than we did. You'll hear lots of people say, 'Oh, it don't make any difference.' But they'll tell you that and they'll feel the same way. And they'll treat these people—some of them treat them much worse." An elderly Creole attempted to explain the ethnic group tendency to isolate themselves from other nonwhites in the following terms: "We just was a different family of people, that's all. I don't know; I can't tell you how. We just try to do the right thing I reckon, just mix with the right kind of people. That's the whole thing of it." Mixing with the "right kind of people" means in large part not mixing with lower-class outsiders, especially Negroes who are, like the Creoles, identified by color.

Another woman, who was making a cake, gave some insight into her attitudes when she divided the batter into six thin layers, explaining that "those three-layer cakes are niggerly!"

"Do you mean niggardly?" she was asked.

"No. I mean niggerly! That they are coarse and rough!" This retort was probably intended to highlight status differences between Letoyants and Negroes.

One of the Creole landlords in Riverville who has relatively small landholdings with eight or ten tenant families expressed empathy toward the Negroes living on his place. He said he did not blame them for leaving and getting homes in town where they had better facilities even though it worked a hardship on the planter. Both he and his wife agreed that a family deep in debt "to the commissary" or plantation store could do better in town where they could get a "fresh start." Undoubtedly, many of their tenants were in debt to them at the small store which they operated on their plantation, but both expressed a warm feeling for the Negroes who had economic difficulties. As landlords, they undoubtedly had occasions for more intimate relations with Negroes than some landholders and Creole tenants generally have.

When Creoles who have migrated and become attuned to a broader society in other environments return to Riverville, they seem to resume social relations very much as they would have done if they had never migrated. In reference to the Negro people, one Letoyant who returned from the North said: "Well, I don't know if anyone told you this, but I can work with them [Negroes], teach with them, live with them, and yet when you hit the river, you can see other [Negro] people on the street, and immediately there is something that you feel differently. You have come back on the river, yet I can have [Negro] friends of mine with me. You think of them [Negro people of River-ville] as one of the people on the place." This informant resumed her old interaction patterns in the environment where she was socialized, indicating the influence of environment upon attitudes.

A woman from a prominent Riverville family who married a fellow Letoyant and moved to an urban community in an adjoining state expressed understanding and tolerance of Negro people. When she was living in the urban community, she exerted much leadership in behalf of the nonwhite population. In one instance, she went to the welfare office to plead for an increase in the allotment of a Negro who had cancer. She described her efforts in the following words: "The hospital gave her special care in this cancer department but not medicine. And I took care of that part and I would send her food. I have solicited clothing for her and her little girl, and bedding—I mean sheets, linen, and such as that. I would always try to get for her. And I stuck with her until she died. And it all happened within this year that I was chosen Mother of the Year." This recognition came from the State Federation Club for Colored Women, an organization consisting primarily of professional people. The recipient of the prize said that she was "very happy, nervous, and surprised, and everything." The rewards of interaction in another environment were sufficiently gratifying to outweigh the costs.

There seems to be, then, a wide variation in the Letoyant reaction to Negroes. Men who work primarily with Negro men have a better insight into the Negro situation and more firsthand information about and association with them. Women, however, who seldom work side by side with Negroes or oversee them, have more resistance and hostility, as well as prejudice. Therefore, these findings support the hypothesis that prejudice tends to be reduced when individuals from two groups have close or intimate contacts. On a professional basis, such as in the Federation of Women's Clubs in the border town, there is more acceptance of Negroes. This finding supports the hypothesis that contact reduces prejudice when members of the interacting groups have similar socioeconomic statuses—a hypothesis that is further examined in the next section. Moreover, the presence of other Creoles in a community strengthens discrimination against the Negroes; a small number of Creoles do not seem to have the degree of avoidance of a colony. The costs of interaction are usually high when there are groups of fellow Creoles present with which one can associate in the traditional manner.

THE SOCIOECONOMIC SPECTRUM

The image which the Letoyant Creoles in the rural community have of Negroes approaches a stereotype. When Letoyants go out of the community to Southern City or other large urban communities where they come into contact with Negroes who are higher on a socioeconomic scale, their image of the Negro is altered. One Riverville woman said that when her daughter came back from Southern City she could not refrain from drawing parallels between the Negroes there and those in Riverville. After quoting her daughter, the woman commented about Riverville Negroes as follows: "The ones we have here are degenerate. They don't care about getting ahead, but spend everything they have. They don't care about their children, either—whether or not they are clothed or fed properly. They live for the day. On weekends they go to the honky-tonks, and when the places on the other side of the river close at midnight, they come over here to the other one. We meet them going home on Sunday morning when we are going to church. They take all the children with them. There are more children than adults in those places. If they would only enforce the law that children could not be in those places! I haven't anything against someone just because their skin is dark, but they are low-class people—degenerates." This observation lends support to the hypothesis that contact tends to reduce prejudice between groups with similar socioeconomic status but intensifies prejudice where statuses differ.

Riverville Negroes are also believed to be shiftless. On one occasion, a Negro passerby asked a landowner for some of the vegetables she was gathering. The housewife curtly refused the request, and when the man had passed out of earshot, she exclaimed, "The nerve of them tenants, walking up and down the road doing nothing while I'm hoeing the garden." She proceeded to give her opinion of the "good-for-nothin's" by adding, "They are too lazy to help themselves, and they wouldn't help you if you ask them to lend a hand, but they are bold enough to ask for a batch of mustards!" Another woman described the work habits of Riverville Negroes: "When they work, they hoe a little and then rest. One planter has an overseer who watches to see who is resting, and then he takes thirty-five cents an hour off that man's pay. They don't care how they do the work. When they are picking cotton, they get paid by the pound and they work harder.

Still they pick only the full bolls and skip the others, or they drop some and walk right over it. Sometimes they skips part of a row to catch up with someone they want to talk to." Again, this observation, made by a higher-class woman of lower-class persons, is supportive of the hypothesis on status, similarities, and differences.

Negroes are also said to be unclean and uncouth. Although cleanliness is not, strictly speaking, a social class phenomenon, lower-class people have comparatively few opportunities and facilities to promote cleanliness, especially in rural areas. One Riverville Letoyant used the term *nigger* in reference to the Negro who is not clean. She said after a "nigger" learned to take care of himself and dress properly and appeared neat and clean, he was no longer a "nigger" but raised himself to the status of "Negro." In this informant's opinion, a person may be in rags and patches, but he could be clean because to the white people dirtiness is repulsive, and they associate dirtiness with the Negro. Consequently, this mother stresses the paramount importance of cleanliness to her children. If they want to have an identity of which they can be proud, they have to be careful not to be dirty. Two other Creole women commented about an incident where they met someone who was dirty. When a new store was opened in Indianola, free doughnuts and coffee were being served, and two Letoyant friends decided to take advantage of the invitation. Later they remarked that there was "a big old stinking nigger woman in there who should have washed before she come in." In a tone of disgust, one woman announced, "I wouldn't sit beside those people, and I don't blame the whites who don't want to, either!" Her companion added, "They can't get rid of that smell they have!"

The "rough" behavior of the lower-class Negroes is also a topic for discussion among Creoles. "Even animals wouldn't live like that—fighting and clawing and cursing," declared one Letoyant woman. "I can't have that rough tough stuff!" she added. "Those low-down darkies even beat their women." Young couples who quarrel may be reminded by a parent that their behavior is undesirable. One boy's mother said, "I told him to stop it. They'll be popping each other next—just like the darkies!"

What is more, the Negroes are said to have low morals and "to change husbands and wives just like they do clothes!" Illegitimacy is just "one of those things." When one Negro woman expressed sympathy for another with the exclamation that "That poor lady has a baby nearly every year," the Letoyant woman responded, "As though *she* deserved sympathy."

Letoyants may occasionally take advantage of Negroes on the assumption that the latter, being in another social class, are not as discriminating in food or manner. A Creole recalled an incident when she had sent thirty-six chickens into town to be dressed, and her son was later asked to bring the birds home. She remarked on "how little time it took to get the chickens," but when she opened the packages, the chickens were already thawed out.

"We couldn't eat them," she said.

"Didn't you offer any complaint?" she was asked.

"No. They'd have said that the boy lingered on the way, because it was a very hot day."

"Thirty-six chickens were a big loss. What did you do about it?"

"Oh, I put them in the deep freeze, and when they were solid, I sold them to the tenants."

These generalizations are based primarily upon Letoyant attitudes toward the Riverville Negroes who are low on the socioeconomic scale since they are predominantly tenants or day hands.

There are, of course, Negroes in the South who enjoy a comparatively high status. In the Riverville area such Negroes are primarily teachers. Concerning them, one Creole expressed the opinion that they were fearful of "offending people and losing their jobs" and consequently they seldom acted as leaders. Although they are educated and in a financial position to exert leadership, in the informant's estimation, they appear to be interested in investing in new cars and other prestige symbols.

There is evidence, however, that even in Riverville some Letoyants, particularly in the upper social strata, identify in some measure with Negroes. In the living room of one home, there is an autographed picture of Joe Louis. Television programs featuring

Negro performers are very often given preference over other programs, and there is some expression of pride in the accomplishment of Negro entertainers and athletes. But the Negroes with whom Creoles profess to have more than a cursory acquaintance are those who have achieved status. Evidence in Riverville supports the hypothesis that prejudice is not reduced by contacts between divergent status groups.

## RELIGION

Although the church in Riverville appears to have a broader scope of influence than as a strictly religious institution, there are times when religious values are subservient to other values. Belonging to the Catholic Church gives status in the community, and the practicing Catholic who is active and belongs to church organizations tends to have high status. Logically, then, a Negro convert who is a practicing Catholic should automatically be eligible for church organizations and for participation in social events sponsored by church groups. But the Creoles are loath to associate with the Negroes at church fairs, dances in the school hall, gumbo suppers, and parties, in large part because of socio-economic differences and semicaste barriers.

Although the church records in Riverville attest that the Letoyants christened their slaves, there is no trace of a Negro burial in the Riverville cemetery. Sometime in the late nineteenth century the church in Riverville became known as a church for the Creoles. Letoyant reaction to Negroes in "their" church was sufficiently strong, even in the mid-twentieth century, for some of the Frenchmen to express their feelings. More than one person is reported to have said that he "wouldn't go to church or to school if they'd sent us black priests and nuns," and that he "ain't gonna confess his sins to no black man."

As noted previously, the Riverville clergy made an effort to follow the bishop's exhortations to encourage converts. Negroes who came to services in the Riverville church reported reactions of hostility from the Creoles. Two Negro converts who went to church services reported that there was "a swelling of resent-

ment" when they stepped inside the church door and that everyone stared at them. Another family who knelt in the rear pew said
that they encountered such unfriendly glances that they were
"frozen out." Still another Negro said that she was treated "like
dirt" when she went into that church. A Creole family, in the
Frenchman status category, explained the difficulty they had in
accepting Negroes in church: "Now we have a family down
here. This boy is grown and he is bold. He's going to instructions
to church. That's fine if it is for the religion and for instruction,
and we would all be glad if it is that. But we feel like it is to get
with *the people*. You see, his sister did the same thing. She became a Catholic, but she's living wrong. She's had children . . .
and she doesn't practice her religion. We just don't feel that they're
serious about their religion. Now they asked our cousins to be
godparents. They went to Father and told him they couldn't be
responsible for them. If they would be a  godparent, that's what
it meant. But she was already living this kind of life, and they
would rather not. Since she's baptized she has already had babies
and she's still going out. It didn't make any difference. She don't
live like a person who wants to be religious."

A Letoyant woman who became concerned over a Negro handyman during his last illness asked him before he died if he wanted
to be a Catholic. He reportedly said, "Whatever you think." The
woman said, "I thought he had lived as a Baptist all his life and
it would be better for him to be buried from that church." She
proceeded to interest a white Baptist preacher to preside at the
Negro's funeral. The reaction of her friends and relatives was that
she "must be crazy getting mixed up in the business of them
common people—and getting a *white* preacher when there's all
kinds of deacons here." According to the woman who arranged
for the funeral, she was subsequently asked by several other
Negroes to help arrange funerals for their old folks.

Religion is one of the key marks of differentation among
Creoles and Negroes. Letoyants would prefer to continue using
religious affiliation as an index of ethnic identity and would like to

have some assurance that a Negro convert is not using religious identification to enhance his social status.

## EDUCATION

Letoyant children who are learning their identity run the risk of becoming intimate with classmates who are not ethnic group members. This may be rewarding to Creole parents who have children going to school with whites; however, it is disturbing if the children are in school with Negroes because intimate contacts tend to reduce the barriers to interaction that parents have forbidden. Creole parents voice their resentment of their children's association with Negroes in the public schools. A Letoyant boy who was playing truant from school in Riverville was excused by his mother on the grounds that he "didn't like school since he had to be with those black faces. The blacks are too rough." Another couple, classified as Frenchmen, related that their son, who had been eating an ice-cream cone during recess, stopped to talk to a friend, and a "darky come along and took a bite—smarty like!"

Still other Creole parents recalled the following admonitions they had given to their daughters when they went to the Riverville public school: "Well, we always told them that they were not the same, but that they [the Negro children] are human. We want them to treat them nice—be nice to them. Don't get in anything with them. They go on trips. Now, they are with the teachers. They take care of them, but I don't trust them, so whenever they plan trips, she don't go out anymore. The principal said that they must go, but I said if he had a fifteen-year-old girl, he wouldn't let her go either, so I think the parents should see where their daughters are, where they are going, and who they are going with. My girl used to tell me all the time, 'Mother, you don't trust those people.' I say, 'No, let's not trust them. I trust you, but you don't know the things you ought.' "

Much of the opposition to the public school system is that Creole children must perforce associate not only with Negro children, but particularly with Negro teachers who have high status by virtue of their position in the school. In Riverville, few Creoles were initially prepared by education to be hired in the public school system. As they became better educated and more Creole teachers were added to the staff, Creoles who had formerly attempted to send their children away to boarding schools were placated.

A Creole interpreted the situation at the Riverville public school as follows, "The teachers who were not from here did not understand this place and they made remarks about our children and scolded them for being standoffish." He went on to say that Creole children who first went to the public school would naturally asssociate with one another because "anyone who goes into a strange situation, he usually looks around for some props." A Negro teacher observed that the "French people don't associate much with the Negroes. They all sit together in the classrooms and play together during gym periods. The teachers have to make them mix with the other students." A Negro student at the high school gave his impression of the interaction: "When those mulattoes first start to school, they all sit together on one side of the room. They don't say nothing to us, and we don't say nothing to them. Later on during the school year, when they see we are completely ignoring them, they come sneaking around trying to talk to one of us." Negroes also have the impression that the main reason some Creoles do not finish at the school is that they do not like the idea of a black person telling them what to do.

Another criticism of the public school concerns the type of materials children are forced to use. A Letoyant mother said, "If we could just have the nice books and things. The books over there are so old. They don't have any cover on them, and they're all to pieces. Our children have to use them. Now that's the only thing. We would like to have good books and teachers for our children. Other than that, as you know yourself, the people on the river doesn't mix too much one way or the other."

There is little indication of conflict among Creole and Negro faculty members in the Riverville public schools. On the contrary, a harmonious working relationship appears to be present among them. To a certain extent, this type of attitude is carried over into their personal relationships, but outside of the school setting the association tends to be on a superficial level. In public, the Creole teacher treats the Negro teacher as his colleague and can be found in friendly conversation with him. He will invite him to fund-raising dances or benefits sponsored by the Catholic church; however, the Negro teacher is rarely invited home for a social visit. Even when the Negro receives such an invitation, he is skeptical about accepting it and may refuse to go.

The strong feeling generated between Creoles and blacks in Riverville over the school situation is evident in an incident related by a Letoyant woman. "We always is to ourselves, the Creole people as they call us. No dark people at all—not one. When one tried to come to our school, we had someone to send them back. And they accepted going back, too. But now, these high schools, and these teachers; they just changed, you see. You know where my daddy got his education? In his mother's back yard. They had an old Frenchman from across the waters to come and live here, and educated those children right in the back yard."

The woman went on to relate a telephone conversation with an unidentified caller. The caller asked, "When your granddaughter finish there, do you intend sending her to the public school here?"

"I said, 'Well, I don't think so.'

'What's your reason?'

'I don't have to give you my reason.'

"She say, 'Well, since your granddaughter isn't going, I would like to know why.'

"I say, 'Well, since you insist, I will give you my reason. I'll tell you why. From now on, I intend for my family to continue their education in Catholic schools, because every one has been in Catholic schools so far, and myself, too.'

" 'Good!' she said. 'I like your talk fine.'

"I said, 'Well, I hope so.' "

The incident reveals the resentment on the part of some of the Negro people toward the Letoyants because of the isolation of the children whose parents can afford to send them away to school.

Creole parents admit they would prefer to send their children away. The wife of a day hand said, "If I was able to send my children off to school, I wouldn't send them here. But it's better than nothing, so I send them here." She continued, "Once they go to this Catholic high school, they grow up there. They're around fourteen years old when they get out of that grade school. And they've learned so much—how to be nice and how to be good. They very seldom goes wrong even if they do mix with the Baptists and others, you know—people not like the Catholic."

Children who have not completed high school are impressionable and have been socialized as Creoles. Then in high school, they must accord status to Negro teachers, and they are obliged to interact as peers with lower-class students who allegedly have different behavioral norms. Therefore, in the opinion of many Letoyant parents, the rewards of educational attainment are hardly worth the cost outcome of a public school education.

RECREATION

Recreation, like the school, is an area of interaction that promotes intimacy and often generates strong intergroup feelings, particularly on the part of Letoyants who are attempting to maintain status, and who deplore Riverville's limited recreational facilities. One informant said, "If you goes to the recreation center the lower classes have fights and shoot at each other." She went on to comment that Riverville had no good movies, no decent dance hall, and all that the people could do was to have an occasional ball game or a visit. Although Riverville has several places that are called recreation centers, only two are frequented. They are private commercial ventures each consisting of frame structures with storage space and one large room where crowds can gather to dance, enjoy hard and soft drinks with snacks, and occasionally view a movie. Although both halls are operated by Letoyants, one restricts clientele, while the other is less exclusive. The upper social classes go to these places, as a rule, only when they have reserved them for some special occasion.

An upper-class Creole woman noted, "Just any and everybody

goes to those places, and there is fighting and kicking. I wouldn't want to earn my living like that. Of course, people *are* going to spend their money that a way, and somebody might as well get it." (As the Negroes view this situation, the Creoles would like to profit financially from recreation enterprises, but they are reluctant to mix socially with the Negroes.)

Creole reluctance to associate with Negroes informally at recreation centers is also evident when the Negroes wish to patronize the Riverville church fair. Whatever financial contribution the Negroes might make is considered offset by their intermingling at games or at the meal. A white resident of Riverville, who lived on a plantation that had predominantly Negro tenants, tested the Creole reaction to the Negroes by inviting two Negro boys, whom he chanced to meet, to accompany him to the fair. The boys hesitated, but their host reassured them by telling them that they were his guests. When they reached the fairground, the white man was welcomed and led to a table. He had to remind the Creole women who met him that there were two boys with him. After some consultation, the women placed the three of them at a large table that was nearly vacated, and they seated no one else at this table, even though the other tables were filled.

Pressure was put on the owner of one recreation place called Frenchie's to admit Negroes after the NAACP became active in Riverville. An old-family representative remarked that the NAACP "sent all kinds of darkies down here to try to get into the hall. It was some commotion." There were "darkies from Riverton, Centerville, Indianola, and every other place. We *never* had that many darkies here before!" The NAACP "put them up to it." Then three of the Letoyant plantation owners who "were in cahoots" with the NAACP "came and took Joe over to the lodge and told him he'd have to sign some papers that the place was open to everyone or else he'd have to make it a private club." Joe preferred the latter; the sign Private Club is tacked outside, and a framed charter or license hangs on the inside wall. "We don't want to get mixed with the NAACP any more," concluded the informant. Other small landowners sympathized with Joe. "He had a lot of trouble," said one landowner, "and feeling was high over it."

Creole parents, like other American parents, are especially protective of their daughters. Since a proportionately larger number of girls than boys marry outside the ethnic group, parental concern has some basis in fact. A Negro visitor who spent several weeks in Riverville commented that she had never seen a Creole girl or woman at a recreation facility frequented by Negroes; however, on some occasions the Creole males did recreate with the Negroes. Creole parents who have girls of high school age are particularly sensitive to their interaction with Negro male teachers. No doubt parents are fearful that the teachers who enjoy status by virtue of their position will unfairly use informal excursions or recreation to decrease the social distance between Creoles and themselves.

USE OF SANCTIONS AGAINST CREOLE DEVIANTS

Letoyants who marry Negroes tend to have difficulties. The Frenchmen refer to them and their children very much as if they were "has-beens." Reacceptance by the ethnic group is not simple. In the urban environment, ostracism is not nearly as likely as in the rural environment; however, out-group marriage does have the effect of impairing close family bonds. A Riverville couple who were asked about some of their nieces and nephews who had moved away and married outsiders answered simply: "We never hear from them. They married into the *munde couleur* [world of color]." The couple went on to express indignation at the way "people are ruining themselves."

Another rural Letoyant couple said, concerning one woman who had married a Negro, "Well, she was raised over there on that plantation among those people, and her parents weren't educated, and they felt they had to let them girls take up with these people and play with their children. Of course, they could have sent them to their friends or their people where they could go to Catholic schools. They didn't *have* to do that."

A Creole male who left his first wife and began to cohabit with a Negro woman by whom he had several children was completely ostracized by the Riverville Creoles. These children are considered Negroes rather than Creoles. One of them took instruction in the Catholic faith, but, like other Negro converts, she was not warmly welcomed by the Creoles.

Another family expressed their impression of the consequence of out-group marriages to Negroes as follows: "Once the Negroes have a French girl, they mistreats them terribly. They beat them. They give them fine clothes and cars, and everything they want that a way, but they are not allowed to go out with their own people or to look at anyone else. They will just kill her if they attempt to be out with anyone else or their own people. They were always taught that, and as the days go on, I can see it. I know that. So many have told me that same thing. That's the way they treat them."

In urban areas remote from Riverville, where the semicaste barriers between Creoles and Negroes are not pronounced, Creoles who contract out-group unions can cultivate friends and associates among Negroes. But such unions in the area of Riverville may lead to ostracism and rejection by the ethnic group. This penalty is, in itself, a forceful lesson for young Creoles undergoing the process of socialization.

### Blacks' Perspectives of Creoles

What the Negro thinks of the Letoyant Creole is, in large part, a reaction to the esteem or disesteem that the Creole has for the Negro. If Creoles tend to esteem Negroes, Negroes will, in turn, be disposed to have favorable opinions about Creoles. But if Creoles generally hold Negroes in disesteem there is a strong likelihood that the Negro's perspectives of Creoles will have strong negative overtones.

Negroes are not, of course, all in the same social class, and among Negroes there are varying attitudes toward each other on the basis of class distinctions. Thus, the classic study of the American Negro by Gunnar Myrdal, reported in 1944, revealed that Negro upper social classes were characterized by many traits that were in complete contrast to those of the masses of lower-class Negroes; moreover, the upper classes strove to retain their distinctiveness. In fact, the upper classes were often the most severe critics of their people, and their criticisms of the lower social classes approximated the commonplace Negro stereotype.[7] These Negro upper classes, who have been disproportionately composed of the same kind of racial admixture that is found among the Letoyants, behave toward the lower classes in much the same way as the Creole acts toward the Negro.

## NAME CALLING

Because of distinctive Creole racial characteristics, as well as intergroup attitudes, Negroes call the Creoles by such names as *Creole, Frenchie, Frenchman, yellow,* and *mulatto.* The last two names are regarded by the Letoyants as deprecatory. An old Negro man attempted to explain the rationale behind the use of this terminology: "I want to tell you something about this mulatto race here—between the colored and white. Now I won't speak of it in any bad way, daughter. It was the white man, and the colored woman; that's the beginning of those mulattoes. I could explain it to you more plainer, but I'm kind of ashamed. Well, I'll tell you. You take the male breed of something—fowl or hogs, or horses that way—and take the female breed, the same breed. . . ." The implications were the Creoles were not a pure race but sprang from an illegitimate union.

A similar reaction was expressed by a Negro woman who was annoyed by a Creole man working in the same house with her because, she said, he was "putting on airs." In a disdainful tone the man said to the Negro woman, "Why in the world don't you go back to Africa where you came from?" The Negro woman quickly rejoined, "You're so right. I done got Africa, that's where I come from. But you? You ain't got no place to go back to." Another old Negro man said, "There *are* few of them that realize and put themselves on the same quality—with me. But they're very few of them. The rest of them, why, they'll try to class up with the whites." A Negro woman married to a Creole man expressed

[7] Gunnar Myrdal, *An American Dilemma* (New York: Harper, 1944), 703.

similar attitudes when she commented, "You know, those people over there on the other side of the river think they are better than the other people. They don't call themselves colored—they say they are Creoles. Well, I've had one for thirty-six years and he isn't any different than any other man." All of these remarks reflect the Negroes' resentment of the status aspirations of the Creoles.

In southern urban communities, Creoles are called by additional names. Thus, in one city they are called *giches*. When a Creole from this community was questioned about the meaning of the term, she said, "I don't know exactly what it means, but we know who they're talking about when they say it. It's just the bright ones who have what they call good hair. They call you a giche and they call you Frenchmen. But you know, some of the people from the river hated to be called Frenchmen. Now they say they're just French—that they have French blood. They used to call themselves Frenchmen. I mean if you went up to them and asked them about it—like if they get mistaken for Italian or something like that—say, 'Well, what are you?' They'd say. 'I'm a Frenchman,' instead of saying just plain Negro. But they don't like this giche thing, and I don't either, but they take it. I mean they can't do anything about it, because that's what the people call them."

Negroes, then, give vent to their hostility toward the Letoyants from time to time. They particularly resent the efforts of the Creole to maintain social distance, and they speak disparagingly of Creole status aspirations. Since Letoyant Creoles, at least those in the vicinity of Riverville, are not amenable to changing their attitudes toward the Negro and a status differential does exist, interaction between the two groups has not reduced prejudice. On the contrary, interaction tends to generate increased hostility and resentment.

COGNIZANCE OF LETOYANT CREOLE ATTITUDES TOWARD BLACKS

Negroes sometimes express bitterness about the behavior of some Letoyants toward them. One small landholder who was hired to chop cotton noticed that there was a sign outside the

Creole employer's house in large letters, NO NIGGERS ALLOWED. Another Negro informant said that he knew friends who could not sit at the same table with the Creoles with whom they worked. They had to sit on the back steps or in the garage, and the Creoles "handed out food to them like they were dogs." The Negroes felt that if the Creoles did not want to eat with them, they could at least sit at a table by themselves, and the Creoles could eat either later or first. With strong feelings another Negro said, "I would rather eat beans with a stick than work for them tallow-faced s.o.b.'s." And still another Negro said, "You are all right as long as you are in the field working with them, but otherwise they treat you like dirt."

Negroes are particularly resentful of the Letoyant attitude towards Creoles who intermarry with them. A Negro woman married to a Letoyant male said that her husband's brothers and sisters do not claim him any more. They did not tell him about his mother's death, and she was buried five days before he found out about it. At the time of the mother's funeral, one of the brothers asked, "Does my brother still have that black woman?" When he received an affirmative response, he said, "Well, he doesn't need to be with us." The wife said the only time her husband's people had been to her house was when they came to get him to sign some papers to sell some property. Another Negro commented, "Creoles think they are so much until one of their girls marry a Negro and then they act like they don't even know her."

Negroes are also sensitive to their virtual exclusion from the Catholic Church in the vicinity of Riverville, and the number of converts to Catholicism has been negligible. A priest who had been in Riverville for a long time said he was called to the bedside of a very old Negro man. The dying man said he had never really given up his Catholicity. He had been given the "cold shoulder" at church and his self-respect as well as the indignation of his wife and children caused him to go to the Baptist church. His children and grandchildren were Baptists, but he still retained his allegiance towards Catholicism, and he wished to receive the last rites of the Church.

Segregation at the recreation place known as Frenchie's is another source of friction between the Negroes and Creoles in Riverville. The informant, an old Negro man, said, "Some of the bright people don't like to associate with the dark people. We have this private place that the owner didn't want the dark people to go to, but he has found out that he is just losing money by letting the bright people go there, and he decided he'd let the dark people go there, too. Well, one night we went over to a fair in the school yard and Joe said he'd let all us dark people, you know, go to this place, if we cared to go. And he didn't want at first all the people to mix. I told him that I was not going because I know he didn't appreciate us over there. And Joe's nephew had three other men with him and they were darker than him and they bought up a lot of whiskey and drank. After Joe thought they had spent all their money, he told the nephew that he'd have to take those black boys out of his place. So the nephew gave him a cussing out and left. Haven't been back since. I saw his nephew about two weeks ago, and asked him had he been back there. He said that he wasn't going back. And if his nephew—he'd treat him like that—I know how he would treat me."

Negroes sometimes disavow any important differences between themselves and Creoles. A Negro informant said, "Why do those Frenchmen think they are so important? White folks treat them the same as they do all Negroes." Yet, in the forms of polite address used in the vicinity of Riverville, Negroes show deference to Creoles. In addressing or referring to a dark Negro, they say, "Joe Doe." For a Creole they say, "Mr. Doe," and for a white they say "Mr. Joe." (The Creoles themselves say "Mr. Joe" to refer to fellow Creoles who have status within the group.)

REACTION TOWARD CREOLES

Despite expressed hostility and resentment, Negroes recognize that some Creoles treat them with respect and friendliness. Concerning this differential behavior, a Negro woman said, "Some of them have something to say. You know, kind of behind your back. They don't tell you anything to your face. But *some* of them acts friendly towards you." Negroes give evidence of their ambivalent attitudes in their behavior toward Creoles. Thus, when Negroes are serving as waiters or as cooks to both Creoles and fellow Negroes, they have been observed to show special courtesy toward Creoles. One informant noted, "Service is prompt and the interaction is comparable to the Negro-white relationships in the South. In these situations, the Negro takes the initiative by asking, 'What can I do for you, sir?' and 'Will there be anything else for you, sir?' Regardless of age, this pattern seems to be prevalent."

In Riverville, where the cleavage between Negroes and Letoyants is most pronounced, Negroes emulate Creole behavior in their attitudes toward those who become converts to Catholicism; converts are often regarded as having overstepped the group's boundary. Conflict within the group becomes most pronounced if the convert attempts to take on some of the Creole's attitudes toward his fellow Negroes. The only persons with whom he can share social activities are fellow Negroes, yet he is seldom found engaged in friendly conversation with them. Creole Catholics do not accept him as a social equal, and he therefore becomes something of a marginal person—a member neither of the Creole group nor of his own Negro group.

Despite the rejection, however, Negro imitation of the Creole extends to the area of religion. One of the Baptist churches in the Riverville vicinity is named after Grand Pere's patron saint.[8] Moreover, the Riverville Negro is, at times, critical of his own people because they are not regular in their church attendance. One educated Negro commented: "If the Baptist church had a white man like the Catholic church to tell him to come to church, he would come. The priest only has to tell his people one time to come to church and they come every Sunday. But the poor colored minister begs and begs and only a few people come each Sunday."

[8] It is interesting to note that one Baptist church, like the white cathedral in Indianola, is called St. Mary's, since Baptists ordinarily do not venerate the Virgin Mary as a patroness. The naming of the church seems to indicate a status-conscious emulation of whites as well as of Creoles.

The most obvious indication that the Negro emulates the Creoles is the occasional claim of a very dark Negro to being a Creole. One woman with pronounced Negroid features, who was asked some questions by a Negro social worker, replied, "I don't understand American talk too well because I am Creole." The Negroes, at times, also claim to be descendants of the Letoyants and talk about the great material prosperity in their early history. Yet, these same people recall with some degree of satisfaction the Creole's loss of land. One Negro remarked on this situation as follows: "While the colored people were admiring their blue eyes and straight hair, the white man took their land. And some of them are working for the white man for only a few pennies a day!" This informant, who had classified herself as a Creole, commented further, "I don't think I'm any better than the people across the river. Those mulattoes aren't any good, but I feel sorry for them because they don't have a color or a race. They're neither black or white. They don't want to say they're black, and the white people won't let them say they're white."

Negroes, like the Creoles, give verbal approval to the value of an education; however, they are less educated than the Creoles. When talking to a well-educated Negro woman, one of the Riverville Negroes said, "I don't have as much education as you, but I can hold you in conversation." The educated woman had the impression that this comment reflected envy and was an attempt to rationalize. If education were truly valued, the informant believed, Negroes would have taken more advantage of the educational opportunities available to them.

If, as the Negroes observed, the Creoles "ape the ways of the whites," the Negroes also "ape the ways of the Creoles." In the struggle for status, it is not uncommon to aspire to the nearest attainable level and to envy those who have attained a higher status. Such aspirations and experiences do affect the image one group holds of the other.

Toward the Creole, then, the Negro has mixed feelings both of envy and of emulation. The Negro uses derogatory names and expresses hostility toward the Creole. On the other hand, when

face to face with Creoles, Negroes often take a subservient attitude
and behave as though they were in the presence of their superiors.
In urban communities where the Negro population has proportionately more educated and professional people than in rural
areas, the attitudes are markedly different. But Indianola has very
few Negroes who can be classified as upper-class, and within the
vicinity of Riverville and Indianola the attitudes and images just
described prevail. Letoyant Creoles from Riverville take their
attitudes with them wherever they migrate, and they probably
generate negative images in the Negroes with whom they come
into contact, at least until such time as they become exposed to
Negroes who enjoy a higher class status than those in Riverville.
Repeated contact of Creoles with Riverville, however, does
much to reinforce the attitudes which currently prevail there and
to perpetuate them among the Creoles who migrate to other communities. Therefore, the image which Negroes have of Letoyant
Creoles throughout the South is probably contingent upon the
behavior of the Creoles towards them, and the Negroes' behavior
toward the Creoles is, in turn, based upon the attitudes just
described.

## Conclusions

Letoyant-Negro relations involve a number of variables. They
have to be interpreted in the light of the semicaste structure of
the Riverville area where there are in reality caste barriers between the Negro and the Creole just as there are between the
Creole and the white. These barriers are not easy to overcome
in the efforts of each group to attain a higher status, and there is
a strong tendency to emulate the group with a higher status despite the obstacles to attaining that status.

Even in Riverville, where the "official Letoyant Creole attitude"
originated, there are variations in attitudes toward Negroes. Plantation owners, particularly if they have Negro tenants, have a
different perspective from the Frenchmen, who pride themselves
on maintaining tradition, probably because place of residence in

Riverville also makes a difference. In some sections of the community, where all the property is owned by small farmers and where there are no Negro residents, traditional attitudes are much stronger than on large plantations. Po' folks who live on a large white-owned plantation and work with Negroes are much more tolerant and accepting than those who work on plantations where no Negroes reside or are employed. The Frenchmen, who are extremely conscious of caste distinction, are quick to note inconsistencies between the actions of the Letoyant planters and what the "big fellows" say. For instance, a Frenchman commented that "there's only one dark fellow that can go into Joe's house, and he goes to the back door!" It could be, of course, that the planter's wife had a voice in saying who would enter the house through the front door. Moreover, the purpose of the Negro's entry into the planter's house is undoubtedly to perform some type of chore rather than to pay a social visit. "Little fellows" are much less likely than "big fellows" to employ Negroes to perform chores in their homes.

The planters initially supported the NAACP and supplied leadership locally until the disturbance at the recreation center. At a political rally, all Rivervillers, regardless of color, were invited to a lodge and everyone stood in line to be served. There was no evidence of any order of precedence or of a color line.[9] It was at the lodge that the proprietor of Frenchie's was "put on the carpet" by the planters for not admitting blacks. Until the revolt of the Frenchman over the latter incident, the planters had supported every NAACP project.

Whatever social contacts exist between Negroes and Letoyants are made predominantly by the men. Frequently, Letoyant men attend dances and other social activities with Negroes. Moreover, in the vicinity of Riverville, there has been a higher incidence of Creole males marrying Negro women than Creole women marry-

---

[9] In this instance, the planters acted in the capacity of "volunteer Negroes," that is, they identified with the blacks in assuming leadership roles. None of Riverville's Creoles, however, could be classified as a race leader, in the strict sense of the term.

ing Negro men, a pattern that is reversed in urban places, particularly outside the South.

All of the hypotheses on intergroup interaction and contact were
supported by the findings. Differences in social status between
Negroes and Creoles contribute to the continuance of prejudice,
especially in the Creole. Creoles are not susceptible to change, at
least in the rural environment, and where contact does occur it
tends to reinforce prejudice. Intimate contacts that might reduce
prejudice are avoided in recreation and to some extent in the
public school. Moreover, the rewards for group interaction and
for lessening prejudice are not commensurate with the penalties
associated with loss of separate identity and of social status.

# Chapter 11

# Southern Creole Image Projected to Whites by Letoyants

The self-identity of Letoyant Creoles in the South is related to their image among whites as well as among Negroes. The whites' image, in turn, is contingent upon the manner in which Creoles view them and the relationships between the two populations. All the variables mentioned in Creole-Negro relations, namely, social class, age, and rural-urban residence, are also operative in Creole-white relations.

The Caucasian image of the Letoyant is further related to historical experiences. In a history-conscious environment where plantation homes have been preserved and where a first-generation Letoyant plantation is included in the pilgrimages to places of interest in the area, knowledgeable whites cannot feign ignorance of Letoyant history. As a Creole who was being registered to vote said, "The whites knowed the difference between Creoles and Negroes because we never was slaves. The whites knew we had voted before, but had just stopped, but the blacks had never voted; they had been slaves." And he continued, "We were always property owners and paid taxes, but not the darkies; slaves never owned nothing!" Educated and knowledgeable whites in Indianola also know the origin of the Creoles.

The same hypotheses regarding Creole-Negro intergroup relations are tested here in regard to Creole-white relations; however, the Creole occupies the lower social status in reference to the dominant white population, and Creole emphasis is, as a consequence, just the opposite of what it is in regard to the Negro. Like the Creole attitudes toward the Negro, the white attitudes toward the Creole are not readily susceptible to change; therefore, it is hypothesized that whites will become more prejudiced after an interaction experience than they were at the outset. Since

227

intimate contacts tend to reduce prejudice, the Creoles will endeavor to promote such contacts while the whites will be opposed to them. Interaction of upper-class Creoles with economically secure whites will tend to reduce prejudice, but interaction of lower-class Creoles with whites, nearly all of whom feel that they enjoy more status than the Creoles, will intensify prejudice. Creole-white interaction, finally, will be weighed in terms of the rewards received by the respective individuals and groups as well as by the costs they incur, and the resulting relationships will produce at least minimally satisfactory reward-cost outcomes.

### CREOLE CONCERN FOR WHITE IMAGE

In their relationships with the whites, the Creoles are concerned about how they are regarded by those above them in the social status hierarchy, and they act quite differently than they do toward the Negro. Instead of maintaining or increasing social distance, Creoles view it as desirable to bridge the semicaste barriers that set them apart from the dominant white population representing power and prestige.

There are certain things which Creoles never share with outsiders, particularly with whites. In an effort to project a favorable self-image to the dominant population, they attempt to conceal the deviants who are perpetual law breakers and the unmannered who are categorized as "no count," as well as those who are simply indifferent or nonperceptive about social relations. In the latter category, a Letoyant woman who was spreading tales about how a fire was started in a house on the river was censured by her friends and relatives. One relative said, "No one out here is going to set a house afire. She said that house was set afire to warm the cats. Even though it had happened, you don't go down there telling that to those white people. Even though it is true, and I don't believe it is. Even if she *knew* that, oh, you don't say it. She oughtn't to start something like that. And she shouldn't have told it to those kind of people." Embarrassment in the presence of whites is also quite painful because the situation is publicized outside the ethnic population and particularly to the dominant group. The Creole woman who was harassed about her intentions regarding the public school in Riverville (see p. 213) regretted the presence of a white man at the time of the call. She said, "The white man was sitting right here, drinking his coffee. He wasn't hearing what she was saying, but he was understanding according to my answers."

One of the chief concerns of the Letoyant Creoles is the image their white acquaintances have of them; however, they are not insensitive to their image among other whites who have little, if any, firsthand acquaintance with them. The latter concern stems, in part, from the image disseminated by a novel about the Creoles written by a well-known Louisiana author who resided in Riverville at the time he was writing the novel. Creoles believe the novel projects a highly unfavorable image because of the chief character's ambition to have her illegitimate son (fathered by a white man with whom she had very little acquaintance) pass into the white population.

Caucasian strangers to Riverville tend to conjecture about the Letoyants. A discharged veteran of World War II, for instance, who had read the novel, visited Riverville and got into a conversation with a Creole couple outside the church. The incident was related by the husband in the following words: "It happened that we were going to church on Friday evening and a young man stopped and talked with us. He'd just come out of the service from up North, and he had some business here. He always heard of this place, and he wanted to come out here and see for himself. He wanted to ask some questions, and then he was telling me what he had heard and everything.

"I told him, 'Well, I don't know,' I says, 'but it's just like I tell you what I know of it.' And I say, 'What you've seen since you've been stopped here?' Because all the different people were passing, going to church.

"I said, 'Oh, yeah, the people going to the Stations of the Cross.'

"He say, 'Well, they all with white nuns.'

"I said, 'Yes, and our pastor is white,'

" 'Well, then?' he said.

"I said, 'Well, I guess you heard that story long years ago. You going to be surprised to read that book!'

"He said, 'That old book didn't tell the truth. That's why I wanted to come here myself, just to see.'

"I said, 'Well, they are called a Negro.' I don't know what I said. 'But I don't consider myself one of them,' I said, 'because my grandparents were not that. They had these people to work for them. They had slaves. And they had those people to sell them. They'd sell them like they sell cattle. They would buy them . . . my grandmother's mother and father. But when they set them free, the other people left. They wouldn't stay with them.'

"He say, 'No, you all are not Negro. You all are white,' he said. 'But he has that in his book, and that's why his old book didn't sell. He even changed the name on it. Gave it another *big* name to see if it wouldn't sell, and it still didn't sell.' He said, 'When I passed here, I said to myself that I'm so glad this book didn't sell, because he didn't tell the truth.' Then he said, 'Well, when the troops came by, none of the girls didn't marry them?'

"I says, 'No.'

"He says, 'Why not?'

" 'Because they wouldn't have it.'

"He says, 'What do you mean?'

"I says, 'They just wouldn't have it. They couldn't walk to town and draw a license to marry one of those boys. They wouldn't have it.' "

This incident reflects Letoyant Creole sensitivity to their public image. They emphasized to the stranger that they would not have marital relations with whites without benefit of clergy and that they were a religious people who adhered to church norms. If they are to be confused with either whites or blacks, they prefer the former.

Apart from strangers, there are basically three categories of whites about whom the Creoles express concern: the few whites who reside in Riverville or who live close to them and know them;

the lower-class poor whites who live in the hill country near Riverville; and the whites in towns and cities who represent varying statuses and who have varying degrees of acquaintance with them. Each of these categories is treated more at length in the discussion of white perspectives of the Letoyants.

Although the semicaste system in the South has limited conflict between Creoles and whites, it has also limited opportunities for sympathetic contact and firsthand acquaintance between them. Creoles are especially conscious of this lack of interaction and communication, and like many southern middle- and upper-class Negroes[1] would like the whites who are in positions of dominance and who are relatively unacquainted with them as persons to learn that there are refined, educated Letoyants.

Letoyant Creole attitudes toward whites are expressed in broad generalizations as well as in specifics. These attitudes need to be viewed in the light of the experiences of the Creole informants and those of the whites to whom they are referring. Although the broad generalizations reflect general attitudes, Creole reactions to specific incidents afford special insights into Creole-white relations.

## LETOYANT CREOLE PERSPECTIVES OF HOW WHITES VIEW THEM

Some history-conscious Creoles from old families express resentment against all Caucasians who do not accord them their rightful status. For the most part, these Creoles are in the non-affluent middle classes. One woman voiced the attitudes of the Frenchmen as follows: "As far as the American white man is concerned, if your skin isn't white, you're not supposed to have nothing. Don't be a Mexican, don't be anything. They should have their foot on your neck! That's their belief. They have that from England. It's down deep. I guess they can't help themselves. But they couldn't see that. Now, these people always wanted this

[1] Cf. John Dollard, *Caste and Class in a Southern Town* (New Haven: Yale University Press, 1937), 73.

land. They wanted everything we had. Americans were foreigners to us, you know. Well, anyway, Louis was very good about loaning people money, and so forth and so on. I don't know if it was a plot. I don't know what happened, but the Americans wanted that land. Bad! So he borrowed. Louis give his name and he stood for the man. The man couldn't pay; they grabbed his property. And that's how we lost that big place there."

The transfer of Louis Letoyant's plantation, Whitefield, to white owners, occasioned many comments about Creole attitudes toward the white planters. A Creole planter's wife expressed chagrin that Mr. White had been able to induce one of her relatives to sell his share of the homestead, which the family subsequently tried to repurchase. "We've been trying to buy that land, but Mr. White won't sell it," protested the informant. The narrow strip in question did divide a Creole planter's holdings, but, what was much more significant, it represented a loss of land to the whites.

Other prosperous Creoles also voiced resentment against Mr. White and family. Miss Marie White, who noticed Grand Pere's portrait unframed and disintegrating in one of the Creole homes, had the portrait restored and displayed on White's plantation. During the centenary celebration of the Riverville Catholic Church, the portrait was on exhibition in the school hall. After the celebration, however, when the portrait had been taken back to the White plantation, some out-of-town Creoles asked to see it. This circumstance caused a Letoyant landholder to voice her opinion as follows: "Those were Grand Pere's people, and they wanted to see that picture. It belongs to them. They left it in the house when they moved and that Miss Marie what wasn't even a Catholic come and got it. They used to have all those old treasures themselves, but when Miss Marie come around, they just gave her anything!"

Another landholder expressed hostility over the inclusion of the plantation homes of whites in the centenary publication. "That's supposed to be our centenary, not those white folks," protested the woman. "Why didn't Father put in the pictures of *our* homes?"

She went on to complain: "Them rich white folks can't even support a priest; we supports them!" The last remark referred to the housing in Riverville of the priest who is in charge of the mission chapels attached to the Riverville parish church.

Riverville Creoles are particularly sensitive to the behavior of local whites in the presence of other whites. When large numbers of white people visit Riverville and attend the annual church fair, the Creoles say that the wives of the local white planters are not as likely to recognize them as they are at other times. One Creole woman said, "There is a distinct coolness on the part of the whites at such times. They are afraid of being labeled 'nigger lovers.'"

Some persons of old-family stock profess not to bear any ill feelings toward the whites today or even toward their ancestors who dispossessed them of their lands. In referring to a deceased white planter, a woman remarked: "He was a good businessman and when people couldn't pay their debts, he got their land; he had a right to it!" Another Creole expressed similar attitudes; however, since this investigator's association with this informant was a very brief one, he may have been saying what he thought a white person would expect to hear. At any rate, he voiced the type of reaction which the white people believe most Creoles have. He said: "I believe as long as the colored people stay in their place, I believe they'll make it."

The ambivalence of Creole attitudes is revealed in their comments about the future of their children. A Creole father remarked that the young white people in the South are "generally idealistic," but when they marry and start to raise a family, "they get just like their parents." One father said that the white child must make the overtures if he wishes to play with Creole children and make friends with them. Creole children are taught to be very cautious and not to make the first friendly gesture. A playing relationship tends to generate intimacy, particularly among children, and subsequently to reduce prejudice; therefore, the white child, who in this instance is the more prejudiced, must be willing to make the first overtures. Any intimacy and subsequent prejudice reduction generated by play relationships are jeopardized when the white person becomes a parent—that is, one who is expected to transmit southern folkways to the next generation.

One Creole woman thought that most white people do not make distinctions based on the social class level of the Creole children. She was hopeful that the democratic principle of esteeming a person for his own sake might be found in the desegregated school. Since she had few socioeconomic resources, she may have been overplaying the democratic principle and relying too much upon the white's lack of discernment of Creole in-group status. She expressed herself as follows: "White people who accept colored people—accept all colored people. They don't just distinguish between those what has and those what hasn't. If my children goes to the white schools in town rather than to the school out here with the blacks, they will be accepted by the white folk for what they are worth rather than for their social class figure and the position their families have."

BUSINESS AND THE PROFESSIONS

In Riverville, the Creoles have varied reactions to the white resident planters. There is more criticism of one white planter, whose property adjoins that of many small Creole farmers, than of other planters. One common impression is that he is intent upon enlarging his plantation at the expense of the Creoles. Some Creoles believe that older landholders who are "not all right in the head" either borrow from this white planter or let him pay their taxes—which he does in an effort to eventually acquire the land. Once when there was a dispute over the ownership of a strip of land, the white man summoned the Creole contender to court annually, contesting his claim. Since the white planter paid a lawyer a retainer fee, it was not prohibitive for him to continue bringing up the case, but the Creole landholder, who had to hire a lawyer, eventually paid out more in legal fees than the land was worth and gave up his claim. Efforts of the Creole's descendants to regain this land have been fruitless.

The cleavage between Creoles and whites regardless of economic status was evident when a white planter insinuated that the Creole planters might take undue advantage of a chance to violate rules and to use grain provided by the federal government for fodder to fatten cattle for the market. A Creole planter responded that he had more grain than usual and suggested, "Let the little fellows have it." The white planter answered, "The little fellows can take care of themselves. You go ahead and take the chance to make some money." This suggestion was taken as an insult by the Frenchman, who said, "Mr. White might as well have spat in my face. He's trying to get a stick to hold over the heads of the leaders so he can tell them how to vote. They're riding for a fall, and the only way to save the situation is for the independent little farmer not to get committed!" This episode indicates the basic distrust Creoles have of the whites, particularly those in positions of power.

Another issue that causes contention between the Creole and white landholders is the question of cotton acreage. For many years, the cotton allotment was established, and anyone who planted more acreage than he was allowed was ordered to plow under the excess planting. One Creole who had this experience said that the men from the Indianola office "wink at the big landowners who measure their allotment generously, but the little fellow has to have the exact measurement or the man from town makes him plow the excess under." A Creole landholder who had a large holding was told that he had planted three acres in excess. He did not take the man's word for it but went into Indianola to speak to the men in the offices. When he explained his predicament, he was told, "Just leave it for this year. You'll have a slight increase in acreage next year and then it will be just right." This Creole got the impression that if one were in disfavor with the people in power, one would have to plow up the cotton, but if one voted according to their wishes, they would give one a break. His reaction was, "I don't owe anything to any man, and I don't make any promises how I am going to vote. When people do you favors, you make promises how you are going to vote, and they can tell how you voted even with those machines because you have numbers." This was another incidence of a relatively large landholder who distrusted the white power structure and who did not want to accept favors from the whites in power lest he be obligated to play politics with them.

Even in Riverville among people who have large landholdings, the issue of racial equality enters into the commonplace. One man who had property adjoining a white plantation said that the white man's cows kept coming through his pasture and tearing down his fence. When the Creole reported this incident to the white planter, he was told that the cattle would be moved to another pasture if the incident happened again. The Creole responded, "I may not have fixed the fence very well," a remark indicative of his deference in a conflict situation. The Creole landowner went on to say, however, that if his cows broke a fence and went into the white man's pasture, he would have to make the overture and inform the white man immediately what had happened, whereas, when the situation was reversed, the burden of seeking relief was his responsibility.

The small landholder who has difficulty in maintaining a steady cash income is particularly sensitive to the power of the Caucasians in the vicinity. One "little fellow" said, "We might be able to find work to do in town, but the big chiefs want to keep us in our places." He went on to explain that a white planter and farmer, with large landholdings, "sells his mustards in town, but they won't buy mine, and he pays eight or nine dollars a day to the fellows that pick them for the market." In recent years, the Creoles have gotten a fair market price for their cotton, but according to some of the older farmers, "there was a time when we got a lower price than the white plantation owner."

Until the fall of 1954 the local committeemen who carried responsibility for much of the farm program were white men. By order of the federal government, however, restrictions were at this time placed upon the reelection of the same committeemen. Consequently, two Creole men were selected at an open meeting. News of the outcome of the meeting was brought home by one man who was obviously delighted with the choice of two fellow

Letoyants and proceeded to elaborate on their qualifications. Since 1954 the Creoles have profited in many respects by the efforts of the federal government to equalize opportunities in the deep South.

The Creole who works for the white planter often gives a much more favorable picture of social relationships than the one who is a fellow landholder. A Creole renter had very positive attitudes toward his white landlord; he related that he "brings the truck home in the evening and takes it back in the morning. No rent is paid for the house, and there's a big yard to raise chickens and ducks. There is garden space for a patch of corn, and they pays for the salary." Concerning the same white planter, an informant said, "When the heavy frost and sleet come a few weeks ago, he asked whether we had provided for our cattle. We had. The Sunday before, he had taken the truck and bought twenty-five bales of hay that he stored in the barn. Our neighbor down the road was depending on pasture. When Mr. Clay asked him, the cattle had been in the barn all day and had had nothing to eat. Mr. Clay went to get several loads of hay from bales that had been broken, and hauled it in the cold to this man's barn."

The Riverville women from the tenant farmer or renter categories who worked in the plantation homes of the whites sometimes express dissatisfaction with the working conditions or with their pay. One woman said, "We were never supposed to say, 'What will you give me?' or 'How long do you want me to work for what wages?' or 'When do you want me to work regularly?' You worked when you were sent for, and at the end of the day you were supposed to be satisfied with what they gave you. Now there are not enough women who work in the big plantation homes, and sometimes they have no one for the cooking, but they expect us to come when they send for us."

In southern towns and cities Letoyants and other nonwhites who have skills as carpenters, bricklayers, or plumbers, have had unequal opportunities because the labor unions would not hire nonwhites with these skills. Instead, they were relegated to mixing the mortar, carrying the bricks, and doing other lower-paying jobs. A city Creole who was working on a construction job related that he was once nailing some pieces of wood together when he was accosted by a white foreman who asked him what he was doing with a hammer and nail. When the Creole responded that he was fixing a mortar box, the foreman warned him not to do any carpentering. The Creole resented not only his exclusion from labor unions but even more the constant reminder of his relatively powerless position.

Letoyants are distrustful, at times, of banks and of the financial power structure. One old woman said, "I keeps everything pinned right here in my bosom." Another old woman who kept her money in her house lost all of it in a fire. A Creole planter said, concerning the financial structure: "No colored man is going to protest unfair treatment too loudly, because if he does, he will be unable to borrow money for his crops. If you make an enemy of a white planter, the board members of the bank will just say you are a bad risk, and you will not get a loan."

Creoles also depend upon the whites for medical and legal assistance. They usually consider it a good policy to have friendly relationships with these professionals because risks are high if doctors and lawyers, in particular, are indifferent or unfriendly. A Creole man who became violently ill when traveling in the state was taken to the clinic of a doctor who was a stranger. According to the man's family, the doctor gave the sick man an injection, after which delirium resulted. The family wanted another doctor called in for consultation, but the doctor in attendance refused on the ground that the clinic was his. The family hastened back to Riverville and talked to Mr. White. As a result of his intervention, another doctor was put on the case. It was too late, however, according to the family, and the sick man died within two days. Another Creole, who was in a veterans hospital for tests, complained that when he was being discharged, he "was so thoroughly sat upon" by the person in charge that he refrained from inquiring further about his report and returned home very discouraged, without knowing what disposition had been made of his case. He felt that he had been talked to in "a degrading fashion," and had been given a sheaf of "legal looking papers and asked to sign them without time to examine them." Because of the pressures, he signed a statement concerning permanent and total disability, and subsequently received a routine letter saying that his disability was not total and that he was not eligible for any "pension."

Segregation in health facilities in the South throughout most of the twentieth century was particularly annoying to the Creoles. Thus, the mother of a child with a speech defect was encouraged to take the girl for therapy to a teaching clinic at the college in Indianola. When she took the child the first time, the teacher looked at her and asked if she were colored. When she received an affirmative response, she told the mother that the child could not be treated on the campus. There was, however, an office where therapy was given to nonwhite children. The mother resented her child's being treated in a place apart from other children with similar defects, especially on a college campus. Members of another Creole family who had a relative in the state hospital were distressed when they paid her a visit. The informant said, "She was put on a ward with all those dark people in the hospital. The staff could see that she wasn't like the rest of those people." Although segregation in hospitals is no longer enforced by labeling wards as nonwhite, in effect some wings of a hospital are still used predominantly for nonwhites. The Creoles are not always accepting of the segregation in the waiting rooms of the professional offices, and on occasion they sit in the section that has been traditionally reserved for the whites. Some of the older Creoles, however, look with disfavor on forcing acceptance. One elderly woman said, "If one is worth respecting, he will get respect."

In legal business, also, Creoles can experience the effects of inequality. A landowner who insured his cotton crop was told that the insurance cost would be $28.45, but when the bill came the decimal was misplaced, and the bill was for $284.50—an error that, if ignored, would add $156.05 to the estimate, and, if challenged, would be embarrassing. The landowner, who took the latter course, said that the "mistake in the figuring" cost him "just lots of trouble," and that he had to go to a lawyer. If he had found no lawyer to handle the case, or if the lawyer had been "in cahoots" with the chiseler, the Letoyant Creole could have been coerced into paying the large sum.

The strain of inequality is evident also in business dealings with merchants. Once when this investigator accompanied two Creole women to a store in a large city, there was a very frosty reception. The clerks who were not busy were, nonetheless, hesitant to give service. When the investigator remarked about the incident to the women afterwards, one of them said, "Those people are not used to us Catholics. Up here, they can't tell the difference between us and the blacks." The other woman went on to relate that although they are "nicer to us in Indianola, they still are not friendly in some places." She related an incident about her daughter's attempt to return a dress that the mother thought was more suitable for a nightclub than church attendance. The mother insisted that the girl return it and explain that she had been high-pressured into making this selection by the clerk. The girl begged her mother to keep the dress, but her mother insisted. At the store, the girl "got the run around." She was first told to "speak to the man in the white shirt about making an exchange," but this man ignored her. She finally decided to make another selection and then insist upon an exchange; however, the exchange was made with great difficulty. Other Creoles describe similar situations. Once the investigator waited twenty minutes for a Creole woman to return from the store where she was making a small purchase. The woman, explaining the delay, said that she had made her selection, but when she took it to the cashier, she was told to go back to the clerk in the department where she made the selection. That clerk would not give her attention but carried on a leisurely conversation with someone else and made her wait. The segregation of facilities in places of business is also very inconvenient to the Creole. One mother said that it was very inconvenient to take small children to town because they "are liable to want to use the bathroom at any time, and the stores do not permit the colored to use the restrooms."

Store owners who do not give overt evidence of discrimination are more likely to have Creole customers than others who have lower prices. When the owners of an Indianola grocery store died rather suddenly, a Creole man and his wife commented, "They were good people; they talked to *the* people." Then, as an afterthought, the wife added, "Course, I guess that was good business." One planter's wife, who had been in a car accident and who walked with difficulty, spoke appreciatively of the service she received from some store owners who came to her car to ask her what they could do for her. She said, "It may have been a business proposition, but it was a nice gesture."

The embarrassment which Creoles sometimes experience when whites are attempting to identify them was expressed by one Creole: "When I go to a store in town, people look at you, and talk in whispers, or laugh—trying to figure out who you are. Sometimes they makes mistakes and puts people what aren't colored in the coloreds' section; then they are in trouble. When you are in California, and they don't know who you are, they treats you like everyone else. You can go into a picture studio and they takes you in and puts you in the nice chairs like others. Here in town, they acts like they are afraid to touch you when they takes your money, and they puts you in the back or somewhere in a separate place."

As the Creole sees the white business and professional people, there is a general tendency to limit, if not restrict entirely, clerical and white-collar jobs and to deny skilled workers entry into labor unions. Although there are white doctors, lawyers, social workers, and merchants who relate positively to them as persons, the Creoles sense the social distance between themselves and the people in power, and they tend to be distrustful of overtures that may have political implications.

POLITICS

One of the principles underlying the Creole's relation to the law is that it is a white man's law and that it is unwise to testify against an ethnic group member. As one Creole leader said, "We can have those persons who are no count, but just let them get a raw deal from the police! As we say, 'let them get railroaded.' We got quite a bit of jealousy. As long as it's gossiping on each other, it's all right, but from the outside, it doesn't sound so good." He continued, "A good many years ago we had a prosecuting attorney who used to get up and criticize the defendant as much as the plaintiff, so around through here, that caused the people whenever they had any differences among themselves, they used to try to settle them privately. The attorney would berate the defendant because he was half white and he'd treat him as though he was a slave. That was one of the things that caused some of the people to compromise about going to court against one of his group. We seemed to think that going to court was trying to 'down the group.'"

A priest who was a resident in Riverville for several years felt strongly that troublemakers should, at times, feel the arm of the law. He said, "Some people have a reputation of being lawless and the people in town are getting too lenient with these people. They get a little bit patronizing. After all, it's just a colored man doing something to another colored man. They keep him in jail a day or two and let him out." The troublemaker is regarded as "just a bad nigger." When the priest insisted that a boy who had attacked a girl at a dance be brought to justice, he was given the "run around." At the district attorney's office he was told to see the sheriff. At the sheriff's office he was told to see the district attorney. Therefore, he waited until the police jury was meeting and put the case to them. Even there, the attitude was, "Those are colored people. They have their own laws. They just live that way." When the priest insisted on justice, the boy was arrested, but he was kept in jail only two days and then he was released to the white planter on whose property his family lived. Although he was released on bail, he was never brought to trial. In some way his family probably settled matters with the officials.

One important Creole planter who was not a Letoyant did take the law in his own hands and was able to "get away with it" because of his relationships with the "powers that be" in Indianola.

This planter allegedly shot and killed three of his fellow Creoles over theft of his property.

In another instance, the priest attempted to call in the law. He observed a school girl being accosted by three boys when she tried to pass them on her bicycle at some distance down the road from the church. When the priest called loudly to the boys to desist, one of the boys fired a gun into the air. In the excitement that followed, the girl bypassed the boys. The priest wanted the boys to be apprehended. He asked his Creole housekeeper who they were, but she denied knowing them. The father of the girl who was attacked was then advised by the priest to take the matter to the police in Indianola. Because of pressure from the priest, the case was eventually heard and one of the boys was convicted. Much later the priest discovered that the charge against the boy was that he had fired a shot at a white priest. The priest's interpretation of the situation was that the girl's father did not trust the white man's law and therefore charged that it was the priest who was attacked.

When the lawbreaker is a white person, Creoles are reluctant to take action against him. Thus, when three servicemen broke into a Creole home and attacked a young girl, who was alone at the time, no one responded to the girl's screams. Her uncle, who lived next door, heard the screaming but, according to relatives, was afraid to go to his niece's assistance since white men were involved. A Creole who was working in the fields nearby eventually came to the back door of the house, and the servicemen ran out the front door as he entered. There were conflicting reports as to the manner in which justice was secured in this incident. The Creole relatives of the girl said that they attempted to get legal redress for her, but the district attorney said he didn't know what could be done about it. Then they went to the priest and he appealed to the local authorities who said that the military had jurisdiction. After much communication with a general, a trial was held in the Riverville school and the offender was sentenced to forty years.

The indignation expressed by the Creoles against the soldiers who attempted to rape the Creole girl was especially strong because the girl in question was a "good girl" and not one who was "free with her favors." In indignation, one of the Creoles said, "If this were a colored man and a white woman, the white men from town would be out here and the colored man would be strung up in no time. But since it is this way, they may not bother to do anything about it."

Another Creole gave his brush with the law as the precipitating factor in moving away from Louisiana. He described the incident as follows: "I came up here because I got into some trouble with some white people. I thought my neck was better than staying there and taking a chance. They claims I done something I didn't do, but you know, a white person's word against my word down there—yours ain't worth nothing. So I left there. I didn't take no chance, because one man already done told a lie on me. I got out on a bond, and I just jumped the bond. And I had my own home down there. So I sold the home and asked my cousin Joe—he underwent my bond—to sell my house and take his money and send me the rest."

A fugitive from the Riverville area related a similar experience:

"When I first started working on the train I was a water boy. I worked up to where I could fire. I got to where I could handle the locomotive pretty well. So, the first thing I know, the engineer got sick and they place me in the locomotive. Every now and then I'd work from locomotive engineer man back to fireman.

"Now braking is a kind of a dangerous job. You have to watch close. You can't be looking at something else and doing your work, too. It was a logging train, and sometimes them logs is longer than the car. The car couples up. Well, you got to squat down and keep your head out of the way. I've seen fellows just get their heads mashed off, and killed right away. I was firing. And I was getting ready to go to the mill. So I run and I come back and I told him, 'He's dead. He mashed his head between them logs.'

"And the engineer told me, he said, 'He fell? Go see what happen to him.'

"So I run and I told him. I come back and I said, 'He's dead.'

"He said, *'Dead?'*

"I says, 'Yeah, he's dead. He mashed his head between them logs.' And that engineer just fell out.

"I said, 'What are you going to do?' I said. 'Blow the whistle! You got to blow for help!'

"He said, 'I can't blow that whistle. You have to blow it for me.'

"So I went to blowing the whistle. We were about two miles from the camp. So then, we had to go to the camp to call, so we could move this dead man, you know.

"And when we got back to the camp, he say, 'Say, I knowed that was you who did it that time because you blowed too many death whistles.' Said, 'You wasn't caught.' Said, 'This time, I know it was you.'

"I said, 'Well, let's get outta here.' He ain't caught me yet, and I best not let them catch me."

When a Creole is involved with a white man in an accident, especially where the law is called in, the Creole may decide not to risk seeking justice because he has so often been a scapegoat. The odds are so great in the white man's favor that the Creole may feel that his life depends upon a quick escape. The reaction of a Creole who accidentally ran over an intoxicated white man who had fallen in the road was the exclamation, "My God, it's a white man." To leave the scene of the accident or to risk facing the law is not a simple decision for the Creole.

One way of effecting legal changes is through the exercise of the franchise. Letoyant Creoles had enjoyed the franchise during Reconstruction but lost it in the years following.[2] A white resident of Riverville, who is sympathetic toward the Creoles, explained

---

[2] The free people of color were first denied the suffrage in 1812 when Louisiana restricted the franchise to whites. Following Reconstruction, other measures were taken. In 1898 the constitutional convention disfranchised 90 percent of the nonwhites through the "grandfather clause," whereby all persons whose grandfathers had not been qualified voters were deprived of suffrage. Theoretically, Riverville's nonwhites were not affected, but an education qualification and the white primary which regulated the activities of nonwhites in the Democratic Party did so, until the United States Supreme Court decision in *Smith* v. *Allwright* in 1944. Cf. Charles Roussève, *The Negro in Louisiana* (New Orleans: Xavier University Press, 1937), 47, 137.

that there was only one polling place near Riverville until the early 1950's, and it was on the other side of the state highway from Riverville. He told how, on election day, the "hillbillies hung around the place and were so dreadful that none of the colored cared to undergo the humiliation." In order to register, moreover, the Creoles had to go to Indianola, and that was another ordeal.

There were several reasons why the Creoles were willing to "stick out our necks," as they expressed it, and to try to exercise their franchise in 1950. Their school children had no bus service. One side of the river road had never been graveled and was impassable in bad weather, and the few white persons in the ward were making demands of the politicians that seemed contrary to the common interest. A five-mile stretch of road behind the Riverville woodland where only two families, both white, resided had been graveled because a white school teacher traveled that way to school. The Creoles were dissatisfied over such use of their tax money.

About this time, the NAACP began to function in the Riverville area. Both Creoles and Negroes were urged to register and go to the polls, and the NAACP officials promised to be on hand to take legal action if necessary. The second Letoyant Creole to register chuckled as he related his experience in these words:

"When I went in and asked to register, some white dame raised her eyebrows and then got up and left her desk. I told her to come back and get her purse that she left behind or she'd be yelling that the fifty cents in there was missing. She took the purse and left in a huff. The people around there told me they didn't register no colored. I said they might as well start because plenty of colored would be in to register in the next two days. The NAACP would have the FBI around from Washington, and we meant business."

This independence was evidenced when gravel was to be put on the unimproved road along the west bank of the river in 1951. No amount of persuasion could induce the residents to shorten the road along which their homes were built. Twenty-five years earlier, however, the white voters were largely responsible for shortening the road on the opposite side of the river when improvements were made there.

In Riverville's precinct, one that is geographically much larger than the community boundaries, 52 percent of the voters in the 1960 gubernatorial election were Creoles. This represents only 21 percent of the Creoles eligible to vote in the precinct, a percentage that does not compare favorably with nonwhite voting throughout the state. When a voter registration drive began in 1960, 26 percent of the Negroes of voting age were registered.[3]

In 1963 nonwhites were placed on the jury list in Indianola for the first time since Reconstruction days, when twenty nonwhites were added to the three-hundred-name list. By 1967 sixteen Creoles were running for political offices and that year three were elected. One was elected constable (the first nonwhite constable since 1870), one as a member of the democratic executive committee, and one as a justice of the peace. All three were direct descent Letoyants and recognized leaders among their people.

Another instance of Creole-white interaction involving the local power structure was Creole participation in the county fair. The differential treatment which Creoles received from the authorities led them eventually to refrain from any participation. A prominent Creole man who was on the committee said that he voted against using that "old barn where the colored were supposed to set up exhibits." This was to remonstrate against the decision to segregate the nonwhite from the other fair entrants. One Creole woman remarked, "At one time folks entered cakes, and canned goods, and clothes in the fair and judges couldn't tell whether they belonged to the colored or not. The colored won so many prizes that they were separated and had their own exhibits. A Shetland pony was given as a prize but a colored child has never gotten one as a prize." While such experiences as these generate Creole resentment and support the hypothesis that interaction among groups of different statuses intensifies rivalry and leads to increased

[3] By 1964 the percentage in the state had risen by 6 percent to 32 percent; no comparable data are available for Creoles. "Negro Voters: A Loud Voice," New York *Times*, November 22, 1964, Sec. E, p. 5.

prejudice on the part of individuals opposed to change, they are not as vital to Creole morale and well-being as the right to exercise the franchise and, in particular, the equal protection of the law.

EDUCATION

Educational opportunities, like economic opportunities, are closely associated with status, and the denial by the whites of equal educational opportunities on the high school and college level was cause for Creole concern and resentment. Creoles had their own Catholic elementary schools in most places, and in a few instances secondary education was available to them in the Catholic segregated system. But Creoles had to be financially able to send their children out of the state for a quality higher education.

In Riverton, the educational situation was especially acute because there were two elementary schools on the church parish property, one serving the white children and the other the non-white children, with the Sisters who taught in the two schools living together. Since enrollment in the white school was always less than that in the nonwhite school, the white school was closed in May, 1964. When the Sisters who were to teach the nonwhites returned to Riverton in the fall of that year, they were coolly received by some of the white families. There was too much opposition from the whites to transfer the nonwhite children to the structure that had been used by the white children, a structure that was in better condition and much more convenient both to teachers and pupils than the other.

The unequal opportunities of Creoles in the Riverville area prior to desegregation was the subject of comments from the Creoles. One white Riverville family with a school-age child was allegedly reimbursed by the state for transporting the boy to school in Indianola, since there was no white school in the immediate vicinity of his home nor any school buses running between Indianola and Riverville. The Creole informant said that she, too, had no high school available to her, but she was forced to leave home and live with an aunt in Centerville in order to attend high school; however, her parents were not eligible for any re-imbursement for her high school education.[4]

The Head Start Program, which was federally sponsored in the mid-1960's, was viewed by the nonwhite school officials as highly desirable for nonwhite children, but in Indianola the program received little or no publicity, probably because it would have to be integrated, and the townspeople were not amenable to integrating their preschool children. The Riverville program was able to be integrated because one of the teachers was a white woman who brought her little boy along to participate in the program. Creoles' reactions to the integration of the Catholic school in Indianola and their attitudes toward the closing of their own elementary school in Riverville with the subsequent enrollment of Creole children in the Riverville public school are discussed later.

A Letoyant girl born and reared in a border city voiced perspectives that reflect confusion about the status quo. She first gave her observations on the Civil Rights bill saying, "Why don't they just make all the people see that the Civil Rights bill is what the Constitution's always said. Why give us a separate bill? We're still a separate people. Besides, in Louisiana it isn't different. Maybe in some parts, but not where I live. We can go to a few drive-in movies, but who wants to always go to drive-in movies? We're still doing the same things. There aren't too many people going to the schools. Maybe because they just don't want to. I guess they don't even want to go to the schools. They're too attached to people in their own schools, anyway. So why leave them? No use

---

[4] Efforts to desegregate the schools in the state met with stiff opposition. Although the Supreme Court decision on equal educational opportunities was handed down in 1954, it was 1960 before the decision began to be implemented in the South. Not until 1962 was any appreciable effort made to desegregate some of the schools. By 1965–66, the percentage of nonwhite students attending integrated schools in Louisiana was .9 percent. Moreover, the Louisiana Teachers Association was the last of the state education associations affiliated with the National Education Association to eliminate racial restrictions for membership, an action taken in 1966. Cf. "Integration and Free Choice," New York *Times*, April 23. 1967. Sec. 4, p. 2; *Education U.S.A.*, Washington, D.C.: National School Public Relations Assn., December 1, 1966, p. 80.

in going to the schools if you feel you're getting a good education at the school you are. Why change and go to a school just for the integration sake when nothing else is integrated?"

Recent desegregation in the public schools, particularly on the higher levels, seems to be a clear case of the costs of segregation outweighing the rewards for the whites. The withdrawal of federal financial support to the state school system is more costly —in terms of dollars and cents—than the whites can afford. Therefore, the rewards of perpetuating tradition have had to yield to excessive financial costs.

RELIGION

Studies of nonwhite churches, particularly Negro churches in the United States, show that while the Negroes oppose segregation as enforced discrimination, nearly all prefer their own churches to inferior status in white congregations.[5] Racial prejudice on the part of the white population is not the only reason for this preference. The sermons given to white congregations, especially to those who are not lower-class, are not always understood by the less well-educated nonwhites, and the emotional response of the nonwhites to a moving message is often distasteful to middle-class whites.[6]

The Church, as has been seen, is a very important force in the lives of the Letoyant Creoles. They take religious obligations seriously and, at the same time, enjoy the opportunities which church services provide for negotiating community business and for associating with their neighbors. The Riverville church is, in a special way, their own church.

Although Riverville's few white people attend church services there occasionally, they also go into Indianola. When they are in Riverville, they generally occupy the front pews and seldom linger after services to visit. They attend church fairs, but rather than

[5] Liston Pope, "The Negro and Religion in America," *Review of Religious Research*, V (Spring, 1964), 145.
[6] Joe Gray Taylor, *Negro Slavery in Louisiana* (Baton Rouge: Louisiana Historical Association, 1963), 148.

working with the Creoles during the fair, they send a contribution to show community spirit and to support the church.

The white priests and religious who work with the Letoyants generally enjoy status because of their education and background. Their Caucasian origin can be viewed either as an asset or a liability. It is an asset because they can negotiate matters as equals with the dominant population, and they sometimes assume the role of mediator between the Creole and white populations. On the other hand, race is, at times, a barrier to intergroup relations. The clergy and religious serving the Creole population can never, strictly speaking, be identified with it because of this physical barrier. The priest who worked in Riverville for twenty years remarked that he had sometimes been told to his face, "You are a white man"; apologies followed almost immediately. "We know you are a priest and we wouldn't want to do anything to hurt a priest." The implication was, however, that they would not be hesitant to retaliate against a white person who was not a priest or religious.

One elderly Creole woman voiced her support of the priest and Sisters in Riverville. She said, "When we'd be collecting for the fair, some people wouldn't give anything. They ain't doing nothing for the church. They'd say, 'That's for the priest to do what he wants to do.'

"I said, 'Listen, it isn't your business. Your business is to help your church—your community. The Sisters toiling and fighting with your bad children. You don't even appreciate a bit.'

"When they tell me all those things, I put them on the list. Some promised, and some preached. That's the way I put it. And when I turn my list in, I say, 'Father, so and so preached!' "

Many Creoles are quite critical of the use made of church funds, but others assume a protective attitude toward the pastor. A middle-aged woman related an incident in the parish hall when the old pastor was asked about the disposition of some money. She thought the questions were phrased in a very harsh way and constituted an insult. She said she felt like going and putting her arms around the pastor because of the way he was being attacked by prominent parishioners. She was much less judgmental than others, who may have been reflecting the racial differences between pastor and critics.

The church in Riverton, which has a mixed congregation, approximately half white and half nonwhite, has problems peculiarly its own. Some white parishioners accuse the priest of paying too much attention to the nonwhites, and threatened to leave the church if he continues to be partial to them. A new pastor in Riverton, who distributed communion to the people in the order in which they went to the rail, was upbraided by some of the white parishioners for giving the nonwhites communion ahead of them. The priest responded that the whites should come to the head of the communion rail if they wanted to go to communion first, saying, "I can't tell one from the other anyhow." This same pastor attempted to resolve the segregation in the church pews but was not able to carry out his intention. The white people sat in the middle of the church, the Creoles on one side, and the blacks on the other. After services, the white people customarily went out the center door, the Creoles out one side door, and the blacks out the other side door. The priest intended to close the two side doors permanently, but the upheaval in the parish caused him to reconsider this maneuver. When the people of the parish contributed their services in repairing church property, the priest had to exercise diplomacy in the assignment of tasks because members of the various groups refused to work with one another. They preferred to come in shifts and work together without sharing the work with the other racial groups.

The same insistence on the preservation of social class distinction was evidenced when a group of Mexican farm laborers were bussed to the church in Riverville because they were unwelcome at the church in Indianola which had a white congregation. The Riverville people were incensed. A Creole Frenchman said, "Our people put on a suit for Sunday and clean up, but these fellows wore overalls and were dirty, and didn't speak English. They even had numbers on their overalls and looked like convicts. Father even preached in Spanish. When he started a second sermon, some of us got up and walked out." These laborers, who were in

Riverville at the time of the church fair, were encouraged by some Creoles to spend some of their evenings at the fair. When some of them paid to dance, they were indignant that none of the girls would dance with them and tried to get their money refunded.

Attached to the Riverville church are two chapels, one of them about midway between Riverville and Indianola. It serves only the white planters in that area, most of whom are related. A Creole family that formerly lived in the vicinity of this chapel said that they were forced to miss church services in bad weather before the roads were hard surfaced because they could not make the trip to the Riverville church and they were not welcome at this chapel. Any effort to close the chapel and force the planters to go to the Riverville church has been strongly resisted by the whites.

The second chapel attached to the Riverville church has also come to have a totally white congregation. Initially, however, it served all the Catholics in that area, many of whom were either Creole or predominantly Indian. A Creole woman whose family property has been in the vicinity of this chapel for many years decided to attend services there again. At that time, she was asked by an old lady not to return, but she told, with some delight, the response of an old Indian woman who was also requested to go to services elsewhere. "Aunt Marie just looked at her and said, 'Shoo away from me: I come to serve God.'" According to this informant, white parishioners had the body of an old Negro man removed from the cemetery near this church, and there are stories told about his disturbed spirit haunting the cemetery. Some of the Letoyants who formerly attended church in this area are known to have ceased practicing their religion because they were unwelcome in church and have no way to go to Riverville; some have become Baptists, since the Baptist church was the only one in the area which they felt free to attend.

In a sense, the Church and its adjunct, the school, have played nondeliberate roles in the segregation of Creoles. Efforts of individual white churchmen to effect changes were largely unsuccessful, and the Church and its spokesmen usually adapted to the prevailing pattern.

THE SOCIAL AMENITIES

The system of etiquette that evolved in the deep South to regulate behavior among racial groups has its counterpart among the Creoles. As people of color, they are expected to show deference to the whites. Two of the chief ways in which deference is shown are "presentation rituals" in which the actor concretely depicts his appreciation of the recipient and "avoidance rituals" which take the form of proscriptions and taboos and imply what an actor must refrain from doing lest he violate the right of the recipient to keep him at a distance. Deference behavior tends to be honorific, that is, in many ways, more complimentary than the actor's sentiment may warrant. The recipients sense that they ought not take the actor literally or force his hand. The higher the class, the more extensive and elaborate are the taboos against contact.[7]

The Creoles who were Letoyants on both sides of the family were never noted for their spirit of deference as were some of the Letoyants who did not have the same "purity of lineage." Both Creoles and whites recall the instance of a nonwhite man who came into the area immediately before the Civil War and who was said to "have the grace to adjust to whites and to be acceptable to the Letoyants at the same time." During the Reconstruction he became a deputy sheriff and recouped the fortunes which he lost during the Civil War without losing the respect of those who suffered losses and whose property he acquired. He was sufficiently well known into the twentieth century for chronicles to have been written about him by those who had firsthand acquaintance with him.

A typescript by a southern writer described this man as follows, "He could not sign his name, but he was endowed with business ability, and tact to know how to get along with the white man in a part of the South where the conditions of slavery were most exacting and where the character of the negro was thoroughly

---

[7] Erving Goffman, "The Nature of Deference and Demeanor," *American Anthropologist*, LVIII (June, 1956), 479–87.

understood." The writer went on to say that this emigrant to the South "knew his place at all times and under all circumstances, and his family were reared in the same way." The commentator then gave some illustrations of the avoidance rituals employed by this family: "If his white friends paid him a visit on business, they were entertained royally in a separate house from the one occupied by himself and erected for that purpose. He would be the head waiter assisted by his family and yet so gracefully and hospitably done you could not but respect the man." This prominent man had race horses. After the races when it was customary to go to the jockey club for a drink, he again knew the avoidance ritual. The writer said, "Often I have seen him invited to the bar to take a glass of wine or toddy with the prominent [white] men in the country. He always waited until his friends had finished, then with his hat in his hand, he would step up to the bar, pour out his wine, and light a Chesterfield with glass in hand, drink to the health, and happiness of them all. If a cigar was passed to him, it was never lighted in the presence of the company, but he waited until he was on the street where he felt he had reached his level." The last observation about the man's sentiments is undoubtedly the white man's perception of them, for deference behavior does not always reflect the true sentiments of the actor.

The children of this prominent man were said to engage in much deference behavior. A white man from Indianola who has business dealings with the Creoles in Riverville said that "years ago, when transportation was not so good, the white folks from town who did business in that area, used to try and stop over at Joe's [the son of the immigrant]. He set a good table. They waited on you and didn't eat with you." Joe's son, however, assumed a different attitude. Drummers and other whites who came through the area were welcome to eat with him, if they wished to sit at the same table, but he did not provide separate facilities for them, and he was not inclined to take a subservient role.

Another white business man in Indianola spoke with approval of the behavior of this particular family. He said that when he went to the Riverville area on business, the family would "put me up in a bed which they said no one but a white man had used." He spoke of the practice of serving meals at a table apart. He noted also that when the younger generation of this family (one that had inter-married with the Letoyants) came to a parade "they knew better than to push to the front of the walk to see it. When my family came along, they pushed their little children back to make place for us. My wife said she could tell they had class." Getting off the sidewalk to make way for a white person was a part of the whole etiquette ritual of the deep South. If the nonwhites did not of their own accord show their deference, however, the white per-sons were not expected to push them off.[8]

Deference was also shown by avoiding personal contact even by shaking hands.[9] The nonwhite person is never supposed to proffer his hand; however, if a white person makes the offer, it is courteous for the nonwhite to accept it. A white woman from a poor home, who married a wealthy landholder, was a subject of comment because when she went to the church fair in River-ville, she was "nice and shook hands around with everyone." The informant made very clear, however, that this woman did not have the training in etiquette between the ethnic populations that one from a high socioeconomic level would have. Most women who attend church functions only "chat in a friendly fashion; they draw the line at social contact." Women, as indicated earlier, have many more taboos in their interaction with nonwhites than do men. If the women themselves are unaware of these social norms, the Creoles may call them to mind. Thus, when this investigator made a visit to a Creole home to obtain some information, the man of the house stood in the doorway but did not invite the investiga-tor to enter the house. Intent upon securing information from a well-known informant, the investigator complained, "Aren't you going to invite me inside out of this cold wind?" The Creole man responded, "I'm sorry, Sister, but I can't ask you in. My wife is not

[8] Bertram W. Doyle, *The Etiquette of Race Relations in the South* (Chicago: University of Chicago Press, 1937), 55.
[9] *Ibid.*, 56.

here, and you would be a white woman coming into the home of a colored man. In the deep South, it isn't the thing to do."

Whites expect the Creoles to show certain kinds of deference. A professional person, for instance, may expect a nonwhite client to offer the facilities of his home for a weekend fishing trip and to prepare meals for him. A white professional who requested a client to come to his home and prepare and serve a Thanksgiving dinner generated much feedback from the Creoles. The woman of whom the request was made generally showed a degree of deference, but she was not particularly adept in the kitchen since she lived alone and cooked only for herself. She attempted to enlist the assistance of some friends and relatives, all of whom had upper-class status, and none of whom would oblige her. Another Creole woman who married into the Letoyant clan and was well known for her hospitality was asked by a professional person in Indianola to prepare a fresh-milk product for his breakfast daily. She asked, "I'm twenty miles away. How will I get it to you?" He responded, "I'll leave that to you." This is another instance of the expectations of the whites that their nonwhite clients observe presentation rituals.

Presentation rituals, of course, are not always demanded. They are also proffered. A white man who took a visitor to see a Creole woman's house commented that "what she called a 'drink' turned out to be a big chicken dinner." The hostess "couldn't bring herself to sit down and eat with us," but "insisted upon buzzing around and serving."

Presentation rituals may also take the form of bestowing gifts upon the whites. Under the French Black Code, neither the free people of color nor the slaves were allowed to receive gifts from whites.[10] With the change in Negro-white etiquette, particularly in recent years, white recipients may exchange gifts with Creoles. When this happens, the Creole's gift nearly always has more value than that given by the white person. A relative of a Letoyant who made a practice of sending dressed fowl at holiday

[10] Alice Dunbar-Nelson, "People of Color in Louisiana," *Journal of Negro History*, I (October, 1916), 364.

seasons was criticized by her relatives with the remark, "Those rich folk don't need those turkeys. What do they care about all that fussing she makes?"

Presentation rituals cannot always be distinguished from hospitality. Thus, when a prominent Creole man was sick, two of his friends paid him a visit, and while they were there, a white business confrere also came along. The latter was offered a "good drink." After he left, the Creole visitors said jokingly, "When the white fellow comes, he gets treated royally—wined and dined, but the poor colored fellow isn't so lucky."

Creoles who follow the traditional patterns of deference undoubtedly have fewer conflicts with whites and project the expected image of nonwhites that traditionalists prefer. Those Creoles who do follow traditional patterns of etiquette may entertain the sentiments of one old man who said, "Everyone is nice to me, and I am nice to everyone, but *I knows how to act.*" Even among the older people, too much display of deference is regarded as ingratiating and lacking in self-esteem. A Creole who rents his property to a white man in preference to his own people is believed to be "fooling around" and runs the risk of "being beaten out of the property."

Alterations in deference patterns, particularly by the younger people since implementation of the Civil Rights laws, have caused some strained relationships between elderly Creoles and their white friends.

## White Perspectives of the Creole

### CATEGORIES OF WHITES

*Riverville Whites.* The Caucasian's image of the Letoyant Creole, like that held by the Negro, is derived from associations with the Creole and from the Creole's image of the white. The white persons residing in Riverville, for instance, are more familiar with status gradations among Creoles than are the whites in Indianola or elsewhere in Louisiana. Moreover, the Creoles probably vent their feelings against Riverville whites much more freely than they do against others.

For several decades, Riverville has had fewer than a dozen white households, and the whites who live there observe the day-to-day human relationships within the community. They meet with the Letoyants when farm officials visit Riverville, and they are well aware of obvious status differentials. Moreover, they cooperate with Creole planters in controlling the geographic mobility of tenants who are not self-supporting.

White Riverville planters are, furthermore, aware that many of the "little fellows" pride themselves in being Frenchmen and that being of old-family stock in Riverville is comparable to having ancestors who came on the Mayflower. The white planters' wives appear to be less aware of class distinctions among the Letoyants than are the men, probably because they do not work as closely with the nonwhites as do their husbands.

*Poor Whites.* Letoyants have always distinguished the poor whites from those with more economic resources. The so-called po' whites began coming into the large urban areas of Louisiana about 1840, and they competed with the already established free people of color. Mutual antagonism developed that resulted in accentuating racial differences. The legislation aimed at restricting the freedom of the free people of color prior to the Civil War received its impetus from the poor white who constituted a sufficiently large proportion of the population to influence state legislation.[11]

Some of the poor whites escaped the economic hardships in the city and shuttled back and forth between Louisiana and Texas. In 1850 one railway promoter estimated that 63,000 emigrants had gone into Texas. These people, who were too poor to own either land or slaves, kept herds of half-starved cattle. They planted patches of corn and a few rows of cotton. In behavior they were described as "rough, dirty, and profane: the women dipped snuff and smoked pipes, and the men, often drunk, quar-

---

[11] Roussève, *The Negro in Louisiana,* 46–47.

reled murderously with knives and pistols." [12] In the barren piney woods along the trails between Louisiana and Texas, many emigrants stopped to plant a crop or were stricken by sickness and never left the area. Some retired into the forest, built log cabins, and lived by hunting, fishing, and, occasionally, herding cattle for Texans.

Although poor whites are, like other race-conscious people, believed to be inordinately proud of being white, they have no outstanding pride of ancestry. Their ancestors had no fortunes, and they are not greatly concerned about increasing their own material goods. Since poor whites allegedly have a meager stock of values and spiritual resources, they go out looking for new experiences or "thrills." Particularly in the plantation areas, these whites are a rootless people with weak kinship ties, lacking the permanence of residence necessary to build up neighborhood bonds.[13]

In the area of Riverville, the poor whites living in the nearby forest in the piney woods are avoided by the Letoyants. One Creole planter said, "It's a good thing we have rich white folk here and not the po' whites." The poor whites are called "hillbillies," "white trash," and "peckerwoods" by the Creoles. They are the ones with the "Ku Klux Klan mentality" who "raise a storm" over any "colored news" in the weekly paper. One small community in the hills is said to be so prejudiced that a nonwhite person dares not stay there after dusk. The feeling of animosity between the Letoyants and these hillbillies was intensified because the impoverished poor whites had the right to vote through the twentieth century, but the rich Creole plantation owners who paid taxes and contributed to the local economy were denied this right.

*Other Whites.* Other white persons who were established in the Riverville area, either on plantations, farms, towns, or cities,

---

[12] Roger W. Shugg, *Origin of Class Struggle in Louisiana* (Rev. ed.; Baton Rouge: Louisiana State University Press, 1968), 45–46.

[13] Edgar T. Thompson, "Purpose and Tradition in Southern Rural Society," *Social Forces,* XXV (March, 1947), 277–78.

were not threatened by the Creoles in the same manner that the poor whites were. The economically secure whites had ample opportunity to display their superiority without resorting to attacks on nonwhites.

Whites who have business dealings with the Creoles discern a real difference between these people and other nonwhites. Evidence of this knowledge is found in remarks such as the following: "They are different from the ordinary Negro"; "those people are from high-class ancestry, and they kept intermarrying and would not have anything to do with the nigger"; "those yellow niggers are as clean as a pin; you can go into their houses and find the bare floors spotless, but niggers are niggers"; "the place is unique, and everyone here recognizes that if they get to know it; only those who become acquainted with the people there really recognize the difference between them"; "they're distinct, just like the Chinese are not anything like niggers; they have none of that loudness and roughness like niggers have. They are just nice."

A white attorney in Indianola said that he recognized a difference in status among the Creole population. He noted that the local weekly paper listed the succession of property in the county, and, as a lawyer interested particularly in land, he made a point of reviewing the deeds of succession as they were filed. Concerning a recent deed, the lawyer said, "That last landowner that died down there had an inventory of over $115,000. He had two or three tractors, machinery, truck, and everything. He was a good man, as far as I could observe. I don't know nothing about his personal conduct, but go look at his succession."

An elderly status-conscious white woman from Indianola who was well informed about the history and class distinctions among the Letoyants commented upon the different life style among the Creoles living in Indianola. She said, "These people are class conscious, and they do not associate with any and everyone. One colored man who built a house on the corner found himself hemmed in eventually with what he called 'a jumpin' joint' (dance hall) on one side and a beer joint on the other. He deplored the neighborhood and would not associate with anyone who frequented these places. He said some of the patrons of the joint bragged about drinking with whites but those whites were only 'po' white trash.' He wouldn't be seen with any of them."

Although the editor of the weekly county newspaper, when questioned about criteria used in printing news about the Creoles, responded that the majority of them did nothing that was newsworthy, he, nevertheless, reflected a knowledge of social class among the Creoles in his selection of news. The particular issue that prompted this query was publicity on a family reunion, a very common occurrence among Letoyants. News releases of their social events—marriages, birthday parties, scholarships, and selection of homecoming kings and queens—always concerned the affluent upper classes. The lower classes were mentioned primarily in the routine listing of misdemeanors for legal offenses or in news stories about these incidents.

The reaction of the white people in the vicinity to the Creole people of importance is evidenced also by the Riverville homes visited when work is being done on the river. The engineers and overseers on any county job along the river will choose to have coffee or lunch in the home of a Creole who enjoys status with them. One woman who is exceptionally hospitable attributed the manner in which she is treated by whites to her behavior. She commented that she is treated very well not only by the people in the area but even by strangers. She gave an account of a trip to the North where the Pullman porter gave her much attention, but she suspected that her son had tipped the porter. Two white men in the same car with her were also exceptionally courteous, and she said she knew no one influenced these men. Her concept of being a Christian woman and a good citizen is to share with others, and she believes that this gives her status that can be discerned even by those who have not experienced her generosity.

WHITE STEREOTYPES OF THE CREOLE

Although many southern whites, particularly in the Riverville area, are knowledgeable about Letoyant history, they nonetheless include all Creoles in their generalizations about other non-whites in the area. Thus, in exploring the attitudes of whites toward the Creoles, the responses were often relevant primarily to Negroes, or included Negroes as well as Creoles.

The white Southerner's attitude of protectiveness toward the nonwhite probably stems from the patriarchal relationships which existed earlier between master and slave, and its tenacity is explainable in terms of the imbalance in power between whites and nonwhites in the deep South. Even the whites who are highly distrusted by nonwhites may protect the latter during racial disturbances in which they are not directly involved.[14]

*The Good Darky.* The image which southern whites have of non-whites whom they say they respect is that of a "good darky." One white man who was aware of changing attitudes among the races commented, "There was a time when the Negro would take the outside of the walk when they saw a white man coming, but they don't do that anymore." Another white person reiterated the same idea saying that "there are very few respectable niggers left, even though they keep their places." This informant went on to say that at one time segregation extended even to the school hall where sections were reserved for white patrons, but now "times have changed because you just sit anywhere."

There are nonwhites who continue to observe some of the norms of racial etiquette or at least give that impression to the whites with whom they associate. A nonwhite man from Indianola who had been in the service said to a white professional man, "Them white Yankees don't know their place. That white man put his hand on my shoulder and started talking. I said, 'White man, take your white hand off me.' " The professional man to whom he was relating his experience then observed, "The setup here is like the English social system. These people know their place."

Many middle- and upper-class whites in Indianola and the vicinity of Riverville believe that the Creoles have learned to "keep

14 Gunnar Myrdal, *An American Dilemma* (New York: Harper, 1944), 680.

their place." One informant said, "The old folks on the river know their places. We never let them clerk in the stores and they don't expect it. They are good nurses and cooks. An old man took care of my grandfather until he died and we thought he was a wonderful nurse, but we never let them clerk." (The prediction that the Creole has no aspirations to engage in other than service occupations has not been supported since the opening up of new job opportunities following the enforcement of Civil Rights legislation.) A white politician made the following comment about the relationships between Indianola whites and the Letoyant Creoles: "The yellow nigger is being recognized today. We make them a part of conferences and committees. They can vote, and they might jeopardize matters if you don't recognize them."

There are whites who stereotype Creoles as having strong qualities such as "loyalty to their families and industriousness and valuing an education for their children." These whites think that all Creoles "know their place and do not want any change." Many of these whites, particularly the women who deal with non-whites in education and social work as well as some of the white housewives who employ Creole domestics, would never stoop to overtly offending them or being discourteous, at least according to the southern rules of etiquette. In fact, they are quite critical of their white confreres who are discourteous. An office girl, who did not offer a chair to a nonwhite who had an appointment with her employer but curtly dismissed the man with the words, "He is too busy now," was severely criticized. Nevertheless, these whites find it difficult to understand why the Creole occasionally shows resentment of traditional southern interracial etiquette. One school official expressed some consternation over the reaction she received when she addressed an elderly Creole, whose name she did not know, as "Auntie." She said the woman responded, and with some emphasis: "I am not your aunt. My name is Mrs. Brown."

By many southern whites, the Letoyant Creoles are probably stereotyped, with all the traditional derogatory characteristics usually attributed to nonwhites in the South. One planter's wife said that whites have certain virtues and vices and so do the Negroes, but the mulatto has the worst of both. This is very negative racial stereotyping. Despite efforts to maintain their distinct status, then, even the upper-class Creoles are generally reckoned as "niggers" by the whites. Social distance, in particular, is important to maintain. The whites in Indianola are so intent on having their children observe the rules of racial etiquette that they had a mass meeting to determine whether or nor they could permit a nonwhite orchestra that had been engaged to play at a high school prom to perform. Even though an orchestra does not associate closely with the dancers, the parent population expressed great concern.

In an area where surnames are spelled in such a fashion as to connote racial identification and where people who have been in contact with one another for a long period of time are aware of mixed ancestry (even of Creoles who are "extracted whites" with blond hair, blue eyes and fair skin), a person known to be a member of a nonwhite population is ipso facto relegated to a position of inferiority. Even Caucasian-appearing Creoles tend to be seen as having, in full degree, all the stereotyped traits usually attributed to the Negro.[15] In fact, Caucasians who have a high degree of prejudice are usually more accurate in identifying minority peoples and more confident of the accuracy of their judgment than are those who are not as deeply prejudiced.[16]

*The Defenseless Subordinate.* Since nonwhites, including the Letoyant Creoles, tend to repress their resentment and hostility toward whites, they have created the appearance of defenselessness. To a certain extent, they are responsible for their image as defenseless subordinates since they avoid going where they will

[15] See the study of fifteen photographs where there was no decrease in stereotyping as the subjects moved from the most Negroid Negroes to the most Caucasian Negroes. Paul F. Secord, William Bevan, and Brenda Katz, "The Negro Stereotype and Perceptual Accentuation," *Journal of Abnormal and Social Psychology*, LIII (July, 1956), 78–83.
[16] Gardner Lindzey and Saul Rogolsky, "Prejudice and Identification of Minority Group Membership," *Journal of Abnormal and Social Psychology*, XLV (January, 1950), 37–53.

be embarrassed. Class-conscious Creoles also refrain from violent expressions of resentment against discrimination and insults. They avoid situations where discrimination can be expected and resort to subterfuge to avoid unpleasant contacts with whites.[17] But a suppressed minority in a position to accept realistically the power structure and to know it cannot win by "bucking the law" awaits its opportunities to give the whites their due. Creoles have been known to react against whites who live in the community over some slight matter with a hostility and aggression out of proportion to what the incident would warrant.

When Letoyant Creoles encounter trouble with the white power structure, however, they have a choice between attempting to defend themselves and enlisting the assistance of powerful whites. They generally choose the latter alternative, for they know that no nonwhite is sufficiently influential to assist a group member who is in trouble with the law. One landholder admitted, "No matter how much money you has, you still have to depend on the white folks if you need help in town." He went on to note, "Everybody knows Joe has money, but when his boy got in trouble, could he do anything? No, he has to call on Mr. White!"

Although Creoles choose to play the role of defenseless subordinate and to seek the assistance of white persons when they are in trouble, they nevertheless resent white persons assuming the role of defender without a careful appraisal of a situation. Thus, Mr. White is criticized for keeping some of his tenants "out of the pen" and for securing welfare assistance for others. Priests, too, are occasionally accused of being too "soft-hearted" and of defending someone who misrepresented facts and should, in the opinion of other Creoles, have taken the punishment he deserved rather than appeal to the whites.

WHITE APPREHENSIONS

*Reverberation from Civil Rights Legislation.* Opportunities for discerning Creole-white relationships were increased at the time of

[17] Cf. E. Franklin Frazier, *Black Bourgeoisie* (Glencoe, Ill.: The Free Press, 1957), 25.

the Supreme Court decision on desegregation in the schools (1954) and subsequent attempts to enforce it. A prominent white business-man made the following observation immediately after the deci-sion: "We believe that the Supreme Court decision ignores the fact that for good or ill, the white South pays almost all the taxes that go to the school system, and that he who controls the purse had better be considered in making plans. It is this factor that makes us declare the decision may well turn out to be a disaster for the Negro." A white schoolteacher made similar re-flections: "The Negro has made tremendous advances in this state and in the South in the past fifteen years and that leads me to say that segregation for both races is best. Segregation has and is working in the South which contains two-thirds of the Negro population. The population of the Negro people in the United States is fifteen million. The population of the Negro people in the South is ten million. In Minnesota, with 14,022 Negroes, 1 out of every 200, it certainly wouldn't be the same situation as compared with Mississippi with a population of 90 out of every 200." A third similar observation was made by a white woman: "I think the decision of the Supreme Court is taking away state rights, and I believe our country was founded on the principle of democracy for the people and by the people, and I believe that you people, our colored people, will agree that Louisiana has done all they could to give equal opportunities to all people re-gardless of color, race, or creed. And we should give everybody equal opportunities but I have been living around the colored people all my life and I don't believe that they want to go to our white schools." The observations of the last three commentators express their reactions to all nonwhites, not specifically to Creoles. But the Creoles, like the Negroes in the South, resented the South's segregation policy.

When, in 1965, the implementation of Civil Rights legislation was evaluated, it was found that Louisiana, Mississippi, and Ala-bama had complied less than any of the other states.[18] Moreover, the

[18] "Week in Law: Rights Act Compliance Grows," New York *Times*, March 28, 1965, Sec. E, p. 6.

individuals most committed to segregation were aged eighteen–twenty-nine, the ages where young parents are generally found.[19]

Following the federal government's efforts to protect the civil rights of minority peoples, the whites in Indianola made several attempts to improve opportunities for the nonwhites. They erected and staffed a new branch library, named after a Negro educator and designed to serve only nonwhites, and they erected a new, modern high school for nonwhites. When the conviction of four nonwhite youths for murder was set aside because nonwhites had not served on juries for many years, changes were made in the selection of jurymen.

Opposition to change, however, was evident. Although the signs segregating restrooms in public depots were taken down by order of the Interstate Commerce Commission, they were later restored in accordance with state legislation which the local authorities in Indianola regarded as having precedence over the federal directive. The Ku Klux Klan was revived, crosses were burned on several occasions, and a Citizens' Council was founded. The latter organization was equivalent to the States' Rights Committees set up in other parts of the South. However, the defeat at the polls of a proposal to have a sales tax in the county to replace any federal funds lost by refusing to comply with desegregation indicated that there was a price beyond which citizens would not go to maintain the status quo.

In general, whites view nonwhites as their social inferiors and resist alterations in the intricate patterns that have been devised to keep the social distance between whites and nonwhites. In many respects, Creoles are more of a threat than Negroes simply because Creole norms and values more closely approximate those of the whites. Moreover, Creoles express offense at interracial social barriers. A white employer's interpretation of Creole behavior was stated as follows: "One failing of those people is they're very social, and they want to get on your equal. But I

[19] "18–29 Group Leads Segregationists," New York *Times*, September 23, 1962, Sec. L., p. 55.

hold her just like this. I trust her. She's kind. I give to her. I let her sleep here in my room when we are gone. She's faithful. I have no worries or doubts about her integrity or honesty. And she doesn't know what it is to stop. She stays till four and four-thirty every day. She's what I call a wonderful servant. But she wants to get on your equal." Another white woman said she was aware of Creole aspirations from her maid's associates. Once her maid, who was attempting to get some extra assistance in serving at her employer's party, urged a relative to help her. The relative reportedly responded, "I'm just as white as they are, and I won't kowtow to them." Still another informant related the "boldness" of some nonwhites who were attending a state college with her daughters at the time the desegregation laws began to be implemented: "There were only eighty Negroes registered, and they surely don't know their places. A boy sat down next to my daughter in the dining room, but she gave him a good hard look and moved." All of these incidents point to white sensitivity to an interaction that borders on the social.

*Miscegenation.* One of the whites' greatest apprehensions is that increased social contacts without the safeguards of traditional etiquette will lead to miscegenation. Since the Creoles are a racial amalgam, fears of miscegnation with them are almost invariably raised by the whites.

There were a few cases of Creole-white extramarital unions in the last century, some of which involved very prominent white families. One elderly white woman said, "My mother's grandmother had one son who did not get married. And he had two of these griffe women. They are bright mulattoes. He had been with them, and when he died he left everything he had to these two women who took care of him. And that's the way they started using his name." Another white woman from an old French family said, "The white people seldom talk about miscegenation nor do they discuss their cousins down the river, although they know that they are related. When an old man died, a six-year-old white girl remarked, 'He looks just like grandpa.' " The girl's mother said that there *was* a striking resemblance; however, the girl's father objected strongly to the child's remark.

In 1964 a much publicized marital relationship between a Letoyant woman and a white man occasioned conversations on the subject. The woman was put in a penitentiary for breaking the state miscegenation law. In discussing this incident, two Creole women observed that after the woman's release from prison, she went to California where she was able to live with the white man as his wife. Two other incidents where Creoles were lynched were recalled during this discussion. In one case, a Creole orderly in a hospital negotiated with a white nurse to pilfer some hospital property. When the incident became public and the stolen goods were traced, the Creole was arrested and put in jail, but he was lynched before the case was tried. Another incident concerned a Creole man who was allegedly making love to a white woman. He was forcibly taken from his home and lynched without any incarceration or formal accusation. Sexual relations occur mostly between Creole females and white males; these relations are not strongly resented by the whites, for they follow traditional patterns. The offenders are not subject to the same harassment or physical danger as are Creole males who violate this norm.

Whites seem to have an inordinate fear of intimate social contacts with nonwhites, particularly Creoles, lest they lead not only to the reduction of prejudice, as was hypothesized, but also to the disintegration of the complex system of etiquette that has long been part of the southern pattern of social interaction. Creoles are amenable to changing these mores, but whites oppose change; therefore, white prejudice, rather than being reduced, is often augmented.

# PART III
# The Diaspora

Establishing an ethnic identity and maintaining it for two centuries in the place of origin and its vicinity is, without doubt, a noteworthy achievement. But when an ethnic population experiences an exodus from the homeland, preservation of identity becomes increasingly difficult.

Letoyant society was bound to be affected by such changes in America as greater mechanization of farming accompanied by increasing productivity and the decline of the family farm; greater emphasis on higher education; and the general population movement of a permanent or semipermanent nature from the rural South to urban centers, with the nonwhite migration rate twice that of the white. Instead of following general trends, the Creoles might have reinforced isolation and attempted to preserve the heritage of the past by emulating the Amish, who remain relatively unaffected by technological changes and live apart from others. But the Letoyant Creole population can no longer be contained in the vicinity of Riverville. Moreover, the Creoles were never wedded to agriculture or hesitant to utilize the new technology.

Part III deals with the Letoyant diaspora from the "Promised Land" of Riverville and its effects on ethnic identity. Chapter 12 delineates the factors responsible for the Creole exodus from the South; it describes the migration process itself, both interarea and out-migration, within the framework of migration theory. Chapter 13 treats factors in the choice of settlement outside the South and settlement patterns, particularly in "colonies," as a means to preserve ethnicity. Finally, Chapter 14 discusses the impact of colonization on Creole identity and values.

# Chapter 12

# The Exodus from the Farm

Initially, the Letoyant Creoles who left Riverville settled within Louisiana. Prior to the Civil War they were concentrated in Riverville, where they prospered economically, except for a few intervals such as the depression of 1837. From the time of the invasion by Union forces in 1862 until 1900, however, the economy of Louisiana suffered. Federal troops were not withdrawn until 1877, giving the state a Reconstruction period longer than any other. Bankrupt plantation owners and farmers were often forced into the city to seek a livelihood; the Letoyants also sought to alleviate their financial troubles in this way, especially by going into nearby Indianola. Most of the Creoles, however, remained in the immediate vicinity of Riverville where they could rely upon relatives for mutual assistance.

Industry developed slowly in Louisiana. About 1890 when timber began to be cut and processed near Riverville, some Creoles found employment in the lumber industry and settled in the adjacent rural areas. Then at the turn of the century the discovery of oil near a northern Louisiana town stimulated Creole mobility; however, the subsequent discovery throughout the state of other oil deposits as well as sulphur and natural gas early in the twentieth century had little discernible effect on Letoyant Creole mobility.

World War I uprooted many Louisianans, including Letoyants, who never returned to reside in their place of origin. In the postwar years, the growth of the livestock industry and timber processing created more economic opportunities near Riverville than were available previously. Newly discovered deposits of oil and gas, salt, and sulphur in the state attracted labor from rural to urban places, but few Creoles sought jobs in these industries; however, they did gravitate toward urban communities at this time. Some of them eventually became proprietors of small businesses such as grocery stores and dry-cleaning plants serving the predominantly nonwhite population; others found work in the building trades or as mechanics; and still others became handymen or domestic servants.

The great depression that began in 1929 not only halted out-migration from rural places, but also reversed the trend of population mobility from rural to urban places. During these troubled years Riverville lived up to its reputation as a homeland for many Creoles, especially those who had precarious positions in the cities. Both Riverville and Riverton had a population increase from in-migrants during the depression.

Mobility throughout the country was greatly accelerated during World War II by war industries as well as by troop movements. The demand for agricultural products simultaneously boosted the economy in rural areas and militated against out-mobility from Riverville and Riverton, at least for economic reasons. Only after this war did the Creole exodus to urban places outside of Louisiana take place on a sizable scale.

Young adults could not establish themselves on farms, and economic opportunities in the urban areas of Louisiana were not particularly enticing. Many of the young people who had been uprooted by the war never attempted to settle in the South when they finished their military service. Even those young adults who preferred to remain in the South, especially in rural areas, found it difficult to be economically self-supporting and to establish families of their own without parental assistance.[1]

During the war and its aftermath there was a redistribution of the Negro population that had been predominantly rural and southern. In 1940 the South had 77 percent of the nation's total

---

[1] Since young adults have had more educational opportunities than their parents, they follow the apparent trend toward greater mobility for the better educated. See Elizabeth M. Suval and C. Horace Hamilton, "Some New Evidence on Educational Selectivity in Migration to and from the South," *Social Forces*, XLIII (May, 1966), 539.

Negro population; by 1950 this population had decreased to 68 percent, and by 1960 to 60 percent.[2]

Louisiana ranked seventh in the states that lost population through out-migration between 1950 and 1960, with a net migration loss of approximately 92,000 nonwhites and a population gain of about 42,000 whites, making a total population loss of 50,000. Despite the out-migration rate of nonwhites who were predominantly Negro,[3] however, the rate of nonwhite natural increase was sufficiently high to make the net loss of nonwhites between 1950 and 1960 less than one percent.

Louisiana's nonwhite population, constituting about one-third of the total in 1950 and 1960, has traditionally been rural; however, in the intervening years it became predominantly urban. In 1950 the nonwhite population was approximately 77 percent rural, but by 1960 it had become 62 percent urban, a greater increase in urbanization than in any other southern state.[4] There was, moreover, an increase in the rural nonfarm population in the state with each successive decade 1940–60.[5]

Riverville, like other rural places in Louisiana, suffered population loss; of the 2,195 living Creoles who were born there, 79 percent have moved away. Riverville residents recall with nostalgia the heyday of their homeland. An elderly Creole reminisced: "They was people—they was houses all along that river—where

[2] *Social and Economic Conditions of Negroes in the United States* (Bureau of Labor Statistics Report, No. 332, October, 1967), 4. The South, according to the census definition, includes the states of the old Confederacy as well as Delaware, the District of Columbia, Kentucky, Maryland, Oklahoma, and West Virginia.

[3] The census definition of nonwhites includes American Indians, Japanese, Chinese and other Eastern peoples, while the definition of Negro includes persons of Negro and mixed Negro-white or Negro-Indian descent, unless in the latter instance the Indian ancestry predominates.

[4] The nonwhite population as a percent of the total was 33.1 in 1950 and 32.1 in 1960. Vivian W. Henderson, *The Economic Status of Negroes in the Nation and in the South* (Atlanta: Southern Regional Council, 1963), 6, 8.

[5] By type of residence, the state's percentage distribution of the nonwhite population of the country was as follows in 1940, 1950, and 1960 respectively: urban, 2.4, 2.8, 3.1; rural nonfarm, 1.2, 1.3, 1.5; and rural farm, 3.0, 1.5, and .4. Daniel O. Price, "The Negro Population of the South," *Rural Poverty in the United States* (Washington: Government Printing Office, 1968), 13.

old man Joe lives. People living all along both sides of that river. And today you go there, they's no houses—nobody's living there. They got an old man living there—that's all." Another informant made a similar remark: "Ten years ago, people living all along this river. People just gone on and wandered away. Children grew up you know and left, and the parents died, and some followed them and all. Aw, we don't ever have labor any more in this place. Have to haul labor from town."

## Factors in Migration

### SOCIAL CONDITIONS

Social conditions, in general, are not conducive to the Letoyants' remaining in the South. As has already been noted, Creoles are sensitive to a marginal position that is often compounded by racial visibility in a color-conscious environment with a long tradition of discrimination against nonwhites. Although their lack of social acceptance by the whites has been a factor in strengthening ethnic group ties, it has not contributed to their sense of dignity and honor. Lack of social acceptance per se probably would not rank high as a cause for group out-migration; it is, nonetheless, a contributing factor, just as it has been and continues to be, paradoxically, a factor in geographic isolation.

Political powerlessness in the past has also been resented; the Creoles who represented the majority in the ward where Riverville is located had little to say about the spending of their tax money, and Creoles were subject to unequal treatment under the law. Furthermore, political inequality led to the development of a Creole substructure for handling serious deviancy that permitted some deviants to "get away with murder" since justice was uncertain under the white man's law. Even such simple matters as procuring a driver's license might have racial overtones. Although much of this type of discrimination has been alleviated, it has not disappeared.

Inaccessibility of professional services in Riverville, as in other rural places, also led to out-migration. Riverville has few medical services. A clinic was established near the public school by the Public Health Service after a Creole leader supplied the land and the lumber. Every week a doctor from Indianola comes to the clinic and offers services. There are, however, no dental services, and anyone who needs medical care after diagnosis is advised to go to Indianola for assistance. When an old person becomes too ill or too feeble to take care of himself, his children who have moved from Riverville usually insist that he join them in the place to which they have migrated. Men eligible for services under the Veterans Administration also move from Riverville to a community which has a hospital offering such services.

Particularly since World War II, Creoles have been concerned about educational limitations in the South. One parent said, "Marie knew everything they had to offer at that high school. She was one of the best students. When she left here, though, she discovered she didn't have the equivalent of a high school education. In Western City the schools are better and the children are smarter." Higher education in the vicinity of Riverville was, until recently, out of the question.

Young people whose families cannot afford to send them away to college and who are not prepared for work that requires a college education have constituted the bulk of the out-migrants from Riverville. These adolescents are ready to enter the labor market, and there are few opportunities for them in Riverville or its vicinity. One parent commented: "Our children all have finished their education. If they could make a living here they wouldn't go. All they can get is ten dollars a week, and the only jobs open to them are in the kitchen, caring for children, or nursing in homes. They have a high school education and could clerk, but they are never hired." Many parents maintain that their children would have preferred to remain near Riverville if they could have earned a "decent living" there.

The few young Creole couples who have purchased property and remained in Riverville in the last two decades have financial resources and are educationally prepared to offer services in demand. Some of them attended the vocational school in Indianola.

But those who chose to study in fields where there are no job openings are forced to find work elsewhere. One mother, commenting on this situation, said, "A lot of the kids take up different work and they can't do it on the farm. They go to school and they learn different trades. You know how industrial work is down here. They just don't have any. They have to go where they can do different work—unless they are mechanics. Now the few people that bought land and got married and stayed here—they are mechanics or agriculture teachers and things like that. Other than that, all the youngsters go away. They just don't stay."

The lack of health facilities and of educational opportunities, until very recently, and the relatively low social status accorded nonwhites have, then, been factors conducive to out-migration. Nonwhites in Louisiana, like those in other states where the plantation economy was formerly dominant, remain in a lower position than nonwhites in other parts of the South.[6] For a proud people with a rich heritage, social inequalities cannot be discounted.

THE ECONOMY

Economic factors are probably most responsible for Creole out-migration. Although the percentage of nonwhite to white median family income remained the same between the 1950 and the 1960 censuses (42 percent),[7] during that decade rural nonwhites suffered a sharp percentagewise drop in median income as compared to urban nonwhites.[8] Therefore, predominantly rural parishes with a high proportion of nonwhites suffered the greatest loss of in-

---

[6] See James D. Cowhig and Calvin L. Beale, "Socioeconomic Differences between White and Nonwhite Farm Populations of the South," *Social Forces,* XLII (March, 1964), 362.

[7] Henderson, *The Economic Status of Negroes in the South,* 14.

[8] By type of residence, Louisiana's nonwhite income, as a percentage of white income, was 64.0 for rural farm males in 1949 but only 38.7 in 1959, a decline of more than 25 percent. For females the corresponding percentages were 70.1 and 49.5, a decline of nearly 21 percent. This is based on individuals fourteen years of age and over with income. Income may not be earnings; therefore, it cannot be attributable solely to employment or related directly to employment status. Price, *The Negro Population in the South,* 30.

come. The parish of which Indianola is the seat, which includes all of Riverville, had the lowest median income per family of any parish in the state in 1962.

Riverville Creoles have, of course, a wide range of income. Until the late 1950's, rural farm Creoles were classified as landowners, renters, sharecroppers, or day hands, with income ranging correspondingly from high to low. Ten large landowners, seven of whom are Creole, are properly referred to as planters. These planters, like all farm managers, are the least mobile, as contrasted to farm laborers, who are the most mobile.[9]

After five years of poor crops (1954–58) and erratic farm prices, renters and sharecroppers did not have financial reserves to continue meeting their expenses. Many of them, particularly those working marginal land, migrated. The percentage of household heads classified as renters and sharecroppers decreased appreciably between 1954 and 1964. In 1954, 27 percent of the Riverville Creole household heads were in those categories; in 1964, only 8 percent. The biggest increase was in those categorized as "other" —the retired who no longer farmed but rented enough land for a home and garden, nonfarm workers who were not property owners, and those on welfare. The percentage of day hands, 11 percent, and of landowners, 53 percent, decreased by only 1 or 2 percent.

Renters and landowners with small holdings found it increasingly hard to compete with large landholders, as farming became mechanized and new techniques were introduced. Although a few farmers say that they can make a living on sixteen acres, others believe that at least twenty-five acres are needed to make a "fair living," provided the land has a reasonable amount of cotton-raising sandy soil.

Some of the out-migrants who were renters were undoubtedly averse to using new techniques that increase productivity, but even had they been willing, the expense entailed in employing these

[9] Cf. James D. Tarver, "Occupational Migration Differentials," *Social Forces,* XLIII (December, 1964), 232.

techniques, for the most part, precluded their use. A sympathetic Creole made the following comment about the tenants who moved from Riverville: "After they make the crop, they got to pay for the poison and they got to pay for the fertilizer. And when they finish, they ain't got nothing. They just living. That's all. You can't tell where they are—from one place to the other. They live in one place today, tomorrow they are in another. They are scattered all over the world. They ain't got nothing to do here."

Effective and economical use of machinery necessitates large farm holdings. Since the Creoles in the first half of the twentieth century were primarily small farmers, they could not afford to compete with the planters who had more acreage and who could profit by investing in machinery. The division of farmland among successive generations of Creoles decreased the acreage per farm and made it uneconomical to invest in such machinery as cotton pickers and irrigation devices.

Since nearly one-fourth of the farmers in Riverville have holdings of fewer than twenty acres, they undoubtedly need supplemental sources of income. More and more Creoles have, since 1964, obtained gainful employment in Indianola while continuing to farm.

The sharecropper-debt system, after a series of poor crop years, was in effect a type of peonage. Debts incurred over a few years became impossible to liquidate. Sympathetic Creole landlords who were themselves under financial strain did not deter their tenants from moving to the city. Moreover, as landlords utilized new farming methods and agriculture became increasingly mechanized, the demand for human labor decreased.

The preponderance of out-migrants from the area has been young adults. The apparent affluence of Creoles who have moved out of the South is believed to be a major influence. "The children from here have visited their relatives in Northern City and Western City or, if they have not visited, these relatives have been to Riverville," said one observer. "The children see how well off their relatives are," he continued, "because they come with good cars, have pictures of their homes, and talk about their jobs that afford them a decent income."

In referring to the young adults who leave Riverville for jobs in urban areas, another informant remarked. "I don't know how they do it. Perhaps they scrimp and save all year to come back here with a roll of bills and a new car. But they *do* come back here with a roll of bills. They probably have just started to make payments on the car. No one around here could do that well. Our young people see them and want to leave also." There was, then, not only a push from the rural areas but also a pull to the cities.

POPULATION PRESSURE

Population pressure may be thought of as the difficulties a people encounter in attempting to make a living—difficulties arising from the nature of the environment, that is, the abundance or scarcity of natural resources; the state of development of technology by means of which the natural resources can be utilized; and the number of people to be supported in this environment by those in the economically productive years.

Environment and technology in the area of Riverville have already been discussed; however, their effect on population has not been highlighted. The improvement in farm methods has increased the yield, but simultaneously decreased the number of persons needed to produce this yield, resulting in a "surplus" farm population. The subsequent pressure, intensified by the comparatively high proportion of dependents, is generally relieved by rural out-migration. Therefore, increased farm mechanization accompanied by a high ratio of dependents forced many people, particularly small farmers, into the urban economy. Consequently, some 30 percent of the Letoyant Creoles now have urban residence in Louisiana; and slightly more then 50 percent are living in urban places outside the state (Table 15).

The proportion of dependents in rural areas was undoubtedly a factor in out-migration from these areas. In 1964, for instance, Riverville had a nonsymmetrical population pyramid with a solid base, except for the age category under five, but very little taper-

*Table 15*

RURAL-URBAN RESIDENCE OF CREOLES BY SEX, WITHIN
LOUISIANA AND ELSEWHERE, 1964

| Residence | Males | Females | Total | Percent | |
|---|---|---|---|---|---|
| Urban | | | | | |
|   Outside La. | 1911 | 1773 | 3684 | 50.75 | |
|   Within La. | 1044 | 1046 | 2090 | 28.79 | |
|   Total Urban | | | | | 79.54 |
| Rural (La.) | 729 | 756 | 1485 | 20.46 | |
|   Total Rural | | | | | 20.46 |
| Totals | 3684 | 3575 | 7259 | 100.00 | 100.00 |
| Total in La. | 1773 | 1802 | 3575 | 49.25 | |
| Total outside La. | 1911 | 1773 | 3684 | 50.75 | |

ing of the pyramid as the population became older (Fig. 5). Such a distribution, with comparatively many Creoles in the unproductive years of youth and old age, puts pressure on those in the economically productive middle years to provide for their young and old dependents.

*Figure 5*

CREOLE POPULATION LIVING IN RIVERVILLE
BY AGE, SEX, AND TYPE OF DESCENT, 1964

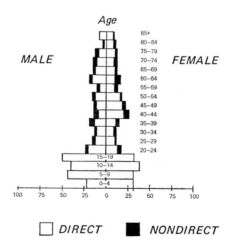

One means of assessing this kind of pressure is the dependency ratio, based upon the number of individuals under eighteen and aged sixty-five and over per one hundred individuals in the intervening years. In Louisiana the highest ratio of Creole young dependents (79.5) is in rural areas. In urban places it is much lower (49.7 in Louisiana and 37.3 outside the state). The high rural dependency ratio is related to the proportionately few Creoles in the productive years, and to the large number of children because of the relatively high birthrate, while the relatively low urban ratio in places outside the South is due in large part to a slight postponement of marriage [10] and to the high proportion of young people who have incomplete families. For the older dependent population the trends are the same, but the differential is even more marked (Table 16). This relatively high Letoyant Creole rural ratio of elderly is attributable to their reluctance to leave their homeland where the majority of them are property owners, and to the tendency of rural Letoyants to have their aged parents live with them. For all dependents, both young and old, rural Louisiana Creoles have a ratio of 105.7, compared to 62.1 for urban Louisiana Creoles and 43.2 for Creoles in other urban places.[11]

Since 1930 there has been a gradual decrease in the proportion of young Letoyant Creole dependents, from a ratio of 114.0 in 1930 to a low of 47.4 in 1964, whereas the population of the country as a whole has witnessed a gradual increase from a low of 48.9 in 1940 to a high of 66.9 in 1964. Both the Creole and the United States populations have shown an increase in the proportion of aged dependents at each five-year interval since 1930, with the total Creole ratio always lower than that of the country, reflecting the greater longevity of the white population. In 1964 the comparative ratios were 17.3 for the country and 11.0 for the Creoles (Table 17).

[10] The median age of marriage for males by residence is approximately: 22.1 in rural areas, 22.8 in urban Louisiana, and 23.5 in urban places elsewhere. For females, the corresponding ages are 20.8, 20.9 and 21.8 years.

[11] The total population of Louisiana Letoyant Creoles has a relatively advantageous dependency ratio at 77.7 compared to 91.1 for the total Louisiana population and to 85.3 for the country.

## Table 16

DEPENDENCY RATIOS * OF TOTAL CREOLES BY RURAL-URBAN RESIDENCY, IN AND OUTSIDE LOUISIANA, 1964

| Age Category | Rural Louisiana | | | | Urban Louisiana | | | | Urban Elsewhere | | | |
|---|---|---|---|---|---|---|---|---|---|---|---|---|
| | M | F | Total | Ratio | M | F | Total | Ratio | M | F | Total | Ratio |
| Under 18 | 276 | 298 | 574 | 79.50 | 330 | 310 | 640 | 49.65 | 490 | 468 | 958 | 37.25 |
| Aged 65+ | 90 | 99 | 189 | 26.18 | 71 | 90 | 161 | 12.49 | 74 | 80 | 154 | 5.99 |
| Total Dependents | 366 | 397 | 763 | 105.68 | 401 | 400 | 801 | 62.14 | 565 | 548 | 1112 | 43.23 |
| Population 18–64 | 363 | 359 | 722 | | 643 | 646 | 1289 | | 1347 | 1225 | 2572 | |

* Ratio based on individuals under eighteen and sixty-five years or over per one hundred individuals eighteen–sixty-four years of age.

Table 17

DEPENDENCY RATIOS OF THE U.S. AND CREOLE POPULATIONS: 1930–64 *

| Year | Total U.S. Dependency ratio | Total U.S. Change from earlier date | Creole Dependency ratio | Total Creole Change from earlier date | Ratio of ratios: U.S. to Creoles | Under 18 yrs. U.S. | Under 18 yrs. Creole | 65 yrs. and older U.S. | 65 yrs. and older Creole |
|---|---|---|---|---|---|---|---|---|---|
| 1964 | 84.2 | +2.0 | 58.4 | −3.4 | 1.4 | 66.9 | 47.4 | 17.3 | 11.0 |
| 1960 | 82.2 | +8.1 | 61.8 | −3.9 | 1.3 | 65.4 | 51.3 | 16.9 | 10.5 |
| 1955 | 74.1 | +9.4 | 65.7 | −4.1 | 1.1 | 58.8 | 57.3 | 15.3 | 8.4 |
| 1950 | 64.7 | +0.3 | 69.8 | −6.7 | 0.9 | 51.3 | 62.9 | 13.4 | 7.0 |
| 1945 | 64.4 | +4.6 | 76.5 | −14.0 | 0.8 | 51.4 | 71.8 | 13.0 | 6.0 |
| 1940 | 59.8 | −3.6 | 90.5 | −13.7 | 0.7 | 48.9 | 85.6 | 10.9 | 5.0 |
| 1935 | 63.4 | −4.4 | 104.2 | −15.0 | 0.6 | 52.3 | 99.2 | 10.0 | 4.7 |
| 1930 | 67.8 | (X) | 119.2 | (X) | 0.6 | 58.6 | 114.0 | 9.1 | 5.2 |

(X) Not applicable.
* U.S. figures from *Population Estimates* (Bureau of Census, Ser. P–25, No. 321, November 30, 1965), 2. Latest figures for Creoles are for 1964; for U.S. they are for 1965.

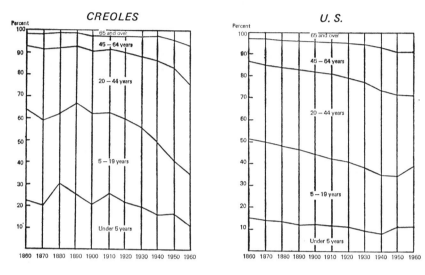

Figure 6

A CENTURY'S CHANGE IN AGE DISTRIBUTION

U. S. AND CREOLE POPULATIONS

A comparison between the Letoyant Creole age distribution and that of the total United States population over the last century (Fig. 6) shows a higher proportion of young dependents among Creoles until about World War II (Table 17), and an increasing number of aged dependents since that time.

## THE MIGRATION PROCESS

In looking at the chief factors in Letoyant Creole migration, namely, social conditions, the economy, and demographic pressures, a few migration trends are evident. The direction of out-migration is from rural to urban areas and from the urban South to other parts of the country. A closer analysis of out-migration shows the extent to which Creole trends approximate general trends. Moreover, since the South, particularly the rural South, has been the seedbed of the Letoyant ethnic group, the extent of migration from the South leads to conjecture about the future of both Riverville and the ethnic population that originated there.

Everett S. Lee advances several points relative to out-migration that are apropos.[12] Migrants, he maintains, never completely lose the characteristics which they share with the population of origin. This contention is central to the major hypothesis of the Letoyant study, namely, that they have established an identity of their own in their community of origin to which they adhere regardless of where they are dispersed. Chapter 14, on the impact of colonization on Letoyant values and identity, is concerned with the validity of this hypothesis. Lee also contends that migrants take on some of the characteristics of the population at destination. Letoyant Creoles who identify with Negroes or pass into the white population assume these characteristics more completely than others. This phenomenon, too, is discussed in Chapter 14.

There is also a tendency, Lee maintains, to migrate at certain stages of the life cycle: at the time of maturity and the search for marriage, and at periods of family disruption by divorce, widowhood, or death. Some evidence of the migration of young adults who are seeking jobs prior to marrying or immediately after marriage has already been noted. Moreover, the elderly who are unable to care for themselves are sometimes persuaded by their children to move where there will be a responsible relative. Supporting evidence for this trend comes primarily from interviews and observations; moreover, a breakdown by age brackets of the population in reference to place of birth and place of last residence substantiates these findings.

Lee's hypothesis that migration takes place in distinctive streams that have a marked place of origin and destination is tested in the present chapter, with the emphasis on destination within Louisiana since the home of the Letoyants is the focus of this chapter. All of the descendants of the Letoyants living in 1964, excluding those who married into the population, were categorized according to place of birth and place of residence as well as by

[12] Everett S. Lee, "A Theory of Migration," *Demography*, III (No. 1, 1966), 47–57.

age and sex. The results were tabulated by volume of redistribution to determine the size and type of out-migration streams and variations in selective characteristics.[13]

CREOLE INTERAREA MIGRATION

*Rural Migration.* Most of the out-migration from Riverville to other rural places with populations under twenty-five hundred is in reality mobility up and down a short stretch of river between Riverville and Riverton. Church parish boundaries are the best indication of community lines because of the role of the church in the lives of the people. In the Riverton community are some Letoyants who have lived on East River for many generations. They consider Riverton their home community, but they also recognize strong ties with relatives in Riverville.

Among the Letoyants who were born in Riverville and migrated to another rural community, where they resided in 1964, there were more females than males and more older persons than younger persons. Only 4.9 percent moved to rural places, 5.9 percent of the females and 3.4 percent males.

On the southern tip of Riverville's boundaries are many former residents of Riverton who have moved to Whiteside Plantation in order to work for cash by the day. Since Whiteside is on the periphery between Riverville and Riverton but within the Riverville parish boundaries, families who have lived in Riverton for many years tend to return there for Sunday services to meet their friends and relatives. Some of the Riverton people now residing in Riverville have intermarried with the Riverville population and reside there. Creoles born in Riverton constituted about one-fifth of the 1964 population of Riverville, with no difference in migration by sex.

A small rural community west of Indianola also has several

[13] For much of the analysis in this chapter pertaining to migration theory and to Riverville see Florence Alwilda Strom, "The Out-Migration Pattern of a Colored Community in the South" (M.A. thesis, Trinity University, San Antonio, Texas, 1966).

Letoyant families. Like Riverton, this community has a sizable white population and a rather sizable Negro population, and an effort is made by the Creoles to maintain their separate identity. In Riverton they succeeded to the extent that they maintained, until 1966, a separate school on the church grounds and customarily have special places in the church. In the more distant community beyond Indianola the Letoyants have been less successful in maintaining their separateness in both the school and the church. The people of Riverville who allude to their relatives in the latter community comment that some of them have been absorbed by the white population.

Apart from these two communities, where a number of Letoyant families settled, the migration to rural places has been scattered. When inquiries were made about relatives who had moved to farms in remote or sparsely settled parts of Louisiana, the Creoles always averred that these relatives were in danger of losing touch with the mainstream of the population because of their isolation.

*Figure 7*

*DISTRIBUTION OF U. S. AND CREOLE*

*POPULATION BY URBAN RESIDENCE*

*1850 – 1960*

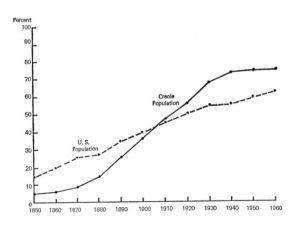

In one instance a Creole woman moved across the Louisiana border into Texas and married a Negro. She reared a large family and today has over one hundred descendants in this community (located after statistics were processed). Although she is welcome to visit her relatives in Riverville, the people of Riverville feel strongly about visits by groups of "Negroes" who claim descent from them, and they make disparaging remarks about Letoyant relatives who have married down the social ladder.

*Urban Migration.* The Letoyant Creole population became more urban than rural between 1900 and 1910, but the urban residents were primarily still Louisianians. (Fig. 7). In contrast to both the Negro and the white United States population, both showing about 7 percent farm residence in 1964, the Creoles were nearly 20.5 percent farm residents [14] (Table 18). In 1964 the Creole population was almost 80 percent urban, with about 29 percent within Louisiana and 51 percent outside the state. There were more males than females in urban places outside Louisiana, but more females than males in the Louisiana population, both urban and rural (Table 15).

For the most part, migration to urban communities in Louisiana is within an eighty-mile radius of Riverville. Indianola, about seventeen miles from Riverville, has one of the largest Letoyant populations, and Centerville, fifty-eight miles to the south, also has a relatively large Letoyant population. Another larger urban center to the north of Indianola attracts a sizable number primarily because of its industrial plants.

[14] Although nonfarm can refer either to rural or urban places, here it refers only to the latter. The rural Letoyants traced prior to 1965 were in the farm communities of Riverville or Riverton, and the adjoining rural farm areas. Moreover, the definition used in the 1950 census classified as farm residents all persons who were reported as living on farms in answer to the question, "Is this house on a farm?" The farm population so defined gradually came to include many persons living on places on which no agricultural operations had been conducted recently, or on places where the farm products were solely for the use of the occupants. Although this definition was refined in the 1960 census by the addition of subsequent questions (see *Farm Population* [Bureau of Census, Ser. P–27, No. 28, April 17, 1961], 1), the Creoles in question would undoubtedly have classified themselves as farm residents in the 1950 census.

*Table 18*

FARM-NONFARM RESIDENCE OF NEGRO, CREOLE, AND WHITE POPULATION, 1964 *
(U.S. and Negro populations in thousands)

| | Residence | | | | | |
| | Farm | | Nonfarm | | Totals | |
| Population | Number | Percent | Number | Percent | Number | Percent |
|---|---|---|---|---|---|---|
| Negro | 1,421 | 6.85 | 19,318 | 93.15 | 20,739 | 100.00 |
| Creole | | | | | | |
|   Direct Descent | 1,353 | 21.22 | 5,024 | 78.78 | | |
|   Nondirect Descent | 132 | 14.97 | 750 | 85.03 | | |
|   Total | 1,485 | 20.46 | 5,774 | 79.54 | 7,259 | 100.00 |
| White | 10,983 | 6.60 | 156,063 | 93.40 | 167,046 | 100.00 |

* Creole population included in U.S. totals. Data on U.S. Negro and white populations from *Population Characteristics* (Census Bureau, Ser. P–20, No. 142, October 11, 1965), 1, 17.

IN- AND OUT-MIGRATION OF CREOLES

*Riverville.* A few in-migrants to Riverville are persons who were born there and spent their productive years working elsewhere. When they reached retirement age, they came back, purchased property which they improved, and again took up residence. A few young couples who had earned a living elsewhere moved back to the community when their parents needed help on the farm, provided they could secure additional income, usually through driving a bus or doing janitorial work. Some young people in the productive years who have returned to Riverville are accused of being lazy and of looking for an easy living even though they are helping their parents operate a farm. In another instance a young man who returned to Riverville from an urban Louisiana community allegedly "got in some bad trouble there so he came back to the country and decided to stay." Some "age-able" people who are eligible for old age assistance return to Riverville and live on tenant property. Occasionally they do a little labor to supplement their income.

Although lack of educational opportunities led to out-mobility, the opportunity to attend a Catholic school in a community with other Creoles was also a factor in mobility back to Riverville as long as the school was in operation. One mother who lived in Texas said she had contemplated moving back because her children were growing up in "an atmosphere that is not Catholic." If her husband could find work in Riverville, the family would "move back tomorrow."

An analysis of out-migration and in-migration to Riverville by age and sex reveals that the rate [15] of out-migration increases sharply with adolescence and decreases after fifty. In the age bracket seventy to seventy-four, however, there is another sharp increase in out-migration primarily because children who are living elsewhere insist that elderly parents have someone live with them; therefore, parents move to the communities where their children have settled. The in-migration curve is relatively high in the school years, primarily for the farm population that originated in Riverton. The next sharp increase is for women between fifty and sixty-nine, many of whom are widows. There is some in-migration of males, but less than among females. After age seventy this migration decreases for the reasons noted above.

Findings show an out-migration [16] of 79 percent for the Creoles born in Riverville; however, 21 percent of the 1964 residents of Riverville had not been born there. Female out-migration rose above or paralleled that of the male except for the forty–forty-four age bracket and declined in the final stages of the life cycle while that of the male leveled off (Table 19). Of all places of Letoyant residence, Riverville suffered the highest out-migration —nearly four times as great a loss as Riverton. Approximately 35 percent of the out-migrants from Riverville went to southern towns and cities; 32 percent went to Northern City; 19 percent to Western City; less than 5 percent to other rural areas; and .6 per-

[15] The migration rate is based upon the number of individuals in a given category moving to a place other than place of birth divided by the total in the category, e.g., age or sex.
[16] This rate is cumulative, covering total out-migration because the time factor could not be considered. See Strom, *The Out-Migration Pattern of a Colored Community in the South.*

Table 19

MIGRATION OF LIVING DIRECT DESCENT CREOLE POPULATION, 1964

| Place * | Birthplace | | | | | Residents in 1964 | | | | | Net Gain or Loss † |
|---|---|---|---|---|---|---|---|---|---|---|---|
| | Total | Stayed There No. | % | Moved Away No. | % | Total | Born There No. | % | Moved There No. | % | |
| Rural | | | | | | | | | | | |
| Riverville | 2195 | 485 | 22.1 | 1710 | 77.9 | 611 | 485 | 79.4 | 126 | 20.6 | −1584 |
| Others | 1203 | 462 | 38.4 | 741 | 61.6 | 742 | 462 | 62.3 | 280 | 37.7 | − 461 |
| Towns | | | | | | | | | | | |
| Southern | 1085 | 543 | 50.0 | 542 | 50.0 | 1207 | 543 | 45.0 | 664 | 55.0 | + 122 |
| Others | 3 | 0 | 0.0 | 3 | 100.0 | 6 | 0 | 0.0 | 6 | 100.0 | + 3 |
| Cities | | | | | | | | | | | |
| Western | 302 | 295 | 97.7 | 7 | 2.3 | 1129 | 295 | 26.1 | 834 | 73.9 | + 827 |
| Northern | 177 | 164 | 92.7 | 13 | 7.3 | 699 | 164 | 23.5 | 535 | 76.5 | + 522 |
| Southwest | 3 | 0 | 0.0 | 3 | 100.0 | 80 | 0 | 0.0 | 80 | 100.0 | + 77 |
| Southern | 247 | 128 | 51.8 | 119 | 48.2 | 663 | 128 | 19.3 | 535 | 80.7 | + 416 |
| Others | 136 | 116 | 85.3 | 20 | 14.7 | 752 | 116 | 15.4 | 636 | 84.6 | + 616 |
| Total Known | 5351 | 2193 | 41.0 | 3158 | 59.0 | 5889 | 2193 | 37.2 | 3696 | 62.8 | |
| Unknown | 1026 | | | | | 488 | | | | | |

* Classification based on population as follows: Rural, under 2,500; Town, 2,500–49,999; City, 50,000 and over.
† Net gain or loss based on the difference between the Creole population born in a place and those residing there in 1964.

cent to Southwest City. (No data were available on about 8 percent.)

The pattern of selective characteristics by age and sex shows the heaviest concentration of out-migrants to be between the ages of twenty-five and fifty. Female redistribution is highest in the twenty to twenty-five age bracket and second highest in the elderly age brackets; moreover, females have a greater tendency than males to migrate toward rural areas. In directional trend, the male redistribution is toward the North while the female redistribution favors the South. In Riverville, then, out-migration appears to be patterned. Noticeable streams of migrants from Riverville, as the largest single place of origin, have moved toward urban places in a ratio of about twenty to one. Variations in the streams are discernible by age and sex, with the largest out-migration among Creoles in the economically productive years, especially at the beginning of the family life cycle. Conversely, nearly one-fifth of the resident population of Riverville is composed of in-migrants. Some of these in-migrants are not direct descent Letoyants, but have married into this population or migrated from Riverton. The chances are that a large proportion who were born there will eventually move out.

*Other Southern Centers.* Riverton, the only large rural settlement other than Riverville, has had a little less out-migration than Riverville. About 62 percent of the living Creoles who were born there have moved away compared to 79 percent of those born in Riverville. Out-migration is highest for males between ages thirty-five and sixty-four; the rate for females is slightly higher in these years. In-migration is greatest for young people under twenty-four years of age, especially those under age ten who move there with their young parents who are attempting to establish themselves. In-migration is slightly greater among those over seventy than in the preceding age brackets, with females having a higher rate than males, probably because of their greater longevity.

Early out-migrants from rural places generally went to Indianola, where people without land could secure work either as skilled or semi-skilled laborers or as domestics. Some went to Southern City, the largest metropolis in the state. Here a few of them lost identity with the group or disregarded some basic norms. One, for instance, achieved distinction as the first nonwhite notary public in the state of Louisiana; his obituary noted that he was single and Protestant. Another Letoyant became very prominent among the "Zulus," that is, Negroes who march in the Mardi Gras festivities with blackface makeup. No Riverville Letoyant would parade with blackface makeup, nor would he countenance participation in its sponsoring organization. Later migrants to Southern City seem to have retained their identities and communicated regularly with their relatives in Riverville. This city is not, however, one of the major migration centers.

A city in northern Louisiana that was settled relatively early by the Creoles has attracted comparatively large numbers of migrants. Here they live in predominantly segregated city blocks [17] where a high proportion of them are property owners. Here, too, there are residential clusters around the vicinity of one of the two Catholic churches that serve the nonwhite population. Travel to Riverville is frequent, and close ties are usually maintained between relatives, both here and in Riverville.

Another city, Centerville, that is within a two-hundred-mile radius of Riverville, did not attract the Letoyants in appreciable numbers until World War I. Most Centerville Creoles live in a segregated neighborhood and attend churches that serve the predominantly nonwhite population. Centerville has a new residential area that is less segregated than the areas near the heart of the city, but the migration to Centerville in recent times has been relatively slight.

Approximately half of the Letoyants born in southern towns—almost exclusively in Louisiana—remain there. The rate of in-migration accelerates by age bracket from twenty-five to fifty; then there is a little decline, and an upward swing again at sixty-five. By sex, there is little difference except between the ages of

[17] Only 8 percent are living in blocks that have less than 80 percent nonwhite household heads.

twenty and twenty-four when females migrate sooner than males. Out-migration follows the same trend by age and sex, with a sharp increase at age twenty-five, a decline at fifty, and an upswing at sixty-five. Since more of the 1964 residents of southern towns moved there from another place of birth than were born and remained there, there has been a gain of 5 percent in in-migration.

Southern cities with populations over 50,000 have only one-tenth as many "native-born" Letoyants as southern towns with populations between 2,500 and 50,000, but approximately the same number of persons born in southern cities remain there (52 percent) as in southern towns. There is, however, a much higher rate of in-mobility into southern cities. Approximately 81 percent of the 1964 residents of these cities are not living in the place of their birth. The rate of in-migration increases sharply for Letoyants between the ages fifteen and nineteen, with the male rate higher than the female rate through the twenties, and the increase becomes high at ages thirty to thirty-four. Out-migration is never high at any specific age level, but it is highest among the very young.

Out-migration from place of birth is marked among Louisiana-born Creoles; approximately two-thirds of them migrated, a proportion 2 percent higher than that for all Creoles regardless of place of residence. Out-migration is patterned, as was hypothesized. Distinctive streams of a predominantly urban trend have formed, and noticeable differences exist in life-cycle stages. There are also some differences by sex. Since nearly all Letoyant out-migrants are from the South, the patterns among them reflect the general patterns of out-migration (Table 19).

Of all Creole out-migrants on whom data are available, slightly more than 6 percent moved from place of birth to a rural community; this move may have been only a few miles along the river between Riverville and Riverton. About 28 percent moved to urban towns or cities within the state of Louisiana, and nearly 32 percent moved outside the state, again to urban centers. The pattern was definitely toward urban areas, with a slight preference for out-of-state mobility.

Age and sex patterns are not as marked among all Louisiana

migrants as for Riverville migrants because of the variations in types of communities. Rural areas experienced a higher rate of out-migration while urban areas experienced a higher rate of in-migration. In-migration to towns and cities tended to accelerate by age brackets from the time adolescents finished high school until about age fifty. It started a little earlier for cities than for towns; the male rate of in-migration into cities during young adulthood was higher than for females, while more females than males in their twenties tended to migrate to towns. Among older persons, after sixty-four particularly, there was an increase in out-migration from towns; however, this trend was not notice-able in cities.

There is, then, migration within the South, with more mobility toward cities and towns; however, older persons who were reared in rural areas and who may have relatives and friends there tend to migrate back if they can be independent. Young adults who are attempting to earn a living show the highest rates of out-mobility from rural areas and toward the towns and cities. Many of them, of course, migrate outside the South.

## EFFECTS OF OUT-MIGRATION

Out-migration of Letoyants from rural places to urban com-munities in Louisiana affects the composition of the ethnic popula-tion. This composition, in turn, has an effect on the future size of the population as well as its dependency ratio. The relatively high fertility in rural communities is suggested by the proportion of young dependents and the low rate of in-migration. Louisiana towns have more young dependents (35.1 percent) than Louisiana cities (29.1 percent); however, cities have a higher proportion of Creoles in the vital productive years (63.2 percent) than towns (57.2 percent). Both towns and cities have the same proportion of aged dependents, namely 7.7 percent.

The in-migration rate for Louisiana towns is 58.4 percent, while that for cities is 82.1 percent. For both combined, the rate is 65.3 percent. Out-migration, however, is also high at slightly more than 51 percent for towns as well as for cities. Even though the mobility into urban Louisiana would seem to indicate that the Creoles would keep their southern roots, it is doubtful that those who move into these urban centers will remain there. If prevailing trends persist, more than half of those born in the urban places will later migrate out of the South.

The out-migration of southern Creoles from the South where they have been concentrated until the last few decades poses some serious threats to ethnic survival. Since Riverville has special significance as the place of origin and of return for those who migrate, its survival has particular relevance. Out-migration as a cause of extinction is a well-supported hypothesis.[18]

From the demographic viewpoint, the homeland is not approaching extinction. Even more important than demography, however, are the prevailing attitudes toward Riverville of the 78 percent of the living Creoles born there who have migrated away and of many others whose parents or relatives have roots there. Property is not sold to outsiders, as a rule, and when the present older population disappears, there is a strong likelihood that Creoles from other communities will move into Riverville and settle on family property, or that the property will be sold to other group members who intend to settle on it. It might become greatly revitalized if it actually contains reputed mineral resources.

Riverville will probably continue to be a kind of Mecca to which Letoyants who live elsewhere return to reinforce their sense of identity and learn about their heritage. Ties of out-migrants are maintained by frequent communication and particularly by visits during holidays and vacations. Traditions and values tend to endure if such ties are maintained. It is improbable that Riverville will suffer the fate of E. Franklin Frazier's Gouldtown in New Jersey, despite the high rate of out-migration. Gouldtown was socially and physically out of harmony with

[18] Cf. Kingsley Davis, *Human Society* (New York: The Macmillan Co., 1949), 157.

Anglo-Saxon environment in the North. Riverville seems to be embedded in the southern scene.[19]

Letoyant Creole survival in the urban environment is important since 80 percent of the living Letoyants are urban dwellers, and more than 50 percent are living outside of Louisiana. Within the state, communication and visits to Riverville strengthen ethnic ties; however, the solidarity and the transmission of traditional values rest largely in the hands of those who have migrated from the state. In the next two chapters emphasis is upon the settlement patterns and the impact of resettlement upon Creole attitudes.

[19] E. Franklin Frazier, *The Negro in the United States* (New York: The Macmillan Co., 1957), 198.

# Chapter 13

# Colonization Patterns

Southern out-migration has a temporal or historical pattern as well as a spatial one. The historical pattern first emerged during Reconstruction, but lacked emphasis and focus until the end of the century when the rate nearly tripled. The fluctuations were attributable largely to social conditions and the demand for labor. Until World War I, nine-tenths of the nonwhite population lived in the South, and four-fifths of those in the South were in rural areas. During the World War I years, the demand for unskilled labor in northern industry stimulated out-migration for the first time in about ten years, and the migrants settled where industry was located.[1]

Both whites and nonwhites were given an impetus to migrate from the South during World War I; in fact, for the first time since the 1880's, white out-migration actually exceeded that of nonwhites. The restriction of foreign laborers by the immigration laws passed in the 1920's also served as a stimulus to migration. However, the depression of the 1930's had an adverse effect on migration; nonwhite out-migration from the South dropped almost 50 percent. The rate of out-migration increased again in the 1940's, and the volume of migrants veered sharply to the West, where defense industries had been established.[2]

Since 1955 the South has reversed the trend of out-migration. In the period 1950–55, the South had a net loss of 1.7 million

[1] E. Franklin Frazier, "Conditions of Negroes in American Cities," *Transactions of the Fifth World Congress of Sociology* (Louvain, Belgium: International Sociological Association, 1964), 133.

[2] Hope T. Eldridge and Dorothy Swaine Thomas, *Population Distribution and Economic Growth, United States, 1870–1950*, Vol. III of *Demographic Analysis and Interrelations* (Philadelphia: The American Philosophical Society, 1964), 90–91.

persons; however, between 1955 and 1960 there was a gain of about 300,000. The reversal took a sharper upswing between 1960 and 1965 when there was a net migration gain of 750,000 which reflects the growing industrialization of the region.[3] The change in net migration rates to and from the South, as defined by the census, is attributable primarily to white migration patterns, for nonwhites were still leaving the area in relatively large numbers. Between 1940 and 1950, Louisiana's net migration rate was 0.2 for whites and −17.0 for nonwhites. During the 1950's the state was one of the five in the South to have a net in-migration of whites.[4]

Trends in Negro migration are pertinent to Creole migration because Creoles are generally included in the Negro category, especially by whites who know nothing of Creoles. Also, migrating Creoles who are dark-complexioned will tend to look for the economic opportunities open to the Negro in the places to which they migrate. However, migrating Creoles who wish to avoid being categorized as Negro usually avoid settling in places that have a large Negro population.

The Negro—and Creole—out-migration pattern has been toward urban centers, and also away from the South. In 1910, 89 percent of the Negroes were in the South; by 1960 the percentage was 60 percent; by 1969 it was 52 percent. In 1910 only 8 percent of the Negroes lived in the twenty-five largest cities, with the leading ones being in the South: New Orleans, Memphis, Washington, Baltimore, and Atlanta. By 1960 almost 32 percent of the Negroes lived in the twenty-five largest cities: in the North, New York, Chicago, Philadelphia, and Detroit; in the South, Washington and New Orleans; in the midwest, St. Louis; and on the west coast, Los Angeles.[5] The Letoyant Creoles settled

[3] "Estimates of the Population of States: July 1, 1965," *Population Estimates* (Bureau of Census, Ser. P-25, No. 348, September 16, 1966), 2.
[4] C. Horace Hamilton, "The Negro Leaves the South," *Demography*, I (No. 1, 1964), 278, 284.
[5] Ben J. Wattenberg, *This U.S.A.* (Garden City: Doubleday & Co., 1965), 270–71; 1969 data from "The Social and Economic Status of Negroes in the United States, 1969," *Current Population Reports* (Bureau of Census, Ser. P-23, No. 29, 1970), 3.

in sufficiently large numbers in two of these cities to classify the settlements as colonies, even though residents of the central cities were not always in contiguous residential areas. The third colony does not have a large Negro population, nor have Creoles established residence in any appreciable numbers in the other six major cities having large Negro populations.

Letoyant Creoles, like Negroes, have migrated out of the South toward urban centers in the North. Negro migration northward is about evenly distributed between the Northeast and North Central regions; Creole migration is primarily toward the North Central region. In the Northeast, fourteen out of fifteen Negroes live in urban centers; in the North Central States, sixteen out of seventeen, and in the West, ten out of eleven. In the South, however, only three out of five (60 percent) Negroes are urban.[6]

## CREOLE CHOICE OF SETTLEMENTS

For the most part, early Letoyant Creole out-migrants went to urban centers in Louisiana or across the state boundary. Such out-migration still goes on, but today out-migrants tend to go greater distances. One of the Negroes in Riverville observed that when Creoles move, "they goes a fur piece," that is, "someplace off yonder where they can jump the color line."

Letoyants have not migrated to any extent to many of the cities that have shown an explosive growth in nonwhite population. Although the nonwhite population of Philadelphia doubled between 1940 and 1960, that of New York City increased nearly $2\frac{1}{2}$ times, and that of Detroit tripled,[7] none of these cities received many Letoyant in-migrants. In fact, the twenty-nine states and the District of Columbia that showed a gain of nonwhites between 1950 and 1960 included only one state to which the Creoles migrated in appreciable numbers during that decade.

[6] Wattenberg, *This U.S.A.*, 271.
[7] Charles E. Silberman, "Negroes in Our Cities," *Readers Digest*, LXXXI (August, 1962), 53.

Like the nonwhite migration pattern, the Letoyant pattern of out-migration from the South was almost completely toward urban places. Of the 3,696 living Letoyants who are known to have moved from place of birth, 2,085 moved to cities outside the South. Letoyant choice of settlement, however, has been distinctive in that the population has been disposed to form its own rather closely knit subcommunity. Over 70 percent of the living Letoyant Creoles who moved to cities outside the South settled in three places, called here Northern City (40 percent), Western City (26 percent), and Southwest City (4 percent). The percentage settling in the latter city has been small, but it seems to have potential for further Creole settlement.

Although migration to Northern City was initiated immediately after the Civil War by a few of the descendants of Grand Pere's younger siblings, this migration was negligible until after World War I. After the second World War, migration accelerated. But the high rate of Negro migration to Northern City as well as the in-migration of southern "hillbillies" made this community a less desirable place than it had hitherto been. Creoles still migrate to Northern City, especially if they have relatives there, but the bulk of the present southern out-migration is not northward bound.

In 1964 Northern City had 699 resident Letoyants, 23.5 percent of whom had been born there. A high proportion of the population born in Northern City (92.7 percent) remains (Table 19). However, the population composition of Northern City is not symmetrical because the base is not in proportion to the rest of the pyramid (Fig. 8). There are slightly more males than females, especially among the middle aged. The Creole population in Northern City is predominantly between the ages of twenty and forty. Families are not large, primarily because many parents have not yet completed the childbearing years. The relatively small number of children in Northern City may also reflect a general trend toward smaller families.

Southwest City and Western City are both places where contemporary Creoles have settled. The westward movement did not

Figure 8

CREOLE POPULATION LIVING IN NORTHERN CITY
BY AGE, SEX, AND TYPE OF DESCENT, 1964

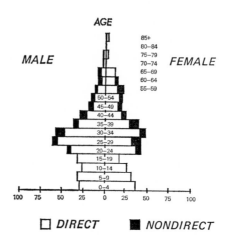

□ DIRECT    ■ NONDIRECT

gain momentum until after World War II when Creole servicemen who fought in the Pacific became acquainted with the West and saw it as a likely place of settlement. Following the war they had money to invest in automobiles and homes, and many of them decided to settle in the West. Young Creoles on their own for the first time may attempt to make a living in Southwest City. If this fails, they go to Western City, where they are likely to find relatives and friends to assist them. In both of these communities the Creoles have established colonies where identification with less privileged groups is minimized and where status can be more readily achieved than in the South.

In 1964 Western City had a population of 1,129 Creoles, 26 percent of whom were born there. An even higher proportion of Letoyants born in Western City (97.7 percent) remained there than the proportion remaining in Northern City. Figure 9 reveals a comparatively solid base with the exception of the age groups under five. Since information on Western City births for 1964 did not include approximately the last five months of that year,

Figure 9

CREOLE POPULATION LIVING IN WESTERN CITY
BY AGE, SEX, AND TYPE OF DESCENT, 1964

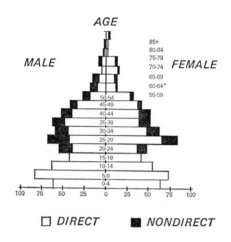

□ DIRECT    ■ NONDIRECT

the bar for that age group is probably more symmetrical than it appears on the pyramid; however, national population trends show a decline in births after 1960. Figure 9 also indicates a relatively high number of Creole women in the age bracket between twenty-five and twenty-nine. The population in Western City is, then, a relatively young one with more older women than older men—a trend that reflects the greater longevity of women.

Since the Creole population of Southwest City in 1964 was only eighty persons, none of whom was born there, it is too small to depict on a pyramid. Although this city is a stopover point en route to the West, and has special appeal for Creoles who prefer not to settle in large cities, many Creole migrants to the West go there directly.

FACTORS IN SETTLEMENT SELECTION

INFLUENCE OF RELATIVES

Unlike the Negroes, who often migrated as single persons or in families with female heads, Letoyants generally moved as families with male heads. Only in recent years has the out-migration of adolescents or single adults been sizable, and when they do migrate, they are encouraged by their parents to migrate to the large urban centers where appreciable numbers of Creoles have already settled, where relatives and friends can assist them to get a start financially, and where group members can serve as a means of social control.

Youths who migrate from Riverville after finishing school generally join siblings in one of the colonies. If the migrant is the eldest child, he may join aunts, uncles, or grandparents. Sometimes an out-migrant depends upon Creole friends for a place to live and for advice on a job.

A job situation in Northern City was depicted in the following terms: "Where my daddy work, just about my whole family is working there, and they hardly have anybody from the city working there. It employs about forty people. And the man like the way the people from here work, and ever time some other one would come off the river, he would tell them to bring them over. Until right now, I'll bet you twenty-five of the forty people is working at that particular factory as far as the people from home you see are here."

Creoles who obtain positions of responsibility tend to give preference to their own people if they have any voice in hiring workers. One such situation was described in the following words: "In those small factories like where Mr. Joe's son work it's most of the people he got in. He got to be foreman, and the boss man know that the people here . . . if they know you're from the river, they're willing to make a way for you because they figure the folk from here work better than those people from up there. They have a reputation for being better workers."

Single adults with households of their own sometimes act as patrons of nieces and nephews who wish to settle in a place where they can earn a living. One middle-aged man in Western City has had a relative in his household almost constantly over the last fifteen years. His mother came to live with him after the death of his father. When she became bedridden, a sister in

Western City took the mother into her home, and the bachelor brother launched one niece and nephew after the other until they got married and established their own households.

CATHOLICISM

If the Creoles had migrated to areas where Catholicism would have contributed to their minority status, it would have been one more impediment to social status, and, under such circumstances, they might have been tempted to conceal their religious identity, if not to reject it. In communities where Catholicism is strong and influential, however, identification with it is an asset. Some of the Creoles identify themselves as Catholic when applying for jobs in the belief that stating their religious convictions gives the impression that they are honest.

Whether the religious complexion of a city consciously played a role in the choice of places of settlement is uncertain. However, the relative importance of Catholicism in the colonies is reflected in the proportion of Catholics in a city's total population. Northern City has always been an important metropolis with a high proportion of Catholics, about 42 percent in 1965. Southwest City and Western City were settled by the Spanish, and have a long tradition of Catholicism. Southwest City is more than 38 percent Catholic; Western City is approximately 19 percent Catholic.

A resident of Northern City voiced her impression of the association between religious identity and choice of a place of settlement as follows: "Being a Catholic is quite a big thing, but you know people here are essentially Catholic anyway, so this is what we would want. A lot of us are excommunicated for different reasons but we all still go to church. Because this is where the group is going to be. And hoping, I guess, that we can all finally be able to die a Catholic. That is instilled in us."

In the parishes where they attend church the Creoles sometimes find difficulties stemming from their racial visibility. Thus, in Northern City, Creoles who reside in a predominantly Polish parish met with unexpected opposition when they expressed an interest in joining a church organization. An interracial marriage between a Creole man and a Polish woman intensified prejudice, but in time the Creoles came to be accepted in the parish. To this day, however, clusters of ethnic populations that are traditionally Catholic still exhibit racial prejudice in Northern City.

In Southwest City, where segregation is practically nonexistent in churches as well as in residential sections, Catholicism is more of an advantage than a disadvantage to the Creoles who moved there. As Creoles improve their economic status, they move into better residential areas. There never was any problem, however, about Creole acceptance into the Catholic community in Southwest City.

Although Western City Creoles do not tend to settle in predominantly Latin neighborhoods nor attend churches where Spanish is spoken, they are sometimes identified as Latin because of their complexion and do not experience discrimination in their churches. Since, however, Spanish-speaking people constitute the largest minority group in Western City and are relatively low on the socioeconomic scale, the chief advantage the Creoles have in being identified with them is in not being classified as nonwhite.

In Western City many of the Creole homes have very large stickers on the front doors reading, "This is a Catholic home." In some instances, stickers are displayed as a deterrent to the Jehovah's Witnesses, who attempt to gain entry into homes and win adherents. But the stickers also identify the Creoles as Catholics to neighbors and visitors.

LATIN MILIEU

Historically, Northern City had very little Latin influence, particularly when the Letoyants first went there. Since World War II, however, there has been an increase in the Latin population. Latins in Northern City have been primarily the people of Mexican origin, who follow the crops and subsequently settle in the North, or Puerto Ricans, who have filtered into the community from the east coast, or Cuban refugees. Since the Creoles tend to settle in neighborhoods where their color is deemphasized and where

Catholicism is strong, they have come into rather close proximity with the Spanish-speaking elements of Northern City.

The settlement where Latin atmosphere is greatest is Southwest City. Here people with Spanish surnames comprise more than a third of the total population, and Spanish is recognized as an official language. This Latin atmosphere was undoubtedly a consideration in the choice of this city for settlement.

Although the population with Spanish surnames in Western City amounts to slightly less than one-fourth of the total population, the Latin atmosphere of the city affords distinct advantages to the Creole. A Louisiana Letoyant commented: "In the West they do not make many distinctions. Everyone goes where he pleases in churches and in buses. Those people is dark, too, and you can't tell who is colored and who isn't. They has people of all kinds, and they do not make the coloreds go to one part of the church or sit in special places."

In an environment that has an appreciable number of Latins, Creoles are likely to be identified as such rather than as Negroes. While the Latin classification is often associated with low socio-economic status, that type of association is, perhaps, less damaging to status identification than identification as Negro. Moreover, in places where a Latin atmosphere prevails, there is usually a high incidence of Catholicism also.

ECONOMIC CONSIDERATIONS

*Occupations.* Since the Creoles come from a predominantly rural background, where the older migrants had rather limited educational opportunities, they could not be expected to find high-status, well-remunerated jobs. Among the early migrants there was a tendency to seek work in the church or in a hospital, school, or other institution operated by priests, brothers, or nuns. To be a housekeeper, janitor, or handyman in such an institution is deemed more prestigious than to do the same work elsewhere.

Identification as nonwhites also sets limits to the occupational choice of the Creoles, especially the males who are traditionally the breadwinners. Compared to white migrant males, nonwhites are in a particularly disadvantageous position. Nonwhite male migrants, regardless of their social origins, are in relatively low-ranking manual jobs as operators, service workers, or laborers. Moreover, nonwhite males are not likely to progress to higher-status jobs, according to Otis Duncan's study of occupational mobility. Nonwhite men whose fathers have higher level occupations are likely to move down, but white men are likely to stay at the same level as their fathers.[8] Migration seems to compound occupational inequality, and nonwhites often augment welfare rolls in communities where they settle in large numbers.

But Creoles seldom move into areas where they have no "connections." If they have no relatives, they may use their church affiliation to get initial jobs at a church plant, hoping to move to more remunerative work. For the most part, however, relatives help in getting jobs. Many relatives not only work on the same job but live together, sometimes in apartments within the same large dwelling.

Approximately 55 percent of the Creoles in Northern City are semiskilled and the vast majority of them work in some kind of manufacturing. Occasionally they become foremen or supervisors in a manufacturing plant. About 14 percent are engaged in unskilled occupations chiefly as maintenance workers. Another 14 percent are skilled either as policemen, firemen, or bus drivers; however, the majority of the skilled workers are not direct descent Letoyants but Creoles who intermarried with them. The remainder of the Creoles are either proprietors (of liquor stores or barber shops, for instance) or professionals. Occasionally both husband and wife will be employed, perhaps in positions of different status. Some Northern City Creoles have received recognition for their job performance: as model worker in a manufacturing plant, as foreman, or as superintendent with the authority to

[8] Otis Dudley Duncan, "Patterns of Occupational Mobility Among Negro Men," *Demography*, V (No. 1, 1968), 11–22. These findings are based on 1962 data.

hire workers. A few of them have savings that they can invest in property, homes, apartment houses, or stores.

Creoles in Southwest City, like those in Northern City, are generally recognized as an industrious people. Approximately one-third of the gainfully employed Creoles are in skilled occupations, predominantly as carpenters. Another one-third are semiskilled; most of them work in the same automobile repair shop. Other semiskilled occupations include work in dry-cleaning shops, checking at wholesale drug companies, and manufacturing. Slightly less than one-third are unskilled either as janitors or as service-station attendants.[9]

Although Western City has a paucity of jobs for untrained people, Creoles have not experienced the same disadvantages as unskilled Negroes, because the majority of the Creoles who migrated there have either had skills or been able to acquire them with the assistance of relatives and friends. Creoles are predominantly self-supporting. About 35 percent of the family heads in Western City are skilled workers, with carpenters predominating; 10.4 percent of the Creoles are semiskilled clerks, and another 10.4 percent are housewives. Nearly 15 percent of the household heads are retired. Less than 10 percent are unskilled, chiefly in maintenance work, and less than 5 percent are professionals.[10] Compared to Creoles in the other two large colonies, those in Western City are better off financially.

*Homes.* In Northern City the majority of the Creoles are not homeowners. Only 9 percent live in blocks where 80 to 100 percent of the dwellings are owned by the tenants; none is found in the blocks where the percentage ranges from 60 to 79. Seventy-nine percent of Northern City Creoles live in blocks where less than 40 percent of the homes are owned by the dwellers (Table

[9] A complete occupational census was obtainable for Southwest City through an up-to-date city directory. Information on occupations in the other cities is based on a variety of sources.

[10] These percentages are based upon one-third of the Creole population in Western City. Information was taken from church parish census cards.

20). The majority of those who are owners probably came to Northern City financially prepared to make investments, or they are industrious, long-time residents of Northern City.

Southwest City has the highest proportion of owned dwellings: 24 percent of the families in Southwest City live in blocks where ownership by the dwellers is from 80 to 100 percent; and another 29 percent live in blocks where ownership is between 60 and 79 percent, making a total of 53 percent of Creoles of Southwest City probable homeowners. Homes in Southwest City, however, are often little more than unpretentious adobe dwellings of low economic value when contrasted to Creole homes in Northern City.

In Western City about 14 percent of the Creoles families live in blocks where ownership ranges between 80 and 100 percent and another 14 percent in blocks where the percentage of owned dwellings is between 60 and 79. More than two-thirds of the Creole dwellers in Western City are probably not homeowners. Since the median age of Western City Creoles is relatively low, these young couples are only getting started in an occupation; therefore, the low percentage of homeownership is not surprising, nor is it necessarily a reflection on their ability to be economically self-supporting.

Dwellings in Western City are in better condition than those in either of the other two settlements. About 12 percent of the Creoles in both Northern and Southwest City live in blocks where 1 to 39 percent of the dwellings are not sound, whereas only 1 percent of the residents of Western City live in such neighborhoods (Table 20). Rents are higher in Southwest City. One skilled Southwest City mechanic pays over $100 per month rental on his home. Average rental prices there range from $83 to $57 per month. In Western City, average rents are slightly less, ranging from $73 to $60 a month. Rents in Northern City are lower than those in the other two communities.[11]

---

[11] Based upon average contract rent as given in block analysis data in Bureau of the Census publications.

## Table 20

CREOLE HOMEOWNERSHIP AND CONDITION OF DWELLING IN SELECTED COMMUNITIES *

| Creole Dwellings by Community | Percentage of Owned Dwellings by Block | | | | | | Percentage of Sound Dwellings by Block | | | | | |
|---|---|---|---|---|---|---|---|---|---|---|---|---|
| | 0–19 | 20–39 | 40–59 | 60–79 | 80–100 | Total | 0–19 | 20–39 | 40–59 | 60–79 | 80–100 | Total |
| Percentages in | | | | | | | | | | | | |
| Northern City | 30 | 49 | 12 | 0 | 9 | 100 | 6 | 6 | 15 | 13 | 60 | 100 |
| Southwest City | 0 | 12 | 35 | 29 | 24 | 100 | 6 | 6 | 6 | 23 | 59 | 100 |
| Western City | 10 | 30 | 32 | 14 | 14 | 100 | 0 | 1 | 6 | 8 | 85 | 100 [a] |

* Based on block analysis in 1960 census. Percentages of owner-occupied dwellings for the total city in Northern City is 34.3; in Western City 46.2; in Southwest City 69.1. Percentages of sound dwellings in Northern City is 84.7; in Western City 91.1; in Southwest City 89.3.

## RESIDENTIAL SEGREGATION PATTERNS

Although the Creole settlement in Riverville was, in effect, self-segregated, segregation eventually became an important consideration when the Letoyants migrated to other places. In the early migration to cities in the South, segregation was not particularly important, for in the old southern cities Negroes lived on side streets or along alleys back of the residences of whites; domestic servants often resided in the back of the house.[12] In Southern City many Creoles still live in mixed neighborhoods.

The degree of residential segregation between whites and nonwhites has been increasing since the Civil War. In the North this trend may be partially the result of rapid increases of Negro population during periods of scarce housing supply during the two world wars, combined with economic and social practices of the Negroes which limited their ability to compete for housing outside Negro residential areas.[13]

Between 1940 and 1960 a direct relationship began to develop between the percentage of a city's nonwhite population and its segregation patterns: the higher the percentage of nonwhites, the higher the degree of residential segregation.[14] Karl Taeuber's segregation index refers to the distributions of white and Negro residents of a city, or to the minimum percentage of Negroes or whites who would have to change the block in which they live in order to produce a distribution in which the percentage of each race living on each block would be the same throughout the city. The higher the index, the more concentrated the racial populations. A city block containing only whites or only Negroes would have an index of 100. Segregation indices based on the 1960 census for three of the Creole colonies are as follows: (1) Northern City, 93; (2) Western City, 82; (3) Southwest

---

[12] Leo F. Schnore and Philip C. Evenson, "Segregation in Southern Cities," *American Journal of Sociology*, LXXII (July, 1966), 58–59.

[13] Karl Taeuber, "Negro Residential Segregation: Trends and Measurement," *Social Problems*, XII (Summer, 1964), 50.

[14] *Ibid.*, 48.

City, 77. The respective percentages of Negro population in these three settlements are 24, 17, and 7.

The index does not in itself indicate either causes or effects of segregation, nor does it imply that race relations are better or worse in Northern City than in the other cities. However, there is a relationship between the degree of segregation as measured by the index and the proportion of the Negro population in each of the cities.

In each of the three major Creole settlements, the census provides data on the nonwhite and white household heads per total dwelling units in a city block. The location of Creole dwelling units affords information on the extent to which Creoles are segregated in housing. Creoles in blocks that are predominantly white are probably passing. Those in predominantly nonwhite blocks are undoubtedly being identified as nonwhite or Negro; however, they are not necessarily neighboring with Negroes. The discussion of each of the settlements notes the degree of Creole segregation in housing.

*Northern City.* The Letoyant settlement here has peculiarities that distinguish it from other major places of settlement. It was the first distant place to which Creoles went in relatively large numbers. As will be noted in more detail later, it was also a settlement where early efforts to cluster around a particular church failed, primarily because of the rapid turnover of population and the influx of Negroes into the neighborhood. Research on areas of Negro residence in Northern City shows that in 1950 there was a concentration of Negroes in the southern section with a small scattering north of the business district. By 1960 the southern residential sections doubled in size, and the section in the north spread rapidly westward. One settlement in the northeast was relatively isolated from other areas of non-white residence. The boundary line between the northern and southern residential sections probably contributed to the tendency of the Creoles to settle in neighborhoods where household heads were either predominantly Negro or predominantly white; only

6 percent live in blocks that are not in either of these categories, i.e., where the percentage of nonwhite units ranges from 20 percent to 80 percent (Table 21).

Visiting between Creoles living in the white northern sections and those living in the nonwhite southern sections assumed a one-way pattern; Creoles in the north often visited in the south, but those living in the south were not encouraged to visit their relatives and friends in the north. A Creole who purchased property in the south made the following comment concerning settlement in Northern City: "But now, it comes to actually, I think that once you settle in a town like this, that it's more or less . . . your activities are more or less based on what you expect of any city of this type. But now, when it comes to any particular interest in the river people, they *are* pretty much divided according to sections, depending on how you want to live. I was under the impression that a lot of the river people settled as a group. But I'm sure you have found out that they have spread; I think there have been ten or fifteen who moved to another area. Even though quite a few river people settled in this area right here where we are, basically, the ones I know are relatives to a great extent."

*Southwest City.* Various accounts have been given of the choice of Southwest City as a place for Letoyant settlement. According to one account, the first to settle there was working for a bus company. His work took him westward and he liked what he saw as he appraised the city. Shortly after he made his home there, a brother joined him and later a nephew. This was the nucleus of the settlement. Another account of the settlement credits the interest in this city to servicemen who were stationed in adjacent areas or who visited this city during their years of service. Compared to other settlements, Southwest City has a small Letoyant population; however, the city itself is not very large.

In Southwest City the Letoyant Creole population is highly concentrated in blocks that are predominantly white. Fifty-three

## Table 21

### RESIDENTIAL PATTERNS OF CREOLES IN THREE MAJOR SETTLEMENTS BY DEGREE OF WHITE-NONWHITE SEGREGATION

| | Percent of Units with Nonwhite Heads per Total Dwelling Units in a Block * | | | | | | Total units with known addresses within city limits | Total Creole units in Metropolitan area † | Percent known units in Metro. area |
|---|---|---|---|---|---|---|---|---|---|
| | 0 | 1-19 | 20-30 | 40-59 | 60-79 | 80-100 | | | |
| Western City | | | | | | | | | |
| No. Creole units | 7 | 17 | 36 | 27 | 24 | 39 | 150 | 250 | 60 |
| Percent | 5 | 11 | 24 | 18 | 16 | 26 | 100 | | |
| Northern City | | | | | | | | | |
| No. Creole units | 19 | 11 | 0 | 2 | 1 | 20 | 53 | 120 | 44.2 |
| Percent | 36 | 21 | 0 | 4 | 2 | 37 | 100 | | |
| Southwest City | | | | | | | | | |
| No. Creole units | 9 | 5 | 1 | 12 | 0 | 0 | 17 | 27 | 63.0 |
| Percent | 53 | 29 | 6 | 12 | 0 | 0 | 100 | | |

* Degree of segregation as defined in 1960 census. Figures based on block analyses of that census. Northern City has the highest percentage of nonwhite occupied housing units, 20.2 percent; Western City has 14.8 percent; Southwest City has 2.6 percent.
† Metropolitan area here includes communities (often incorporated) contiguous to the city or engulfed by it.

percent of the Creole population there lives in blocks where there are no nonwhite heads; another 29 percent live in blocks where 1 to 19 percent are nonwhite, making a total of 82 percent of the Creole dwellers in Southwest City occupying housing units where there are under 20 percent of the household heads classified as nonwhite (Table 21). Some of the latter may be married to Latin girls, for the classification by block is based upon the race of the household head.

The older residential sections of Southwest City apparently have no zoning regulations. It is possible to find a very modest dwelling that might be classified as "upper lower class" adjacent to a home that is quite pretentious. Informants in Southwest City maintain that there is no strict segregation. Indian or Spanish-speaking people mix rather freely with "Anglos." A few Creole families live in a section that is predominantly nonwhite, but it is a new development with modern dwellings and well-cared-for yards. Many Creole homes in Southwest City are adobe houses, and some of them are in obviously upper-middle-class neighborhoods. The newer arrivals to Southwest City live in the lower socioeconomic areas. The first Letoyant family to move to Southwest City now lives in a neighborhood that is exclusively white, and the probability is that these Creoles are recognized as white. They appear to be in more favorable economic circumstances, judging from their living quarters, than any other Creoles in Southwest City.

*Western City.* Segregated areas in Western City, like those in some other metropolitan centers of the West, have sizable numbers of ethnic minorities other than Negroes. Orientals, who are classified by the census as nonwhite, tend to live in their own residential sections as do substantial numbers of Spanish-speaking inhabitants, many of whom are Mexican.

Negroes were reputedly among the original settlers in Western City; however, they were not numerically very strong until after World War II. Now they have settled in predominantly nonwhite areas. Few Creoles initially settled in these Negro neighborhoods. They tend to live in an area south of the city along one of the major freeways.

Five percent of the Creoles live in blocks where the 1960 census block analysis recorded no nonwhite household heads, and another 11 percent in blocks where there are 20 percent or less nonwhite household heads. These 16 percent could be passing as whites. Approximately 26 percent of Western City Creoles reside in blocks in which 80 to 100 percent of the household heads are nonwhite. An additional 16 percent reside in blocks where 60 to 79 percent are nonwhite, making a total of 42 percent residing in blocks where the household heads are 60 percent or more nonwhite. The overall picture in Western City reveals a scattering of Creoles in blocks where the percentage of nonwhite household heads varies from none to 100 percent with the greater proportion being the blocks where more than half are white (Table 21).

Colonization patterns, then, reflect the importance of the major elements of Letoyant identity. They settle where family strengths can be utilized to meet their needs and where their racial heritage will not place them at too great a disadvantage. Moreover, they tend to capitalize on the religious aspects of their ethnicity. Since they have a predominantly Latin origin attributable to their French and Spanish forebears, they have also chosen to move to communities where the Latin element is more of an advantage than a disadvantage. Economic considerations, which were a primary factor in out-mobility from the South, are important, and both religion and family give assistance in finding jobs. Once the Letoyants establish their reputation in a place of work, they locate jobs for other Letoyants and vouch for their industriousness and reliability. A few of them have attained professional stature; however, the majority are still working their way up the occupational ladder. Although they probably have retained esteem for land and homeownership, not many are financially able to make such an investment. The fact that a high proportion of out-migrants from the South have settled in a few cities, even though they are dispersed within the central cities, supports the hypothesis that Letoyant Creoles make an effort to retain ethnic identity when they leave the South. This hypothesis is further explored in the next chapter where more attention is given to the impact of colonization upon ethnic identity and values.

# Chapter 14

# Impact of Colonization on Creole Identity and Values

As the Letoyant population grew in size and became geographically dispersed, the attraction of the individuals born into this population to their ethnic group came to vary with the extent to which the group satisfied their needs. In Riverville and the surrounding area, Creoles seldom relinquished their identity because the only other sizable group with which to identify was the Negro population. There was definitely more status attached to being Creole than to being Negro in the environs of Riverville. Moreover, there was a strong chance that Letoyants would have a special status simply because of their ethnic heritage.

Letoyant Creoles who migrated away from their homeland, particularly outside Louisiana, where their ethnic identity was not likely to be recognized, had to confront the question of ethnicity anew. Like other migrants,[1] the Creoles questioned the repression and contradictions of a society broader than their homeland and wondered whether the possibility of wider identification was a threat to or an enlargement of themselves. They were faced with several options: Were they to maintain their Creoleness with its identifying characteristics of preferred in-group marriage, strong Catholicity, uncertain and peripheral racial origin, and ties to Riverville? Would this option entail becoming psychological isolates in an urban milieu? Or would it be more rewarding to attempt integration with either the Negro population or the dominant white population?

One young migrant who questioned his identity attributed his attitudes, in part, to intergroup relations in the South. He said, "We have, say, three-way segregation down there on the river.

[1] Cf. Helen Merrill Lynd, *On Shame and the Search for Identity* (New York: Harcourt, Brace, & Co., 1958), 255.

There's this group, this group, and this group [Negro, Creole, and white]. But I can see that this group has a way of life which is much different from the other group that also had a way of life. So *they* identify with *that* group and remain close. Now, however, when we left this group, the migrants went to various parts of the country. We were exposed to a much different environment here, and we found out that in many cases we weren't so much on the ball. When we analyzed our situation back in that river group, we felt that we were losing ground if we continued to identify ourselves here solely on those bases. We're not being recognized fully here, and we don't have a strong enough force to make any notable achievements in that particular area, so then immediately we have to identify with something else."

The confusion often faced by Creole migrants in a new and complex environment was also voiced by a Northern City informant as follows: "Could I live in the South comfortable? No, no, not to be frank with you, no. But I can't live in the North comfortable, so it doesn't matter. I'm serious when I say this. I haven't lived comfortable in a long time—since I been able to think, you know. I think there is a sort of developmental stage within the people from the river. This is why we all live in different areas, too. One of the big factors that we haven't brought out is that many of us think differently about a lot of things. I think there is a commonness up to a certain point. Then there's a deviation."

Migration has, then, led Letoyant Creoles to engage in introspection about their identity and the feasibility of retaining ethnic group ties. They have to depend upon the wider society for meeting many of their needs, just as other migrants who valued group solidarity have done.[2] Yet, to relinquish all sense of ethnic identity would undoubtedly be psychologically hazardous; mutual

[2] Cf. Phillip E. Hammond, "The Migrating Sect: An Illustration from Early Norwegian Immigration," *Social Forces*, XLI (March, 1963), 277-78.

assistance, at least, is expected from ethnic group members, especially relatives and friends.

Insight into the reactions of ethnic group members toward one another was afforded by residents of the colonies. A young woman whose ethnic origin was similar to that of the Letoyants and who married into the family remarked upon Creole response when meeting another group member: "What I have noticed about the river people here [Northern City] is the minute they meet someone . . . they might not've known you personally, but if you're from that part of Louisiana, they say, 'Oh, you're from home!' " A Creole companion then added, "And actually, they all come up and start . . . almost hugging and kissing again." The attention given visitors from Louisiana or new migrants led one resident of Western City to complain that he no longer had many visitors because more recent arrivals, who had more news and more social contacts with Louisiana, were preferred.

Shared ethnicity is usually sufficient basis for rallying support in time of need. A Northern City informant remarked on this tendency: "I think this. If anyone's in trouble here, and they're from the river, they're tied. It's the thing that would hold them through." Thus, one ethnic group member would hardly be expected to testify against another. And in case of unemployment, sickness and bereavement, ethnic group members are usually supportive of each other. Even in the temporary absence of a spouse, assistance may be proffered. More than one informant remarked that he had received repeated calls from friends and relatives at such times, expressing concern and extending invitations. One experience was related as follows:

"Marie called and asked, 'Well, aren't you going to come over?'

"I said, 'Oh, yes I am! Just wait.'

"Later her husband came by and said, 'I knew Joe was out of town, and just came by to check on you. And if you need me, call.'

"I said, OK, I would if I had to, and just left it like that.

"Right now, if I need help, I'd have to call him. He call me about two or three weeks ago. He use to call me quite often and say, 'I called to see how you're doing.' And maybe I wouldn't see him for six months or a year or something."

## Residential Patterns and Social Interaction

Robert E. Park's contention that social relations are frequently and inevitably correlated with spatial relations [3] has been supported in numerous empirical studies and seems appropriate to apply to the Letoyant Creoles who have moved out of the South. If social relations within a group are valued, then residential clustering is a means of providing for frequent social contacts and of rendering mutual assistance. If, moreover, places of residence are within easy walking distance of a church, such circumstances may attest to the continued importance of Catholicism.

The highest incidence of Letoyant residential clustering appeared to be in Northern City, especially in the northern section where there is little likelihood that they will be taken as non-whites. In fact, all of the Letoyant Creole dwellings in Northern City blocks listed by the census as having no nonwhite household heads are in this area. South of the central city, where Negro residence is more prevalent, Creoles occasionally live adjacent to one another, but clustering is less pronounced (Fig. 10).

In Southwest City the clustering pattern is not particularly evident (Fig. 11). This is probably attributable to the liberal zoning policy in this city, as well as to the population's general acceptance of relatively dark-skinned Spanish-speaking people. There is, then, less threat of identification with Negroes in Southwest City than in either Northern or Western City.

In Western City clustering is quite pronounced. Letoyants tend to live just south of the central city. Those in a northern section of this area are nearly always renters; as they purchase property, they move toward the central and southern sections of the area.

[3] Otis Dudley Duncan and Stanley Lieberson, "Ethnic Segregation and Assimilation," *American Journal of Sociology*, LXIV (January, 1959), 364.

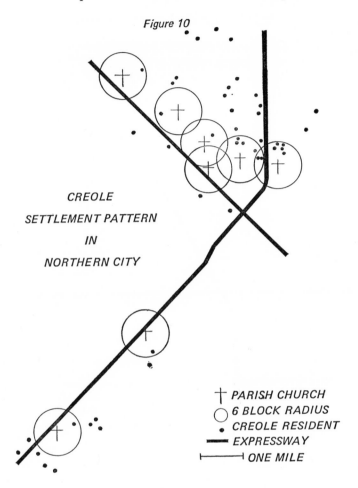

Figure 10

CREOLE

SETTLEMENT PATTERN

IN

NORTHERN CITY

† PARISH CHURCH
◯ 6 BLOCK RADIUS
• CREOLE RESIDENT
▬ EXPRESSWAY
⊢―――⊣ ONE MILE

The northern boundary of this area has large, well-maintained homes that were, for the most part, converted into apartments when a freeway was constructed in the vicinity. Parish churches in the area are close together and relatives often belong to the same parish. Creoles make an effort to visit with relatives on Sundays much as they did in Riverville. A few Creole families live to the west of the central city, but most of them have passed into the white population and have lost rapport with

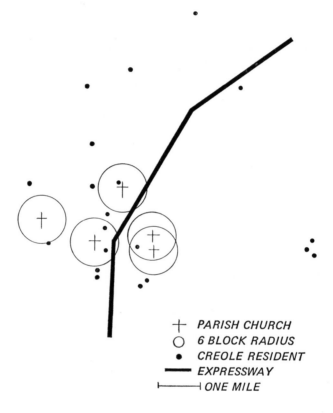

Figure 11

CREOLE SETTLEMENT PATTERN
IN SOUTHWEST CITY

+ PARISH CHURCH
○ 6 BLOCK RADIUS
● CREOLE RESIDENT
━ EXPRESSWAY
⊢━━━⊣ ONE MILE

the others. The Spanish-speaking section of Western City is to the east of the Creole settlement area (Fig. 12).

Such places of rendezvous as social clubs encourage Creole interaction. Western City, for instance, has two such clubs. One is operated by a Letoyant from Riverton and the other by two Letoyants from Riverville. The latter lease the club as an auxiliary business enterprise and relatives take shifts in operating it. It is frequented by the Creoles and, at times, reserved for their functions. Moreover, it is not uncommon in Western City for Creoles

Figure 12

CREOLE SETTLEMENT PATTERN IN WESTERN CITY

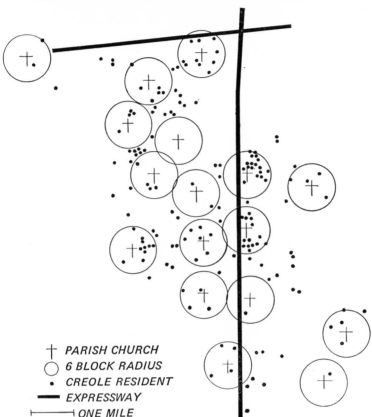

+ PARISH CHURCH
◯ 6 BLOCK RADIUS
• CREOLE RESIDENT
▬ EXPRESSWAY
⊢⎯⎯⎯⎯⊣ ONE MILE

to rent a dance hall for particular group functions. One Western City informant commented that he could attend a dance at least once a month and meet only his Creole friends and relatives. Creole men often congregate at places of business. A barber shop in Northern City is said to be a hangout for them, and a tavern operated by a Letoyant in the same city serves this purpose also.

There are, moreover, occasions that contribute to social interaction, such as recitals and graduations, where attendance is generally by invitation. Other occasions are religious ceremonies. Funerals, for example, attract large numbers of Letoyants who come not only to pay their respects to the deceased but also to meet relatives from Louisiana and receive firsthand news from home. Weddings ordinarily take place at Mass, and, as in Louisiana, acquaintances often show their interest by attending the ceremony even though they are not invited to a reception nor are gifts expected from them. Christenings are usually attended primarily by relatives and close friends who join the family at home after the ceremony. Sunday Mass, however, is undoubtedly the most important religious occasion for social interaction.

## CATHOLICITY

Letoyant Creole informants in the South indicated that their people could be found in the vicinity of churches. "Our people are mostly where the churches are," observed one, who was giving this investigator advice on locating Letoyants who had migrated. Another informant said that if she wanted to find some of her people in Northern City, she knew which Sunday service to attend at a particular church. If Southern informants did not explicitly give assurances of the strong Catholicity of Creole migrants, they implied that living in the vicinity of a church was a clue to the importance of religion in the lives of the migrants.

The Letoyants who first migrated to Northern City did settle in the vicinity of the only Catholic Church that at the time served the nonwhite population, and the descendants still attend this church. Since this church was well established when the Creoles first migrated and since they came in very small numbers initially, no apparent effort was made to establish this church, which was already identified with the Negroes, as a special meeting place for Creoles.

When the wave of migrants went to Northern City in the World War II years, Letoyant migrants preferred to live in a neighborhood that had been predominantly Jewish and that was being infiltrated by other ethnic peoples. A few of the more affluent Creoles purchased land near the parish church—an ornate, spacious Gothic structure—and, early in the 1950's, the parish came to be a gathering place for Creoles. Those who lived in other parishes often requested permission from church authorities to have christenings and marriages in this church, and visitors to Northern City who wished to see Creole relatives or friends were advised to attend a particular Sunday service at the church.

Some of the Letoyants were employed by the parish as janitors and as machinists. When the Creoles in the city wanted to hold a dance or social gathering, the janitor asked for the use of the parish hall. After one dance at which Creole exclusiveness was sufficiently offensive to cause the Negroes to complain, the pastor expressed unwillingness to condone this practice, and, subsequently, church property could not be used to promote Creole social relationships. As the neighborhood around this Northern City church became increasingly Negro, the Letoyants moved out, leaving the parish with only two Creole families, both of whom were property holders.

When the Letoyant Creoles failed to make this church a center for group interaction, and as Negroes infiltrated the parish neighborhood, the Creoles relied more than before upon the strength of blood ties and upon places of recreation leased or operated by themselves to maintain group solidarity. The 1964 map of Northern City with a six-block radius (walking distance) drawn around churches in areas of Letoyant concentration did not reveal any tendency to use churches as a focal point for their residence (Fig. 10).

In Southwest City, where the Letoyants are more scattered than they are in the other two major settlements outside the South (Fig. 11), the churches are located near the center of the community. Only one-fourth of the Letoyant households are within a six-block radius of a church, nor did any knowledgeable informant claim that efforts were made to use the church as a nucleus for Creole activities. The comparatively small number of Creoles in the community, the relative lack of zoning in residential neighborhoods, and the close blood ties among the early settlers may have made such a meeting place less important than in other settlements.

More than in any other major settlement outside the South, the Letoyants in Western City settled near churches. The six-block radii were found to be so close to each other in half the instances that few Letoyants in the area of concentration were not within walking distance of a church. The geographical proximity of the churches, however, rather than a conscious desire on their part to settle near a church probably explains this settlement pattern. If the church were consciously meant to be used as an ethnic meeting place, there would have been greater concentration of Creoles near fewer churches (Fig. 12).

The proximity of Letoyant homes to freeways became apparent when their residences were plotted on city maps (Figs. 10, 11, and 12). Although this phenomenon may have been coincidental, it is probably related to a preference for residence in areas where freeway construction contributed to the devaluation of property, particularly sound dwellings, and also to convenience in transportation.

While the hypothesis that Letoyants initially tended to settle near churches in the places to which they migrate was true, it is no longer supported by evidence. Moreover, the hypothesis that the church is used as an ethnic rallying point now has little support. No doubt some Letoyants do arrange to attend certain services and to meet afterwards, but the size of the out-migration and their geographic distribution within the large colonies no longer makes it feasible to utilize the church extensively in this way. Practices of preempting church facilities for ethnic activities were discouraged among early out-migrants from the South and apparently have not been attempted to any extent in recent years.

Although migrant Letoyants do not seem to be making conscious efforts to settle near churches where they can attend services frequently as well as use the occasion of a church service to interact with one another, there are other indications that they adhere to their religious values. Pastors of the churches attended by Creoles are usually aware of group cohesiveness and identify them as exemplary Catholics. A Northern City pastor said of them, "They are deeply religious, and when they meet up with injustices and things that are hard to bear, religion is their recourse." And a Western City pastor commented, "In regard to the Creoles, I wish I had a whole parish of them." Pastors frequently commented favorably on the support Creoles give the church, their patterns of child rearing, and the efforts they make to bring their affianced who are not Catholics into the church.

Migrant parents seem to take the responsibility for their children's religious upbringing seriously. One midwestern mother related her experiences as follows: "There was only one Catholic church in town, and we found a sign on two pews in the back marked For Colored. My children stayed in the back pew with us when other little children used to be in the May processions, First Communions, and all these other activities. So we decided to send the children to live with Mama Marie and to the Catholic school in Riverville where they could learn the importance of their religion and take part in religious activities."

Another parent expressed his ideas about the difficulties in rearing children to cherish religious values in Northern City, saying: "In the city children have many more distractions—things that they can do rather than practice their religion. Of course, it's got to be in the home brought out to the children that they must do something. You have to get them started. 'Cause if you are going to let them look at the TV and listen to the radio and go to the movies and do some things like that, when they know it's time to go to church, to study their catechism, or things like that . . . well, I think it is harder in the city."

Parents express particular concern about their children who have contracted civil marriages. Old people who reminisce about the joys and sorrows of their lifetime usually place a child's deviancy from Church norms, especially in the area of the family, high on the list of sorrows. When asked about the marriages of his children who were reared in Northern City, one father replied, "Well, they's two of them that's separated, and they remarried again. I pray and hope they'll straighten this thing out before they die. The rest of them [eight children] stick with their husbands and wives."

As already noted in the treatment of the Church in the Southland, the highest percentage of regular religious observance, as measured by attendance at Sunday Mass and reception of the Eucharist during the Easter season, is among Letoyant Creoles in urban places outside the South, namely 94.4 percent as compared to 91.1 percent in urban Louisiana and 81.4 in rural places

*Table 22*

RELIGIOUS OBSERVANCE OF LIVING CREOLES BY COMMUNITY TYPE *

| | Religious Observance | | | | | | | |
|---|---|---|---|---|---|---|---|---|
| | Regular | | Irregular | | Non Attendance | | Totals | |
| Community Type | No. | % | No. | % | No. | % | No. | % |
| Rural Louisiana | 874 | 81.4 | 78 | 7.3 | 121 | 11.3 | 1073 | 100 |
| Urban Louisiana | 521 | 91.1 | 35 | 6.1 | 16 | 2.8 | 572 | 100 |
| Urban Elsewhere | 285 | 94.4 | 13 | 4.3 | 4 | 1.3 | 302 | 100 |
| Totals | 1680 | 86.3 | 126 | 6.5 | 141 | 7.2 | 1947 | 100 |

* Data derived from 1964 parish censuses. Urban Louisiana is represented by Indianola and Urban Elsewhere is represented by fifteen parishes in Western City.

(Table 22). The data on religious observance outside of Louisiana was derived primarily from Western City, where up-to-date parish censuses were available. Moreover, the religiosity of Western City Creole migrants is noteworthy because these migrants are at the ages when religious delinquency tends to be highest, late adolescence and the thirties (Table 8).

There are, of course, Letoyants who do not acknowledge religion as an essential component of ethnic identity. When questioned specifically about religion as an index to group identity because of its relationship to moral behavior, a Letoyant from Northern City said, "Naw, it's not an index of group identity, I don't think. But I think it's an index for training. I think just about everyone from the river . . . I would say are pretty good Catholics. As a matter of fact, I can't think of anyone who isn't. I can't think of one who let their religion go."

Even though religion, as such, is not consciously regarded as an index of identity by migrants, nor as a means to serve group ends, Letoyants nevertheless equate both interracial and inter-faith marriages with "mixed" marriage. Moreover, all the rites of passage, such as christenings and marriages, are performed in the church, and the official sponsors or witnesses are generally members of the Creole population, a practice that serves a dual purpose of maintaining group boundaries and of reaffirming group identification.

## RETAINING TIES WITH THE SOUTH

Origin in Riverville is an identifying characteristic of the Letoyant Creoles, even of those born and reared elsewhere. Residents in the colonies express their feeling of identification with Riverville and their Louisiana relatives in various ways. A Northern City Letoyant commented: "I think this interest is more or less a human type of interest, more or less where all of us—you know even if we never lived to any extent in the place—where we are born. We seek that place out." Another Northern City Letoyant believed that identification with the homeland would lead her to render assistance to any Creole who needed it. She said, "If I was to see someone I knew from the river and barely knew him and if he were in trouble I think I would assist him, you know, without even thinking about it."

"The basic thing I would identify with any person from the river is a common interest," noted another Letoyant. "Sometimes Joe comes over, and says, 'Let's go meet some river people.' It brings almost inexpressible nostalgia that we have quite a bit in common, and we would like to know about what's going on on the river. This is one of the things. Then Joe calls me and asks, 'Did you get a letter from the river?' The minute my sister calls, I ask her the same question. So I think that everyone is concerned with their home. Even if you were just born there and never lived there to any degree, you are concerned with that place."

Riverville is a favorite place for vacation. Rivervillers estimate that 90 to 95 percent of the people who ever lived there come back to visit, even if they have no relatives there. Northern City Letoyant parents say that their children are relatively confined during the year since they cannot play with "just anyone." But on the river the children have this freedom. In Riverville and other Louisiana settlements, Southwest City Letoyants claim to find relief from the Spanish accent and the frequent recurrence of Spanish in conversations.

Trips to Louisiana from Northern City and from Southwest City are usually by car. Sometimes children are sent to Louisiana to vacation with relatives for the summer and are joined by one or both parents later when parents have scheduled vacations. Creoles who are driving to Louisiana and who have space in their cars take friends and relatives along with them. One Northern City family has frequently driven to Riverville for the weekend. The young people take turns driving through Friday night and arrive in Riverville about noon on Saturday. After a day of relaxation with their family and friends, they start the trek back to Northern City Sunday afternoon and arrive in time for work Monday morning. Due to the greater distance involved, Western City Creoles cannot travel to Louisiana by car except during the summer months when they have vacations. They are more likely to send a plane or train ticket to a parent or sibling to allow him to visit in Western City.

Letoyant Creoles in the colonies, however, recognize that some change has taken place in their perspectives. One Creole said, "I think basic group interest as far as I am concerned is much different, say, from my father's view and very different from my grandfather's view." This informant implied that the explanation of his viewpoint is that he has spent so many years of his adult life outside the South and his education had, in large part, also taken place elsewhere. To him Riverville is a birthplace in which he has "a human type of interest," but he acknowledged that he has a more cosmopolitan viewpoint as a consequence of his broader associations in Northern City. "I think when you are exposed to much more, you become a part of something," he said, and then concluded, "You begin to identify with certain movements." Although this informant did not disavow his interest in the place of ethnic origin, he did indicate some of the difficulties he had had in maintaining perspective after his experiences outside the South.

## RACIAL IDENTITY

One of the strongest factors in the retention of ethnic identity by migrant Letoyants is their racial visibility. An educated Northern City Letoyant attempted to explain the rationale underlying her people's idea of race: "Well, as I was just saying, that to try to understand these people, you must remember the white man thinks that one drop of Negro blood can make you a Negro. Same thing happens with this group. A drop of white man's blood makes him superior to the black man. And this, I think, is what makes the wanting to be married in our own group. In other words, feeling superior is still that I'm better because I have that drop of white blood or that Spanish, or that French, or that Italian. It adds something different. As I was saying, about this drop of blood. You walk into a restaurant here. There might be one Negro sitting there when the second Negro goes in and sits near that other Negro. I don't know whether it's strength in unity . . . but it's the same thing with this drop of blood. I have it. You have it. We have something, and there's strength and a feeling of belonging. In other words, we're the same."

According to this reasoning, if a "drop of Negro blood" makes a person Negro, by the same logic, a "drop of white blood" makes a person white. Since there is a proclivity for people to associate with others of similar racial origin, those "bright" Letoyant Creoles who have relatively light skin color and "good" features might have a desire to profit by advantages derived from resembling the dominant group, if not to identify with that group. The Caucasoid phenotype, particularly whiteness, represents personal dignity and affords the possibility of participating completely in American social life. Darkness, however, imposes limitations and implies inferiority. To the nonwhite population in the United States, the Negroid phenotype is the core of a profound group identity crisis, inasmuch as the white world built up the rationale for reducing the nonwhite man to a less than human status by virtue of his Negroidness. Color was, moreover, the basis of the distinction in colonial times for holding a black bond servant for life, but for limiting the term of years for which a white bond servant could be held.[4] While color is only *one* factor in the status of nonwhites, it does symbolize other factors.

SOCIALIZING CHILDREN

If migrants who have been reared in the South have problems regarding their identification, children who are being socialized outside the South undoubtedly have still more difficulty. Like second-generation immigrants, Letoyant children have to reconcile cultural and racial differences at a time in their lives when their concept of themselves is being developed. When a child is exposed to discrimination, he is almost certain to experience shame and an uncertainty about his identity. If he sees this shame in his parents and his people, it is often even more damaging than his own.

Racial overtones in discrimination are especially painful to the Letoyant child who has been taught that he is not Negro. In the urban setting, in particular, where the child meets with appreciable numbers of both white and Negro children, he is likely to permit himself white self-ascriptions more frequently and until a later age than he would if he were in the South. The southern Creole child is infrequently treated as a peer by the white child

[4] Cf. Eric Lincoln, "Color and Group Identity in the United States," *Daedalus*, XCVI (Spring, 1967), 5–9.

and is consequently hesitant to take on white self-ascriptions, for if he unwittingly revealed them he would run the risk of embarrassment. Moreover, the southern child's Creole identity is often reinforced through associations with other Letoyant Creoles. But outside the South the child may be treated as a peer by white children and not recognized as Creole. Therefore, the burden of socializing the child outside the South to his ethnic origin and identity is greater than it is where the child associates primarily with fellow Creoles.

The experiences of a fair-complexioned Letoyant girl, whose family lived in a border state between the North and South where de facto segregation in education prevailed, provides insight into the confusion and humiliation that Creoles sometimes experience during the socialization process. Since much segregation exists in both Northern City and Western City, the experience also has relevance to these colonies.

Two of the girl's experiences were related by her mother as follows: "One day coming from school, my daughter was walking along the street with two dark students, and a lawyer's father, an elderly man, was walking down the street. My daughter and these other two students, they were walking on the sidewalk— three abreast, which they shouldn't have, but anyway she's real fair—truthfully she's every bit of your complexion—light hair with freckles—and this old man coming down the street, when he saw this child in the middle of two dark girls, he turned around to see what was going on. And he fell off the sidewalk.

"And the lawyer became very upset about his father falling off the sidewalk because he went in and told his son that these children, students, pushed him off the sidewalk. But it's not true. He looked around to see this child. Well, she really stood out from the other two, you know, and he fell down from the sidewalk and so they reported it to the police.

"So the police came over and talked to us, and we finally dug into it until we found out exactly how everything happened. That was one incident, and the child was very hurt over it. She just cried.

"Not long after that, she went back to school and a lady was passing in front of the school, and there was a large truck in front of the school parked on the right-hand side, and this child walked across the campus. As she was going across the campus, it attracted this lady in the car driving so, until she wrecked her car. She ran into the truck, wondering what that child was doing going to that school.

"So a lot of talk sprang from that. And so she was very upset again. So she came in that day from school. When she found out all what they said—the woman wrecked her car because that white girl was going to the colored school, and all that—she came in and told her dad. She said, 'Daddy, I'm not going to that school anymore.'

"I say, 'Why?'

"She said, 'Well, I'm not black enough to be black. I'm not white enough to be white—and I'm not going to school anymore. Unless you send me where there's more like me, I'm not going to school.'

"Her daddy took her serious, because she was really upset. So her dad, thinking and stirring his coffee, said, 'Well, baby, if you tough it out this year, daddy will send you where you will feel more comfortable.'

"So, as a result, she went to prep school and came out as salutatorian—the first on record there from out of state."

Although all minority group parents have to teach their children how to regard people of other ethnic origins, skin color complicates the issue for the Letoyant parent, particularly in the colonies. Where there are limited opportunities to associate with fellow Creoles, the responsibility of helping a child discover his identity is even more serious. The mother of a family living in a community with few other Creoles described how she attempted to socialize her children: "The people on the river teach their children to love their people. I taught my children to love *all* people regardless of color. I also taught them to respect people for who they are. Having good training and a Catholic background, I stuck with the Catholic Church, too."

## IDENTIFICATION WITH NEGROES

Letoyants who are not particularly group-conscious, particularly if they are dark-complexioned, may identify in varying degrees with Negroes in urban centers. This identification is more likely to occur where Creoles live and work with Negroes, especially if there are infrequent opportunities to associate with other Creoles. Thus, a family that settled in a community where there were no other Creoles began to identify with Negroes. When questioned about their attitudes, family members responded that they made class distinctions rather than color distinctions and that any Negro with similar class values was acceptable to them and that they mixed socially with such persons.

Letoyant migrants who are sensitive to their Negro friends, especially those whom they knew in the South, are hesitant to disassociate themselves from these contacts when they migrate. One old man in Northern City reflected this when he answered a question about the tendency of those Creoles who pass to ignore other Creoles who make no such effort. "It does make a whole lot of difference in a way. It's kind of foolish. We associate with the colored here and with the Creoles. Our children married Creoles, and stuff like that. When we come here, we met a whole lot of people living here who knew us and we'd have to ignore them. And they were close friends that we knew down there, you know. I don't see no difference here because in a way, you do all these things together. You ride the streetcar, you ride in your car. You go to the show, you sit down where you want. You go to a restaurant, you sit down and eat where you want. The only advantage is the colored people here that pass for white can get better jobs."

Letoyants born and reared in the colonies who have limited opportunities to associate with fellow Creoles or who have not been socialized to differentiate themselves from Negroes are likely to deemphasize Creole ethnicity. Southern Letoyants who have migrated to other regions of the country may react in similar manner, particularly if they have a higher education. In the opinion of a well-educated Letoyant, education has given him a broad perspective. "I've had better schooling," he said, "and I've been exposed to different types of environment. I think I've begun to have a real understanding of ourselves [Creoles] as to our status, what we are, how we are accepted, what people think of us, and where should we be if we want to become individualistic." He explained that he had obtained more of a world view than his ancestors and added that "there are limitations in being just local figures," confined to the Southland. "You aspire as much as anyone else in any field you endeavor—even in international endeavors," he maintained. "But when you think of the river, you think of local thinking. But you are exposed to much more, and you become a part of something bigger. You have to identify with certain movements."

This educated informant continued his analysis as follows: "So some of us reverted to Negro, and some of us here reverted to white. Now even in the white identification, as far as I'm concerned, there isn't too much achievement. The ones who reverted to the Negroes are the ones who are doing better economically. There are basic moral differences, in family type of life. I can't feel very comfortable with the other group, really, on those particular bases. But the Creole cause is a dying cause. Five hundred people—where do we stand? Louisiana doesn't want us, and we're in the middle. I admire my family, the way they brought me up, morally and everything else, I really do. But educational-wise, they were far behind. I think this was our dilemma."

The uneducated man's observation that the Letoyants who pass for white get better jobs is contested by the educated man's contention that those who "reverted to the Negroes" have fared best economically. A third Northern City resident supports the latter contention, and adds that the Creole who fares best is the one known to be "colored" but who looks white and "lives decently." She says, "When you take the river, right away you've got the Creole mixture—mixed blood. In our society, let's face it, appearances mean a lot. It won't, ten years from now. But today, appearances mean a great deal. There are lots of river people holding jobs that if they were dark Negroes, couldn't get the same jobs. So, therefore, they can get ahead much, much faster than other people coming from the South. They're going to work, and they have these opportunities working with them so they haven't got as much trouble getting jobs. And if they live decently, they don't have to trouble to say anything."

The economic factors associated with identification as Negroes cannot be minimized, then, especially at a time when concerted efforts are being made to concur with Civil Rights legislation, and when Negroes are endeavoring to instill pride of race in their own people. Creoles are not averse to taking advantage of economic opportunities open to Negroes. A Letoyant residing in Alaska requested and received a loan from the Small Business Administration, an agency to assist Negroes to become proprietors. Another Letoyant, who was reared and educated in Northern City, was listed at one time as the editor of a Negro magazine and wrote articles on black separatism for other Negro magazines.

When Letoyant Creoles move out of the Deep South into larger communities where they are not readily recognizable, their status is likely to be related to skin color. In Northern City, where the residential lines between Negro and white neighborhoods are rather rigidly drawn, any upper social class Riverville Creole who moves into a Negro neighborhood will probably be identified as nonwhite. This is particularly true if he marries a Negro. One well-educated resident of Northern City, a descendant of a respectable old Riverville family, who married a Negro and later moved into a Negro neighborhood, made the following observations: "My people in Northern City consider me a nigger. We *can* greet down here [in Riverville], like I told my husband. He was shaking this person's hand the other night, and he couldn't shake the hand at home. Down here, the very same people who used to feel inferior to Joe Letoyant's grandchild, is going to go North [Northern City] and feel superior!"

The percentage of Letoyants identified as Negroes because of marriage with Negroes is, nevertheless, relatively small. Of the living "outsiders" who have married Letoyants, only 21.3 percent of the males and 12 percent of the females are predominantly Negroid. Letoyant Creole females are, then, more likely than males to be classified as a Negro because of marriage to one (Table 23).

## "PASSING"

In the South, where individuals are known to belong to families identifiable as Creole, the incidence of losing group identity through passing into the Caucasian population is not great. In the areas where Letoyants live in appreciable numbers, they are recognizable by the peculiar spelling of their names. The proximity to friends and relatives is a deterrent, and, furthermore, the chances of remaining in the area where one has been reared, particularly if it is not urban, and remaining unrecognized as Creole are negligible. Ethnic group members can not readily be convinced of the desirability of severing ties with family and relatives.

When Letoyants move to the colonies, the same pressures are not operative. Under these circumstances, what is the incidence of passing? This question cannot be answered without taking into account the implicit assumption that only nonwhites can pass into the Caucasian population; is it, however, accurate to apply the term *passing* to people who do not consider themselves non-white? Although most Creoles acknowledge that they fall into the nonwhite category, some of those who pass equate nonwhite with Negro and do not admit to being either.

The incidence of this passing in the colonies can be gleaned from the addresses of Letoyant families who live in blocks where the census reports no nonwhite household heads. In the 1960 block analysis, census enumerators asked members of a household to make this classification themselves whereas in earlier census block analysis the enumerator made the classification. Moreover, occupied housing units were classified as white or nonwhite by the color of the head of the household. In the nonwhite category were Negroes, American Indians, Japanese, Chinese, Filipinos, Koreans, Asian Indians, and Malayans; however, no provision was

## Table 23

### Ethnicity of Living Nondirect Descent Population by Generation and Sex, 1964

Ethnicity

| Generation | Other Creole M | Other Creole F | Negro-White M | Negro-White F | Negro M | Negro F | Caucasian M | Caucasian F | Other M | Other F | No Data M | No Data F | Totals M | Totals F |
|---|---|---|---|---|---|---|---|---|---|---|---|---|---|---|
| 3 | 0 | 1 | 0 | 0 | 0 | 0 | 0 | 0 | 0 | 0 | 0 | 0 | 0 | 1 |
| 4 | 2 | 9 | 2 | 0 | 1 | 1 | 1 | 0 | 0 | 0 | 2 | 4 | 8 | 14 |
| 5 | 27 | 37 | 6 | 4 | 7 | 3 | 1 | 2 | 5 | 1 | 21 | 8 | 67 | 55 |
| 6 | 61 | 66 | 30 | 17 | 32 | 13 | 16 | 6 | 2 | 2 | 81 | 51 | 222 | 155 |
| 7 | 45 | 45 | 17 | 6 | 24 | 10 | 19 | 9 | 3 | 1 | 82 | 45 | 190 | 116 |
| 8 | 9 | 9 | 3 | 3 | 4 | 3 | 2 | 2 | 0 | 0 | 14 | 5 | 32 | 22 |
| Total | 144 | 167 | 58 | 30 | 68 | 30 | 34 | 19 | 10 | 4 | 200 | 113 | 519 | 363 |
| Percent Known Ethnicity | 45.1 | 66.8 | 18.2 | 12.0 | 21.3 | 12.0 | 12.2 | 7.6 | 3.2 | 1.6 | | | | |

made for Creoles. A household head who did not identify with one of the established categories was listed as "other."

Letoyant residents of city blocks listed as having no nonwhite household heads may have been passing. However, they may also have classified themselves as Creole, and since this was not one of the prescribed categories, the enumerator could have listed them as white rather than other because the category *Creole* as popularly used generally refers to whites and also because the Letoyant Creoles often have Caucasoid phenotypes. Letoyant respondents may also have identified with whites without really intending to deny their ethnic identity simply because they do not identify themselves with Negroes. Another explanation may be that Letoyant women were married to Caucasians, and the classification by blocks used only the household head's racial origin.

The percentage of Letoyant residents in city blocks which the census reports as having no nonwhite household heads is as follows: In Southwest City 53 percent of the Letoyants are in such household units; in Northern City, 36 percent; and in Western City, 5 percent. Southwest City has a large number of Spanish-speaking people with whom the Letoyants share a swarthy skin color and Catholicity, and a very small Negro population. In Southwest City when a pastor was asked whether or not he regarded the Creoles as "colored," he responded, "People here consider them as 'half and half.' We don't consider them colored strictly speaking because the colored people here are not Catholics, and these people come to Church and make their Easter duty."

Northern City probably has a higher incidence of strong feelings about recognition of group members than either of the other two large colonies. Western City has a very low incidence of identification with whites but a proportionately large Letoyant population. The few Letoyants in Western City who are identifying with whites are, to all intents and purposes, no longer group members.

In Northern City, where there is a noticeable cleavage between Letoyants residing in the relatively segregated northern section and those in the predominantly Negro southern section (mentioned in Chapter 13), there is much rivalry, suspicion, and jealousy. A Northern City Letoyant who lives in a neighborhood that is partially white and partially Negro complained about the lack of communication among his relatives who live on the north side, saying, "Some of my closest kin don't visit me because I don't go for white. They just don't even visit me. Like my sister's daughter who lives up there. They're passing for white. They live over there, and they don't bother about us. They come over to see me once or twice and took me with them to the river when my sister died. But they don't visit me here."

Almost anyone who lives on the north side is suspected of attempting to pass for white; however, this is not necessarily the case. Strictly speaking, if the north side Letoyants intended to pass, they would undoubtedly disassociate themselves completely from other group members who are not passing and cultivate white friends; however, they do not necessarily do this. In fact, they keep somewhat aloof from the north side neighbors who are not Creole. One of these north side Letoyant Creoles commented that she did not know her neighbors, she never talked to them, and she had no plans for making their acquaintance. The same type of relationship obtained in another north side block where a Creole has white neighbors. There is seldom any greeting or passing the time of day in that neighborhood. Creole mothers of small children on the north side rarely allow their children to play with neighboring children; when several Creole families occupy the same flat and there are a number of small children of the same age, they generally find playmates within the house or in their own yard.

Letoyants who deplore the passing of other ethnic group members maintain that the majority of the passers are looking for a higher status because they have not attained status in any other way. A Northern City Letoyant commented: "And I don't see any difference in those people leaving here and going up there and living in the conditions and surroundings that they're living and the Puerto Ricans or another class of people who come here and you hear write ups on what they're doing. I mean their conditions—

the way they have to live. I wouldn't want to live in that neighborhood. I'm seeking to better myself. That particular neighborhood —is not one to be desired. Even if I owned the building, it's not one that I would want. Some of those people who are doing that, you remember, are not the people who own these old plantations down here. They're the people—who—in the first place are escaping poverty, so perhaps this looks like something big to them. You take the actual people who are well off, to the degree that people are well off here, they don't go up there and pass. It's your sharecroppers or your former sharecroppers, and to them perhaps —I can't see it, but to them—they are better off."

A Riverville man commented in a similar vein, saying, "Well, a lot of those people [who pass] don't have anything to do with the majority of the people from home. And what will happen, they will usually marry into some common class of white people. And a lot of them will go to destruction. But still that particular group eventually is lost from the rest of the people. But most of the people, when they move away, if there are only five or six families to one city, they stay in close contact with each other, their friends. They may have a few dark ones, and a few white people as their friends, but they'll, as a whole, stay together. All their talk is about home, longing to be home, looking forward to be home. They all try to send their children back home where they might meet up with some of the people from home."

Many of the Letoyants who pass, including those who have intermarried with Caucasians, still visit relatives in the South. Sometimes, Caucasian spouses express curiosity about the racial origin of the Letoyants, particularly when they visit Riverville where nonwhites predominate, but no instances of broken marital unions are known to be attributed to such visits. A Northern City informant whose relatives were passing was questioned about the attitudes of these relatives when they visited in the South. He responded: "Down there they go among their people." Then, he added jokingly, "But I'd like to know what they going to do if they got to heaven. Are there two different places for them? That's what bothers me."

Creoles who are Caucasian in appearance and who pass into the white population are not necessarily rejected by their Letoyant relatives. One informant talking about a relative who had married a white girl commented, "People go at face value. If you have a better life as white, and you can be white, then do it." Letoyants who pass as white and fail to recognize and greet their relatives and friends on the street do cause hard feelings and are criticized. Moreover, even those who express tolerance for passing acknowledge the threat that it holds for ethnic group survival.

## CHOICE OF MATE

In-group marriage has been a Letoyant value from the time of the second generation when the Letoyants began crystallizing their unique identity. Group boundaries, as defined in this study, extend to those who can trace their descent directly to a Letoyant from at least one parent as well as to those not so descended (the non-direct descent) who marry into the population—whether or not the latter make an effort to identify with the ethnic group. Out-group marriages always pose the threat of diluting ethnicity, particularly if spouses who are outsiders fail to identify with the group or if the group rejects them as is the case with Negroes.

During the first generations, when marriages to cousins within the third degree of kinship were proscribed by the Catholic Church, out-group marriages could be expected, and their incidence was not necessarily a reflection on the strength of ethnic ties. But as the population increased in size and there were increased possibilities of choosing Creole spouses not within the proscribed degree of kinship, the number of in-group marriages may be regarded as an index of the importance attached to preserving ethnicity.

A long-range view of Creole marriages over the last century reveals that about two out of every three (67.7 percent) are endogamous (Table 24). Among the living, married Letoyant population, the percentage of endogamous unions is 68.6 (Table 25).

Based on the population living and married in 1964, the pro-

*Table 24*

PERCENTAGE OF NONDIRECT DESCENT UNIONS TO DIRECT
DESCENT UNIONS OCCURRING AFTER 1865 BY PLACE
OF FIRST MARRIAGE

| Place | Nondirect Descent No. | Percent | Direct Descent No. | Percent |
|---|---|---|---|---|
| Rural | | | | |
| Riverville | 167 | 19.6 | 851 | 80.4 |
| Others | 104 | 24.1 | 431 | 75.9 |
| Towns | | | | |
| Southern | 195 | 35.3 | 553 | 64.7 |
| Others | 1 | 50.0 | 1 | 50.0 |
| Cities | | | | |
| Western | 98 | 63.6 | 154 | 36.4 |
| Northern | 58 | 41.1 | 141 | 58.9 |
| Southwest | 9 | 75.0 | 12 | 25.0 |
| Southern | 61 | 47.3 | 129 | 52.7 |
| Others | 71 | 74.0 | 96 | 26.0 |
| Total Known | 764 | 32.3 | 2368 | 67.7 |

*Table 25*

IN-GROUP AND OUT-GROUP MARRIAGES BY PLACE OF FIRST MARRIAGE
OF LIVING, MARRIED POPULATION, 1964

| Place of Marriage | Total | In-Group Marriages No. | Percent | Out-Group Marriages No. | Percent |
|---|---|---|---|---|---|
| Rural Louisiana | | | | | |
| Riverville | 776 | 677 | 74.2 | 99 | 25.8 |
| Riverton | 337 | 290 | 72.1 | 47 | 27.9 |
| Urban Louisiana | | | | | |
| Towns | 647 | 478 | 47.8 | 169 | 52.2 |
| Cities | 183 | 122 | 33.3 | 61 | 66.7 |
| Urban Outside Louisiana | | | | | |
| Northern City | 198 | 139 | 40.4 | 59 | 59.6 |
| Southwest City | 21 | 12 | 14.3 | 9 | 85.7 |
| Western City | 250 | 152 | 21.6 | 98 | 78.4 |
| Elsewhere | 163 | 92 | 13.5 | 71 | 86.5 |
| Totals | 2575 | 1962 | 68.8 | 613 | 31.2 |

portion of in-group unions by place of first marriage is as follows: Nearly 75 percent of the unions in Riverville and 72 in Riverton (both of which are rural and where the largest number of marriages have been contracted); about 48 percent in Louisiana towns; 33 percent in Louisiana cities; slightly more than 40 percent in Northern City; 22 percent in Western City; 14 percent in Southwest City, and only 13 percent in urban places where the Letoyant Creoles are scattered outside the South (Table 25).

Northern City has an even higher percentage of in-group marriages than do Louisiana cities. Although Western City and Southwest City have comparatively low proportions of in-group unions, out-group unions in both places are often contracted with persons of similar racial and ethnic origins. In the Southwest City, for instance, practically all out-group unions are with Latin peoples.

The choice of out-group partner by sex and by community, based upon the living married population, also affords some insights into patterns by place. Statistics show that Creole women are more likely than men to marry outsiders (Table 23). The incidence is greatest in places where the Creoles are scattered without colonizing and without the social mechanisms to facilitate close interaction among marriage-age Creoles. Nearly 60 percent of the women in these places chose outsiders for husbands. Western City also has a high rate, 52 percent. In Louisiana towns the percentage is 40 percent, and in cities in the state it is 36 percent. In Riverton the percentage is 31 percent.

There are only three places where more males than females married outsiders—Southwest City, where 40 percent of the males married outsiders, compared to 24 percent of the females; Riverville, where the corresponding percentages are 33 and 23, and Northern City, where the percentages are 28 and 26. In Southwest City, the imbalance in the ratio of the sexes is probably responsible for the differential since only 37 percent of the Creoles there are female. In both Riverville and Northern City, however, factors other than sex distribution must be taken into account because these places have only a 3 percent difference, at most.

An examination of the known ethnicity of the living non-direct descent population shows that 45 percent of the males and 67 percent of the females are "other Creoles," that is, Louisiana people of mixed racial origin who can trace their origin to French or Spanish-born ancestors (Table 23). When these outsiders are combined with those other outsiders of mixed Negro-white ancestry (who can claim no French or Spanish blood), the percentages are even higher—63 percent of the males and 79 percent of the females. This means that only 34 percent of the nondirect descent males and 21 percent of the nondirect descent females are of dissimilar racial origin.

Migrants nearly always voice the opinion that it is desirable to marry a fellow Letoyant, even when they themselves have chosen outsiders as mates. There appears to be an increasing acceptance of outsiders with similar racial and cultural traits, even though they are not ethnic group members. Thus, some ambivalence can be detected in the remark of a Northern City Letoyant married to a Louisiana-born Catholic woman of mixed racial origin. He said: "It is much easier to marry within *your own people* and your own religion. Being brought up Catholic, going to a Catholic school, you are exposed to religious teaching. And this is something you come up with and not something you question too much, you will find. In the marriage department you are looking for the right basic things—things that you have in common." Since this informant married a woman who shared his religious beliefs and who was of similar ethnic origin, he may have been extending his ethnic group boundaries to include his spouse, even though most Letoyants would not have acknowledged her as a group member except through marriage. Similarity of racial origin between the informant and his wife was not specified as important, but it undoubtedly is a major factor in the choice of spouse.

Statistics on out-group unions with Caucasians may be viewed as a clue to the incidence of passing. In using them, however, other considerations must be kept in mind. Letoyants who are Caucasian in appearance may decide to pass on occasion, even though they have no desire to lose their ethnicity, while others may deliberately pass, severing ties with relatives and friends. Some Letoyants who marry Caucasians make no apologies for their ethnicity, associate freely with Creole relatives and friends, and take their spouses to Riverville to visit. However, the statistics do afford some insight into their preferences for Caucasian mates.

Among the living nondirect descent Letoyant population, 8 percent of the females and 12 percent of the males are Caucasian. These statistics need to be interpreted, however. As already noted, in this study any outside mate of a Letoyant is considered a part of the nondirect descent population, regardless of intent or lack of intent to be so identified. Furthermore, every outsider known to have had a marital relationship, even a temporary and illicit one, with a Letoyant Creole is included. Among the Caucasian females are a high proportion of Mexican-Americans, many of whom probably have Indian admixture but who are classified as Caucasian in the 1960 census. These females, predominantly in Southwest City, resemble their Creole husbands in appearance and have a Latin, Catholic heritage.

The incidence of marital unions with Negroes may similarly be regarded as an index of Letoyant identification with that population for even though non-Negro partners in an interracial union do not necessarily identify as Negro, the likelihood is greater for Letoyants than for whites simply because the former have Negroid ancestry. Since Negroes are regarded by Letoyants as less desirable than Caucasians, those who contract unions with Negroes pose a greater threat to identity because these couples run a greater risk of being rejected by the Creoles. Again, Letoyant women have a higher proportion of out-group marriages to Negroes than do the men. The nondirect descent living population contains 21.3 percent Negro males and 12 percent Negro females (Table 23).

According to the data, based upon approximately two-thirds of the nondirect descent population whose ethnic origin could be ascertained, out-group marriage does not appear to be any more threatening to ethnic identity than it was a century ago. Two out of three living Letoyants prefer to marry within the population, and more than half of the outsiders are "other Creoles." Nevertheless, there are some indications that out-group marriage is higher in urban than in rural places, and Letoyants are becoming increasingly urbanized. If this trend toward urbanization continues, there will probably be more out-group unions, particularly if the trek continues toward Western City, where the rate of out-group unions is 78.4 percent. Moreover, an analysis of exogamy by date of marriage might reveal an acceleration in the incidence of out-group marriages that is not discernible in the statistics for the total living, married population. Since much of the information on outside spouses was obtained through interviews with persons who did not know dates of marriage, data are too fragmentary to reveal these trends.

### Image of the Letoyant Creole Migrant

In places to which the Letoyants have migrated they are recognized as a people with roots in the South. Their speech, surnames, preference for vacationing in the South, and versatility in performing a variety of jobs—such as might be expected of farm operators—contribute toward their image as Southerners. In addition, they are usually regarded as a mixed racial people. Letoyant Creoles are also recognized for their industriousness, cleanliness, strong family ties, and religiosity.

Wherever the Letoyants have moved in large numbers, they are generally acknowledged to take pride in being self-supporting and to be willing to do almost any kind of available work. "Every person that I've ever met from the River," said one informant, "he was skilled, semiskilled, or he knew something to do to make a buck." Another informant elaborated on the qualities of Rivervillers by saying, "They will work, provided they can find something to do. They can operate a tractor. You take any skilled job where you have to stand in line to get a job. Laboring job. That's what I'm trying to say. Just a common laborer. Of course, some of them are hired. Some guys know carpenter work. They know how to labor—handle a hammer and a saw."

The informants then went on to compare the people from Riverville with other nonwhites in Northern City who are also looking for work. One of them commented, "Now you take people up here. They're either kicked out of school . . . just any number of things could happen to them. They never had a job before, they don't know what to do. You'd be surprised at the young children." The second informant substantiated the remarks of the first informant and added, "This guy from the river, first he can hammer, and he can saw. But here is a guy with a certificate who can hammer, and who can saw. And these guys from the river don't have this. But yet, they [the employers] will give this guy from the river the job over this black boy. Let's put it that way. They going to give this guy the benefit of the doubt. And you know this guy from the river is going to work as hard as he can to make a living. This is in him. I don't know. They are industrious people in that respect. They are going to prove themselves."

A young Northern City Letoyant remarked that he thought a Creole man's "central goal is to make sure his family is well provided for." He went on to explain, "I think this is something that is inherent in the average river man that comes to Northern City. Whereas you find that most of the people on relief are from broken homes, this type of situation, where there are eight kids and the father is married to another woman and the woman is married to another man, just isn't found among my people. I think it is an innate crime for a river man not to provide as good a life for his family as he can. I don't know where it came from, but it is there."

A Northern City pastor concurred, saying, "We have had many Creoles in this parish over a period of years and I have observed that the Creole father is *undoubtedly* the head of the family. It is not that women are not industrious or that they do not earn money. It is just that the man must have always been dominant. Women learn this from their parents and pass these attitudes on to their children."

Regardless of income and socioeconomic levels, Letoyants have a reputation for cleanliness. A well-educated woman in Northern City remarked that she did not accept as equals her lower-class fellow Creoles, but she went on to acknowledge some of the desirable qualities of the lower classes saying, "I think these people are clean. Cleanliness follows them to a certain extent. Even *those* people. Maybe I'm wrong, because even here I don't associate with them and I can't say that I know how their homes look. But I know when they come to church, they're always neat. And from just pure observation—social gatherings—I would say they make a better appearance than some of the other people."

Attitudes toward religion were frequently expressed by Creole informants. An elderly man revealed his attitudes when he reminisced about his experiences, saying: "From where I lived to church it was two miles, and you had to walk. Well, when I did get a chance to get an old car, there wasn't no road to run the old car on. So I couldn't get there no way. After I got to the city, it was so convenient. Looked like it was just a pleasure to go to Mass. And then after I started going to Mass, if I'd miss Mass on Sunday, it'd look like everything went wrong the whole week. I had to make Mass that Sunday whether I did anything else or not. I was working at night and I'd pass by and get my children and my wife and say, 'Well, let's go to Mass.' "

Religiosity is also evident from devotional practices. Another devout old man in Northern City expressed his sentiments as follows: "I go to retreat all the time. Yeah, I've been making retreat for thirty-five years. I gave my children all the good example I can. I go to church all the time, and me and my wife go to church and try to live right. You never hear me cussing, swearing . . . nothing like that. They've never seen me drunk in my life because I never been drunk in my life."

On the basis of the empirical data available—church records, census analyses, settlement patterns, and informants both within and outside the ethnic group—the Letoyant migrants seem to have retained, in large part, their distinctive ethnicity with the characteristics peculiar to it. They still evidence pride in their cultural heritage and reflect their traditional values. However, there are indications that their ethnicity is becoming diluted by continual migration, increasing identification with other racial populations, and especially by out-group marriage.

# PART IV
# Epilogue

The final chapter indicates the extent to which the data presented support the hypotheses. It also looks to the future by summarizing the findings of a thesis on the self-perception of Letoyant Creole children in the South and by pointing out further research possibilities.

It is followed by an Appendix directed primarily to scholars interested in the methodology of this study and in the prospects for further research. The methodology concerns only the sociological aspects.

*Chapter* 15

# What Future for the Creoles?

A Backward Glance

THE IDENTITY PROCESS

In an age of alienation, research on the Letoyants affords new empirical evidence of the strong urge men have to belong to a relevant group whose members provide social and psychological support to one another. Like numerous other hybrid populations, the Creoles have had to develop an identity and to struggle for status. A study of these people in their natural habitat over two centuries supports the hypothesis that a people who possess a marginal status in a society tend to develop a sense of identity and bonds of solidarity to meet the basic social need for belonging to a meaningful group.

Among the factors contributing to the development of the Letoyants' strong sense of identity were: a territory in Riverville; an affiliation with the Catholic Church with high priority attached to its norms; distinguishing racial characteristics deemphasized because of the onus attached to Negroid traits by the larger society; descent from one of the first French settlers through whom they could lay claim to the title of Creole; and ties of blood and marriage.

Territoriality is usually deemed important in the process of developing a social group, for it contributes to a sense of identity and of solidarity.[1] Ethnic groups, in particular, tend to establish territorial boundaries within which they experience a feeling of belonging and where they are not continuously reminded of their inferiority by the dominant group. Here they are free in some

---

[1] Cf. Robert Ardrey, *The Territorial Imperative* (New York: Atheneum, 1966); Muzafer Sherif, *Reference Groups* (New York: Harper & Row, 1964).

357

measure to set their own goals, enforce their own norms, and develop and perpetuate their own social institutions. Negroes in the United States, for example, have, from time to time, emphasized the need for a territory where they could have such advantages. Marcus Garvey's "back to Africa" movement claimed over half a million Negro supporters in 1923.[2] More recently, there have been proposals to create within the United States a Negro state. The Letoyants have always recognized the importance of a territory they can designate as a homeland. It has afforded them a place to develop ethnicity, to socialize their children with little or no outside interference, and to interact freely in comparative isolation. Their interaction with the sizable Negro population in the vicinity of their homeland as well as their relationships with the Negro in the colonies supplies empirical data on intergroup relationships among nonwhites, an area in which comparatively little research has been done.

As a group develops, it delineates its own meaningful norms. According to Creole norms, group members are to conduct themselves in such a manner as to contribute to the group image of a proud, respectable, self-reliant, and cohesive people. A group's norms accepted from the larger society may be modified to contribute to a group's distinctiveness. Thus, the Letoyants used Catholicity as one of their distinguishing characteristics in the area of their homeland by rather effectively excluding the darker people from membership in "their" church. Conformity to church moral norms, moreover, was expected of Creole group members who aspired to high status within the group.

Identity and ethnicity are nearly always associated with racial origin if for no other reason than that physical characteristics afford a relatively simple, visible handle by which to categorize people. Any trait that detracts from the status accorded a group will probably be minimized; on the other hand, it may be prized as a mark of distinction in defiance of the norms and values of the larger society. Color, specifically, contributed in a special way to

[2] C. Eric Lincoln, *The Negro Pilgrimage in America* (New York: Bantam Books, 1967), 170.

the marginal status of the Letoyants; it was a visible barrier to their acceptance by the larger society in the color-conscious deep South. Since the Letoyants accepted many of the values of the dominant society, such as Catholicism in colonial Louisiana, a strong male familial role, and an appreciation of material goods, the Letoyant Creoles (in contrast to the American Negro, who has recently defied the color norms of the larger society by declaring that "black is beautiful") minimized the denigrating feature of dark skin to the extent that the forebear who initially introduced Negroid strains was "forgotten" by a people who place great value on genealogy.

Another norm of the larger society that the Letoyants accepted is the importance of history and tradition. A contributing factor to their identity and status is their descent from one of the original French settlers, a circumstance that gives them a claim to the title of Creole. Concomitant with their pride of ancestry is the value placed on the tie of consanguinity. Blood relationships, no matter how remote, can have great binding force. The Creole esteem for tradition and their tendency toward self-perpetuation through in-group marriage and love of progeny attest to the relevance of their ethnicity.

Ethnic peoples generally have the ability and the requisite interest to resolve their problems of identity. The Negro, for instance, has not only introduced the slogan "black is beautiful" but has also begun to emphasize the desirability of reinforcing black solidarity through some forms of segregation such as campus housing. This type of self-determination has been used by the Creoles, who resorted to self-segregation in Riverville early in their history.

The process by which a people achieves identity and develops and preserves solidarity is of great relevance to marginal peoples experiencing alienation in complex societies. The Jews who had a sense of identity before going to Israel had to create a political society in a territory that they wrested from the Arabs and to develop their own social structures, such as the kibbutz. Although the Letoyants went through a similar process, discernible in the unfolding of their group experience, it was a more gradual one, characterized by persistence over two centuries.

Letoyant Creole solidarity is evident in their family system with preference for in-group marriage, an ability to reconstruct genealogy despite the intricate web of relationships, and patterns of frequent communication and visiting as well as mutual aid; emphasis on tradition and recalling the glories of the past; preservation of the homeland and resistance to its invasion by outsiders who attempt to purchase land; and an identification with a common religion and a high degree of conformity to its norms. By relying on the social institutions of the family and the Church, with its adjunct, the school, in a political milieu that was neither intolerable nor overly oppressive, the Creoles succeeded in giving their members a sense of unique identity and a feeling of belonging to a meaningful social group.

EFFECT OF DISPERSION ON IDENTITY

When identity is closely associated with place of origin, outmobility from that place can be a threat to identity. It was hypothesized that Creole solidarity and sense of ethnic identity would be weakened as they moved from the vicinity of their homeland to distant places. The hypothesis was not supported by the available data on certain indices of ethnic persistence, namely, consciousness of common place of geographic origin, mutual aid, racial identification, religious observance, and family solidarity. The hypothesis was supported in a limited degree by residential patterns and by a proportionately greater incidence of out-group marriage than prevailed near the homeland.

The Letoyant exodus from Riverville began shortly after the Civil War when economic circumstances forced some of them to seek a livelihood in urban places. For the most part, however, this early migration was to nearby settlements, and they usually retained ties with the homeland. But about the turn of the twentieth century, and especially in the World War I Era, migration assumed greater proportions and large numbers of Letoyants left Louisiana. Even these early migrants, who did not have the means to travel back to Louisiana with any frequency, usually identified with their place of origin. The greatest exodus, however, was after World War II, when the Creoles, like other nonwhites, experienced pressures that uprooted large numbers of them from their southern moorings. They were a part of the nonwhite stream migrating from the rural South to urban areas throughout the country. As such, the Creole population with its well-defined parameters affords an in-depth view of this phenomenon and an opportunity to study the extent to which mobile individuals with strong ethnic ties are likely to experience a weakening of the bonds of ethnic solidarity and a loss of identity. In reference to the ethnic index of identifying with the homeland as place of group origin, particularly with the river, migrants are strong. The river is, moreover, a favorite vacation land. Creole migrants recognize the river as their place of origin; they think that experiences as an ethnic people in that place undoubtedly contribute to their tendency to settle in colonies. Their resulting proximity admittedly facilitates interaction among members of the group and contributes to cohesiveness. Furthermore, mutual support, especially in finding employment for fellow Creoles and in rendering assistance in times of crises, is promoted by this proximity.

Phenotypically, some out-migrant Creoles are identified by outsiders as Negroes, and others are identified as Caucasian; however, Creole phenotypes, for the most part, contribute to the preservation of ethnicity since observant outsiders probably surmise that these people have an unusual origin. Those outsiders who become acquainted with the Creoles—the clergy (from young curates to cardinals), employers, school teachers, and neighbors—generally recognize them as distinctive.

When Creole migrants are asked to identify themselves, they can hardly say that they belong to *the* people since that would not be meaningful to strangers; therefore, they ordinarily say that they are colored. To them, being colored is a way of saying that they have mixed racial background, for they do not regard colored as synonymous with either Negro or white. Although they have a special pride in their claim to being Creole, they are hesitant to make such claims to strangers, particularly to whites who may call themselves Creole and who specifically exclude persons with Negroid strains from that classification. Creoles may, like other "hyphenated Americans" such as the Mexican-Americans and Polish-Americans, who adhere to their national origin for generations beyond the one that migrated, call themselves French-Americans, or simply Frenchmen.

That Letoyants have retained their Catholic identity is evident from statistics on religious observance as well as from knowledgeable "outside" informants. Creole homes and cars often display religious objects and stickers. Moreover, they view their Catholicity as an asset. The colonies have a relatively high proportion of Catholics, and Creoles believe that their adherence to the norms of their church contributes to their status. Although their homes in the colonies were not found to be clustered around churches as was popularly believed, neither were the homes at any great distance from churches.

Family solidarity remains prominent. A study of the incidence of family dissolution through desertion and divorce reveals relatively low figures among out-of-state migrants—3.0 percent for the males and 3.9 percent for the females. For rural Louisiana Letoyants the percentages are 10.2 for males and 2.2 for females while for urban Letoyants the percentages are 5.0 percent for males and 6.2 percent for females. Family solidarity and the strong role of the Creole male are also apparent in the colonies where males are the chief means of family support and where they are noted for their versatility in work and for their industriousness.

Nevertheless, out-mobility presents dangers to the preservation of Creole ethnicity. Great geographical distance from the homeland, which is in some respects the repository of ethnic values, precludes frequent visits by the migrants. Even though migrants have attempted to settle in colonies where they have opportunities to exclude outsiders in social affairs and to interact with one another, much of the interaction is through communication media rather than face to face, and there is, necessarily, more interaction with outsiders than occurs in the rural Creole population.

In Louisiana towns where Letoyants have settled in appreciable numbers they generally live in segregated neighborhoods and attend services at predominantly nonwhite church parishes. Nearly everyone is acquainted with his fellow Creoles and has opportunities to interact with them socially. In towns where outsiders have identified individual Letoyants as such from childhood, the size of the community is a deterrent to disclaiming ethnicity. In these towns, Letoyants who associate freely with Negroes and marry them may experience the same rejection from other Creoles that prevails in Riverville. Therefore, in Louisiana, the smaller the settlement and the greater the size of the Letoyant population, the less the likelihood that they will reject their identity.

Place of residence in the three major settlements outside of Louisiana is an index of Letoyant identification with both whites and other nonwhites. Moreover, it affords an empirical measure of the social phenomenon of passing about which there is much conjecture but little hard data. Only 8.8 percent of the 397 known households in the colonies were classified as having no nonwhite heads, and one-fourth of them were in Southwest City, where the segregation index is low, where zoning is not stringent, and where those who might be passing are probably identified as Latins. This index is less reliable when applied to Creole identification with non-whites since the census includes not only Negroes but all non-whites in that category, and since Creoles often refer to themselves as colored. Only 3 Creole households (.8 percent), all in Northern City, were in blocks where all household heads were categorized as nonwhite. Combining the 8.8 percent listed as white and the .8 percent as nonwhite makes a total of less than 10 percent. This low incidence lends little support to the hypothesis that Creoles who move from the vicinity of their homeland tend to lose their identity.

The hypothesis has more support if it is assumed that Letoyant Creoles residing in blocks that are within 20 percent of the areas having all-white or all-nonwhite household heads are identifying with the dominant population. In addition to the 8.8 percent of the Creoles in blocks where all household heads are listed as white,

8.3 percent are residing where 80–99 percent of the household heads are so listed, making a total of 17.1 percent who might be passing. Another 15.1 percent reside in blocks with predominantly nonwhite household heads making a total of 15.9 percent in all or largely nonwhite residential areas. If this assumption that Creole residents in a block are identifying with the predominant population is valid, then 33.0 percent may be identifying with other populations, and the hypothesis is, in part, supported.

Out-group marriage is also generally perceived by ethnic peoples as hazardous to the preservation of ethnicity. Thus, the incidence of out-group marriage among Jews in the United States has led to the belief that if the trend continues, the survival of the group is threatened. Letoyants voice the same fears. Although the percentage of out-group marriages for all Letoyants is approximately the same in the second century of their history as in the first, despite the population increase and dispersion, a close examination of this phenomenon lends limited support to the hypothesis that migration weakens ethnicity. An examination of the extent of out-group unions of living Creoles by place of first marriage reveals that over 50 percent of the unions in all urban places are of this type, compared to 26 percent in Riverville and 28 percent in rural Riverton (Table 25). The differential between towns with populations under 50,000 and cities is not, however, in direct relation to size. Nor is the differential in direct relationship to distance from the vicinity of Riverville. Southwest City, which has the highest ratio of out-group unions, is not as far from Riverville as Western City and has a smaller total, as well as Creole, population than either of the two colonies. Moreover, Louisiana cities have a higher ratio of out-group unions than Northern City. The hypothesis that out-migration from the homeland weakens ethnicity is, then, only partially supported by the index of out-group marriage in that Creoles residing in urban areas are more likely to marry outsiders than are rural Creoles.

Out-group marriage per se does not imply a weakening of ethnicity. On the contrary, some spouses teach their children the

Creole norms, visit Riverville and its vicinity to see relatives, become converts to Catholicism, and attempt in a variety of ways to identify with the Letoyant Creoles. If the outside spouse is of mixed racial origin like the Creole, there are fewer risks that he will be rejected by the Letoyants than if he were either white or Negro.

For the most part, Letoyants who marry outsiders do choose spouses who are of similar racial origin. Approximately 63 percent of the nondirect descent males and 79 percent of the females are reported to have both Negroid and Caucasoid extraction, and the majority of them are Louisianians who can be classified as "other Creoles." About 21 percent of the outside males and 12 percent of the females are reported to be predominantly Negroid, and another 12 percent of the males and 8 percent of the females are Caucasoid, with the remaining outsiders having varied racial backgrounds. Therefore, on the basis of the evidence on outside unions, the hypothesis has only partial support.

If one great cause for concern to Letoyant purists is the incidence of out-group marriage, especially on the part of migrants who have been socialized in the South to place a high value on their ethnicity, of still greater concern is the socialization of the next generation. Transmission of ethnicity by imparting the wisdom of the past to successive generations assumes great relevance when an ethnic group becomes geographically dispersed and particularly when the responsibility rests on only one parent.

## HINTS OF THE FUTURE

Identity formation in the young Letoyant Creoles is so crucial to group preservation that it deserves special emphasis. For the child, identity means a sense of continuity and social sameness that bridges what he "*was* as a child and what he is *about to become* and also reconciles his *conception of himself* and his community's recognition of him." In early childhood, identity is family-bound, but later the child incorporates his experiences outside the family, particularly with his age-mates. The child looks for a sense of valid identity, "a sense of being a particular person with a satisfactory degree of congruence between who he feels he is, who he announces himself to be, and where he feels his society places him." [3]

Confusion about identity on the part of the Letoyant child could be expected to occur most frequently when his family resides in a place where there are few opportunities to associate with fellow Creoles. Since half of the living Letoyant Creoles now reside in cities outside the South, their children would seem to be the most exposed to identity confusion. Those who reside in colonies, of course, have more ethnic group members in the vicinity with whom to associate and probably more occasions to do so than those who are relatively isolated from their fellows.

Even within Louisiana, in settlements where relatively large Letoyant populations live in proximity to one another and commute regularly to Riverville, children experience identity confusion. This is particularly true where there is a dark Catholic population and where the Creole children mix with darker children who share their religious values. But it may also be the case in a more limited fashion where children are not Catholic. A teen-age girl from a community on the Louisiana border who was asked the ethnic identity of her best friend responded, "My best friends are dark children. I go to church with mostly people from the river. Everybody is from the river that I go to church with, but most of my school friends aren't from the river. I guess because I've always been here and most of the kids at my school from the river haven't always lived here. They came up later and mostly stick together. I'll be with them sometimes, but we don't do things together. I've always just been here and I know the kids better 'cause I've gone to school with them longer."

Children born in Louisiana settlements where they associate with large numbers of Negroes may not only have Negro friends but also look askance at Creole classmates who have been born on the river and who keep their social distance from the Negroes. A

[3] Lee Rainwater, "Crucible of Identity: The Negro Lower-Class Family," *Daedalus*, XCV (Winter, 1966), 200–201. First quotation from Erikson, as cited in Rainwater.

teen-age Creole informant made several observations about the interaction of Creoles and Negroes in her home town. She said that when Creoles first move from the river they usually form cliques and stay together, and that leads the Negroes to avoid them. Moreover, she said that Creoles are always "brighter" than the Negroes and that Negroes do not think that Creoles have "the soul that all Negroes have."

If a Creole will "act as a Negro," she continued, "then he's accepted. The only way that people from the river aren't accepted is if they act different. When they clique together and refuses to call themselves Negro and say that they're Frenchmen is when people don't accept them. But if he acts just like anybody else and he doesn't go around calling himself a Frenchman and he doesn't go around with Frenchmen, they accept him." Even the Creoles who begin by forming cliques eventually associate with Negroes "because being up there so long they couldn't help but want to do things that all the rest of the children do. So now they go to some of the school activities and have a few friends. And each clique now has a few Negroes in it." The informant concluded by noting that the first ones to begin associating with Negroes were boys because "boys run around and do things together."

Letoyant parents, particularly out-migrants, have long attempted to control the dating and friendship patterns of their offspring, but they have not always been successful. One informant said that she was chagrined when her grandmother, who was visiting her, told a dark boy who had arranged to pick her up that she had already gone. She waited and waited, and when her date didn't come, she finally went on to the dance by herself. There she saw the boy and accosted him, asking, "Why didn't you pick me up like you promised?" He responded, "But I *did* call for you, and Mama Marie told me you had already gone."

When queried about the attitudes of elderly relatives, a teen-age respondent said: "A boy who was born on the river moved to the city when he was a little boy, and there were a lot of Negroes there. So they're in contact with Negroes and he brings his girl friend down to the river to meet his grandmother and grandfather, and they don't mind. Some of them just don't mind, but some of them do. I guess it's really how *all* the people think about it and everything. They don't mind that he'd introduce her to everybody. Some people would just turn off, or just ignore them, or something like that. Others would just meet her, and then comment about it later. But then that's because these people have been down there on the river all their lives, and they've never been up here except to visit their own people. After a while the boy won't even want to go down there, maybe after his grandmother and grandfather have died. He has his and her family, so there'd be no reason to go back down there."

The informant continued by noting that although "Creoles keep thinking of this—where they're from, and they more or less love to be with their kind, they'll get out and they'll gradually bring their dark friends into it, because if they love them, they'll want them to meet their other loved ones. But not at first. I guess they'll have to be particular about who they bring to meet, because of some of their relatives. The very old relatives . . . they didn't let them meet them. They just have to get in the environment or the atmosphere where there are darks, and where you have to be in contact with them, and then they'll think about the world's changing and everything else."

The last informant's great-grandparents live with her family. The old people cherish their ethnicity and have attempted to impart their own attitudes and sense of identity to the younger people. Although Louisiana-born great-grandchildren know the expectations of their elders, they accede to these expectations more by occasional external conformity than from real conviction. Judging from the attitudes of young Louisiana informants who do not live on the river, Letoyant ethnicity is not particularly relevant to many teen-agers.

The relevance of preserving a distinct identity was questioned by a Louisiana teen-ager, born and reared away from the river. She thought her people were inconsistent in stressing uniqueness

when they observed the decorum prevalent among southern
Negroes and expected by the whites, saying: "You know, the
Creoles always had to go through the colored door, so they've
always been with the colored people. So they'll mix more and still
think the white man is on that side. When they've always had to
go to the colored door, naturally they keep with the darks before
the whites. I guess that they're always so quick to say, 'Yes, sir,'
and 'Yes Ma'am,' and you know, all this bit. A lot of them have
had to work for whites and they always say, 'No sir,' and 'Yes
Ma'am,' and all that mess."

There are, moreover, indications that Creole children living
on the river, and in Riverville itself, are encountering an identity
crisis. The Creole school, attached to the church in Riverville,
was an institutional safeguard that contributed to a child's feeling
of security in his identity. There he associated with his own
people through the years of elementary school and seldom had
occasion to be with other children. But the closing of that
school in 1966 forced the children to have broader contacts. They
were then enrolled in either the local public school, where students
are nearly all Negro, or the parish school in Indianola, which has
a predominantly white enrollment.

That some change in self-identity may be taking place among
Creole children in Riverville was evidenced in a study conducted
in December, 1967.[4] Creole students in grades five–twelve who
were attending either the public school in Riverville or the Catholic school in Indianola responded to an attitude questionnaire
that had three measures of prejudice—a stereotype measure, a
social distance measure, and a forced choice question relating to
type of school preferred (all white, all Negro, integrated)—and
an open-ended essay question. The study explored the Creole
children's self-perception as well as their attitudes toward both
Negroes and whites.

[4] For a detailed description of the study, see Sister Helen Rose Fuchs,
"Contact and Prejudice Reaction from the Viewpoint of Colored Creoles" (M.A.
thesis, University of Texas, August, 1968).

An indication of the self-perception of Letoyant children is discernible in the responses of Creoles [5] attending the public school to three stereotype items about themselves: Light colored people are not honest, do not like Negroes, and have bad manners. The greatest consensus was on the first item: 49 percent agreed, 17 percent were not sure, and 34 percent disagreed. Comments made by Creoles on the essay question as well as in interviews indicate that many of them felt their people were being dishonest in not admitting to being Negro. One Creole girl commented: "You [researcher] sound like our parents who are always telling us that we are not Negro. We are Negro and just like the other Negroes here even though most of us are lighter." Another student expressed the same sentiments by declaring, "We don't like the idea of your distinguishing Creoles and Negroes like some of our own people do, since we are all the same. We are all colored people even though some of us are lighter." After the testing, a group composed primarily of Creole high school girls expressed indignation at their parents' injunction that they refrain from associating with Negroes because they were different and from a "better class of people." One girl said, "That was the way it used to be thought of and taught to children, but it ain't that way no more. We is all equal." Another responded, "I don't intend to teach my children that they are better than the next man." No doubt the response to the stereotype about the Creoles' honesty triggered the questioning of identity. Not all of the respondents may have associated dishonesty with a denial of Negroidness, but if they did, then approximately half of the respondents in the Negro school were disapproving of the Creole claim to a distinct identity and another 17 percent were unsure.

Letoyants reacted to the statement that "Creoles do not like Negroes" as follows: 49 percent agreed, 15 percent were not sure,

[5] Two-thirds of the sixty-one Creole children in the public school responded to the stereotype items; no data are available from the twenty-two Creoles in the private Catholic school on these items.

and 36 percent disagreed. Creole denial of Negroidness as well as the traditional stress on Negro inferiority undoubtedly contributed to the students' feeling that Creoles, in general, do not look with favor on the Negro. On the third stereotype, "Creoles have bad manners," however, 81 percent disagreed, 12 percent were not sure, and only 7 percent agreed. This extent of disagreement reflects a positive self-image for those who identified themselves as Creoles and a favorable image of the Creole on the part of the others, as well as recognition of parental success in one aspect of the socialization process.

ATTITUDES TOWARD NEGROES

In order to ascertain perceptions and attitudes of Creole children toward both whites and Negroes, the questionnaire administered to the Creole children contained items regarding both groups. It was hypothesized that contact would reduce prejudice so that those Creoles attending the white school would be less hostile toward whites than those attending the Negro school, and that Creoles going to the Negro school would be less prejudiced toward Negroes than those attending the white school. However, results did not support the hypothesis. The general prejudice score of both groups, computed by taking an average of the stereotype, social distance, and forced choice measures, was similar, indicating little prejudice toward Negroes, and no statistically significant difference in the scores of the two Creole groups on any of the prejudice measures.

On the stereotype item that Negroes are lazy and stupid, 90 percent of the respondents in the public school disagreed, compared to 86 percent of those in the white school. In regard to bad manners, however, there was less disagreement on the part of the children in the public school than there was by those in the private school: 60 percent of the public school children disagreed and 20 percent were uncertain, while 95 percent of the other children disagreed. The differential response on manners is probably attributable to the social class differences between the Negroes with whom Creoles come into contact in the two schools.

The stereotype with which respondents in both Creole groups agreed most frequently was "Negroes can't be trusted." Of the respondents in the public school, 25 percent agreed and 20 percent were not sure. Creole children in the white school expressed less distrust of Negroes: 10 percent agreed to the statement and 10 percent were not sure. The reluctance of Creoles in the Negro school to respond to stereotypes about the Negro may reflect identity confusion and some mistrust. Only 34 percent responded to items on the Negroes, compared to a response of 67 percent on items about the light colored, and 100 percent on items about whites.

On the social distance measure, even though the two groups of Creoles ranked the unpleasantness of situations differently, they both ranked having a Negro marry into the family as the most unpleasant. Since only one-third of the Letoyants in the Negro school responded, however, their responses are probably not representative. For those in the white school, 24 percent would find it unpleasant, 14 percent were not sure, and 64 percent would not find it unpleasant.

Again, on the forced-choice question concerning the preferred composition of the student body, 79 percent of the public school Creoles did not respond, making the representativeness of the responses questionable. Of the Letoyant respondents in the private school, 41 percent gave first preference to a Creole and a white student body while 27 percent preferred a segregated Creole school.

Negro students are the numerical majority at the public school and have been there longer than most of the Creoles; therefore, social activities are primarily Negro. Creoles have a choice between associating in their own groups and being socially isolated from many of the school activities or being acceptable to the Negroes and joining in dances, parties, cliques, and clubs. Consequently, many Creoles are beginning to associate with Negro students. The rewards of insisting on a distinct Creole identity are no longer so great as they were when the Creoles had their own school activities and social affairs and could exclude the

Negro. At the same time, costs of stressing Creole identity are great.

A significant variable associated with degree of prejudice toward Negroes on the part of both Creole groups was the degree of parental approval perceived by an individual. The more students perceived that parents disapproved of their having a good Negro friend, the less prejudice they expressed toward Negroes. Several Creole students in the Negro school voiced hostility toward parents who did not want them to associate with the Negro students. Parents, on the other hand, fear that their children will "forget who they are" by mixing more and more with Negroes. Several parents said that even though their children have to go to school with black people, they do not mix any more than necessary with them, and they maintain that dates with black people are no more frequent than they ever were. Parents pointed out with great pride that not one marriage occurred between a Negro and a Creole attending the Negro school. The comment was frequently made that even though the Creoles go to the black school, they "keep to themselves" in school as much as possible. There was evidence, however, in the gymnasium as well as in informal gatherings in the halls, that some informal association is occurring between Negro and Creole students.

ATTITUDES TOWARD WHITES

An analysis of attitudes toward whites as expressed on the questionnaire indicates that Letoyants in the white school are significantly less prejudiced than those in the Negro school. When the two measures of prejudice, the stereotype and social distance measures, are analyzed separately for the two groups, it is evident that the greatest difference in scores between the two groups is in the stereotype measure. Those in contact with whites in the school situation are less apt to categorize whites unfavorably; however, when it comes to feelings about associating with whites, their attitudes are more similar.

Even though Creoles at the Negro school showed more prejudice toward whites on the stereotype items than those at the white school, for both groups the item "whites can't be trusted" was the most prevalent stereotype of the three. Among the public school Creoles 38 percent agreed with the item and 36 percent were not sure. Among the children at the white school, 33 percent agreed and 19 percent were not sure. When asked about whites hating the nonwhites, 29 percent of the Creoles in the white school and 26 percent of those at the Negro school agreed; however, only 19 percent of the former were unsure compared to 46 percent of the latter. If the two scores are combined, 48 percent of the children in the white school reflect this attitude compared to 72 percent of those in the Negro school.

Comparisons between Creoles in the white and Negro schools on the stereotype and social distance measure reveal interesting differences. The same general rank of items, from least to most agreed with, exists for the two groups on the stereotype items; however, on the social distance measure the two groups ranked the unpleasantness of social situations in divergent ways. A larger proportion of Creoles in the Negro school marked "unsure" on both measures than did Indianola Creoles. Apparently, those going to the white school have more definite ideas as to how they think and feel about whites than do those who have less contact with whites.

For both groups of Creoles, the social situation most unpleasant to them was having a white person marry someone in their family. The Creoles in the white school found it slightly less unpleasant than those in the Negro school: 41 percent of the Creoles in the white school agreeing or not being sure, compared with 51 percent of the Creoles in the Negro school. As in the case of attitudes toward Negroes, when the issue of marriage is raised, much reluctance is shown.

The fact that those Creoles in contact with whites have lower prejudice scores than the others has significance when the contact situation itself is analyzed. Even though white and Creole students are together in class, there is very little, if any, mixing outside the classroom. During recess periods the Creoles associate together and eat their lunch together at cafeteria tables. Four situations were presented on the questionnaire and students were asked if they felt they were discriminated against in these situations. Only 1.3 percent of the entire group of Creoles at the white school reported no discrimination; 51 percent perceived that they were discriminated against in three of the four situations.

When Creole parents were asked how they thought their children were accepted in the white school, the majority commented that the situation was better than they anticipated. The parents were proud that their children were allowed to be in the white school. This overriding sense of accomplishment seemed to lessen the unpleasant aspects of the situation for the children. Parents noted that the Creoles were not yet allowed at social activities and that some of them were mistreated periodically; however, the comment usually followed: "But it will just take time, and we'll have all the rights of the whites."

Even though the situation is very costly to the Creole students in the white school in terms of not being fully accepted, the reward of being able to be in the school at all and having the support and pride of their parents seems to make attitudes toward whites less hostile than those of the Creoles not in the school with whites. The costs associated with being a nonwhite student in the white school, then, seem to be overshadowed by the rewards.

In both school situations the same general mechanism is operating to account for the low degree of prejudice expressed by the students and for the similarity in the scores of the two groups. In each school situation there are costs associated with emphasizing a distinct identity and rewards for identifying with the Negro. In the white school, white students do not distinguish Creoles from the Negroes and frequently Creoles are called Negro. To maintain adamantly that they are not Negro is costly to the Creole students since white students ridicule the distinction. In the Negro school it is also costly to stress a distinct Creole identity since the Negroes in the school dislike the idea of the Creole's being superior because of his "white blood." From remarks made by Negro students during and after the testing period, it was evident that Negroes deny the Creoles a distinct identity.

That Creole children still feel some apartness as an ethnic

population is suggested by their responses on stereotype items concerning trustworthiness of Negroes and whites. Children cannot have close friendships with those they distrust; therefore, the Creole's closest friends will probably continue to be fellow Creoles. Moreover, in both situations they expressed some dislike of marrying outsiders who are either Negro or white, nor have there been any marriages between Creoles and Negroes in the twenty-year period during which Creole children have attended the Negro high school. Marriages between Creoles and whites in the Riverville area are still more unlikely. It may be that Creole teen-agers will become more ethnic conscious when they become parents. If, however, young Creoles continue to move from the South and to acquire a higher education, both of these circumstances will tend to dilute ethnic consciousness.

## AREAS FOR FURTHER RESEARCH

The youth are without doubt the key to the future of the Letoyant ethnic group. To ascertain the effect of closing their Riverville school and their forced intermingling during their impressionable childhood years with other populations will necessitate a follow-up of the children who have been tested. If young Creoles take advantage of the higher education now available to them in the local state university, and if they can engage in the occupations for which they are prepared in that locale, Creole ethnicity may be reinforced. Young Creoles who are being socialized elsewhere and who have many contacts with outsiders run an even greater risk than Louisiana Creoles of weakening or even losing their ethnic identity. This is particularly the case when their parents have been reared in a similar environment or when only one parent has ties to the ethnic group. In order to ascertain the long-range effects of living away from Riverville, a longitudinal study over time is necessary.

Among older Louisiana Creoles, preservation of ethnicity will probably be associated with maintaining ethnic ties and preferably remaining in the South. Out-migration may be checked by the opening up of jobs hitherto unavailable to Creoles or available to only a few of them. The tide of Creole out-migration may be halted or even reversed by the cessation of the rural-urban exodus. During 1968, there was practically no farm-to-city migration, and Calvin L. Beale, the Department of Agriculture's chief population specialist, predicts that this migration wave is about over. Moreover, if the reputed mineral resources on Creole river property are a reality, their extraction may be accompanied by unexpected prosperity in the homeland and strengthened ethnic identity. The importance of the economic factor in out-migration can be ascertained only by a periodic reassessment of the local situation.

For the numerous Creoles who have already migrated or will migrate, the continuation of the trend toward settling in colonies is pertinent to the persistence of ethnicity. If individuals migrate without attempting to relocate in proximity to relatives and other ethnic group members, then they will necessarily have limited opportunities to associate with fellow Creoles. Even if they settle in colonies, risks to ethnicity will continue.

Concerning the Creoles' identification as Catholics, the full effect of closing the Riverville church-related school on their religion needs to be evaluated. The future of the nonwhite parish school in Indianola, attended by most Creole children living there, is uncertain in a period when school participation in federal programs is contingent upon conformity to civil rights legislation. Although Joseph Fichter estimates that approximately one-third of all baptized Catholic infants cannot be traced later through census schedules, records of the parochial school, or catechism classes conducted for children in public schools, this is not the case with the Creole child. Whether future generations of Creoles can be traced through church rolls, as was the case in the past, remains to be seen.[6]

Although early migrants settled in one church parish and attempted to use it as an ethnic meeting place, today Creoles are too scattered for the Church to serve this function. It is difficult to predict what the effect of this dispersal upon attendance at church and the religious observance of the Creoles will be.

[6] Joseph J. Fichter, *Social Relations in the Urban Parish* (Chicago: University of Chicago Press, 1954), 75.

Creoles have exhibited some passivity, as a people, to prevailing social situations, especially the efforts of the Negro to alleviate inequalities. Will their ethnic identity be affected also by the contemporary malaise that affects those to whom social institutions have become more and more meaningless?

One of the most vital issues facing the Creoles as a people is that of their relationships with darker peoples. To what extent is the persistence of their identity contingent upon the continued avoidance of other nonwhites? During the 1950's most Creoles in the vicinity of Riverville were not supportive of Negro organizations that attempted to stage demonstrations to secure equal rights. But now the Creoles are benefiting from the Negro's efforts to secure such rights. Under these circumstances, will the Creoles even in the South come to identify themselves more with Negroes in their efforts to secure full equality? There are already indications that ethnic-conscious Creoles elected to political office are participating in meetings where the political future of southern nonwhites is being probed and that they are identifying in those situations with nonwhites who hold political offices. Outside the South, Creoles have been less reluctant about intermingling in such situations.

Creole relationships with Negroes in situations more intimate than the political, however, are better indications of the future. Although Creole women have intermarried with Negroes more than men, in-group marriage is still preferred. Moreover, among outsiders, Creoles are most likely to prefer mates who are racially and culturally similar. As the Negro gains social status, and as Creole children come to know and accept Negro children in the school setting, there may be an increase in marital unions between Creoles and Negroes.

The Letoyant Creoles as a people have demonstrated how to attain an identity and achieve solidarity without recourse to violence. Both identity and belongingness to a group are particularly relevant in today's complex American society. The full impact of the Creole diaspora upon the relevance of their identity and its persistence remain to be seen.

# Ways of a Researcher

## INITIATION OF THE SEARCH

I first became acquainted with the ethnic population in River-ville in the summer of 1954. That year, in preparation for the celebration of the centennial of the church parish, the people brought old family ledgers, portraits, land deeds, and heirlooms to put on display in the church hall. Prominent in the display was a genealogy of one family compiled in 1880 by a former pastor. The pride with which people pointed out their ancestry and traced their genealogy and their familiarity with the genealogy of their neighbors gave evidence of strong family and group ties.

As a member of the religious congregation which had staffed the parish school since 1889, I had no difficulty in being accepted by the people. They were accustomed to having visitors during the summer and welcomed visits to their homes, especially from the priests and nuns. When classes started in September, however, there were queries about my role in the community. I explained that I was spending a sabbatical in Riverville to learn more about life in the rural South. During the fall of 1954, I received invitations to participate in pecan picking, butchering, cooking, and quilting bees. There were ample opportunities for participating in routine community and family activities and for establishing relationships with the people.

Since the Letoyant Creoles identify strongly with Catholicism, my identity as a religious contributed to acceptance. Moreover, the convent residence was ideal for purposes of observation because it was strategically located adjacent to the school property where most community-wide activities took place. But my role as a nun also implied strong religious values and imposed a certain reserve. Persons who were not in good standing in the church were reluctant to become friendly with me, and those who were in good standing but who disagreed with church norms were probably not as free in discussing these norms as they might otherwise have been. Nor was it proper for me to join groups of men talking over a glass of liquor in the corner plantation store or to mingle with any all-male group, even on the school property.

Although the first phase of the study was largely exploratory, specific information was obtained on types of property ownership, household and farm equipment, and educational level. I kept a diary during my first six months in Riverville, with careful notes made after each day's experience. I made short visits to Riverville between 1955 and 1962, during which years the study began to focus on the nature of the Letoyant Creole ethnic population. Among the specific questions I asked were: (1) How did these people originate and maintain themselves over a period of two centuries? (2) What effect has their marginality had on their establishment of identity? (3) What factors have contributed to their solidarity? (4) What pressures have militated against solidarity? (5) How have these people related to one another and to outsiders? (6) What values have been retained over the two centuries of these people's history?

## GENEALOGICAL DATA

The genealogy of the population from 1767 to 1880, compiled in composite form by a former Riverville pastor, was photocopied in its entirety. But a note in the preface stated that there were minor gaps; occasionally infants and other individuals who did not live to establish families were missing. The original records, written in French script in blank ledgers, were checked to supplement and verify the composite record. A few of these old ledgers had paper too brittle to permit photocopying; others, however, could be copied. Church records of christening, confirmation, marriage, and death were also photocopied in Riverville and in four nearby Louisiana settlements.

After each field trip, the records secured were processed. Complete registers photocopied in Riverville and the adjoining communities of Indianola and Riverton were bound. In other instances, records obtained where the Creoles had settled in colonies were either copied directly on 3 x 5 cards designed for that purpose or dictated on tape and later transcribed. Every individual listed in a bound register was assigned a number serially, beginning with the community of Riverville. In other communities, numbers were assigned only after an individual had been identified as a member of the Letoyant family or as one who had married into the family.

In the case of Creoles who had not settled in colonies, it was not feasible in terms of time and expense to attempt securing records; therefore, relatives or acquaintances were asked to supply information on them, and approximate birth dates were given. Usually it was not difficult to get the ordinal position of children, for Letoyant Creoles are accustomed to visiting one another, and those who have left Riverville almost always return with their children.

From the registers and tapes, index christening cards were typed, with complete data on each person's name, assigned number, names of parents (with assigned numbers of parents, if known), place of birth, date of birth, date of christening, and names of godparents. Space was left on these cards for name of spouse and for place of last residence. One carbon copy was made of each of these records. The first copy was filed alphabetically by family name, while the carbon copy was put in a numerical file.

Both files were extremely useful. Since the cards could be handled and sorted easily, they were ideal for suggesting sources of missing information on genealogy of parents or of spouse or on place of last residence and for recording data. Because of the similarity in names, the numerical file was useful in searching for an individual when an assigned number was known. In one family, for instance, where one daughter was called Laura and another T-tine, the christening names of the girls were as follows: Marie Laura, Laura Victorine, Severine Laura, Victorine Fidelise, and Marie Meline. Any of the first three could have been Laura;

any of the last four could have been T-tine. Again, between 1783 and 1883, thirty-five boys with the same surname were christened Joseph. The recurrence of the same names undoubtedly contributed to the practice of calling children by their middle names or by nicknames. Very often the nicknames were the last syllable of a name. Thus, Theodule became known as Dule, Hippolite as Po-leet, Eulalie as La-lie, and Sephyra as Fear-ah. Other nicknames appeared to be unrelated to the given name: Cheen-o, Jay-co, Tee-tah, Nan-co, and Druie. In the alphabetical file, these names were listed with a cross reference to the christening name.

The form used on christening cards was also used for individuals for whom no christening record was available, including all those entered in a destroyed Riverville record covering the years 1893–1908. Data for these individuals were taken from other sources: school, marriage, or death records; tombstones; family Bibles; or testimony. If an exact date of birth could not be obtained from these sources, an estimated date of birth was entered. Year of birth of spouse was used to estimate the birthdate of a married individual. If the birth dates of siblings were available and the ordinal position in the family known, a more exact date could be estimated. After genealogical charts were drawn, all these estimated dates had to be checked against dates of both parents and siblings.

A form that could be readily handled was also devised for entering data from marriage and death records. The marriage record contained the following information: names of groom and bride; date of marriage; place of marriage; page of the record book where marriage was entered; names of witnesses to the marriage; type of dispensation, if any; parents of the groom; parents of the bride; ethnicity, religion, and place of residence of both bride and groom. A carbon copy was made to permit filing under the names of both parties to a union.

Death records contained the person's number, name, date of birth, place of birth, date of death, place of death, age at time of death, cause of death, residence at time of death, place of burial, parents' names, other relatives, and whether or not a priest had administered the rites of the church at the time of death. The people interred in Riverville since 1920 had an entry in the death register on cause of death—information that was deemed to have potential usefulness in the biological aspects of the study. In some instances, data on cause of death were obtained through interviews. When dates of death could not otherwise be located, the information was often taken from tombstones.

Data from all three forms (christening, marriage, and death) were entered on edge-punched keysort cards coded to facilitate the tracing of genealogy by sorting for parents' numbers. The original intent was to use the keysort cards for processing all the data. The number of Letoyants traced back to common ancestors grew with each field trip, and this method of processing became increasingly time consuming since cards had to be counted by hand. When eighty-column punched cards had to be used to compute coefficients of inbreeding, most of the data from the keysort cards were transferred to the punched cards.

Genealogical charts were made to show the direct descendants of Pierre Letoyant and Marie, through ten generations. Charts were drawn on legal-size manila folders, and generations were color coded. In the tracing of the genealogy, the keysort cards were first sorted to find all the children of the eldest child, Nicholas (known as Grand Pere by his descendants), in the first filial generation. Subsequently, his children were sorted by mother's number to chart multiple marriages and half-sibs. Then the individuals who had the same parents were entered on a chart and deleted from the deck of cards to be sorted. The same procedure was followed to find Grand Pere's descendants by his eldest child and repeated for each of Grand Pere's eight other children, according to ordinal position. When his descendants were all charted, those of his siblings were similarly processed (Fig. 13).

As each manila folder was completed, it was stamped with the name of the progenitor in the first filial generation and given a number. This number was transferred in the color coding of an individual's generation to the index christening cards. The chart

# Figure 13
## SAMPLE GENEALOGICAL CHART

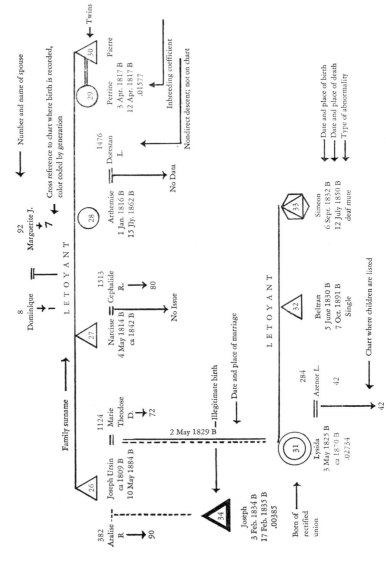

number of a spouse was also entered on the cards of married individuals; the spouse's number was encircled. Through this system, an individual could be located in the index file and then found on the genealogical charts.

A high incidence of group intermarriage was most evident among Grand Pere's descendants (Fig. 14). When a person's descendants were already charted on one parent's chart, the number of that chart was entered where the children would otherwise have been listed on the second parent's chart. In addition, the number of the chart on which the spouse was first listed was entered under the spouse's name, making it easy to trace genealogy once the reference work was done. Similarity of names in several generations necessitated much cross-checking and verifying of information through interviews. For example, both a father and his eldest son with given names of Sylvan married women of the same surname having given names of Leonie and Elodie. With the tendency to drop the first syllables of names, the only way to verify genealogy was to secure names of grandparents as well as parents.

Those who were not born into the population but married into it had only the encircled number on their index cards. Other individuals with similar surnames who were christened in the vicinity of Riverville and who, therefore, might have been related also had cards in the index files; these cards were differentiated from others by the absence of any colored numbers. Supplemental genealogies were drawn up for families where more than one sibling married into the Creole population, and numbers were assigned to the parents to indicate the sibling relationship; however, neither the parents nor the siblings who did not marry into the population were included in the final count of the nondirect descent population.

Although documentary sources, particularly church records, were important in tracing genealogy, interviews were essential not only in identifying lines of descent, even where records were accessible, but also in securing information on Creoles dispersed throughout the country. Except for the composite record in

# Figure 14

FIRST AND SECOND GENERATION LETOYANTS, WITH SECOND GENERATION INTERMARRIAGES

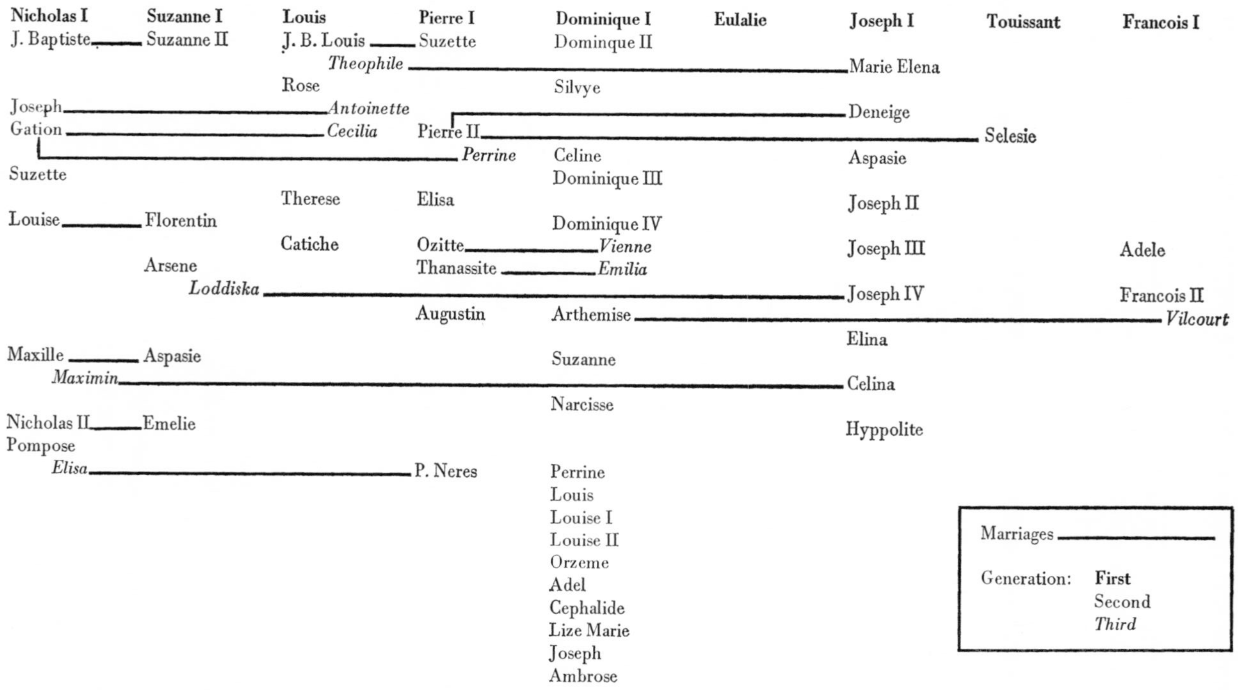

| Nicholas I | Suzanne I | Louis | Pierre I | Dominique I | Eulalie | Joseph I | Touissant | Francois I |
|---|---|---|---|---|---|---|---|---|
| J. Baptiste | Suzanne II | J.B. Louis — Suzette | Dominique II | | | Marie Elena | | |

*Theophile*

Rose

| Joseph | Antoinette |
| Gation | *Cecilia* | Pierre II |

Silvye

Deneige

Selesie

*Perrine*

Aspasie

Suzette

Celine

Dominique III

Joseph II

| Louise | Therese | Elisa |

Dominique IV
*Vienne*

Joseph III

Adele

| Arsene | Catiche | Ozitte |
| *Loddiska* | | Thanassite |
*Emilia*

Joseph IV

Francois II
*Vilcourt*

Augustin

Arthemise

Elina

| Maxille — Aspasie |
| *Maximin* |

Suzanne

Celina

| Nicholas II — Emelie |
| Pompose |

Narcisse

Hyppolite

| Elisa — | P. Neres |

Perrine
Louis
Louise I
Louise II
Orzeme
Adel
Cephalide
Lize Marie
Joseph
Ambrose

Marriages

Generation:  **First**
Second
*Third*

Riverville, information was never provided in the records on more than two generations. With the reoccurrence of names, it became standard procedure to inquire about grandparents. Reliance on records alone would have yielded a population of approximately five thousand rather than one in excess of ten thousand.

## LOCATION OF THE MIGRANTS

In early June of 1963 I made a trip to Northern City, where information I had secured from relatives in Louisiana was helpful in locating Letoyants. I also found telephone directories to be useful. Addresses from these sources were utilized to plot settlement patterns on a map of the city. The churches in the areas of residential clustering were also plotted on the map. I made an effort to secure information from the parish registers as well as from the people themselves. Neither method proved to be highly successful. The population was sufficiently scattered among parishes in close proximity to make the collection of data time-consuming and unrewarding. When the population first went to Northern City, they migrated to the vicinity of one church which did have relatively complete records for the early years but which ceased to be a center of group activity when the parish became predominantly Negro. In 1963–64 I made other trips to Northern City, where I held additional interviews with families whose relatives in Riverville were well known, and where I further explored church records.

I also made several trips to Western City, where Creoles were concentrated in one part of the city and where up-to-date parish censuses were available to supply information particularly on religious observance and occupation. Some interviewing was done, especially with informants whose acquaintance I had made in Riverville or whose relatives had written or otherwise communicated about a visit with me. For the most part, however, I relied on records.

I made two visits to Southwest City. Since a complete city directory had been compiled at the time of my first visit, I obtained information from it on place of residence, occupation, and name of spouse. School records were also useful in Southwest City since most of the Creoles attended one high school.

In all of these settlements, I plotted places of Creole residence on maps noting the location of the parish churches. Subsequently, census data were used in block analyses to indicate degrees of segregation and the extent of home ownership.

## Riverville: 8 Years Later

In a second six-month residence in Riverville in the spring and summer of 1962, I again made personal observations while participating in community activities. On this occasion, many interviews (both structured and unstructured) were taped on a portable recorder, with the consent of the informants. School records were searched systematically for data on educational attainment, parentage of children, and any other pertinent matters.

In July of 1962 I took a census of the church parish in Riverville and devised a face sheet to enter data on landownership, educational attainment, and place of residence of children, parents, and other close relatives. Through the religious censuses from Riverville and other places, information was secured on religious observance by age, sex, and community type, as well as on the degree of participation in church organizations.

Household census forms were devised to record the composition of all known households and the relationship of household members to the head of the family. Where parish censuses were available the data were entered directly on these forms; where they were not, interviews often supplied the information.

Legal documents of several kinds were reproduced: wills, deeds of property transfer, and records of marriages and law suits. Newspaper files in Riverville were useful since they contained a weekly listing of all legal transactions and court hearings. After 1962 these items were clipped from the parish weekly newspaper. Moreover, the local paper carried obituaries and news items on social events such as wedding anniversaries, family reunions, and birthday parties.

A map of Riverville was made from an aerial photograph; every dwelling on the map was labeled as residence, barn, store, school, church, etc. Occupied houses were identified by the name of the family head and by ethnicity, and empty dwellings were noted. Landowners were depicted through a color coding, as were welfare recipients.

## Processing the Data

Every field trip supplied additional entries on individuals who could be traced to the common ancestors or who married into the population. December, 1964, was established as a cut-off date for inclusion into the population because final processing of data in tabular form could not begin until such a date was set. Additional information not affecting the population count was secured by mail and by personal interviews through 1971.

Tape recorded interviews were transcribed, and, in some instances, edited to eliminate repetitiousness. Although Creole speech has a distinct dialect flavor, which was reproduced phonetically by a speech analyst, in the final editing it was decided to regularize the spelling rather than attempt to convey the precise phonetic quality of the speech. All direct quotations used in the final report were either taken from tape or dictated from notes taken at the time of an interview or shortly thereafter. Interview data were filed with newspaper clippings, correspondence, and photocopied materials by topics to facilitate organization.

Throughout the period of data collection and analysis, new research possibilities became evident. The importance of biological data, for instance, was recognized early, and in 1965 there was an opportunity to have inbreeding coefficients computed by a graduate student at the University of Michigan who had written a computer program for that purpose. Since analysis necessitated the use of 80-column cards, other pertinent data were punched into these cards to facilitate the procurement of information on the population at time intervals, by sex, by generation, by place of residence, and by type of descent. Computer programs were written to secure much of this information. Then comparative data on the total United States population as well as the white, the nonwhite, and the Negro populations were taken from demographic sources.

The validity of comparative data necessitated the adoption of the Bureau of the Census definitions for both Negro and nonwhite populations. Throughout the study, *Negro* or *black* is used for people who identify themselves as such, even though many of them are of mixed racial ancestry. *Nonwhite* refers to all non-Caucasians, that is, to populations with Negroid or Mongoloid ancestry. *Colored* is used only in reference to Letoyant Creoles, who often refer to themselves as colored and who generally regard this designation as less objectionable than *black*. The term *Creole* is used in this study only in reference to native-born descendants of French or Spanish colonists who have mixed racial ancestry, even though this is not the popular usage in Louisiana. I refer to the Letoyants as *Letoyants, Letoyant Creoles, the people,* and *Creoles*. Non-Letoyant Creoles are referred to as *other Creoles*.

# Index